THE CHANGE OF POSITION DEFENCE

This book defines and explains the operation of the defence of change of position in Anglo-Australian law.

It is a widely accepted view that the defence is a modern development, the first express recognition of which can be traced in England to the seminal 1991 House of Lords decision in *Lipkin Gorman (a firm) v Karpnale Ltd.* Commentators have accordingly tended to focus on post-*Lipkin* case law in discussing the defence and its many disputed features.

This work takes a different stance, arguing that the defence is best understood by placing it within its broader historical and legal context. It explains that the foundations of the defence can be found in the related doctrines of estoppel by representation, the agent's defence of payment over and the law of rescission. The analysis applies crucial insights from those areas, together with the change of position authorities and broader considerations of policy and principle, to develop a rigorous model of the change of position defence.

The work not only provides a clear and exhaustive examination of the defence, but demonstrates that, properly understood, the defence operates in a rational and justifiable manner within its broader private law context. In so doing, its analysis meets the oft-expressed concern than the defence may operate in an unprincipled way or by reference to 'that vague jurisprudence which is sometimes attractively styled "justice as between man and man"'.

The Change of Position Defence

Elise Bant

HART PUBLISHING

OXFORD AND PORTLAND, OREGON
2009

Published in North America (US and Canada) by
Hart Publishing
c/o International Specialized Book Services
920 NE 58th Avenue, Suite 300
Portland, OR 97213-3786
USA
Tel: +1 503 287 3093 or toll-free: (1) 800 944 6190
Fax: +1 503 280 8832
E-mail: orders@isbs.com
Website: http://www.isbs.com

Hart Publishing Ltd, 16C Worcester Place, Oxford, OX1 2JW
Telephone: +44 (0)1865 517530 Fax: +44 (0)1865 510710
E-mail: mail@hartpub.co.uk
Website: http://www.hartpub.co.uk

British Library Cataloguing in Publication Data
Data Available

ISBN: 978-1-84113-965-4

Typeset by Hope Services, Abingdon
Printed and bound in Great Britain by
TJ International Ltd, Padstow, Cornwall

PREFACE

This book is the revised, updated and expanded version of my thesis entitled 'The Change of Position Defence' which was accepted in satisfaction of the requirements for the degree of Doctor of Philosophy at the University of Oxford in early 2008. Slightly modified versions of chapters three and four were published in the *Lloyd's Maritime and Commercial Law Quarterly* and the *Restitution Law Review* respectively in 2007. My sincere thanks go to the editors and publishers of those journals for consenting to their inclusion in this book.

Of the great many people who provided their assistance during the completion of the thesis and its conversion into this work, there are a number who require special mention for their extraordinary kindness and support. First and foremost, I have been very fortunate in having the guidance of two outstanding thesis supervisors in Professors Andrew Burrows and Robert Stevens. Their insight and encouragement made a huge difference to the process of writing the thesis. Additionally, I wish to thank Professor Burrows for his kind interest beyond the thesis to the wellbeing of my family, a broader concern that meant a great deal to me during the transition from Australia to Oxford and back again. He also provided invaluable guidance on converting the thesis into a book. My debt of gratitude to him is very great.

Outside the supervision context, my thanks go to Professor James Edelman both for his suggestion of the thesis topic and for his enthusiasm and friendship throughout. Dr Birke Häcker provided much appreciated encouragement, feedback and helpful criticism during the early development of the thesis, particularly in the areas of rescission and proprietary restitution. I also extend warm thanks to my examiners, Mr William Swadling and Professor Graham Virgo, whose perspicacity and interest in the thesis transformed the viva process from a rather formidable prospect into a truly enjoyable experience. Their insights greatly informed the revision process that has resulted in this publication. Finally, during the weeks leading up to submission of the manuscript, I was assisted beyond description by the unstintingly generous efforts of my colleague Professor Michael Bryan in reviewing and commenting on the final drafts of this work.

In addition to the intellectual assistance given by those friends mentioned above, I wish to thank the Clarendon Fund and the Banking and Financial Services Law Association for their significant financial support, without which this venture may well not have proceeded. I would also like to acknowledge the ongoing support shown to me by Wadham College and, in particular, my college supervisor Mr Jeffrey Hackney. His ongoing interest in the welfare both of my research and my family was greatly appreciated.

Sincere thanks are also due to Mr Richard Hart for his enthusiasm for this project and for his patience in waiting for it to be completed while my family and I resettled in Melbourne. I am very grateful to him and the team at Hart Publishing for their concerted efforts in seeing this manuscript through to publication.

Finally, this book is dedicated to my husband, Geoffrey Bant, who has been the single greatest factor in its successful completion. Words cannot express my appreciation and gratitude for his love, support and distraction. The book is also dedicated to our two young sons, Jesse and Hayden, whose companionship, humour and adventurous spirits have kept the relative importance of my work firmly in perspective.

The law is as stated on 4 February 2009.

CONTENTS

TABLE OF CASES

TABLE OF STATUTES

Australia

European Union

Germany

1

Introduction and Overview

A Introduction

THE AIM OF THIS book is to define and to explain the operation of the defence of change of position in Anglo-Australian law. It is a widely accepted view that the defence is a modern development, the first express recognition of which can be traced in England to the seminal decision of the House of Lords in *Lipkin Gorman (a firm) v Karpnale Ltd.*[1] In that context, it is usual to attempt to clarify the features of the defence by reference to the recent, post-1991 case law, only dipping into earlier materials to highlight the historical lack of a coherent defence and the kinds of factors that militated against its earlier development.[2]

Against this trend, this work argues that it is preferable to examine the modern case law through an historical lens. To start the story in 1991 is to miss important insights that can help to inform the modern law. The law must develop rationally, in a manner consistent with the existing law and its underlying policy concerns as a whole. Placing the change of position defence within its broader historical and legal context helps us to see how its disputed features might be resolved.

With this in mind, part one of this book does not directly address the change of position defence as we know it today. Rather, it considers other, well-established defences, the examination of which sheds considerable light on the change of position defence. Part one therefore lays the foundations for the comprehensive examination of the modern defence in a manner consistent with the law as a whole—the task of part two of the book.

[1] [1991] 2 AC 548 (HL). In Australia, express recognition of the common law defence came in *David Securities Pty Ltd v Commonwealth Bank of Australia* (1992) 127 CLR 353 (High Court of Australia) but was foreshadowed in *Commonwealth v Kerr* [1919] SASR 201 (South Australian Supreme Court); *Commonwealth Bank of Australia v Younis* [1979] 1 NSWLR 444 (New South Wales Court of Appeal) and *Bank of New South Wales v Murphett* [1983] 1 VR 489 (Victorian Supreme Court). *Cf National Mutual Life Association of Australasia Ltd v Walsh* (1987) 8 NSWLR 585 (New South Wales Supreme Court). Statutory versions of the defence existed in New Zealand and Australia long before express recognition of the common law versions: R Sutton, 'Mistake of Law: Lifting the Lid of Pandora's Box' in J Northey (ed), *AG Davis Essays in Law* (Butterworths, London, 1965) 218; P Watts, 'Judicature Act Amendment Act 1958-Mistaken Payments' *New Zealand Law Commission Contract Statutes Review Report No 25* (Wellington, 1993); E Bant and P Creighton, 'The Statutory Change of Position Defences in Western Australia' (2003) 31 *U Western Australia L Rev* 47.

[2] eg the threat of unbridled judicial discretion expressed in *Baylis v Bishop of London* [1913] 1 Ch 127 (CA) 140 (Hamilton LJ), noted below, at 3.

Although this structure is theoretically necessary, practitioners and students coming to this area for the first time and wishing to take a shortcut, may find it easier, after reading this chapter, to commence at part two, where the features of the defence are identified, examined and clarified. Part two defines the elements of, bars to, ambit of operation and rationale of the defence by reference to the change of position defence authorities, considerations of policy and principle and by drawing on those lessons derived from the doctrines and defences which were the subject of part one. Once familiar with the identified features of the defence, the reader may then want to go back to part one, to see the links and lessons to be derived from a consideration of the law surrounding the change of position defence.

This chapter provides a road map through the book. It commences that process in section B by identifying a core example of the change of position defence, which is used throughout the book as a reference point from which to explore the uncertain parameters of the defence. The section then identifies the four major areas of uncertainty that the book aims to resolve. Section C of the chapter identifies and provides brief explanations of the key assumptions underlying the book, in particular those relating to the structure of claims in unjust enrichment, the connection between unjust enrichment and restitution and the relationship between law and equity. Section D concludes by providing an overview of the structure and content of the book.

B The Change of Position Defence

(1) A Core Case

The starting point in the process of clarifying the characteristics of the change of position defence is to identify an accepted and uncontroversial core example of the defence.

Suppose a claimant made a spontaneous mistake (that is, a mistake in no manner generated or induced by the defendant) which caused her to make a payment to the defendant. Suppose further that the defendant, having no grounds to suspect any mistake, purchased a lavish dinner he would not otherwise have bought but for his honest belief that the value of the payment was irrevocably his. If the claimant subsequently brings an action against the defendant for restitution of the value of the payment, the change of position defence will apply *pro tanto*, to the extent of the change.[3] Thus, if the defendant received £500 by mistake and the price of the dinner

[3] The hypothetical is derived from Lord Goff's example of a defendant who changes his position in good faith by making a gift to a charity: *Lipkin Gorman (a firm) v Karpnale Ltd* [1991] 2 AC 548 (HL) 579. That example is problematic, however, because the defendant's gift may be reversible: see ch 5, at 141–42. Expenditure on consumed goods, which is not reversible (see at 131–32), was accepted as a relevant change of position in *Gertsch v Atsas* [1999] NSWSC 898, (1999) 10 BPR 18 431 (New South Wales Supreme Court) and *Philip Collins Ltd v Davis* [2000] 3 All ER 808 (Ch).

was £200, the defendant will only be required to make restitution to the claimant of the balance of £300. If the defendant spent the full value of the enrichment received on the dinner, the defence will operate to defeat the claim completely.

Stripped to its essentials, the core case demonstrates that the defence applies where:

- a claimant makes a payment to a defendant as a result of a spontaneous mistake;
- the claimant seeks to rely on her personal right to restitution of the value of the money;
- the defendant has changed his position by purchasing goods which he has since consumed;
- in changing his position, the defendant acted in reliance on the security of his receipt; and
- the defendant acted in good faith.

Two final points must be made about the core case. The first is that it is irrelevant to the outcome whether the defendant spent the precise notes received from the claimant or used his debit card at the restaurant to pay for the meal. Both changes count for the purpose of the defence.[4]

Secondly, in our core example, the claimant seeks restitution of a payment caused by a spontaneous mistake on her part. Such claims fall within the category of claim commonly known as unjust enrichment,[5] rather than within, for example, the law of torts or the law of contract.

(2) The Four Main Areas of Doubt

While the application of change of position to the above core case is not in doubt, there remains considerable uncertainty and controversy surrounding the defence. The prospect of its unprincipled operation was a significant barrier to its earlier recognition in English law. As Hamilton LJ stated in *Baylis v Bishop of London*[6] in rejecting the defence, courts are not free to administer 'that vague jurisprudence which is sometimes attractively styled "justice as between man and man"'. If that criticism is not to be merited, there are four main issues that must be addressed.

[4] The defence has succeeded in a number of cases where no attempt was made to trace the value of the receipt into the purchases: eg *Philip Collins Ltd v Davis* [2000] 3 All ER 808 (Ch); *Gertsch v Atsas* [1999] NSWSC 898, (1999) 10 BPR 18 431 (New South Wales Supreme Court); *RBC Dominion Securities Inc v Dawson* (1994) 111 DLR (4th) 230 (Newfoundland Court of Appeal) (although here, the goods were not consumed, discussed in ch 5, at 134–35).

[5] In England, the main decisions are *Fibrosa Spolka Akcyjna v Fairbairn Lawson Combe Barbour Ltd* [1943] AC 32 (HL) 61 (Lord Wright); *Kleinwort Benson Ltd v Lincoln County Council* [1999] 2 AC 380 (HL); *Deutsche Morgan Grenfell Group plc v Inland Revenue Commissioners* [2006] UKHL 49, [2007] 1 AC 558. In Australia, spontaneous mistake was expressly identified as part of the law of unjust enrichment in *David Securities Pty Ltd v Commonwealth Bank of Australia* (1992) 127 CLR 353 (High Court of Australia).

[6] 1913] 1 Ch 127 (CA) 140.

(a) The Reliance Issue

First, it is contentious whether reliance is a necessary element of the defence (the 'narrow' version of the defence) or whether it is sufficient merely to establish that the defendant's good faith change of position was caused by his receipt (the 'broad' version).[7] This can be called the 'reliance' issue. In the core example, the defendant satisfies both versions of the defence. But that will not always be the case.

A key example where the reliance issue is said to matter is where the change of position arises through a supervening act or event independent of the defendant, such as through the theft or the natural deterioration of the received benefit.[8] While the change will count for the purposes of the 'broad version' of the defence, in most cases[9] it will not count for the purposes of the 'narrow version' because the change was not made by the defendant in reliance on his being entitled to the receipt.[10] For example, suppose, in a variation of the core case, the defendant received the mistaken payment but, before he had a chance to do anything (such as purchase a fine meal), the very notes were stolen from his hand by a thief. Assuming the other elements of the core case remained the same, on the broad approach to the defence, the change of position defence would apply. The receipt of the payment certainly was a precondition of his loss: but for his receipt, the notes would not have been stolen. In contrast, the defendant did not change his position in reliance on his receipt and so the narrow version of the defence would not be satisfied.

(b) The Fault Issue

The second major area of disagreement is the extent to which the defendant's fault may operate as a bar to the defence (the 'fault' issue). This debate can be divided into six distinct areas.

First, there is debate over the role of the concept of 'good faith' in the operation of the defence. In *Lipkin Gorman (a firm) v Karpnale Ltd*,[11] Lord Goff stated that the defence should only be available to 'innocent' defendants, who have 'bona fide'

[7] *Scottish Equitable Plc v Derby* [2001] EWCA Civ 369, [2001] 3 All ER 818 [30] (Robert Walker LJ) endorsing AS Burrows, *The Law of Restitution* 1st edn (Butterworths, London, 1993) 425–28; see now AS Burrows, *The Law of Restitution* 2nd edn (Butterworths, London, 2002) 512–17.

[8] *Scottish Equitable Plc v Derby, ibid*; Burrows, *The Law of Restitution* 2nd edn, *ibid. Cf* P Birks, 'Change of Position and Surviving Enrichment' in W Swadling (ed), *The Limits of Restitutionary Claims: A Comparative Analysis* (The United Kingdom Committee of Comparative Law, Glasgow, 1997) 51.

[9] *Cf Gertsch v Atsas* [1999] NSWSC 898, (1999) 10 BPR 18 431 (New South Wales Supreme Court) and *Corporate Management Services (Australia) Pty Ltd v Abi-Arraj* [2000] NSWSC 361 (New South Wales Supreme Court) discussed in ch 5, at 136.

[10] Unless reliance is understood very broadly so that it is satisfied simply by receiving the benefit: Birks, 'Change of Position and Surviving Enrichment' in W Swadling (ed), above n 8, at 50–51. If so, the concept loses much of its distinctive force: *cf* discussion in ch 2, at 30–31, 40–41.

[11] [1991] 2 AC 548 (HL) 580.

changed their position 'in good faith'.[12] Controversy has since erupted in this area, as in others, over the meaning of good faith, the relationship of this concept to dishonesty and knowledge and the role of objective standards of behaviour in assessing a defendant's conduct.[13] For example, in *Abou-Rahmah v Abacha*,[14] a bank suspected that its client might be involved in money-laundering. It received a deposit from the client and changed its position by paying over the amount of the deposit to a third party in accordance with the client's instructions. Had it acted in good faith, given its general suspicions? As we will see in chapter five, the Court of Appeal was split on this issue, with the judges disagreeing as to the operation and content of any good faith requirement.

The second issue concerning the relevance of the 'fault' of the defendant is whether the change of position defence applies to defendants who are 'wrongdoers.' In *Lipkin Gorman (a firm) v Karpnale Ltd*,[15] Lord Goff noted that it was 'commonly accepted' that the change of position defence would not be available to wrongdoers.[16] But the meaning of this label is notoriously uncertain. In this work, a 'wrong' is classified as a breach of legal or equitable duty and thus 'wrongdoers' are those who have breached a legal or equitable duty owed to the claimant.[17] On that basis, there are two kinds of case in which the question arises whether wrongdoers are and should be denied the defence.

The first class of case is where, although having committed a wrong, the defendant is not sued on that basis but in an independent claim in unjust enrichment.[18] For example, suppose, in a variation of our core case, that a claimant seeks restitution from the defendant of the value of a payment transferred pursuant to a mistake induced by the fraudulent misrepresentations of the defendant. The defendant will have committed the tort of deceit. However, the claimant need not rely on the tort: she may decide to proceed against the defendant relying solely on the fact that she entered into the transaction as a result of her mistake. Should the defendant in that case be permitted to rely on the defence where there is evidence before the court that he committed a tort?

The second class of case is where a defendant has committed a wrong against the claimant and is sued by the claimant on that basis. Although many wrongs (such as deceit) involve fault that might itself provide a basis for denying the defendant the defence, it is not always so: there exist many wrongs of strict liability. In that

[12] *Ibid*, at 579.

[13] Notably, in the area of knowing assistance: *cf Barlow Clowes v Eurotrust International* [2005] UKPC 37, [2006] 1 WLR 1476 and *Twinsectra v Yardley* [2002] UKHL 12, [2002] 2 AC 164.

[14] [2006] EWCA Civ 1492, [2007] 1 All ER (Comm) 827, discussed in ch 5, at 158–60.

[15] [1991] 2 AC 548 (HL) 580.

[16] The passage leaves open the question whether Lord Goff accepted that view: Burrows, *The Law of Restitution* 2nd edn, above n 7, at 525; G Virgo, *The Principles of the Law of Restitution* 2nd edn (OUP, Oxford, 2006) 705.

[17] The book thus adopts the arguments of J Edelman, *Gain-based Damages* (Hart Publishing, Oxford, 2002) ch 2 and P Birks, 'The Concept of a Civil Wrong' in D Owen (ed), *Philosophical Foundations of Tort Law* (Clarendon Press, Oxford, 1995) 31.

[18] This analysis assumes that unjust enrichment and wrongdoing are independent categories of claim, as to which see below, at 13–14.

context, the question arises whether the 'innocent' defendant is entitled to rely on the change of position defence in response to a claim for restitution of a benefit wrongfully received. It has been suggested, for example, that an innocent converter should be entitled to rely on the change of position defence to reduce his restitutionary liability in conversion.[19] The same argument has been made with respect to innocent breaches of fiduciary duties (an equitable wrong).[20] This second class of case also raises the question of the ambit of operation of the defence, to which we return below at (c).

A third context in which the fault of the defendant comes under scrutiny is where the claimant transferred the benefit as a result of the duress or undue influence of the defendant. Part of the difficulty in such cases stems from the ambiguous nature of these categories of claim. Although duress and undue influence cases often involve fault, and may even involve breaches of duty on the part of the defendant,[21] it is far from clear that duress and undue influences are categories of wrongdoing per se, in the sense of involving breaches of legal or equitable duties that would, for example, support a claim to compensation.[22] Some commentators have argued that the claims are more properly characterised as coming within the law of unjust enrichment.[23] Given the demonstrated availability of the change of position defence to at least some claims in unjust enrichment (spontaneous mistake), the question arises whether, by analogy with mistake, defendants to claims based on undue influence or duress are entitled to rely on the change of position defence and, if not, why not. This question again overlaps with the third area of controversy, the 'ambit of operation' question, discussed further below at (c).

A fourth context in which the fault of the defendant arises for consideration is where defendants have been involved in illegality. There is little authority in the English change of position case law on this question and what there is raises a number of issues regarding the consequences of illegal conduct.[24] One of the chief

[19] *Kuwait Airways Corp v Iraqi Airways Co (Nos 4 and 5)* [2002] UKHL 19, [2002] 2 AC 883 [79] (Lord Nicholls); R Nolan, 'Change of Position' in P Birks (ed), *Laundering and Tracing* (Clarendon Press, Oxford, 1995) 154; G Jones (ed), *Goff and Jones The Law of Restitution* 7th edn (Sweet & Maxwell, London, 2007) [40-016].

[20] Nolan, *ibid.* *Cf* Virgo, above n 16, at 705. The classification of breach of fiduciary duty as an equitable wrong reflects a fusionist approach to the law, as to which see below, at 14–15. *Cf* P Millett, 'Proprietary Restitution' in S Degeling and J Edelman (eds), *Equity in Commercial Law* (Thompson, Sydney, 2005) 309, 311 (breach of fiduciary duty is not analogous to wrongdoing at common law).

[21] Thus, duress to goods may involve a separate tort of conversion: eg *Astley v Reynolds* (1795) 2 Stra 915, 93 ER 939.

[22] On duress, see *Universe Tankships Inc of Monrovia v International Transport Workers Federation* [1983] 1 AC 366 (HL) 385 (Lord Diplock), cited with approval in *Dimskal Shipping Co SA v International Transport Workers Federation* [1992] 2 AC 152 (HL) 166 (Lord Goff). On undue influence: *Niersman v Pesticcio* [2004] EWCA Civ 372, [2004] WTLR 699 [20] (Mummery LJ).

[23] eg Burrows, *The Law of Restitution* 2nd edn, above n 7, chs 5 and 6; J Edelman and E Bant, *Unjust Enrichment in Australia* (OUP, Melbourne, 2006) chs 9 and 10.

[24] *Barros Mattos Junior v MacDaniels* [2004] EWHC 1188 (Ch), [2005] 1 WLR 247, criticised by AM Tettenborn, 'Bank Fraud, Change of Position and Illegality: The Case of the Innocent Money-Launderer' [2005] *Lloyd's Maritime and Commercial L Q* 6; *Abou-Rahmah v Abacha* [2006] EWCA Civ 1492, [2007] 1 All ER (Comm) 827.

concerns of commentators is that barring such defendants from raising the defence may result in their being disproportionately penalised for what are often technical infractions of the law. In that context, the reasons for, and nature of operation of, any illegality bar are prime areas for clarification.

The fifth sense in which the fault of the defendant may be relevant to the defence is where the defendant induced the claimant's impaired decision to enter into the transaction. Varying our core example, suppose a defendant innocently misrepresented a fact or matter to the claimant which then formed a basis for her decision to transfer a benefit to the defendant. The defendant committed no breach of duty, nor was his conduct illegal. The question arises whether he should nonetheless be debarred from raising the defence because he was in some sense responsible for bringing about the transfer in the first place. This question can also arise in cases of undue influence and duress, where defendants will have often played an active role, albeit with possibly the best of intentions, in bringing about the impugned transfer.

There are strong voices against considering the fault of the defendant in this sense as relevant to the defence.[25] However, the chorus is by no means unanimous, with decisions,[26] academic opinion[27] and legislative provisions[28] supporting the relevance to the defence of the fault of the defendant in this sense. As Professor Birks noted, this area remains one of the 'central questions' of the law of the change of position defence.[29]

The sixth and final sense in which a defendant may be regarded as at fault is where the defendant's change of position was itself the result of careless or reckless behaviour on the part of the defendant. Here, it is not the role of the defendant in *inducing* the original receipt that is in issue, but the quality of the defendant's conduct following his receipt. Suppose a defendant receives a benefit and invests it

[25] *Dextra Bank and Trust Co Ltd v Bank of Jamaica* [2002] 1 All ER (Comm) 193 (PC) 207, adopting the arguments of Birks, 'Change of Position and Surviving Enrichment' in W Swadling (ed), above n 8, at 41 and R Grantham and C Rickett, 'Change of Position in New Zealand' [1999] *New Zealand Business L Q* 77, 77–78; R Grantham and C Rickett, 'Change of Position and Balancing the Equities' [1999] 7 *Restitution L Rev* 162, 162–63.

[26] eg *National Bank of New Zealand Ltd v Waitaki International Processing (NI) Ltd* [1999] 2 NZLR 211 (New Zealand Court of Appeal).

[27] J Beatson and W Bishop, 'Mistaken Payments in the Law of Restitution' (1986) 30 *U Toronto L J* 149; E Bant and P Creighton, 'The Australian Change of Position Defence' (2002) 30 (2) *U Western Australia L Rev* 208, 225; E Bant and P Creighton, 'Mistake of Fact and Change of Position: Sound Advice from the Privy Council?' (2002) 2 *Oxford U Common L J* 271; P Watts, 'Rescission of Guarantees for Misrepresentation and Actionable Non-Disclosure' (2002) 61(2) *CLJ* 301.

[28] Law Reform (Frustrated Contracts) Act 1943 1(2) and (3). There are a number of statutory change of position defences in Australia: Frustrated Contracts Act 1958 (Vic); Trustee Act (NT) 50AAA(2)(c); Trusts Act 1973 (Qld) 109(3); Succession Act 1981 (Qld) 53(5); Perpetuities and Accumulations Act 1992 (Tas) 24(2)(c); Trustees Act 1962 (WA) 65(8); Property Law Act 1969 (WA) 125, considered in ch 10, at 244–54. Detailed consideration of the relevance of fault in the context of the Western Australian legislation is contained in Bant and Creighton, 'The Statutory Change of Position Defences in Western Australia' above n 1, at 65–67. New Zealand also boasts a wealth of statutory change of position defences, the best known of which (Judicature Amendment Act 1958 (NZ) 94B) is considered in *Thomas v Houston Corbett* [1969] NZLR 151 (New Zealand Court of Appeal) and *National Bank of New Zealand Ltd v Waitaki International Processing (NI) Ltd* [1999] 2 NZLR 211 (New Zealand Court of Appeal).

[29] P Birks, 'Change of Position: The Two Central Questions' (2004) 120 *LQR* 373.

unwisely, burns it, or otherwise fails to deal with it as would a reasonable man. Should the defendant's lack of reasonable care in dealing with his enrichment be relevant to the defence? Again, the authorities and commentators are divided.[30]

(c) The Ambit of Operation Issue

The third area of doubt shrouding the change of position defence is the ambit of operation of the defence. This can be broadly divided into two sub-issues. The first is that its application to claims in unjust enrichment is uncertain. We saw earlier that the defence can operate in cases of spontaneous mistake, but that it is doubtful whether it is available in cases of innocently, negligently or fraudulently induced mistake. Nor is it clear whether the defence applies to claims in undue influence or duress, which often are considered as claims in unjust enrichment. It is also uncertain whether the defence applies to 'failure of consideration or basis' claims,[31] or whether it applies to claims for restitution based on public policy grounds.[32] Finally, it is controversial whether the defence applies where the claim is for proprietary, rather than personal, restitution.[33]

The second ambit of operation issue is whether the defence operates beyond claims in unjust enrichment. As we saw earlier, some commentators have argued that innocent converters should be able to rely on the change of position defence to claims in conversion.[34] Whether this is even a possibility depends on whether the defence is limited to claims in unjust enrichment or whether it may extend to other categories of claim where restitution is sought from a defendant. Another possible candidate in that regard is in the area of what may loosely be called 'vindication' claims, that is, where a claimant seeks restitution of a benefit received by a defendant, not on the basis of the commission of a wrong (such as conversion) or on the basis of unjust enrichment, but on the basis of the claimant's continuing proprietary right to the benefit held in the hands of the defendant.[35]

[30] *Cf National Bank of New Zealand Ltd v Waitaki International Processing (NI) Ltd* [1999] 2 NZLR 211 (New Zealand Court of Appeal) and P Birks, 'A Bank's Mistaken Payments: Two Recent Cases and Their Implications' (2000) 6 *New Zealand Business L Q* 155, 164 (carelessness relevant) and Bant and Creighton, 'The Australian Change of Position Defence' above n 27, at 227–28; *Port of Brisbane Corp v ANZ Securities* [2002] QCA 158, [2003] 2 Qd R 661 (Queensland Court of Appeal) [23] (McPherson JA, Davies JA and Mullins J concurring) and Edelman and Bant, above n 23 (carelessness irrelevant).

[31] *Cf* Burrows, *The Law of Restitution* 2nd edn, above n 7, at 524 and Edelman and Bant, above n 23, at 330–31.

[32] *Cf* G Jones, 'Some Thoughts on Change of Position' in AS Burrows and Lord Rodger of Earlsferry (eds), *Mapping the Law: Essays in Memory of Peter Birks* (OUP, Oxford, 2006) 65, 67–74 and Edelman and Bant, *ibid*, at 337–38.

[33] This debate assumes proprietary restitution is possible: see ch 7, at 204–09. Commentators divided on the issue include Burrows, *The Law of Restitution* 2nd edn, above n 7, at 527 (the defence applies) and C Rotherham, 'Tracing Misconceptions in *Foskett v McKeown*' [2003] *Restitution L R* 57, 73–76 (identifying reasons militating against the application of the defence).

[34] Above, at 6.

[35] Millett, above n 20, ch 12, explaining *Foskett v McKeown* [2001] 1 AC 102 (HL) and disputing Rotherham, above n 33.

(d) The Rationale Issue

Underpinning each of the three areas of doubt discussed above is the fact that the rationale of the change of position defence has yet to be conclusively determined (the 'rationale' issue). Some courts and commentators have taken the view that its principal concern is with 'disenrichment': the defence operates to protect the defendant where, as a result of his change of position, he is no longer enriched by his original receipt.[36] Others dispute this analysis.[37]

One of the most important clues to the answer to this question lies in whether courts are prepared to consider non-pecuniary changes of position as relevant to the defence. For example, if a defendant changes his position not by purchasing goods that he subsequently consumes but by commencing a family, does that change count for the purposes of the defence?[38] Unsurprisingly, courts and commentators are deeply divided on this issue.[39] It will be an important aim of this book to address that question as an intrinsic part of the process of defining the rationale of the defence.

C Underlying Assumptions

(1) Introduction

Any work focusing on a defence must necessarily rest on certain assumptions as to the legal system and the superstructure of claims to which that defence potentially responds. This book assumes three substantive points. The first relates to the nature of the category of claim known as unjust enrichment, the second to the nature of the link between unjust enrichment and restitution and the third to the relationship between the common law and equity. This section will both identify the nature of the assumptions made and give some brief reasons for their adoption.[40]

[36] eg Burrows, *The Law of Restitution* 2nd edn, above n 7, at 512–17; P Birks, *Unjust Enrichment* 2nd edn (OUP, Oxford, 2005) 208–12.

[37] eg *National Bank of New Zealand Ltd v Waitaki International Processing (NI) Ltd* [1992] 2 NZLR 211 (New Zealand Court of Appeal); Edelman and Bant, above n 23, at 319–23.

[38] The characterisation of this change as not disenriching is explored in ch 5, at 132–34.

[39] eg *Commerzbank Ag v Price-Jones* [2003] EWCA Civ 1663, (2003) 147 SJLB 1397 [65]–[72] (Munby J), critically discussed in Birks, 'Change of Position: The Two Central Questions' above n 29. Underscoring the uncertainty in this area, Birks contemplates the possibility of a non-disenriching change of position in Birks, *Unjust Enrichment* 2nd edn, above n 36, at 258.

[40] The reasons are set out more comprehensively: Edelman and Bant, above n 23, pt 1 and ch 7.

(2) The Nature of Unjust Enrichment

The first assumption is the nature of the enquiry when a claim is made in unjust enrichment. The basic structure of that claim is (1) that the defendant must have been enriched; (2) that the enrichment came at the expense of the claimant; and (3) that the enrichment was unjust. Once those three elements are established, the question arises whether there is any defence to the prima facie claim.[41] This book focuses on one of the potential defences, the change of position defence.

Of particular importance is the sense in which the third requirement of the claim in unjust enrichment is understood. In essence, there are two different approaches taken by legal systems to the question of 'unjustness'. The first looks to the enrichment of the defendant and asks whether there is any juristic reason for retention of that enrichment, such as a contract, gift or trust. It is described in this book as the 'juristic reasons' approach. A juristic reasons approach has long been adopted in German law.[42] A version of this approach has also recently been adopted in Canada.[43] The second approach to the question of 'unjustness' is that taken in England and Australia. This approach looks for a particular legal reason, such as mistake, duress or failure of consideration, why the defendant's enrichment is unjust. It thus requires the claimant to show a positive reason why the enrichment is unjust, rather than to show (as does the juristic reasons approach) that there is no juristic ground for the defendant to retain the enrichment.

A simple example demonstrates the distinction between the approaches. Suppose I pay money to you thinking I owe it to you when in truth I do not. The juristic reasons approach asks whether there is any juristic reason for the payment. In the example given, the payment is not made pursuant to a contractual obligation, it is not a gift, nor is there any other legal explanation for the payment (eg trust, payment in discharge of a statutory liability or some other legal basis). It follows from the fact that there is no juristic reason for the defendant retaining the benefit that I can recover the value of the payment. In contrast, under the 'unjust factors' approach, it is the mistake that is the key to recovery.

Having previously played a key role in identifying and endorsing the 'unjust factors' approach,[44] in 2003 Birks argued that English law had changed direction and

[41] *Banque Financiere de la Cite v Parc (Battersea) Ltd* [1999] 1 AC 221 (HL) 227 (Lord Steyn) 234 (Lord Hoffmann, with whom Lords Griffith, Steyn, Clyde and Hutton agreed generally). A fifth question is whether the claimant has a right to proprietary or personal restitution.

[42] R Zimmerman and J Du Plessis, 'Basic Features of the German Law of Unjustified Enrichment' [1994] *Restitution L Rev* 14; R Zimmerman, 'Unjustified Enrichment' (1995) 15 *OJLS* 403.

[43] *Garland v Enbridge Gas Distribution Inc* [2004] 1 SCR 629 (Supreme Court of Canada); *Pacific National Investments Ltd v Victoria (City)* [2004] 3 SCR 629 (Supreme Court of Canada). Both cases reinterpret remarks from *Rathwell v Rathwell* [1978] 1 SCR 629 (Supreme Court of Canada) and *Pettkus v Becker* [1980] 2 SCR 834 (Supreme Court of Canada). The recent adoption of the juristic reasons approach is discussed in R Grantham, 'Absence of Juristic Reason in the Supreme Court of Canada' [2005] 13 *Restitution L Rev* 102.

[44] P Birks, *An Introduction to the Law of Restitution* rev edn (Clarendon Press, Oxford, 1989).

now adopted a juristic reasons approach.[45] That view is not shared in this work, for three reasons. The first is that, as a matter of precedent, the 'unjust factors' approach remains the law both in England[46] and Australia.[47] This is emphasised by the fact that both in England[48] and in Australia,[49] claims have been struck out for not pleading an unjust factor. Therefore, while it is true that there are signs of instability in both jurisdictions, the law has not gone so far as to endorse the juristic reasons approach.[50]

Indeed, a number of areas in the general law are almost impossible to reconcile with a juristic reasons approach. A good example is provided by the case of rescission, considered in chapter four. It is there shown that rescission is a predominantly restitutionary process that responds, inter alia, to claims in unjust enrichment.[51] If, therefore, the juristic reasons approach applied in England and Australia, the rescission case law should be amenable to that analysis. As we will see in chapter four, attempts have indeed been made to subject rescission to analysis borne out of the juristic reasons tradition.[52] However, it will be shown that cases of rescission in the common law tradition proceed on the assumption that there *is* an existing juristic reason for retention, which the claimant is trying to set aside. That is the whole point of the exercise. That is, rescission presupposes the existence of a valid contract or gift that the claimant then seeks to rescind.[53] It is difficult to reconcile this model with a juristic reasons approach. No doubt it is precisely for this reason that, in Germany, the law governing the situations in which a contract may be avoided do not form part of the law of unjust enrichment.[54] But this relocation of rescission outside the law of unjust enrichment will not work in England or Australia because, as will be shown, a power to rescind a contract in these jurisdictions is generated by the event of unjust enrichment.

Secondly, the 'unjust factors' approach is preferable in that it makes explicit the underlying reason for restitution. In contrast, on the juristic reasons approach, the ultimate reason for restitution is often obscured and only revealed in the recognition of various exceptions and defences to the general rule.[55] Notably, Birks'

[45] P Birks, *Unjust Enrichment* (OUP, Oxford, 2003). See now Birks, *Unjust Enrichment* 2nd edn, above n 36.

[46] '. . . at least for the moment': *Deutsche Morgan Grenfell Group Plc v Commissioners of Inland Revenue* [2006] UKHL 49, [2007] 1 AC 558 [21] (Lord Hoffman); *Sempra Metals Limited v Commissioners of Inland Revenue* [2007] UKHL 34, [2008] 1 AC 561. See also Virgo, above n 16, at 127–30.

[47] *David Securities Pty Ltd v Commonwealth Bank of Australia* (1992) 127 CLR 353 (High Court of Australia). For a detailed discussion of the relevant case law, see Edelman and Bant, above n 23, ch 7.

[48] *Uren v First National Home Finance Ltd* [2005] EWHC 2529 (Ch).

[49] *Wasada Pty Ltd v State Rail Authority of New South Wales (No 2)* [2003] NSWSC 987 (New South Wales Supreme Court) [16], [31] (Campbell J); *Matland Holdings Pty Ltd v NTZ Pty Ltd* [2004] FCA 710 (Federal Court of Australia) [171] (Kenny J).

[50] The case law is identified and discussed at length in Edelman and Bant, above n 23, ch 7.

[51] Ch 4, at 90–91.

[52] *Ibid*, at 96–101.

[53] *Cf* Birks, *Unjust Enrichment* 2nd edn, above n 36, at 126, who simply asserted, without authority, that a voidable contract is 'immediately invalid'.

[54] BGB paras 142–44.

[55] An example is found in the difficult question of whether restitution should be available in cases involving 'incidental benefits': Edelman and Bant, above n 23, at 160–61.

suggested model of the juristic reasons approach sought to retain the unjust factors at the base of a pyramid of reasoning which helped to explain why, at the apex, retention of the benefit by the defendant is unjust. In this way, Birks sought a 'limited reconciliation'[56] between the unjust factors and no juristic reason approaches. It is not possible within the confines of this book to go into a detailed critical analysis of Birks' pyramid model. However, the obvious point for the purpose of this book is that it expressly acknowledges the fundamental, explanatory force of unjust factors.

Thirdly, in the context of the change of position defence, the transparency offered by the 'unjust factors' approach is particularly to be welcomed. As this book will demonstrate, it often helps to determine whether or not the defence should apply in the context of a particular claim. In contrast, on the juristic reason approach, there is no obvious reason for distinguishing between different classes of claim and attempts to do so arguably undermine the otherwise attractive unity of that approach.

This is demonstrated by analysis of the Privy Council opinion in *Goss v Chilcott*.[57] In that case, Mr and Mrs Goss mortgaged their title to land to obtain a loan. By their consent, the loan was paid to a third party, Mr Haddon. Mr and Mrs Goss intended that Mr Haddon would repay the principal and interest, but he repaid only some interest and none of the principal. The mortgage was subsequently avoided through Mr Haddon's fraud. The lender successfully sought restitution of the value of the loan monies from Mr and Mrs Goss. The relevant unjust factor was failure of basis, the basis being that the loan monies be repaid.

Mr and Mrs Goss unsuccessfully argued by way of defence that they had changed their position by allowing the loan monies to be paid to Mr Haddon. As Lord Goff, delivering the opinion of the Privy Council explained, the defendants had allowed the monies to be paid to Mr Haddon knowing that their receipt was conditional on the loan being repaid. In so doing, they had deliberately taken the risk that Mr Haddon would be unable to repay the money, in which case they would be required to fund the repayment of the loan themselves.[58] The reason for denying the defence in this case is thus linked to the operation of the unjust factor.[59] On the juristic reasons approach, it is much less obvious why the defendants should be denied the defence. For example, Birks, having switched from an unjust factors analysis to a juristic reasons approach, argued that the result is 'problematic'[60] because the defendants had acted in good faith. Yet, it is far from obvious that the defendants merited the defence. Arguably, the 'unjust factors' approach not only better accords with our sense of justice, but helps to provide an explicit and reasoned basis for denying the defence.

[56] Birks, *Unjust Enrichment* 2nd edn, above n 36, at 116.

[57] [1996] AC 788 (PC).

[58] *Ibid*, at 799.

[59] The application of the defence to failure of basis claims is considered in ch 7, at 197–98; see also ch 10 at 244–50.

[60] Birks, *Unjust Enrichment* 2nd edn, above n 36, at 217.

(3) Restitution and Unjust Enrichment

The second major assumption underlying this book pertains to the relationship between restitution and unjust enrichment. As Dr Zakrzewski has explained, a remedy is the right that arises from a court order.[61] To use his terminology, a restitutionary remedy is a court order that replicates a pre-existing right which has the goal of restitution, that is, a goal of giving back to a claimant value that was received by a defendant at the claimant's expense, so as to restore the parties to the *status quo ante*.[62] In this work, however, the word 'restitution' is used more loosely to describe both the pre-existing restitutionary right and the remedy that replicates that right.

On the definition adopted in this book, restitution differs fundamentally from compensation, for example, which is a loss-based remedy. However, it is also distinguishable from another gain-based remedy, disgorgement.[63] An example of a disgorging remedy is a disgorgement order consequent on an account of profits, a remedy commonly encountered in the context of breaches of equitable duties. Disgorgement is distinct from restitution because it strips profits from the defendant, rather than simply reversing a transfer of value from claimant to defendant and is premised on a rationale of deterrence.[64]

Restitution is generated by different causes of action, only one of which is unjust enrichment; in the words of Birks, restitution is 'multi-causal'.[65] Thus, restitution is not a synonym for unjust enrichment, for more than one cause of action can give rise to a right to restitution. Indeed, more than one cause of action may be available on the same set of facts. For example, the law of wrongs is the most common category of claim other than unjust enrichment in respect of which restitution is awarded.[66] Thus, restitution may be available in respect of a wrong such as the tort of deceit (as an alternative to compensation) or for unjust enrichment resulting from the claimant's mistaken payment. Although restitution is available in respect of both claims, they remain distinct. Deceit, as a wrong, is founded on a breach of duty. As we have seen from the core example of the spontaneously mistaken payment, unjust enrichment is not dependent on wrongdoing. Therefore, wrongs

[61] R Zakrzewski, *Remedies Reclassified* (OUP, Oxford, 2005) ch 4.

[62] Edelman, above n 17, ch 3; Edelman and Bant, above n 23, ch 1.

[63] Edelman, *ibid*; Edelman and Bant, *ibid*, 43–48.

[64] *Bray v Ford* [1986] AC 44 (HL) 51 (Lord Herschell).

[65] P Birks, 'Misnomer' in W Cornish and others (eds), *Restitution: Past, Present and Future* (Hart Publishing, Oxford, 1998) and P Birks, 'The Law of Restitution at the End of an Epoch' (1999) 28 *U Western Australia L Rev* 13, 16–20, endorsed by Virgo, above n 16, at 10; Edelman and Bant, above n 23, at 29–33, 86–89. Against are eg G Jones (ed), *Goff and Jones, The Law of Restitution* 6th edn (Sweet & Maxwell, London, 2002) 3, although note the apparent softening of that position in Jones, *Goff and Jones The Law of Restitution* 7th edn, above n 19, at [1-001] fn 1, and AS Burrows, 'Quadrating Restitution and Unjust Enrichment: A Matter of Principle?' [2005] *Restitution L Rev* 257.

[66] There may be others, such as an action seeking restitution to vindicate the claimant's persisting proprietary interest in the asset held by the defendant: Virgo, above n 16, ch 21; *Foskett v McKeown* [2001] 1 AC 102 (HL).

and unjust enrichment are distinct types or categories of claim and restitution is a remedy that responds to both. Further, the measure of restitution may differ depending on the nature of the claim, defences may differ, as may limitation periods and interest awards. In the interests of clarity, it is important not to conflate these different legal concepts by assuming that, where restitution is awarded, it must be in response to a claim in unjust enrichment.

(4) A Fusionist Approach

The final major assumption concerns the relationship between equity and the common law. The approach taken in this book is unashamedly fusionist, in the sense that it proceeds on the basis that the law can and should be capable of being rationally understood notwithstanding the historic divide between the courts of Chancery and the common law. It adopts the view, for example, that claims in unjust enrichment arise both at common law and equity and can be understood in the same way: mistake claims exist both at common law and in equity,[67] and both duress[68] and undue influence[69] are capable of being understood as claims in unjust enrichment. A similar fusionist approach is taken to the law of wrongs. Understood as breaches of duty, wrongs comprise both torts (common law wrongs) and equitable wrongs, such as breach of fiduciary duty.[70] On the approach taken in this work, the jurisdictional genesis of these claims should inform, but not confound, rational legal analysis.

Likewise from a remedial perspective, on the approach adopted in this book, restitution is a remedy available both in equity and at common law, which can and should be understood in the same way. It makes no sense to treat the same remedy in separate categories, according to purely historical criteria.

It follows from adopting a fusionist approach that it will be assumed throughout this book that in the area of the change of position defence, the same defence should apply both at common law and in equity, unless there are good reasons to the contrary. The aim is to identify and define one change of position defence, applicable both at common law and in equity.

Obviously, it is well beyond the bounds of this book to justify this fusionist perspective.[71] However, three points must be made about its application. First, the fusionist perspective is borne from the conviction that like cases must be treated alike. Thus, if the change of position defence is available with respect to cases of spontaneous mistake at common law, so should it be in equity, unless there are good reasons to the contrary. Otherwise, the law degenerates into an irrational series of rules which are conducive to injustice.

[67] Discussed further in Edelman and Bant, above n 23, ch 8.
[68] *Ibid*, ch 9.
[69] *Ibid*, ch 10.
[70] This view is not universally accepted: eg Millett, above n 20, at 309, 311.
[71] The author's views are set out in Edelman and Bant, above n 23.

Secondly, however, this is not to say that it is assumed that one jurisdiction will have automatically generated the same response to the same set of facts. One only has to look briefly at jurisdictions in other countries to realise that there can legitimately be different legal responses to the one set of facts. Rather, the aim is to delineate the most consistent answer to the question of when the change of position defence should apply that fits within the common law as a whole, comprising both those rules developed in the courts of Chancery and those of the common law.

Thirdly, to that end, the book will not only identify the underlying unities between common law and equity relevant to the change of position defence, but any historical differences. The analysis will then be transparent in the reasons advocated for rationalising any differences, a process that must be justified by reference to the law as a whole to yield a single change of position defence applicable both at common law and in equity.

D Methodology and Overview

(1) Introduction

Section B outlined the four major issues surrounding the change of position defence which will be addressed in this work. This section will explain the methodology adopted to resolve those issues and provide an overview of the structure of the book.

In seeking to define the change of position defence, the book will focus chiefly on English and Australian authority, although it also addresses where relevant Canadian, New Zealand and German law, in particular. There are two reasons for what might be regarded as the preferential treatment of Australian authorities. The first is that much of the most detailed primary and secondary material relevant to the change of position defence emanates from Australia and a great deal can be learnt from consistently comparing and contrasting the responses of the two jurisdictions. The second is that, as explained in the preceding section, England and Australia share a common 'unjust factors' approach to claims in unjust enrichment. Unjust enrichment is the accepted category of claim in response to which the change of position defence arises. In that context, it makes sense to draw most heavily from these jurisdictions and to be correspondingly wary of relying on conclusions from other jurisdictions that may be based on different underlying assumptions.[72]

[72] New Zealand also shares an 'unjust factors' approach. However, its change of position defence is strongly influenced by the statutory change of position defence contained in s94B Judicature Act: *National Bank of New Zealand Ltd v Waitaki International Processing (NI) Ltd* [1992] 2 NZLR 211 (New Zealand Court of Appeal), discussed in ch 5, at 148–49 and ch 10, at 251–52. The New Zealand authorities are therefore cited where the point in issue is not affected by the statutory provision, or where the influence of the statute provides a useful point of contrast.

(2) Part One—Foundations

Part one commences by exploring three well-established defences that may arise in response to claims for restitution in unjust enrichment, namely estoppel by representation, the agent's defence of payment over and the doctrine of *restitutio in integrum*.[73] It demonstrates that the same sorts of difficult questions that underlie the disputed features of the change of position defence have also confronted and been considered by earlier courts considering these defences. In particular, it has been a problem familiar to courts faced with a claim to restitution for (what would now be called) unjust enrichment that the position of the defendant has changed following his receipt of the benefit from the claimant. In that context, it is not surprising to find that courts have long been required to answer the same sorts of questions that underpin the disputed features of the change of position defence: what kinds of changes of position should reduce a defendant's liability to make restitution and why; when should a defendant's conduct preclude him from complaining of his change of position; and what is the significance of the defendant's reliance on an act or statement of the claimant in changing his position?

Although the answers of those courts to such questions need not necessarily dictate the final form of the change of position defence, it is a central contention of this book that they should be taken into account and indeed that any deviation should be clearly justified, if the law is not to become internally and unjustifiably incoherent. Part one is entitled 'Foundations' to indicate this concern with precedent and the need to locate the change of position defence within its broader historical legal context.

Part one contains three chapters. Chapter two of part one considers the lessons that may be derived from the law concerning estoppel by representation. It is important to emphasise from the outset that it does so not because estoppel by representation is assumed to be analogous to the change of position defence or, somehow, an early version of it. Rather, it is because, as with cases of change of position, courts faced with the defence of estoppel by representation raised in response to claims for restitution of benefits transferred pursuant to a mistake, for example, have had to consider the role and significance of reliance, the concept of a detrimental change of position and the possibility of the fault of the defendant operating as a bar to the defence. Given the overlap in operation between this form of estoppel and the change of position defence, an examination of its elements

[73] Pt 1 does not address the defence arising from presentation of forged bills of exchange, such as that found in *Price v Neal* (1762) 3 Burr 1354, 97 ER 871 and discussed by Goff and Jones as one of the possible, isolated examples of a change of position defence pre-dating *Lipkin Gorman.* (The other instance is the defence of payment over, considered in ch 3.) This is because the basic elements of that defence—including whether a change of position on the part of the defendant is even required—are highly uncertain. This core ambiguity makes the defence an unhelpful starting point for elucidation of the change of position defence. Goff and Jones have themselves fluctuated over its relationship to change of position: compare Jones (ed), *Goff and Jones The Law of Restitution* 6th edn, above n 65, at [40-019]–[40-020] and Jones (ed), *Goff and Jones The Law of Restitution* 7th edn, above n 19, at [40-001], [40-032].

might well reveal questions relevant to, and suggest means of resolving, the disputed features of the change of position defence.

The analysis in chapter two reveals a number of important lessons for the change of position defence. First, it demonstrates that reliance is a causal concept that would have a legitimate role to play in the change of position defence. Indeed, its breakdown of the causal aspects of reliance suggests a means of reconciling the broad and narrow versions of the defence. Secondly, chapter two raises the question whether, if reliance is required for the purposes of the change of position defence, it must be reasonable. In that context, the examination of the estoppel case law suggests some interesting ramifications of adopting a requirement of reasonable reliance, not the least of which is that it renders redundant any separate requirement of good faith. Thirdly, the analysis reveals that the core feature of a 'detrimental' change of position for the purposes of estoppel is that the change is irreversible, rather than detrimental in a purely pecuniary sense. This clearly offers a prime area for exploration within the change of position defence. Finally, the estoppel case law offers considerable insight into the potential role of fault as a bar to the defence. In particular, it suggests why a defendant's role in inducing the impugned transaction might preclude him from relying on the change of position defence and demonstrates the importance of determining whether the application of the defence would undermine or stultify another overriding legal prohibition or policy.

The same analytical approach taken to estoppel is repeated in the balance of part one. Chapter three of part one considers the payment over defence. It demonstrates that the defence has traditionally operated in response to the same sorts of claims and addresses many of the questions that underpin the disputed features of the change of position defence: what difference should it make in a claim for restitution of a received benefit that a defendant has changed his position following receipt; of what relevance is the fact that the defendant received notice of the claim for restitution before changing his position; what difference should the fault of the defendant make to the availability of any defence? Chapter three identifies and explores the answers to these questions to see what lessons they may offer for resolution of the disputed features of the change of position defence.

The analysis reveals that the same concept of irreversibility that underpins the concept of a detrimental change of position for the purposes of estoppel also founds the concept of a 'payment over'. Further, and again like estoppel, the payment over defence arguably adopts a requirement of reasonable reliance. Finally, the payment over defence appears to take much the same approach to fault as does the law of estoppel by representation. These points of intersection support the view that they form important areas for exploration within the change of position defence.

Chapter four considers the lessons that may be derived from the rescission case law and, in particular, the doctrine of *restitutio in integrum*.[74] It explains that

[74] The precise translation of this phrase is contentious: it is addressed in ch 4, commencing at 92.

rescission is a predominantly restitutionary process that responds, inter alia, to claims in unjust enrichment. Further, it demonstrates that the doctrine of *restitutio in integrum* requires more than counter-restitution and demands consideration of other changes to the parties' positions that may prevent them from being returned to the *status quo ante.* The doctrine therefore addresses the same sorts of problems that are the concern of the change of position defence and offers considerable insights relevant to its disputed features.

In particular, the examination of *restitutio in integrum* suggests a number of possible rationales for the change of position defence linked to the overriding aim of rescission (and restitution) to restore the parties as nearly as possible to the *status quo ante.* The analysis also bolsters the suggestion, made earlier in chapters two and three, that the irreversibility of a defendant's change of position is a key concern in claims for restitution and that there is a means of reconciling the broad and narrow versions of the change of position defence through causal concepts (first raised in chapter two). Finally, the analysis reveals that the doctrine of *restitutio in integrum* has grappled with the same sort of fault-based bars that have arisen for consideration in the context of estoppel by representation and the payment over defence. The doctrine thus confirms the importance of unpacking fault as a bar to the change of position defence and contains some suggestions as to how that issue might be resolved.

(3) Part Two—Definition

Part two of the book turns to the central task of defining and exploring the operation of the change of position defence. It considers the change of position case law together with considerations of principle, policy and the lessons derived from the doctrines considered in part one to determine the contested features of the change of position defence.

Part two therefore does not attempt first to determine what, in principle, the rationale of the change of position defence might (or should) be and then use that rationale to determine the disputed features of the change of position defence, as some other commentators have done (a form of 'top-down' reasoning).[75] Rather, it continues to emphasise the 'bottom-up' approach to legal scholarship prevalent in part one and typical of common law development.[76]

Some readers may regard this as a counter-intuitive structure. For example, it may seem odd that the identification of the rationale of the defence is left to the end of part two. There is no doubt that the identification of the defence's rationale is crucial to its complete definition. Indeed, many commentators have recognised the persuasive power of reasoning downwards from the defence's rationale to

[75] As in Birks, 'Change of Position and Surviving Enrichment' in W Swadling (ed), above n 8.

[76] As in W Swadling, 'The Nature of Ministerial Receipt' in P Birks (ed), *Laundering and Tracing*, above n 19.

determine its disputed features. In that context, it might seem that its natural place is at the beginning of any analysis of the defence. In this vein, Birks argued that 'without some idea of the rationale of the defence, or possible rationalia, it is impossible to think at all about its role, its future development or its application to difficult cases'.[77]

However, the structure adopted in this book rests on the belief that the interplay between rationale and decisions that Birks identified is better respected by avoiding any attempt to identify the rationale before one is clear as to what the decisions have been. Premature rationalisation risks distorting the law. If the wrong rationale is identified, and the other features of the defence are articulated by reference to that rationale, the possibilities for resultant obfuscation of the law are immense. For this reason, this book emphasises reasoning upwards from the cases, placing each piece of the puzzle in place until the final picture is revealed. On that approach, the rationale of the defence is the final piece to be identified to complete the definition of the defence. It is revealed through considering the elements of, bars to and ambit of operation of the defence in the context of the surrounding law. It is for that reason that chapter eight is both the last, and shortest, of the substantive chapters in part two. The hard work in identifying the surrounding pieces has already been done and all that remains is to identify the final part. Once the picture is completed, then the rationale can be used, as suggested, to help guide the application of the defence in future cases and to determine its relationship with other legal concepts.[78]

Part two of the book is divided into four chapters. Chapter five identifies the primary elements of the change of position defence. It demonstrates that, in order for the defence to apply, the defendant's change of position must be irreversible and (anticipatory changes of position aside) must have been caused by his receipt. The analysis then explains that the resolution of the causal question depends on the nature of the relevant change of position, in particular, whether it involves a spontaneous change in the received benefit or is a change that is brought about by the defendant. In the latter case, the defendant must show that he reasonably relied on his receipt. Finally, the chapter concludes that there is no separate requirement of good faith in the defence, it either being generally irrelevant to cases of spontaneous changes of position or subsumed within the reasonable reliance requirement.

Chapter six addresses the relevance of the defendant's fault as a bar to the defence. It shows that even where a defendant can establish the primary elements of the change of position defence, his fault taken together with the broader policy not to stultify the law's overriding prohibitions and protections will often operate to deny him the change of position defence. This limited availability of the defence is confirmed in chapter seven, which concludes that the only classes of claim to which it clearly applies are cases of spontaneous mistake and limited instances of

[77] Birks, 'Change of Position and Surviving Enrichment' in W Swadling (ed), above n 8, at 36, 38; also G Virgo, 'Change of Position: the importance of being principled' [2005] *Restitution L Rev* 34.

[78] The identification of the rationale of the defence plays a pivotal role in determining the relationship between change of position and other defences to claims in unjust enrichment: see ch 10.

duress, undue influence and failure of consideration. Beyond these categories, a combination of the reasonable reliance requirement, the role of fault as a bar to the defence and the policy against stultifying overriding legal protections and prohibitions operate to restrict significantly the application of the defence. This is so notwithstanding that the chapter also concludes that, in theory, the defence operates beyond the category of claim of unjust enrichment.

Chapter eight then considers the rationale(s) of the change of position defence in the light of the identified elements of, bars to and ambit of operation of the defence. It concludes that the rationale of the defence has two aspects, or pincers, both of which must be engaged before the defence can grip. The first is to protect the defendant from the harm he would suffer where an order to make restitution in part or in full would leave him in a worse (including entirely different) position than he was in prior to his receipt ('irreversibility protection'). The second is to restrict the protection afforded to the defendant by reference to the defendant's fault. In particular, the defendant is expected to take reasonable steps to protect himself against the possibility that his receipt might be impeachable. This 'prophylactic' aspect of the defence's rationale has the secondary effect of encouraging defendants in like circumstances to take reasonable steps to avoid the costs (both to them and to claimants) of reversing vitiated-consent transfers.

Part two concludes in chapter nine by summarising the findings of the book with respect to the elements, bars, ambit of operation and rationale of the defence.

(4) Part Three—Ramifications

Part three contains only one chapter. Chapter ten addresses the relationship between the change of position defence and other related defences in the light of its definition in part two.

Chapter ten firstly revisits the defences and doctrines which are the subject of part one. It concludes that only the payment over defence may be properly subsumed within the change of position defence. While *restitutio in integrum* is strongly analogous to change of position, the chapter concludes that it is premature to equate the two doctrines. More must be done to explore and rationalise their differences, differences particularly evident in their treatment of defendants who have innocently induced a claimant's vitiated transfer. Further, the chapter concludes that the defence of estoppel by representation remains sufficiently distinct to demand separate pleading and consideration. This is not to deny that its application may result in the same outcome as flows from the successful application of the change of position defence in some, or even in many cases. But its elements and, potentially, its rationale are different and thus it cannot be properly regarded as subsumed in, or rendered superfluous by, the change of position defence.

The chapter then turns to consider two further classes of common law defence that potentially respond to claims for restitution of a benefit transferred to a defendant, namely the defences of good consideration and bona fide purchase. These defences are 'related' to the change of position defence only in the limited sense that, at first sight, they display apparent similarities with that defence that might suggest a degree of overlap between them. Chapter ten demonstrates, however, that any similarities are superficial and should not be allowed to obscure the clear demarcation between the defences. This conclusion also explains the absence of the defences from part one: responding to dissimilar questions and consequently containing different elements, they are an unsuitable foundation for resolution of the disputed features of the change of position defence.

Chapter ten explains that the label of 'good consideration' harbours two separate bodies of law that operate to reduce a defendant's restitutionary liability: the counterclaim by way of set-off for failure of basis and the defence of receipt in satisfaction of an existing right. Failure of basis and its relationship to change of position is addressed earlier in the book in the context of rescission. Chapter ten briefly reviews that relationship before proceeding to identify the distinctions between the change of position defence and the defence of receipt in satisfaction of an existing right. The latter defence is then demonstrated to have its own characteristics and to address different concerns from the change of position defence.

The next defence considered is the defence of bona fide purchase. The chapter explains that, although the defence appears to share some characteristics with the change of position defence, it traditionally responds to different classes of claim, has a distinct underlying purpose or rationale and therefore operates independently of change of position.

The final defences considered in the chapter are statutory defences that are analogous to the change of position defence. Being creations of Parliament, they can and do reflect different policies and concerns from the common law change of position defence. Their similarities and differences are identified and briefly examined in chapter ten so as to provide a more complete picture of applicable change of position defences. In this way, the book concludes by taking a small but not insignificant step towards the comprehensive mapping of defences to unjust enrichment.

Part One

Foundations

2

Lessons from Estoppel by Representation

A Introduction

PROFESSOR BIRKS INITIALLY described the change of position defence as 'estoppel with the requirement of a representation struck out.'[1] Although he subsequently withdrew from that position,[2] there is no doubt that estoppel by representation and the change of position defence may operate in the same kinds of circumstances and by reference to the same factual elements. A prime example of this overlap is the leading estoppel by representation case of *Avon City Council v Howlett*.[3] In that case, an employer brought an action for restitution of moneys mistakenly overpaid to its employee. For the purposes of the appeal, the employee was treated as having dissipated only part of the overpayment in reliance on the employer's assurances that he was entitled to the amount. The question was whether estoppel by representation operated as a complete defence to the claimant's action. By a majority, the court held that as the doctrine operated as a rule of evidence, it barred the claimant's action completely.[4] Today, the same facts (in particular, those relating to the defendant's reliance and change of position) would invite the defendant to rely on the change of position defence, a plea that may well be successful, albeit only *pro tanto*, to the extent of the defendant's change.

The operational overlap between estoppel by representation and the change of position defence invites the question whether there should be any continuing role for that estoppel where the change of position defence applies. The key to answering that question lies in identifying the rationale of estoppel by representation, a matter of significant controversy. Identification of the proper rationale will in turn reveal the appropriate remedial consequence(s) of establishing the estoppel. In particular, it will dictate whether estoppel by representation should operate as a

[1] P Birks, *An Introduction to the Law of Restitution* rev edn (Clarendon Press, Oxford, 1989) 410; P Birks, *Restitution-The Future* (The Federation Press, Sydney, 1992) 141–43.

[2] P Birks, 'Change of Position and Surviving Enrichment' in W Swadling (ed), *The Limits of Restitutionary Claims: A Comparative Analysis* (The United Kingdom Committee of Comparative Law, Glasgow, 1997) 50–51.

[3] [1983] 1 WLR 605 (CA).

[4] *Ibid*, at 624 (Slade LJ) 611 (Eveleigh LJ).

complete defence and, if not, the appropriate measure of remedial response. It is this question of remedial consequence that makes the continued operation of estoppel by representation alongside the change of position defence so contentious.[5]

Although these are matters of great importance, they are not dealt with in this chapter.[6] This chapter asks a different (and prior) kind of question, namely what light is shed on the contested elements of the change of position defence by examining the core elements of the defence of estoppel by representation? In particular, the role and operation of the concepts of reliance and a detrimental change of position on the part of the defendant are the subject of significant controversy in relation to the change of position defence.[7] In that context, and given the operational overlap between the defences, it makes sense to examine the nature and operation of those elements in the context of estoppel by representation to see what light may be shed on their possible roles and operation in the context of the change of position defence. Notably, this enquiry does not assume that estoppel by representation and change of position are analogous defences and thus, that the elements of one should be reflected in the other. Accordingly, the analysis is not affected by the fact that estoppel by representation may have an entirely different doctrinal basis to the change of position defence and therefore may continue to operate alongside the change of position defence.

This chapter will chiefly focus on the doctrine of estoppel by representation, being the doctrine that most clearly overlaps in its area of operation with the change of position defence. In that context, any references to 'estoppel' *simpliciter* in this chapter and book mean estoppel by representation. However, cases of estoppel by convention, promissory and proprietary estoppel will also be canvassed where constructive, where the legal point in issue does not differ substantially between the varying classes of estoppel. In these cases, the particular form of estoppel will be identified. As the chapter is considering estoppel as a defence only, the representor will be labelled 'the claimant' and the representee 'the defendant', unless otherwise indicated.

This chapter will demonstrate that, indeed, examination of estoppel by representation sheds illuminating light on the potential role of reliance in the change of position defence, as well as the kinds of alterations of position that may attract the defence. It also reveals the significant ambiguity in the manner in which courts respond to fault on the part of defendants who might otherwise be able to rely on a defence arising from their detrimental reliance.

[5] *RBC Dominion Securities Inc v Dawson* (1994) 111 DLR (4th) 230 (Newfoundland Court of Appeal); *Scottish Equitable Plc v Derby* [2001] EWCA Civ 369, [2001] 3 All ER 818; *National Westminster Bank Plc v Somer International (UK) Ltd* [2001] EWCA Civ 970, [2002] QB 1286.

[6] The question is revisited in ch 10, at 224–30.

[7] Ch 1, at 4, 9.

B Elements of Estoppel by Representation

There are three undisputed elements of estoppel by representation.

- The claimant must have made a representation to the defendant.[8]
- The defendant must have acted in reliance on that representation.
- The defendant will suffer detriment if the claimant is allowed to resile from her representation.

It is a matter of controversy whether there is a fourth element; namely, that the claimant must have intended or known that the defendant would rely, or would be likely to rely on the representation. We will not address the existence or otherwise of this element. That is because the element, if it exists, is peculiar to estoppel and is irrelevant to any examination of the change of position defence. The element reflects the (controversial) view that estoppel arises primarily in response to the claimant's 'unconscionable' or 'unconscientious' conduct in knowingly or intentionally inducing the defendant's change of position. There is no equivalent element, disputed or otherwise, in the change of position defence and certainly no argument that the defence arises primarily in response to the claimant's unconscionable conduct. Such an element therefore cannot be expected to inform or shed light on the nature of the change of position defence.

This section examines each of the three core elements of estoppel by representation in turn and considers the lessons that may be drawn from that study for the change of position defence.

(1) Representation

The claimant's representation may be explicit or implicit, by words or conduct. In order to count against a claimant, the representation must be clear and unambiguous.[9] Therefore, the traditional position is that a mere payment does not, in and of itself, contain an implicit representation that the defendant is entitled to the

[8] It is a matter of controversy whether the representation may be one of law. On one view, where the representation is one of law, two assumptions operate to restrict the availability of estoppel: first, the assumption that it is unreasonable to rely on a mere expression of opinion and secondly, that both parties generally are deemed to be in as good a position as one another to investigate the legal position: S Wilken, *Wilken and Villiers The Law of Waiver, Variation and Estoppel* (OUP, Oxford, 2002) 163. Both assumptions relate to the reasonableness of the defendant's reliance, rather than to whether the assumption is intrinsically one of existing law or fact, as to which see further below, at 43–47. Another view is that, being a rule of evidence, the representation must relate to a fact. Whether this is correct depends on the rationale or role of estoppel by representation, a matter beyond this book. For a recent case where estoppel by representation was said to operate notwithstanding that the representation was acknowledged to be one of law, see *Hutchison v Steria Ltd* [2006] EWCA Civ 1551 [89] (Neuberger LJ). For present purposes, however, the controversy is inconsequential: what is relevant is the requirement of an unambiguous representation, not whether it is one of fact or law.

[9] *Low v Bouverie* [1891] 3 Ch 82 (CA) 106, 113.

payment. In general, it is only where the claimant is under a duty of accuracy,[10] or being aware of the defendant's mistake, comes under a duty to speak,[11] that a representation will be implicit in the fact of the payment.

However, it is possible that the requirement of clarity of representation simply reflects a more general requirement that the defendant's reliance be reasonable.[12] It is to the core element of reliance that we now turn.

(2) Reliance

(a) The Meaning of Reliance

Considering the central importance of reliance to estoppel by representation, there is surprisingly little discussion in either the authorities or commentaries as to what reliance means. One notable exception is Professor Elizabeth Cooke, whose monograph *The Modern Law of Estoppel* considers the requirement of reliance in detail.[13] Cooke identifies two aspects to the requirement of reliance. The first is 'reliance in the mind'[14]: the need for the defendant to have made an assumption as to a state of affairs and for that assumption to have been induced or fortified by the claimant. The second aspect of reliance is that the assumption must have caused an action. Both of these elements, one mental, the other practical or outward-looking, must be satisfied in order for reliance to be established.[15]

On this definition of reliance, a defendant who knew the claimant's representation was false at the time he changed his position will not possess the mental element of reliance required to satisfy the estoppel. This is because the defendant will not have acted on the basis of any assumption attributable to the representation. Any subsequent action purportedly based on the representation will be a con-

[10] *Skyring v Greenwood* (1825) 4 B & C 281, 107 ER 1064 (KB).

[11] *Holt v Markham* [1923] 1 KB 504 (CA); *Moorgate Mercantile Co Ltd v Twitchings* [1977] AC 890 (HL); *Pacol Ltd v Trade Lines Ltd ('The Henrik Sif')* [1982] 1 Lloyd's Rep 456 (QB (Comm Ct)), 465 (Webster J); *The Stolt Loyalty* [1993] 2 Lloyd's Rep 281 (QB) 289–90 (Clarke J); *The Indian Endurance (No 2) Republic of India v India Steamship Co Ltd* [1996] 3 All ER 641 (CA) 654–55 (Staughton LJ), discussed in Wilken, above n 8, at 172–74. Australian authorities include *Trenorden v Martin* [1934] SASR 340 (South Australia Supreme Court); *Williams v Frayne* (1937) 58 CLR 710 (High Court of Australia) 736 (Dixon J); *Nigel Watts Fashion Agencies Ltd v GIO General Ltd* (1995) 8 ANZ Ins Cas 61-235 (New South Wales Court of Appeal) 75, 651 (Handley JA).

[12] The reasonableness requirement is considered below, at 43–47. Wilken, *ibid* and P Feltham, D Hochberg and T Leech, *Spencer Bower The Law Relating to Estoppel by Representation* 4th edn (LexisNexis UK, London, 2004). The decision has been taken in this book to cite the fourth edition of this seminal work on estoppel separately from the third edition, A Turner (ed), *Spencer Bower and Turner: The Law Relating to Estoppel by Representation* 3rd edn (Butterworths, London, 1977), of which Sir Alexander Turner had prime authorship. As the authors of the fourth edition themselves note, the new edition is so thoroughly revised and rewritten that it bears insufficient resemblance to the third edition even to bear the same title: Feltham, Hochberg and Leech, *ibid*, at viii.

[13] (OUP, Oxford, 2000) 88–96. See also: K Handley, *Estoppel by Conduct and Election* (Sweet & Maxwell, London, 2006) [1-007]–[1-008].

[14] Cooke, *ibid*, at 89.

[15] Considered further below, at 30–31, 44–45.

scious risk taken in the hope that the claimant will not later seek to resile from her representation.[16] It follows that in this case, the reliance requirement renders redundant any need for a separate requirement of 'good faith' on the part of the defendant. A defendant who knows the falsity of the representation cannot act in reliance on it. There is no such creature as 'bad faith reliance' in this context.

More difficult to analyse in terms of reliance is the case where a defendant suspects, but does not actually know of the falsity of the representation. Suppose a defendant received a mistaken payment but was assured by the payer that it was the correct amount. Suppose further that, notwithstanding the claimant's assurances, the defendant continued to suspect a mistake and consciously took a risk in changing his position in the hope of retaining a windfall benefit. In this case, there are two significant hurdles to proving reliance. First, the defendant must show that, notwithstanding his suspicions, he thought it was more likely than not that the representation was true (and thus formed part of the assumption on which he acted). Even if the representation formed part of the background story that triggered the defendant's subsequent actions, given his suspicions, it will be difficult for him to establish his belief in the truth of the representation so as to prove this mental element of reliance. Secondly, in this example, any action taken by the defendant arguably is not made on the basis of any assumption as to the truth of that representation, but on the chance (independent of the truth or falsity of the representation) that he might retain a windfall. If so, the second aspect of reliance (pertaining to the effect of the induced assumption on the defendant's decision to act) cannot be established.

If, contrary to this analysis, the defendant in the given example could be regarded as having relied on the truth of the representation, then the question arises whether the defendant's reliance should count as a matter of policy given his risk-taking or, perhaps, dishonesty. As we will see in the next section, this is resolved for the purposes of estoppel by asking whether the defendant's reliance was reasonable.[17]

Finally, suppose that, in a variation on the last example, a defendant changed his position in all good faith, notwithstanding his persisting doubts, precisely because he trusted the claimant (and thus her assurances that he was entitled to the mistaken payment). In this scenario, it could be said that the defendant suspended his disbelief, assumed the truth of the representation and acted on that basis. In these circumstances, it does make sense to say that the defendant acted in reliance on the representation, notwithstanding his persisting doubts. However, the same element of risk-taking is present in this case as in the case of the defendant who knows of the vitiating factor, or suspecting it, seeks to retain a windfall benefit. In those

[16] This analysis finds parallels in the 'mistake' v 'misprediction' dichotomy found in respect of primary claims in unjust enrichment. It is beyond this book to explore those parallels, but for discussions of the mistake/misprediction issue see J Edelman and E Bant, *Unjust Enrichment in Australia* (OUP, Melbourne, 2006) 168–70; W Seah, 'Mispredictions, Mistakes and the Law of Unjust Enrichment' [2007] *Restitution L Rev* 93.

[17] At 43–47.

circumstances, the question again becomes whether, given the defendant's risk-taking, his reliance was reasonable.

A good example of the complex interplay between knowledge, suspicion and good faith on the one hand, and reliance and reasonable reliance on the other, is *United Overseas Bank v Jiwani.*[18] In that case, a bank credited the defendant's account with $11,000 twice, the second payment being made by mistake. The defendant checked his account by telephone and by a personal visit to the bank. He then used the extra payment to assist in the purchase of a hotel. When the bank sought to recover the amount of the overpayment, the defendant raised a defence of estoppel by representation. In rejecting the defence, MacKenna J held, among other things, that the defendant knew or suspected that the second payment of $11,000 was a mistake and thus estoppel was not established.[19]

There are various ways in which this finding might be analysed. First, it could be said that, knowing of the mistake, the defendant did not assume he was entitled to the extra $11,000 and therefore did not rely on the bank's representation.[20] Alternatively, it could be argued that, suspecting a mistake and having decided to change his position whether or not the representation was accurate in the hope of retaining a windfall benefit, the defendant either did not assume he was entitled to the benefit, or that assumption did not form a basis on which he acted. Thirdly, it could be argued that given his suspicions, the defendant's reliance was not reasonable. A final possibility is that the defence failed because the defendant did not act in good faith. We return to explore the interplay between reasonableness and good faith in more detail below.[21]

(b) The Role of Reliance as a Causal Requirement

Returning to reliance *simpliciter*, what is the role or function of reliance as a key element of estoppel? Cooke characterises the reliance requirement as one of causation: it seeks to answer the very difficult question when a claimant's representation can be said to have caused the defendant to act in a certain way.[22] Put in overtly causal terms, the concept of reliance again has two aspects: first, the defendant must show that the claimant's representation caused him to adopt an assumption (reliance in the mind) and secondly, that the assumption caused him to change his position (the outward-looking, practical aspect of reliance).

Cooke's characterisation is insightful because it demonstrates that when the question of causation involves human decision-making as it does in estoppel, there are two steps in the causal chain; first, between the representation and the assumption and secondly, between the assumption and the change of position.

[18] [1976] 1 WLR 964 (QB).

[19] *Ibid*, at 970.

[20] Either an implicit representation that the defendant was entitled to the money stated in his account, or perhaps arising from the bank's breach of its duty to accurately state his account: *United Overseas Bank v Jiwani* [1976] 1 WLR 964 (QB) 968.

[21] At 45.

Eliding the two stages into one (did the representation cause the change of position?) obscures that point. The defendant must establish both links in order to demonstrate reliance and may fail at either stage and for different reasons, a point to which we will return below.[23] For example, a defendant may be induced by the claimant's representation to assume that the full amount of the payment received from the claimant is the defendant's to deal with as he pleases. Nonetheless, his subsequent decision to spend the notes on pre-booked tickets is not caused in any way by that assumption. The assumption post-dates his decision to purchase the tickets. Conversely, a defendant may decide to purchase tickets on the basis of his honest but mistaken assumption that a payment received from the claimant is his to deal with as he pleases. However, if the payment was received with a note expressly explaining that it was to be held for the benefit of a third party, it cannot be said that the claimant's representation induced the defendant's assumption: the defendant's mistaken assumption was in this sense 'spontaneous'.[24] A recent example of this kind of case is *Hutchison v Steria Ltd*,[25] where Mummery LJ, with whom Jacob LJ agreed, found that even if there were representations made by an employer as to its employee's entitlement under a pension scheme contained in a booklet and letter provided to the employee, its 'warning that the interpretation of the booklet must be read subject to the [contradictory] Trust Deed and the Rules makes it impossible for Mr Hutchison to establish reliance . . .'.

(c) The Applicable Test of Causation

Even accepting that reliance is a causal concept, it still remains to determine the precise test of causation at each stage of the reliance enquiry.

In theory, the familiar 'but for' test of causation could be adopted at both points,[26] so that the relevant questions to establish reliance would be: but for the representation would the defendant not have made the assumption; and, but for the assumption, would he not have acted as he did? However, it is submitted that, as a matter of principle, the 'but for' test should be treated with caution in this context. That test is useful and appropriate for determining causation in most cases involving involuntary objects. However, it is notoriously less satisfactory when dealing with cases of overdetermination.[27] Overdetermination occurs when there

[22] Above n 13, at 88–96. Also Feltham, Hochberg and Leech, above n 12, at 90.

[23] Below, at 44–45.

[24] Alternatively, it may be unreasonable for the defendant to make that assumption and the defence may fail on that ground: see further below, at 44.

[25] [2006] EWCA Civ 1551 [67]. *Cf* discussion in *Peekay Intermark Ltd & Anor v Australia and New Zealand Banking Group Ltd* [2006] EWCA Civ 386, [2006] 2 Lloyd's Rep 511 [29]–[40] (Moore-Bick LJ, Lawrence Collins J concurring) [66]–[70] (Chadwick LJ).

[26] Cooke herself adopts a 'but for' approach at the second stage of enquiry, but not at the first (relating to the adoption of an assumption): Cooke, above n 13, at 93–96, 105–11.

[27] The problem is broadly, but not universally, accepted: *cf* D Lewis, 'Causation as Influence' in J Collins, N Hall and L Paul (eds), *Causation and Counterfactuals* (MIT Press, Cambridge, Mass, 2004); R Stevens, *Torts and Rights* (OUP, Oxford, 2007) 133–44.

are multiple causes present that are independently sufficient for the result that occurred. A classic example of an overdetermined result used by causation scholars involves two fires that reached a barn at the same time. Each was independently sufficient to burn it down. Applying the 'but for' test seems to provide the counter-intuitive result that neither fire caused the destruction of the barn: but for one fire, it would still have been burnt down by the other. Similar difficulties arise where there are multiple causes that, taken singly, are insufficient to produce the result but, when joined together, are sufficient to produce the consequence that in fact occurred. Suppose there were two small fires that, considered individually, were insufficient to burn down the barn. However, when combined, they were sufficient. Again, application of the 'but for' test would indicate that neither fire was a cause of the barn burning down.

Although cases of overdetermination are fairly rare in involuntary causation scenarios, they are rife in the context of decision-making. Issues of human motivation are notoriously complex. There will usually be a number of factors, both conscious and subliminal, that lead to a decision to act. In that context, it is often impossible to say that a decision would not have been made but for the putative cause. The combination of other factors would or may have been sufficient for the impugned decision anyway. Or the reasons may all have been independently insufficient to induce the impugned decision but become sufficient when combined in one or more ways.

Examples in the case law abound. Two of the more notorious examples of overdetermination come from the areas of misrepresentation and duress. In *Edgington v Fitzmaurice*,[28] the claimant frankly admitted that, but for the defendant's representations, he still would have entered into the impugned transaction because of his own, independent mistake. Likewise, in *Barton v Armstrong*,[29] the claimant admitted that, but for the defendant's threat to kill him if he did not enter into the impugned transactions, he may well still have done so for commercial reasons. In each case, the claimant's decision was overdetermined and application of the 'but for' test would have yielded the conclusion that the putative causes (the defendant's misrepresentation, the defendant's threat) did not relevantly cause the claimant's decision to act. This problem of overdetermination is exacerbated when the affected party is not cognisant of all her motivating reasons for decision and so is not sure what she would have decided but for the putative cause (a problem of 'forensic uncertainty' to which we will return below).

Commentators considering the problem of overdetermined results have argued for a refinement of the 'but for' test known as the 'NESS' test of causation, in which the proposed causal element must be a Necessary Element of a Set of conditions that are together Sufficient to produce the relevant consequence.[30] For example,

[28] (1885) 29 Ch 459 (CA).

[29] [1976] AC 104 (PC).

[30] Hart and Honoré labelled this a 'causally relevant condition': H Hart and A Honoré, *Causation in the Law* 2nd edn (Clarendon Press, Oxford, 1985) 111–17, 122–25, 128–29, 235–53. The test was further developed and popularised as the 'NESS' test through the work of Richard Wright: see in particular

when asking in relation to the overdetermined hypothetical whether it was the defendant's act in lighting a fire that, together with another (independently lit) fire, caused the barn to burn down, the NESS test does not ask whether but for the defendant's act, the barn would not have burnt down. Rather, in determining the cause of the barn's destruction, there will be a number of necessary elements that together were sufficient to produce the consequence: combustible material, oxygen, an incendiary device and a fire of sufficient size are some of the most obvious. If we ask whether the defendant's act in lighting a fire was necessary to complete a set of those conditions together sufficient to produce the result that actually occurred (the barn burning down), the answer will be yes. This is so whether or not there was another, equally sufficient set of conditions that do not include the defendant's act, but do include the other fire.

Given that overdetermination is relatively common in cases of decision-making, it is clear that the 'but for' test is not always going to be an appropriate or useful causal test in that context. The NESS test may offer a better approach in those cases. However, the NESS test has its own limitations. In particular, application of the NESS test breaks down in cases where there are significant gaps in the information or knowledge about the causal process involved in producing the result that occurred. In these cases, it may not be possible to make any causal generalisations about the process that led to the result and therefore it is not possible to determine a set of antecedent conditions that together were sufficient to produce the result that in fact occurred. Without that sufficient set, the necessity of the putative cause to the set cannot be established.

This is the problem of endemic forensic uncertainty. Although it is relatively rare in cases of involuntary causation (we generally understand how fires operate and barns burn, for example), it is far more common in cases of causation in decision-making. When we ask whether a particular assumption (or consideration) was a necessary element of a set of conditions that are together sufficient to produce a particular defendant's decision to act, there will often be no clear answer. It is impossible to identify all the various considerations—perhaps even the core considerations—that weighed in the mind of the defendant. And even if they could be identified, the considerations cannot be quantified, nor their relative role in the decision-making process objectively and scientifically assessed. Neither of these points negate Bowen LJ's famous aphorism that the state of a man's mind is as much a fact, as the state of his digestion.[31] However, they do point to the undeniable truth that to weigh and determine the relative importance of the factors that together prompt a person's decision to act is an impossible task. As Birks noted in

RW Wright, 'Causation in Tort Law' (1985) 73 *California LR* 1735; RW Wright, 'Causation, Responsibility, Risk, Probability, Naked Statistics and Proof: Pruning the Bramble Bush by Clarifying the Concepts' (1988) 73 *Iowa L Rev* 1001; RW Wright, 'Once More into the Bramble Bush: Duty, Causal Contribution, and the Extent of Legal Responsibility' (2001) 54 *Vanderbilt L R* 1071; RW Wright, 'Acts and Omissions as Positive and Negative Causes' in J Neyers, E Chamberlain and G Pitel (eds), *Emerging Issues in Tort Law* (Hart Publishing, Oxford and Portland, Oregon, 2007). The NESS analysis adopted in this work takes Wright's formulation as its starting point.

[31] *Edgington v Fitzmaurice* (1885) 29 Ch 459 (CA) 483.

the context of considering claims based on mistake: 'The problem arises because mental processes cannot be weighed and measured. Will-power has no voltage.'[32]

The final concern with application of the 'but for' and NESS tests in the context of decision-making is the possibility that, even if all the antecedent conditions together sufficient to produce a party's decision to act were capable of being identified and repeated, there is no certainty that the party would act in the same way. The propensity for humans to learn from their mistakes, or simply decide differently on the day, has the effect that the proposition that the assumption was such a necessary element cannot be established.[33] This possibility of indeterminacy undermines the efficacy of both the 'but for' and NESS tests of causation.

Professor Richard Wright argues that humans are no less indeterminate than other things or objects.[34] In his view, it is theoretically possible to list all the considerations, motives and factors that together produce a particular decision to act, and that in theory, the result should always be replicated given those same sets of considerations, motives and factors. Of course that proposition cannot be tested and so does not really get us any further in determining the appropriate test for causation in the context of human decisions.

One does not need entirely to accept Wright's argument to concede that in cases where, as a matter of general observation, there are demonstrated patterns of normal reactive human behaviour, or the particular defendant has proven patterns of behaviour, the 'but for' and NESS tests operate without great difficulty. In these cases, the decision-making process seems more automatic, less of a conscious process, more predictable and thus perhaps more akin to cases of involuntary causation.[35] Suppose a driver is faced with a child running out in front of him on the road and applies his brakes. When we ask, but for the child, would the driver have applied the brakes, we know within reasonable bounds what the answer is. The child caused the driver to apply his brakes: but for her appearance, the driver would have continued on as before. We know this as a matter of observed patterns of general human behaviour. So, too, when a defendant makes regular monthly payments on a mortgage. When we ask whether, but for the claimant's representation that the defendant was entitled to a money payment, the defendant would not have made a particular mortgage payment, we know again within reasonable bounds what the answer is. But for the payment, the defendant still would have made the monthly repayment on his mortgage (because that is what he always does). Breaking reliance down into its constituent elements, the defendant's assumption that he must make the mortgage payments and his actions based on

[32] Birks, *An Introduction to the Law of Restitution*, above n 1, at 157.

[33] A Honoré, 'Necessary and Sufficient Conditions in Tort Law' in D Owen (ed), *Philosophical Foundations of Tort Law* (Clarendon Press, Oxford, 1995) 382–84.

[34] Wright, 'Causation in Tort Law' above n 30, fn 44; Wright, 'Acts and Omissions as Positive and Negative Causes' in J Neyers, E Chamberlain and G Pitel (eds), above n 30, at 298; also JL Mackie, *The Cement of the Universe: A Study of Causation* (Clarendon Press, Oxford, 1974) 131–36.

[35] V Black, 'Decision Causation: Pandora's Tool-Box' in J Neyers, E Chamberlain and G Pitel (eds), *Emerging Issues in Tort Law* (Hart Publishing, Oxford and Portland, Oregon, 2007) 327.

that assumption were unaffected by the representation. And so the representation does not cause the defendant to make the repayment in the 'but for' sense. Courts may also be prepared to assume patterns of behaviour—such as that people spend to the limits of their weekly income.[36] Therefore, it might well be possible to apply the 'but for' or NESS tests with some degree of certainty to situations where there is an established or assumed pattern of behaviour, either in the individual concerned or as a matter of collective observation of how people normally react.

However, this does not mean that they will always be useful tests in other, more complex contexts where there is no established or assumed pattern of behaviour. The proprietary estoppel case of *Gillett v Holt*[37] is a prime example of this. In that case, a boy (the claimant) was befriended by a much older man of superior social status (the defendant). At the defendant's invitation, the claimant gave up his schooling to come to live with the defendant and learn about managing his farming business. Their relationship continued for decades, during which time the defendant repeatedly assured the claimant that the claimant would succeed to his farming business. In reliance on these assurances, the claimant remained in the farmhouse, eventually marrying and raising his family there, and became the farm manager for the defendant's property. The relationship between the parties eventually deteriorated and the defendant sought to have the claimant and his family permanently excluded from the farm. In finding that the claimant had relied on the defendant's assurances, Robert Walker LJ said that it was impossible to speculate what the claimant might have done but for the defendant's assurances.[38] 'It is entirely a matter of conjecture what the future might have held for the Gilletts . . .. The fact is that they relied on Mr Holt's assurances . . .'[39]

Given the identified problems of overdetermination, endemic forensic uncertainty and indeterminacy in cases involving causation in decision-making, the question arises whether an alternative test of causation should be adopted. It is suggested that the most that can be usefully asked, in order to establish the required causal link between assumption and decision, is whether the particular factor, reason or consideration was one of a set of reasons that together appeared adequate to this person on this occasion and on which he therefore acted (the 'a factor' test). The particular reason or consideration must be one of a set of factors that together 'provide an adequate explanation of the decision and that the person who makes the decision would acknowledge . . . were his reasons . . .'[40] On the 'a

[36] As in *Skyring v Greenwood* (1825) 4 B & C 281, 289; 107 ER 1064 (KB) 1067 (Abbott CJ): 'Every prudent man accommodates his mode of living to what he supposes to be his income.' See also: *Lloyds Bank Ltd v The Hon Cecily Brooks* (1950) 72 *Journal of the Institute of Bankers* 114 (KB).

[37] [2001] Ch 210 (CA). Although a case of proprietary estoppel, rather than estoppel by representation, there is no reason to think that the reliance requirement differs either in its role or operation between those estoppels.

[38] Robert Walker LJ expressly noted that the same approach to detrimental reliance applied to cases of estoppel by representation: *Gillett v Holt* [2001] Ch 210 (CA) 233, adopting the approach of Dixon J in *Grundt v Great Boulder Pty Gold Mines Ltd* (1937) 59 CLR 641 (High Court of Australia).

[39] *Gillett v Holt* [2001] Ch 210 (CA) 234–35.

[40] A Honoré, above n 33, at 384.

factor' test, no attempt is made to assemble or identify a set of reasons that together were sufficient to produce the decision to act, nor to assess the necessity of the putative cause as part of a set of reasons. Provided the putative cause was one of the factors the person took into account in deciding to act on the day in question, it will count as a cause of his action.

There may also be policy reasons that favour an 'a factor' test in preference to the 'but for' or NESS tests of causation in cases where a party's vitiated intention is at the heart of the reason for liability, or the application of a defence. In such cases the law might well take the view that, as a matter of policy, where the claimant's actions are demonstrated to have been a factor in the defendant's decision to act, that is enough. This is because in cases where an element of the claim or defence is demonstrating that the party's intention was vitiated, it may reflect a policy to protect the party's autonomy in decision-making. Since no objective measure exists to show at what point a party's intention is sufficiently vitiated to attract intervention, the need to protect the party's autonomy dictates that the bar be set at the level of any non-trivial influence or factor in the party's decision-making. On this approach, it is the nature of the liability itself which calls for a more liberal approach to causation, rather than specifically being a matter of causation.[41] Either approach, though, supports the adoption of an 'a factor' approach in preference to the 'but for' or NESS tests of causation.

This conclusion finds support in the estoppel case law. We have seen that the reliance requirement of estoppel adopts an approach to causation that focuses first on the effect of the representation on the mind of the defendant, then on the effect of that belief on the defendant's decision to act. A wealth of decisions now demonstrate[42] that, provided the defendant can show[43] that the representation influenced (was *a* factor in) the adoption of the assumption by him, or reinforced an existing assumption and that the assumption was *a* reason for the defendant's decision to change his position, then reliance is made out. There is no need for the defendant to show that the representation was the sole influencing factor, or that but for the representation, he would have acted differently. As Robert Goff J

[41] L Hoffmann, 'Causation' (2005) 121 *LQR* 592, 595.

[42] eg *Amalgamated Investment and Property Co Ltd (In Liquidation) v Texas Commerce International Bank Ltd* [1982] QB 84 (CA and QB) (estoppel by convention); *Wayling v Jones* (1993) 69 P & CR 170 (CA) (proprietary estoppel); *Gillett v Holt* [2001] Ch 210 (CA) 226 (Robert Walker LJ) (proprietary estoppel); *Campbell v Griffin* [2001] EWCA Civ 990, (2001) 82 P & CR DG23 [25]–[29] (Robert Walker LJ, President and Thorpe LJ concurring) (proprietary estoppel); *Hutchison v Steria Ltd* [2006] EWCA Civ 1551 [117] (Neuberger LJ) (estoppel by representation). The causal question between the varying classes of estoppel does not differ: see discussion below, at n 44 and 57. Australian authorities include *Austral Standard Cables Pty Ltd v Walker Nominees Pty Ltd* (1992) 26 NSWLR 524 (New South Wales Court of Appeal) 540 (Handley JA) and *Byron Shire Council v Vaughan (No 2)* [2000] NSWLEC 216 (Land and Environment Court of New South Wales) [25]–[26] (Lloyd J). Commentators include Turner (ed), above n 12, at 103; J Munro, 'The New Law of Estoppel' (1993) 23 *Victoria Uni Wellington L Rev* 271, 295; Wilken, above n 8, at 185; K Handley, above n 13, at [5-012]. *Cf* Cooke, above n 13, at 93–96, 108–11, M Spence, *Protecting Reliance: The Emergent Doctrine of Equitable Estoppel* (Hart Publishing, Oxford, 1999) 50–52.

[43] See below, at 39–40.

stated in *Amalgamated Investment and Property Co Ltd (In Liquidation) v Texas Commerce International Bank Ltd*:

> . . . it is, in my judgment, no bar to a conclusion that the other party's conduct has been so influenced, that his conduct did not derive its origin only from the encouragement or representation of the first party. There may be cases where the representee has proceeded initially on the basis of a belief derived from some other source independent of the representor, but his belief has subsequently been confirmed by the encouragement or representation of the representor. In such a case, the question is not whether the representee acted, or desisted from acting, solely in reliance upon the encouragement or representation of the other party; the question is rather whether his conduct was so *influenced* by the encouragement or representation (I take the word 'influenced' from the judgment of Bowen LJ in *Edgington v Fitzmaurice* (1885) 29 Ch D 459, 481) that it would be unconscionable for the representor thereafter to enforce his strict legal rights.[44]

While the reference to 'sole' influence may be regarded as rejecting any requirement that the putative cause be independently sufficient to bring about impugned decision, the facts of the case demonstrate that the 'but for' test of causation was also being rejected. In that case, the defendant bank assumed that the claimant's guarantee was binding because of an internal error attributable to persons within, or documents held within the bank. Notwithstanding this, Robert Goff J found that the claimants' course of conduct influenced the bank's mistaken belief, in the sense that it operated to confirm and reinforce it. It made no difference to this finding that the origin of the mistake lay within the bank's own organisation and thus that, but for the claimant's course of conduct, the bank would have remained mistaken. That is, it did not matter that the result (the mistaken belief) was overdetermined.

Robert Goff J's reference to *Edgington v Fitzmaurice*[45] emphasises this rejection of the 'but for' test. *Edgington* is the leading authority in the area of misrepresentation where, again, the causal question is the effect of a (mis)representation on the decision of a party to act (or omit to act). In that case, the claimant frankly admitted that he would not have purchased the shares in the company had it not been for his own mistake. However, another factor which influenced his decision was the defendant's misstatement in a circular. Each member of the court in *Edgington v Fitzmaurice* held that this influence satisfied the causation requirement.[46] In addition to the passage relied upon by Robert Goff J, Bowen LJ stated:

[44] *Amalgamated Investment and Property Co Ltd (In Liquidation) v Texas Commerce International Bank Ltd* [1982] QB 84 (CA and QB) 104–05. Note the erroneous reference to Bowen LJ, discussed below at n 46. This was an estoppel by convention case. However, the nature of the causal link required in such cases, that is between the acts or representations of the claimant and the adoption (or continued adherence to the assumption) on which the defendant subsequently acts, is of the same nature, and shares the same difficulties of overdetermination, endemic forensic uncertainty and indeterminacy, as found in estoppel by representation: see further below, at 57.

[45] (1885) 29 Ch 459 (CA).

[46] Robert Goff J's reference to Bowen LJ is mistaken; the passage is from Cotton LJ at 481, stating: 'It is not necessary to show that the misstatement was the sole cause of his acting as he did. If he acted on that misstatement, though he was also influenced by an erroneous supposition, the Defendants will still be liable'.

> . . . if his mind was disturbed by the misstatement of the Defendants, and such disturbance was in part the cause of what he did, the mere fact of his also making a mistake himself could make no difference.[47]

Similarly, Fry LJ said:

> But in my opinion if the false statement of fact actually influenced the Plaintiff, the Defendants are liable, even though the Plaintiff may have been also influenced by other motives.[48]

As we have seen earlier, there are good reasons why the same 'a factor' test of causation should be adopted in cases of estoppel as in cases of mispresentation. This is because both doctrines respond to the defendant's impaired decision (impaired by the induced mistake) to act. Indeed, in other cases involving impaired decisions, such as cases of spontaneous mistake,[49] duress[50] or undue influence,[51] the same test of causation arguably applies.[52] In each case, the claimant's decision has been impaired by the mistake, undue influence or duress. Thus, in *Barton v Armstrong*,[53] Lords Wilberforce and Simon agreed with the majority that the relevant test of causation for duress was that 'the illegitimate means used was *a* reason (not *the* reason, nor the *predominant* reason, nor the *clinching* reason) why the complainant acted as he did'. Although asked in different contexts (in some cases, in the context of a claim; in others, in the context of a defence) the causal enquiry remains the same and the same problems of overdetermination, endemic forensic uncertainty and indeterminacy in human decision-making, as well as any policy to protect autonomy in human decision-making discussed earlier, must be addressed.

This section has demonstrated that both principle and precedent support the view that in cases where the party's impaired intention is in issue, the probative cause need only be a factor in the party's decision to change his position. As the Full Federal Court of Australia has stated in a case of misrepresentation:

> Acknowledging that people are often swayed by several considerations, influencing them to varying extent, the law attributes causality to a single one of those considerations, provided that it has some substantial rather than negligible effect.[54]

[47] (1885) 29 Ch 459 (CA), at 483.

[48] *Ibid*, at 485.

[49] Edelman and Bant, above n 16, at 181–83, criticising *Nurdin & Peacock plc v DB Ramsden & Co Ltd* [1999] 1 WLR 1249 (Ch) 1273 (Neuberger J). *Edgington v Fitzmaurice* (1885) 29 Ch 459 (CA) 485.

[50] *Barton v Armstrong* [1976] AC 104 (PC).

[51] This is made clear by the presumed influence cases, where to rebut the presumption of operative influence, the influence must be shown to have had no effect on, or that it was not a factor in the claimant's decision to transfer a benefit to the defendant: *Huguenin v Baseley* (1804) 14 Ves Jun 273, 296; 33 ER 526, 535 (Lord Eldon LC).

[52] Edelman and Bant, above n 16, chs 8, 9 and 10. *Cf* A Robertson, 'Partial Rescission, Causation and Benefit' (2001) 17 *Journal of Contract Law* 163 who argues that the different causal tests in duress and fraudulent misrepresentation rest in a policy against wrongdoing.

[53] [1976] AC 104 (PC) 121: see also 120 (Lord Cross) 'It is sufficient if the illegitimate pressure was one of the reasons for the person entering into the agreement.'

[54] *Como Investments Pty Ltd (In Liq) v Yenald Nominees Pty Ltd* (1997) ATPR 41–500 (Full Federal Court of Australia), quoted with approval in *Henville v Walker* [2001] HCA 52, (2001) 206 CLR 459 (High Court of Australia) 494 (McHugh J).

Of course, if a defendant can satisfy the 'but for' or NESS tests of causation (by, for example, pointing to his normal patterns of behaviour) so much the better. But proof of 'but for' or NESS causation is not a requirement of the estoppel doctrine, any more than it should be a requirement of other doctrines which are concerned with the consequences of impairment of the defendant's decision-making process. That is, satisfaction of the 'but for' test is sufficient but not necessary to establish causation.

(d) Proving Reliance

This position underlies the approach taken in practice by courts faced with the difficult question of how reliance is proved in cases of estoppel. Given the difficulty in adducing direct evidence of the defendant's state of mind, courts have taken an objective approach to proof of reliance, which then recasts the evidential onus of disproving reliance back on the claimant. So courts often ask whether the representation was 'material', that is, the sort of representation on which a reasonable person would rely.[55] If the representation would have induced a reasonable man so to act, and the defendant did so act, then courts generally will be prepared to infer that the defendant was induced.[56] The evidential onus of proof then switches to the claimant, to show that the representation had no effect on the defendant's decision to act. For the same sorts of reasons, courts often ask whether the defendant's act was 'referable' to the assumption: that is, did the assumption provide a reasonable basis for the act of the defendant?[57] If a defendant assumes money is his, that belief forms a reasonable basis for him proceeding to tear up the notes or give them away. If a defendant assumes he is not obliged to carry out repairs, that belief forms a reasonable basis for him failing to carry out repairs.[58] However, an assumption that a neighbour is not permitted to cross one's land does not reasonably support a decision to renovate one's house.[59] The assumption and action are not sufficiently referable one to the other. A court would be unlikely to find in such a case that the defendant's assumption influenced his decision to change his position.

This is what underlies Lord Denning MR's statement in *Greasely v Cooke*[60] that once a representor proves that a statement was 'calculated' (ie of a nature)[61] to induce a defendant to rely on it, and the defendant proves that he changed his

[55] eg *Pickard v Sears* (1836) 6 Ad & E 469, 112 ER 179; *Smith v Chadwick* (1884) 9 AC 187 (HL); *First National Bank plc v Thompson* [1996] Ch 231 (CA) 236 (Millett LJ), discussed in Cooke, above n 13, at 80–83. See also K Handley, above n 13, at [5-001].

[56] This same approach is present in cases of misrepresentation: *Smith v Chadwick* (1882) Ch D 27 (CA) 44–45 (Sir George Jessel); *Gould v Vaggelas* (1985) 157 CLR 215 (High Court of Australia) 236–38 (Wilson J).

[57] Cooke, above n 13, at 93–104, from which the following cited examples are drawn.

[58] *Hughes v Metropolitan Railway Company* (1877) 2 App Cas 439 (HL).

[59] *Costagliola v English* (1969) 210 EG 1425 (Ch).

[60] [1980] 1 WLR 1306 (CA) 1311, citing his earlier decision in *Brikom Investments v Carr* [1979] QB 467 (CA) 482–83 (promissory estoppel). Although *Greasely* was a case of proprietary estoppel, there is no reason to think the reliance requirement is operating differently in this context than in the context of estoppel by representation.

[61] *Smith v Chadwick* (1882) Ch D 27 (CA) 44–45 (Sir George Jessel).

position, then reliance will be presumed and the onus will fall back on the claimant to disprove reliance. Lord Denning expressly disclaimed that the defendant must satisfy the 'but for' test, repeating the view[62] that any answer to that must be 'pure speculation'. Notably, Lord Denning also expressly adopted the same approach to proof of reliance as that taken in cases of misrepresentation,[63] an analogy noted earlier and we will see repeated later in this chapter. In both cases, the causal test is that the representation must have been 'a factor' that induced the defendant to act as he did[64] and the method of proving reliance is tailored to that test.

(e) A Residual, Evidential Role for the 'But For' Test

On the above analysis, it will be very difficult for claimants to disprove reliance. The claimant will need to demonstrate that the representation had no influence on the defendant's decision to change his position. Evidence that would support this would include evidence showing that the defendant certainly would have acted the same way even had no representation been made.[65] To this extent, evidence of what might have happened 'but for' the representation will still be relevant.

Similarly, there are some suggestions in the case law that the 'but for' test may remain relevant in cases where what the defendant seeks to show is that as a result of the claimant's representation, the defendant omitted to act or forewent an opportunity that he might otherwise have taken. However, here it seems adoption of the 'but for' test is motivated by courts' concern to ensure that any alleged lost opportunity was real and not theoretical. So, the defendant is required to point to evidence that the lost opportunity was one that would have been likely to have materialised and been adopted by the defendant.[66] It does not indicate a pattern of more widespread and substantive adoption of the 'but for' test of causation.

(f) The Normative Significance of Reliance

This part has argued, among other things, that reliance is a causal concept designed to establish the necessary links between the claimant's representation and the defendant's change of position. However, if reliance operates only as a

[62] First expressed in *Brikom Investments v Carr* [1979] QB 467 (CA) 482–83.

[63] *Reynell v Sprye* (1852) 1 De GM & G 660, 42 ER 710, *Smith v Chadwick* (1882) Ch D 27 (CA).

[64] In misrepresentation, the leading authority is *Edgington v Fitzmaurice* (1885) 29 Ch 459 (CA). In Australia, see *Gould v Vaggelas* (1985) 157 CLR 215 (High Court of Australia) 216 (Wilson J) 250–51 (Brennan J).

[65] In *Brikom Investments v Carr* [1979] QB 467 (CA) 482, a case of promissory estoppel, Mrs Carr admitted that she still would have gone ahead with signing the lease agreement, even had she not received the assurances from her landlord on which she later sought to found the estoppel. Lord Denning MR described the answer as 'mere speculation' and found reliance made out. This refusal to consider Mrs Carr's own admission suggests that Lord Denning considered that the answer was irrelevant, a view considered immediately below.

[66] *Pacific National (ACT) Limited v Queensland Rail* [2006] FCA 91 (Federal Court of Australia) [838], [859]–[866] (Jacobsen J). See also: Feltham, Hochberg and Leech, above n 12, at 120–21.

causal concept, it contains little normative force. The focus and thus justification for courts' interference in cases of estoppel must lie elsewhere: in the role of the claimant in inducing reliance or in a duty to prevent harm, for example. These obviously are matters that require identification of the rationale of estoppel, a difficult issue beyond the scope of this book. It need only be noted that there does exist an obvious concern underlying the requirement of reliance in cases of estoppel, referred to earlier in the context of possible policy reasons in favour of adopting an 'a factor' test of causation. Reliance in estoppel is concerned to identify whether the particular representation induced or reinforced the defendant's assumption and whether that assumption formed a basis for the defendant changing his position. Traditionally, if those elements are satisfied, the claimant is not permitted to resile from her representation where to do so would cause detriment to the defendant. Viewed from this perspective, the doctrine is, at least in part, concerned to protect the defendant's autonomy and in particular his independent decision-making processes. It is this aspect of reliance that gives the concept its normative force. Consistent with the earlier analysis of causation, it is irrelevant in that context to ask how the defendant would have acted without the claimant's contribution[67]: once the claimant has contributed to the defendant's assumption, on which the defendant acted, that is enough. The claimant is not permitted to resile from her representation where to do so would result in the defendant's change of position operating to his prejudice. On this approach, only where it can be shown that the representation played no role in the adoption of the assumption will the causal link between the representation and the assumption be missing.

(g) Lessons for the Change of Position Defence

Notwithstanding its uncertainties, the foregoing analysis of reliance as a test of causation in estoppel is of great assistance in understanding the potential role for reliance in the change of position defence. This section has argued that in estoppel, the reliance requirement expresses the necessity of establishing causal links between the claimant's representation and the defendant's assumption, on which the defendant then acts. On its face, the reliance requirement does not of itself stipulate which test of causation should apply to each of the stages of reliance (the mental aspect and the outward, practical aspect). The argument has been made, however, that problems of overdetermination, endemic forensic uncertainty and the indeterminacy of human decision-making require that the representation merely constitute 'a factor' in the defendant's decision to change his position, in preference to the 'but for' or NESS tests of causation.

Turning to the change of position defence, the causal links that must be established are between the fact of receipt of the benefit, the assumption induced by that receipt and the defendant's change of position. As with estoppel, there is significant difficulty in determining the extent to which a defendant's change of

[67] *Brikom Investments v Carr* [1979] QB 467 (CA) 482, discussed above, at n 65.

position has been caused by his receipt. Where the change comes about as a result of the defendant's act or omission, and where there is no established or assumed pattern of behaviour on the part of the defendant, the same problems of over-determination, endemic forensic uncertainty and indeterminacy in human decision-making again makes the 'but for' or NESS tests of causation generally inappropriate. In contrast, the concept of reliance, employing the 'a factor' test at both stages of the enquiry, offers a useful causal test between receipt and the defendant's change of position.

Further, given the nature of the causal links between the defendant's receipt and his change of position, a similar concern to protect the defendant's decision-making process that lies behind the doctrine of estoppel, may also be present in the change of position defence. If that is correct then, subject to one caveat, there is every reason for assimilating the tests of causation in estoppel and change of position to a uniform requirement of reliance.

The caveat is that the foregoing analysis suggests that courts should distinguish for the purposes of the change of position defence between independent changes in the received benefit and changes brought about through a defendant's actions or inactions ('defendant-instigated' changes of position). Where there is an independent change in the actual thing received, as where it deteriorates or depreciates due to its inherent qualities, there is no difficulty in applying a counterfactual (or NESS) test of causation. Even where the thing received is affected by an intervening event or third party action, such as through fire or the intervention of a thief, the counterfactual test can still sensibly, albeit predictably, be applied. In this circumstance, one asks whether, assuming the continued intervention of the fire or thief,[68] the benefit would have been lost or damaged but for its receipt. The invariable answer will be 'no'.

But for all other cases, the 'but for' or NESS tests are arguably inappropriate. While they may be relatively innocuous in practice in those cases involving otherwise established patterns of behaviour (the weekly shopping or regular payment of a mortgage), the estoppel case law suggests that the tests should not be used to exclude the change of position defence in cases where the defendant cannot point to a pre-existing pattern of behaviour. Rather, the defendant should simply be required to show that the receipt of the benefit influenced or reinforced his adoption of an assumption, and that assumption informed his decision to act. The same sorts of devices used to ascertain objectively the presence of reliance in estoppel can also be sensibly employed in the arena of the change of position defence. The consequence of this approach would be that the causal link required in reliance is relatively weak and it will be correspondingly difficult for a claimant to disprove reliance. On the other hand, the reliance requirement in estoppel is subject to an important limiting condition, which also may be usefully employed in a change of position context. It is to this limiting condition that we now turn.

[68] Here, it is irrelevant that the thief's decision was voluntary: from the perspective of the parties to the claim, the acts of the thief are of the same determinate quality as a fire, bolt of lightning or bullet.

(3) The 'Reasonableness' Requirement

(a) The Defendant's Reliance must be Reasonable

On the preceding analysis, reliance is a causal concept designed to assist in determining whether a change of position made by a defendant can be attributed, in the case of estoppel, to the claimant's representation and, in the context of the change of position defence, to the receipt of the benefit from the claimant. However, the reliance requirement in estoppel carries a significant limitation that also requires examination. This is the long-standing requirement that a defendant's reliance must be reasonable.[69] For example, in *Freeman v Cooke*, Parke B stated:

> if whatever a man's real intention may be, he so conducts himself that a reasonable man would take the representation to be true, and believe that it was meant that he should act upon . . . it as true, the party making the representation would be equally precluded from contesting its truth . . .[70]

In *Standard Chartered Bank Aust Ltd v Bank of China*, Giles J of the New South Wales Supreme Court went so far as to say that the requirement of reasonableness

[69] *Seton, Laing v Lefone* (1887) 19 QBD 68 (CA) 73 (Lord Esher MR); *Low v Bouverie* [1891] 3 Ch 82 (CA); *Canada and Dominion Sugar Company Limited v Canadian National (West Indies) Steamships Ltd* [1947] AC 46 (PC) 55–56; *Sidney Bolsom Investment Trust Ltd v E Karmios & Co (London) Ltd* [1956] 1 QB 529 (CA) 540 (Denning LJ); *Trane (UK) Ltd v Provincial Mutual Life Assurance* [1995] EGLR 33 (Ch) 38–39 (Cooke J); *Hutchison v Steria Ltd* [2006] EWCA Civ 1551 [93] (Neuberger J); Turner (ed), above n 12, at 82–83, 97–98; Birks, *An Introduction to the Law of Restitution*, above n 1, at 402; Cooke, above n 13, at 80–83; Wilken, above n 8, at 181–83; Feltham, Hochberg and Leech, above n 12, at 105–07; K Handley, above n 13, at [5-008], [5-010]. Australian authorities include *Franklin v Manufacturers Mutual Insurance Ltd* (1935) 36 SR (NSW) 76 (New South Wales Supreme Court) 82 (Jordan CJ); *North West County District Council v J I Case (Australia) Pty Ltd* [1974] 2 NSWLR 511 (New South Wales Supreme Court) 519 (Jeffrey J); *Waltons Stores (Interstate) Limited v Maher* (1988) 164 CLR 387 (High Court of Australia) 397 (Mason CJ and Wilson J) ('unified' estoppel); *Commonwealth v Verwayen* (1990) 170 CLR 394 (High Court of Australia) 414 (Mason CJ) 445 (Deane J) ('unified' estoppel); *Valbirn Pty Ltd v Powprop Pty Ltd* [1991] 1 Qd R 295 (Queensland Supreme Court) 297–98 (de Jersey J, Macrossan CJ and Sheperdson J concurring); *Standard Chartered Bank Aust Ltd v Bank of China* (1991) 23 NSWLR 164 (New South Wales Supreme Court) 180–81 (Giles J); *Australian Securities Commission v Marlborough Gold Mines Pty Ltd* (1993) 177 CLR 485 (High Court of Australia) 506 (Mason CJ, Brennan, Dawson, Toohey and Gaudron JJ); *Byron Shire Council v Vaughan (No 2)* [2000] NSWLEC 216 (Land and Environment Court of New South Wales) [25]–[26] (Lloyd J); *Murphy v Overton Investments Pty Ltd* [2001] FCA 500, (2001) 112 FCR 182 (Full Federal Court of Australia) [68] (Branson J) [96] (RD Nicholson J), decision overturned on appeal on another point in *Murphy v Overton Investments Pty Ltd* [2004] HCA 3, (2004) 216 CLR 388 (High Court of Australia); *Voss v Suncorp-Metway Ltd (No 2)* [2003] QCA 252, [2004] 1 Qd R 214 (Queensland Supreme Court); *Galaxidis v Galaxidis* [2004] NSWCA 111 (New South Wales Court of Appeal) [94], [113]–[16] (Tobias JA) (Giles and Hodgson JJA concurring on this point); *Waterman v Gerling Insurance Co Pty Ltd* [2005] NSWSC 1066, 194 FLR 419 (New South Wales Supreme Court) [91] (Brereton J); *Macquarie Bank v Lin* [2005] QSC 221 (Queensland Supreme Court) [258] (McMurdo J); *Pacific National (ACT) Limited v Queensland Rail* [2006] FCA 91 (Federal Court of Australia).

[70] *Freeman v Cooke* (1848) 2 Ex 654, 681; 154 ER 652, 663. *Cf Downderry Construction Ltd v Caradon District Council* [2002] EWHC 2 (QB (Admin)), (2002) 152 NLJ 108, discussed below, at n 84 and criticised in Wilken, above n 8, at 182.

was 'inherent in reliance, although not always enunciated'.[71] His Honour went on to state, consistent with the foregoing analysis of the elements of reliance, that there are two stages to which the reasonableness requirement applies. First, it must be reasonable for the defendant to adopt the assumption induced by the representation. Secondly, it must be reasonable for the defendant to act in reliance on the assumption.[72] Thus, the standard of reasonableness applies to each step of the causal test of reliance: the mental aspect and the practical, outward-looking act of change of position.

The reasonableness requirement in estoppel does not, however, appear to extend to the quality of the defendant's change of position: provided the defendant's reliance was reasonable it does not matter that the act taken in reliance was foolish or unusual. Therefore, a defendant who reasonably assumes following a representation by his employer that he is entitled to the full amount of a payment made to him by the employer, which assumption is one on which he may reasonably rely, should not be precluded from relying on the defence if he chooses to burn the money, tear it up or otherwise act as no other reasonable person would.[73]

Returning to the constituent elements of reliance, it may be possible that one aspect of demonstrated reliance was reasonable, but not the other. For example, it may be reasonable for a defendant to adopt an assumption, but not to act on it. Therefore, it may be reasonable for a defendant to assume, following discussions with a claimant, that the claimant has the present intention of giving £100 to the defendant. However, knowing that intentions may legitimately change, it will not, without more, be reasonable for the defendant to change his position on that basis, by spending £100 on a lavish dinner. This is not the kind of assumption on which reasonable people rely.[74] Alternatively, both limbs may fail but for different reasons. In *Pacific National (ACT) Limited v Queensland Rail*[75] the managing director of a railway company assumed from the contents of a political heads of agreement made between the Australian federal government and the Australian States, that the Queensland government and Queensland Rail would grant his company certain access rights to the railway on certain terms. While Jacobsen J was prepared to assume that the managing director genuinely held that belief, he found that the assumption was unreasonable given the actual terms of the agreement itself, which clearly contemplated that differing kinds of access rights could be granted and on different terms from those assumed by the managing director. Further, Jacobsen J found that it was unreasonable for the managing director (and through him, his railway company) to rely on that assumption, given that the

[71] *Standard Chartered Bank Aust Ltd v Bank of China* (1991) 23 NSWLR 164 (New South Wales Supreme Court) 180.

[72] It is this limb that will be particularly relevant to risk-runners: see above, at 29–30 and below, at 47.

[73] *Cf* ch 6, at 187–91, considering the relevance of the fault of the defendant in changing his position.

[74] *Waltons Stores (Interstate) Limited v Maher* (1988) 164 CLR 387 (High Court of Australia) 403 (Mason CJ, Wilson J); *Commonwealth v Verwayen* (1990) 170 CLR 394 (High Court of Australia) 414 (Mason CJ).

[75] [2006] FCA 91 (Federal Court of Australia) [824].

agreement was a preliminary one made expressly subject to further negotiation and contract between the affected parties.

(b) *The Standard of Reasonableness and its Relationship to Good Faith*

It is relatively clear from the estoppel case law that the standard of reasonableness, although objectively assessed, is set by reference to the characteristics of the particular defendant, taking into account his personal attributes, education and state of knowledge. For example, in the *Pacific National* case Jacobsen J took into account when adjudging the reasonableness of the defendant's reliance, the fact that the railway company was a 'well resourced, commercially sophisticated rail operator, advised by competent and experienced solicitors'. Likewise, in *Macquarie Bank v Lin*,[76] the reasonableness of the defendant's conduct was assessed by reference to how a reasonable commercial bank would operate.

Interestingly, the estoppel case law does not appear to require that the defendant must have acted both in *honest* and reasonable reliance on the claimant's representation. We saw previously that a defendant who knows that the claimant's representation is untrue cannot be said to rely on that representation.[77] We also saw that it is possible for a defendant to act in honest reliance on a representation, even though he harbours doubts about its truth. The question then becomes whether that reliance is reasonable. However, is it possible for a defendant to act dishonestly in reasonable reliance on his receipt? If so, then there would need to be an additional requirement of good faith underpinning the estoppel case law in order to exclude the dishonest but reasonable defendant from raising an estoppel.

It is submitted that the reasonableness requirement probably assumes, or perhaps subsumes, a requirement of good faith. That is because the reasonable man is honest—and a dishonest defendant is not a reasonable man. It is true that honesty and reasonableness are two different standards. However, the reasonableness standard is sufficiently broad to embrace an honesty element, whereas, as we have seen, the converse is not the case. On this approach, the defendant's conduct is judged against that of a reasonable (here, incorporating honest) person having the defendant's characteristics.

(c) *The Function of the Reasonableness Requirement*

What is the function of the reasonableness requirement in estoppel? One answer suggested by Giles J in *Standard Chartered Bank Aust Lt v Bank of China*,[78] but which must immediately be dismissed, is that the reasonableness requirement goes to show when it will be unconscionable for the claimant to resile from her

[76] [2005] QSC 221 (Queensland Supreme Court). *Cf Scottish Equitable plc v Derby* [2001] 3 All ER 818 (CA) 821 (Robert Walker LJ) (defendant was pensioner inexperienced in commercial matters).

[77] Above, at 28–29.

[78] (1991) 23 NSWLR 164 (New South Wales Supreme Court).

representation. As Professor Robertson has noted,[79] one may agree that it will not be 'unconscionable' (or inequitable or unjust) for a claimant to resile from her representation where it was unreasonable for the defendant to make or act on the induced assumption.[80] But used in this way, the concept of unconscionability is simply being used as a statement of conclusion. Clearly, the reasonableness requirement so far as it relates to the defendant's reliance has nothing to say about the quality of the act of the claimant. The requirement of reasonableness in reliance is focused on the quality of the conduct of the defendant. Used in this way, the label of unconscionability adds nothing to our understanding of the role of reasonableness. It simply signals the conclusion that the claimant should not be estopped from resiling from her representation.

There are two further, possible roles. First, there is the evidential point raised in the last section. It is clearly difficult to prove the effect of a statement on a defendant's decision to change his position. There is often no external fact that can be pointed to by way of support to demonstrate the effect of the representation on the defendant's mind. Accordingly, courts adopt an objective approach to assessing the effect of the representation on the defendant's decision to change his position by asking whether the representation is of the kind on which a reasonable person would rely[81] and whether the defendant's change of position is sufficiently referable to that representation. If these questions are answered in the affirmative, then courts will be more likely to infer that the defendant was induced.[82] Therefore, the concept of reasonableness assists in determining whether the representation has caused the defendant to change his position.

However, this evidential role is not the only part played by the requirement. A court may find through circumstantial evidence that a defendant did in fact rely on a representation, although no reasonable person would have done so.[83] The question then arises whether that unreasonable reliance counts for the purpose of the defence. In general,[84] the answer will be 'no'.[85] The reasonableness require-

[79] A Robertson, 'Towards a Unifying Purpose for Estoppel' (1996) 22 *Monash U L Rev* 115–19.

[80] Other examples of this line of reasoning are contained in *Commonwealth v Verwayen* (1990) 170 CLR 394 (High Court of Australia) 445 (Deane J) and *Australian Securities Commission v Marlborough Gold Mines Pty Ltd* (1993) 177 CLR 485 (High Court of Australia) 506 (Mason CJ, Brennan, Dawson, Toohey and Gaudron JJ).

[81] *Pickard v Sears* (1836) 6 Ad & E 469, 112 ER 179; *Smith v Chadwick* (1884) 9 AC 187 (HL); *First National Bank plc v Thompson* [1996] Ch 231 (CA) 236 (Millett LJ); Cooke, above n 13, at 80–83; Feltham, Hochberg and Leech, above n 12, at 92, 111; K Handley, above n 13, at [5001].

[82] This same approach is present in cases of misrepresentation: above, at 40.

[83] As in *Macquarie Bank v Lin* [2005] QSC 221 (Queensland Supreme Court) [259]–[60].

[84] Where the claimant intends the defendant to act in reliance in the manner in which the defendant did act, he may be unable to complain that the reliance was unreasonable: *Downderry Construction Ltd v Caradon District Council* [2002] EWHC 2 (QB (Admin)), (2002) 152 NLJ 108 and Feltham, Hochberg and Leech, above n 12, at 105–06. *Cf* discussion in *Peekay Intermark Ltd & Anor v Australia and New Zealand Banking Group Ltd* [2006] EWCA Civ 386, [2006] 2 Lloyd's Rep 511 [29]–[40] (Moore-Bick LJ, Lawrence Collins J concurring) [66]–[70] (Chadwick LJ).

[85] *Trane (UK) Ltd v Provincial Mutual Life Assurance* [1995] EGLR 33 (Ch) 39 (Cooke J) (a defendant, honestly but unreasonably believing he was purchasing stocks of green cheese extracted from the moon would not satisfy the requirements of estoppel); *Macquarie Bank v Lin* [2005] QSC 221 (Queensland Supreme Court) [259]–[60]; Wilken, above n 8, at 182–83.

ment is not merely a tool to assist with an evidentiary lacuna, but a separate and substantive requirement.[86] What, then, is its role in this substantive sense?

It is true that an important question in determining issues of legal liability is always whether the claimant contributed to the impugned result. But a second, quite distinct question is, what should be the extent of the claimant's responsibility for the result?[87] This question is not one of factual causation,[88] but goes to the kinds of liabilities, or risks, to which a claimant ought to be exposed. It is here that the requirement of reasonableness most obviously fits. The reasonableness requirement serves to limit the claimant's liability. It plays much the same role in cases of negligent misstatement where, like estoppel, the question is often the effect of a statement made by a claimant on a defendant's decision to change his position. In such cases, the reasonableness of the defendant's reliance becomes a key issue.[89] Professor Spence notes the analogies between estoppel and negligent misstatement and comments that the problem that has plagued both areas is how to set appropriate limits to liability. Although he rejects the reasonableness requirement as an appropriate limitation for estoppel, he does so in part on the ground that it has little support in the Australian authorities,[90] a view now plainly incorrect.[91]

(d) Lessons for the Change of Position Defence

The foregoing analysis again raises interesting questions for the change of position defence. We saw earlier that, as with estoppel, application of the change of position defence can give rise to difficult problems posed by the need to find an adequate causal link between the defendant's change of position and receipt of the benefit. If reliance is adopted for that purpose, the estoppel case law raises the question whether that reliance must be reasonable, both as to the assumption (as to the basis of his receipt) on which the defendant changes his position and the reasonableness of relying on that assumption. The estoppel case law suggests, however, that any reasonableness requirement should not extend to changes made in reasonable reliance on the assumption. In other words, it does not matter if the changes themselves are eccentric or foolish, provided that the assumptions on which they were made were themselves reasonably formed and of a nature on which the defendant might reasonably rely. As we will see in part two of the

[86] Hart and Honoré likewise consider the requirement of materiality in cases of deceit does not relate to the causal requirement that the defendant have been induced by the statement of the claimant, but is an independent requirement: Hart and Honoré, above n 30, at 192–93.

[87] Wright, 'Once More into the Bramble Bush: Duty, Causal Contribution, and the Extent of Legal Responsibility' above n 30, at 1080–82; J Stapleton, 'Legal Causation: Cause-in-Fact and the Scope of Liability for Consequences' (2001) 54 *Vanderbilt L R* 941; J Stapleton, 'Cause-in-Fact and the Scope of Liability for Consequences' (2003) 119 *LQR* 388, 411. The distinction is criticised by L Hoffmann, above n 41, at 598–99.

[88] It is thus often called 'legal causation'.

[89] eg *Fashion Brokers Ltd v Clarke Hayes (A Firm)* [2000] Lloyd's Rep P N 398 (CA).

[90] M Spence, above n 42, at 11–14, 55.

[91] Above, n 69.

book,[92] there are intimations in the recent change of position case law of precisely such a development.

(4) Detriment

(a) The Meaning of Detriment

The final, core element of estoppel by representation is detriment. The classic exposition[93] of the concept of detriment in estoppel[94] was given by Dixon J in *Grundt v Great Boulder Pty Ltd Gold Mines Ltd*:

> One condition [for an estoppel to arise] appears always to be indispensable. That other must have so acted or abstained from acting upon the footing of the state of affairs assumed that he would suffer a detriment if the opposite party were afterwards allowed to set up rights against him inconsistent with the assumption. In stating this essential condition, particularly where the estoppel flows from representation, it is often said simply that the party asserting the estoppel must have been induced to act to his detriment. Although substantially such a statement is correct and leads to no misunderstanding, it does not bring out clearly the basal purpose of the doctrine. That purpose is to avoid or prevent a detriment to the party asserting the estoppel by compelling the opposite party to adhere to the assumption upon which the former acted or abstained from acting. This means that the real detriment or harm from which the law seeks to give protection is that which would flow from the change of position if the assumption were deserted that led to it. So long as the assumption is adhered to, the party who altered his situation upon the faith of it cannot complain. His complaint is that when afterwards the other party makes a different state of affairs the basis of an assertion of right against him then, if it is allowed, his own original change of position will operate as a detriment. His action or inaction must be such that, if the assumption upon which he proceeded were shown to be wrong and an inconsistent state of affairs were accepted as the foundation of the rights and duties of himself and the opposite party, the consequence would be to make his original act or failure to act a source of prejudice.[95]

(b) The Time for Assessing the Detrimental Change of Position

As this passage makes clear, in the context of estoppel by representation, the question of detriment is judged at the moment when the claimant seeks to resile from

[92] Ch 5, at 151–55.

[93] As endorsed, eg, by Turner (ed), above n 12, at 110, in turn approved in *Gillett v Holt* [2001] Ch 210 (CA) 232–33 (Robert Walker LJ) and *Cadbury Schweppes Plc v Halifax Share Dealing Ltd* [2006] EWHC 1184 (Ch), [2006] BCC 707 [30] (Lindsay J). See also: *Central Newbury Car Auctions Ltd v Unity Finance Ltd* [1957] 1 QB 371 (CA) 380 (Lord Denning MR); *James v Heim Gallery (London) Ltd* [1979] 2 EGLR 91 (Ch) 93 (Thomas J) and K Handley, above n 13, at [5-016].

[94] Dixon J himself regarded this element as common to all estoppels *in pais*: *Grundt v Great Boulder Pty Gold Mines Ltd* (1937) 59 CLR 641 (High Court of Australia) 674. In *Gillett v Holt* [2001] Ch 210 (CA) 233, Robert Walker LJ adopted Dixon J's exposition as accurately reflecting the position for proprietary estoppel.

[95] (1937) 59 CLR 641 (High Court of Australia) 674–75.

her representation. The defendant's complaint is not that, prior to that date, he incurred expenses or otherwise changed his position: until the claimant seeks to resile from her representation, those changes are unexceptional and, indeed, may be beneficial to the defendant.[96] What makes the changes legally significant is the fact that the claimant now seeks to resile from the basis on which the changes were made. It is then that the changes of position may operate to the prejudice of the defendant.

The estoppel case law also demonstrates that a failure to appreciate this point of timing can lead to considerable confusion, such as the mistaken belief that the change of position must be inherently detrimental in a pecuniary sense or, conversely, that because an estoppel can arise where the intial change of position is beneficial to the defendant, that it is unnecessary to prove detriment at all. The leading proponent of this second analysis, usually raised in the context of 'waiver' and promissory estoppel cases, was Lord Denning MR.[97] A number of judges have refused to follow Lord Denning's lead and with good reason.[98] As Balcombe J remarked in *Fontana NV v Mautner*,[99] the analysis arguably reveals that Lord Denning MR was 'considering the question of detriment at the wrong point in time.'

This point of timing suggests an important insight for the change of position defence. It suggests that the relevant question in that context may not be whether there has been a positive act of expenditure or some other quantifiable pecuniary detriment incurred at the time of the defendant's change of position. Rather, it is whether, as at the date the claimant seeks restitution of the benefit conferred on the claimant, the defendant has changed his position in such a way that would constitute a detriment to or prejudice the defendant were the defendant now required to make restitution or restitution in full. This is a quite different kind of

[96] Cooke, above n 13, at 99; Wilken, above n 8, at 186–88.

[97] *WJ Alan & Co Ltd v El Nasr Export and Import Co* [1972] 2 QB 189 (CA) 156 ('waiver'); *Brikom Investments v Carr* [1979] QB 467 (CA) 213 (promissory estoppel); *Greasely v Cooke* [1980] 1 WLR 1306 (CA) 1311–12 (proprietary estoppel), followed in *Ogilvy v Hope Davies* [1976] 1 All ER 683 (Ch) 688–89 (Graham J) ('waiver') and *Telfair Shipping Co v Athos Shipping Co SA ('The Athos')* [1983] 1 Lloyd's Rep 127 (CA) 135 (Kerr LJ) ('waiver'), but see also *Societe Italo-Belge Pour le Commerce et L'Industrie SA (Antwerp) v Palm and Vegetable Oils (Malaysia) Sdn Bhd (The Post Chaser)* [1982] 1 All ER 19 (QB (Comm Ct)) ('waiver'), adopted by Phillips J in *Youell v Bland Welch & Co Ltd (the Superhulls Cover Case)* [1990] QB 431 (QB (Comm Ct)) 454 (promissory estoppel) and implicitly adopted in *Vitol SA v Esso Australia Ltd (The 'Wise')* [1982] 2 Lloyd's Rep 451 (CA) (promissory estoppel/ 'waiver').

[98] eg *Fontana NV v Mautner* [1980] 1 EGLR 68 (Ch) 72–73 (promissory estoppel); *Spence v Shell UK Ltd* (1980) 256 EG 56 (CA) (promissory/proprietary estoppel), *Goldsworthy v Brickell* [1987] Ch 378 (CA) 411 (Nourse LJ) (promissory estoppel). In *Gillett v Holt* [2001] Ch 210 (CA) 232, Robert Walker LJ refused to accept that proof of detriment was unnecessary for proprietary estoppel, stating that the 'overwhelming weight of authority shows that detriment is required'.

[99] [1980] 1 EGLR 68 (Ch) 72 (promissory estoppel). Earlier in the same judgment, Balcombe J noted that, given Lord Denning's analysis, it was 'somewhat ironi[c]' that Lord Denning had himself approved the words of that 'great Australian jurist' (Dixon J in *Great Boulder Mines*) in *Central Newbury Car Auctions Ltd v Unity Finance Ltd* [1957] 1 QB 371 (CA) 379–80 (estoppel by representation). Taking a similar view to that adopted in this book is S Wilken, above n 8, at 130–32. *Cf* Cooke, who argues that Lord Denning MR's analysis should be accepted, but in the limited context of cases involving the suspension or release of a contractual obligation, where the representee often will have difficulty in proving any detriment in the sense used by Dixon J: Cooke, above n 13, at 101.

question and potentially opens the door to acceptance of a much wider variety of changes of position as capable of giving rise to the change of position defence, as the next section demonstrates.

(c) Detrimental Changes of Position include Omissions and Non-pecuniary Changes

The kinds of changes that count as detrimental, or able to cause prejudice to the defendant, under the estoppel case law are relatively broad. The concept of change of position in estoppel clearly incorporates omissions to act and foregone opportunities: 'inaction in circumstances where one would otherwise have taken action'.[100] A defendant may change his position by omitting to do something he might otherwise have done but for the representation.[101] This class of change is common in cases where the defendant has been promised by the claimant that he will one day inherit, or receive, certain interests in land held by the claimant. In such cases, it is usual for the court to take into account (and value) opportunities foregone by the defendant in reliance on the promise.[102] Although these are cases of proprietary estoppel, rather than estoppel by representation, it is generally accepted that the question of detriment in both classes of estoppel is the same.[103]

Further, it is clear that the kinds of changes of position that attract the estoppel defence are not restricted to those giving rise to financial loss.[104] In *Commonwealth v Verwayen*,[105] for example, several members of the court accepted that the potential psychological harm to the defendant could constitute detriment sufficient to support a claim in estoppel. Although the judges in that case differed in their characterisation of the instant estoppel, they all were agreed that non-financial detriment sufficed.[106] More recently in *Gillett v Holt*,[107] Robert Walker LJ clearly considered that the claimant's decision to leave school at 16 to take up residence with the defendant, with all the implications that decision contained for the claimant's future training, social connections and employment prospects, would

[100] *Knights v Wiffen* (1870) LR 5 QB 660 (QB), 665–66 (Blackburn J). See also: Feltham, Hochberg and Leech, above n 12, at 118–19.

[101] In such cases, the court will require evidence that the lost opportunity was 'real' and not 'speculative': *Pacific National (ACT) Limited v Queensland Rail* [2006] FCA 91 (Federal Court of Australia) [838] (Jacobsen J) and authorities cited therein. See also discussion of the 'but for' test above, at 40.

[102] eg *Gillett v Holt* [2001] Ch 210 (CA); *Giumelli v Giumelli* [1999] HCA 10, (1999) 196 CLR 101 (High Court of Australia).

[103] *Gillett v Holt* [2001] Ch 210 (CA) 233 (Robert Walker LJ), adopting the approach of Dixon J in *Grundt v Great Boulder Pty Gold Mines Ltd* (1937) 59 CLR 641 (High Court of Australia).

[104] *Newbon v City Mutual Life Assurance Society Ltd* (1935) 52 CLR 723 (High Court of Australia) 732–35 (Rich, Dixon and Evatt JJ).

[105] (1990) 170 CLR 394 (High Court of Australia).

[106] Mason CJ only rejected Verwayen's allegation of psychological harm because it was not made out on the evidence, not because it was not a legitimate head of detriment.

[107] [2001] Ch 210 (CA) 234. Because those changes predated the assurances made by Mr Holt, they did not constitute specific instances of detriment but rather formed part of the background of the case. See also: *Campbell v Griffin* [2001] EWCA Civ 990, (2001) 82 P & CR DG23 (proprietary estoppel).

have counted as a detriment for the purposes of the proprietary estoppel claimed in that case. It is evident from his references to the impact the decision had on the claimant's social and private life that his Lordship was not thinking solely in terms of the pecuniary disadvantages inherent in the decision.[108]

(d) The Change of Position must be Irreversible

The estoppel case law suggests that an important factor in whether a change of position counts as prejudicial lies in whether it is reversible either in money or in kind.[109] We considered the case of *United Overseas Bank v Jiwani*[110] earlier in this chapter in the context of the discussion of the mental element of reliance. It will be recalled that the defendant in that case used the extra $11,000 mistakenly credited to his account to purchase a hotel. One of the reasons given by MacKenna J for refusing to find that the bank was estopped from bringing its claim for restitution of the mistaken payment was that the defendant had purchased a valuable asset (the hotel) in reliance on his receipt. This could be sold or used as security to obtain a loan to repay the $11,000, without thereby occasioning the defendant any harm. That is, the defendant's change was reversible. In support of this view, McKenna J cited a hypothetical example of a customer who uses an overpayment to buy a gilt-edged security that can immediately be resold. In his Lordship's view, this would not constitute a relevant change of position for the purposes of the estoppel defence. He contrasted this case with the example of a defendant who invested part of the overpayment in a company which had since gone into liquidation,[111] or paid it to a third party from whom the money could not now be retrieved.[112] The passage is not entirely clear, because his Lordship mixed with it concepts of causation: in particular, his view that without the overpayment the defendant would still have purchased the hotel. But the examples themselves demonstrate that a separate ground for rejecting the defendant's estoppel claim was that the defendant's change could be reversed.

Similarly, in *Pacific National (ACT) Limited v Queensland Rail*,[113] Jacobsen J was not prepared to find that a railway company would suffer detriment if the

[108] Further examples include *Sullivan v Sullivan* [2006] NSWCA 312 (New South Wales Court of Appeal) [10] (Handley JA) (proprietary estoppel) and *Donis v Donis* [2007] VSCA 89 (Victorian Supreme Court of Appeal) (proprietary estoppel) discussed in ch 5, at 133.

[109] *Spiro v Lintern* [1973] 1 WLR 1002 (CA) 1013; *Jones v Watkins* (CA 26 November 1987); Feltham, Hochberg and Leech, above n 12, at 122–24. In *Sullivan v Sullivan* [2006] NSWCA 312 (New South Wales Court of Appeal) the proprietary estoppel was limited to seven years in duration, being the estimated time it would take for the woman's detriment in giving up council housing to be reversed, assuming she re-joined the council accommodation waiting list immediately following the decision of the court.

[110] [1976] 1 WLR 964 (QB).

[111] Drawing from *Holt v Markham* [1923] 1 KB 504 (CA).

[112] As in *Deutsche Bank (London Agency) v Beriro and Co Ltd* [1895–99] All ER Rep 1164 (CA) discussed below, at 52–53.

[113] [2006] FCA 91 (Federal Court of Australia) [840]: 'once the detriment has ceased or been paid for, there is nothing unconscionable in a party insisting upon the enforcement of its strict legal rights'. See also: *Simm v Anglo American Telegraph Co* (1879) 5 QBD 188 (CA) 207 (Brett LJ): '. . . but as soon

party sought to be estopped (Queensland Rail) were permitted to resile from the assumption, because the alleged detriments were reversible. In particular, his Honour found that at the time Queensland Rail sought to resile from the alleged assumptions, it offered to grant access rights on reasonable commercial terms.[114] Although not expressed in these terms, the offer negated any claim of detriment on the part of the railway company, because it would effectively reverse any detriment that otherwise would be caused if the assumption were denied. Further, Jacobsen J noted that the company still retained the ownership of the locomotives and other assets which it had purchased in reliance on its assumption.[115] It continued to have the use of those assets and, presumably, could sell them to reverse those changes of position.

The question arises to what extent a change must be reversible in order not to count for the purposes of estoppel by representation. Here, the authorities seem reasonably clear that the change must be easily reversible, without significant expense, time or difficulty to the defendant. For example, in *Compania Naviera Vasconzada v Churchill and Sim*[116] Channell J said of observations in earlier cases that suggested an otherwise detrimental change of position that could be 'rectified' through litigation would not be sufficient to found an estoppel,[117] that:

> It cannot truly be said as a general proposition, that a person cannot be prejudiced by having made a payment which he has a legal right to get back from the person to whom he paid it unless it is shown that such person is insolvent. It appears to me that the parting with the money, and consequently the being out of it for a certain period of time, coupled with the trouble and perhaps legal expense of establishing the legal right to get it back may amount to an acting to the payer's prejudice sufficient to establish an estoppel against the person in reliance upon whose statement he made the payment.

An earlier example is *Deutsche Bank (London Agency) v Beriro and Co Ltd*.[118] In that case, the claimant made a mistaken payment to the defendant, who in turn paid the money to a third party. At first instance, the claimant's action for restitution of the payment was refused by Mathew J, inter alia, on the grounds of estoppel by representation. Central to that decision was Mathew J's view, based on correspondence from the third party tabled with the court, that the third party may well have changed his position in reliance on the receipt of the payment from the defendant, so as to afford him a complete defence to any action by the defend-

as Burge & Co had paid off the advance made to them by the National Bank, the Bank was no longer in a position to suffer damage . . . and no ground of estoppel could be maintained for its benefit'. Discussed in Feltham, Hochberg and Leech, above n 12, at 123–24.

[114] *Pacific National (ACT) Limited v Queensland Rail* [2006] FCA 91 (Federal Court of Australia) [842].

[115] See also *Jones v Watkins* (CA 26 November 1987) where the change of position was the purchase of a tractor which had maintained, if not increased, its value.

[116] [1906] 1 KB 237 (KB) 250; followed in *Martineaus Ltd v Royal Mail Steam Packet Co* (1912) 17 Comm Cas 176 (KB) 179–80 (Scrutton J) and *Meng Leong Ltd v Jip Hong Ltd* [1985] AC 511 (PC) 524–25 and discussed in Feltham, Hochberg and Leech, above n 12, at 118–20.

[117] *Carr v London and North Western Rly Co* (1875) LR 10 CP 307 (DC) 317–318 (Carr J); *Simm v Anglo American Telegraph Co* (1879) 5 QBD 188 (CA) 211 (Brett LJ).

[118] [1895–99] All ER Rep 1164 (CA).

ants to recover the amount of the mistaken payment. The claimant's appeal against this decision was unanimously dismissed by the Court of Appeal.

(e) Lessons for the Change of Position Defence

The estoppel case law raises a number of important points for consideration for the change of position defence in relation to what constitutes a detrimental change of position for the purposes of that defence. It suggests that the question of detriment may be one of prejudice, rather than pecuniary loss and should be assessed at the time the claimant seeks restitution of the benefit received, rather than the point of the defendant's original change of position. Further, a key factor in determining whether a change is prejudicial for the purposes of estoppel is whether it is readily reversible at the time of the court hearing. If it is, then no relevant detriment exists and the defendant is expected to take such steps as required to reverse the change (and thus protect himself from the harm that would otherwise flow from the claimant being permitted to resile from her representation). The concept of irreversibility should thus also be considered when determining the kinds of changes of position that should count for the purpose of the change of position defence.

C Bars to the Defence

The preceding sections have considered the core elements of estoppel by representation and the lessons to be drawn from their consideration. They have demonstrated that the core elements of reasonable reliance and detrimental change of position found in estoppel by representation may also be relevant in informing the shape of the change of position defence. Given that estoppel and the change of position defence may share these features, which focus on the position and role of the defendant, it makes sense to consider whether there are any bars to the estoppel defence arising from the defendant's conduct which may also be relevant to the change of position defence.

Accordingly, this final section of the chapter considers whether fault on the part of a defendant operates as a bar to the defence of estoppel by representation and, if so, seeks the basis or rationale for regarding it as relevant to the defence. It will then be possible to consider whether fault might legitimately have a similar role to play in the context of the change of position defence. To that end, this section considers three different kinds of fault. The first is where the defendant is at fault in the broad sense of being responsible for having induced the claimant's representation in the first place. This kind of fault does not suppose that the defendant has acted *mala fide*: the defendant can have acted with the best of intentions and been entirely innocent of any wrongdoing (in the sense of breach of duty). In contrast, the second kind of fault is where the claimant's representation came about as a result of, or in the context of, a breach of duty by the defendant. The third is where the defendant's change of position made in reliance on the claimant's representation constituted, or arose in the context of, an illegal act.

(1) Defendant at Fault in Inducing the Representation

In *Larner v London County Council*[119] the defendant was a serviceman who had been overpaid a wartime allowance by his local authority. The allowance was paid pursuant to a scheme designed to make up the difference between service and civilian salaries. As part of the scheme, servicemen were under an obligation to inform their local authority of any changes in their wartime salaries and the defendant was aware of this obligation. Nonetheless, he failed to advise his local authority of an increase in his service pay and, as a result, they continued to pay him his wartime allowance at an inflated rate. When the local authority sought to recover the amount of the overpayments, the defendant claimed a defence of estoppel by representation. Denning LJ, giving the judgment of the Court of Appeal, stated that 'if the mistake was due to an innocent misrepresentation or a breach of duty by the recipient—he clearly cannot escape liability by saying that he has spent the money'.[120] As the defendant had failed to notify the claimant of his change in pay, and this had led to the overpayments, the defendant was precluded from raising his change of circumstances by way of defence.

Putting to one side for the moment the relevance of a breach of duty, the decision constitutes strong authority for the view that a defendant's role in inducing the mistake founding the claimant's representation operates as a bar to the defence. Not only was this a unanimous decision of the Court of Appeal, the restriction was subsequently adopted by Goff and Jones,[121] and endorsed by, among others, Slade LJ in the seminal Court of Appeal decision of *Avon City Council v Howlett*.[122]

Moreover, there are a number of older cases that provide some support for the *Larner* approach. In *Simm v Anglo-American Telegraph Company*,[123] subsequently referred to with approval by the House of Lords in *Balkis Consolidated Co Ltd v Tomkinson*,[124] the claimants sought to estop the defendant company from denying that they were registered as shareholders in the company. However, the claimants had only been registered because, albeit in all innocence, they had presented a forged instrument of transfer to the company and demanded to be registered. The court held that, for this reason, no estoppel arose.

[119] [1949] 2 KB 683 (CA).
[120] *Ibid*, at 688–89.
[121] R Goff and G Jones, *The Law of Restitution* 2nd edn, (Sweet & Maxwell, London, 1978) 554–55.
[122] [1983] 1 WLR 605 (CA) 620. *Larner* was followed on this point in *Secretary of State for Employment v Wellworthy Ltd (No 2)* (1976) ICR 13 (QB) 25 (Nield J); *Saronic Shopping Co Ltd v Huron Liberian Co* [1979] 1 Lloyd's Rep 341 (QB (Comm Ct)) and cited with approval in *Lloyds Bank Ltd v The Hon Cecily Brooks* (1950) 72 *Journal of the Institute of Bankers* 114 (KB) and *National Westminster Bank Ltd v Barclays Bank International Ltd* [1975] QB 654 (QB) 676 (Kerr J).
[123] (1879) 5 QBD 188 (CA).
[124] [1893] AC 396 (HL) 405–06 (Lord Herschell) 412–15 (Lord Field).

There is also a more ambiguous line of cases where, like *Larner*, a defendant failed to notify a claimant of information which, had it been given, may have changed the nature of the claimant's representation, or caused the claimant not to make the representation at all. The first of the series is *Whitechurch v Cavanagh.*[125] In that case, the circumstances of the original transfer of shares to the defendant were sufficient to raise a doubt as to whether the defendant was their true owner. The defendant subsequently sought assurances from the company issuing the share certificates that all was in order, but failed to notify it of his grounds for doubt. In finding there was no estoppel against the company, Lord Brampton said:

> [No] representations can be relied on as estoppels if they have been induced by the concealment of any material fact on the part of those who seek to use them as such; and if the person to whom they are made knows something which, if revealed, would have been calculated to influence the other to hesitate or to seek for further information before speaking positively, and that something has been withheld, the representation ought not to be treated as an estoppel.[126]

This principle has been followed in a number of subsequent cases. In *Porter v Moore*[127] the defendants induced the claimant to sign a memorandum stating that he had received no notice of any prior charge over certain land. The defendants did not advise the claimant that the particular form of memorandum had been submitted to his solicitors for consideration and that it was the known practice of those solicitors to advise against signing such documents. Citing *Whitechurch v Cavanagh,* and *Low v Bouverie,*[128] Swinfen Eady J held that the memorandum raised no estoppel against the claimant, as,

> no reasonable person would have acted upon it, knowing the circumstances as the mortgagees' solicitors knew them, and that the circumstances attending the obtaining the trustees' signatures to the memorandum and down to the date when it was acted on are such as to estop the mortgagees from praying in aid any estoppel.[129]

In *Doey v London and North Western Railway Company*[130] the claimant sent precious items with the defendant railway, which were damaged in transit. By statute, the defendant as carrier was not liable for damage to any items over a certain value unless the claimant declared their nature and value and paid or undertook to pay certain specified extra charges. Although the claimant told the defendant's clerk that he wished to have the goods insured, he did not notify him of their value (which was over the statutory limit) nor correctly or sufficiently specify them. The clerk accepted them for carriage and, on the assumed basis that they did not exceed the statutory limit, charged the usual sum for insurance. The claimant argued that the defendant was estopped from denying the existence of a special contract by which the railway agreed to forego the protection of the statute.

125 [1902] AC 117 (HL).
126 *Ibid*, at 45.
127 [1904] 2 Ch 367 (Ch).
128 [1891] 3 Ch 82 (CA) 106 (Bowen LJ).
129 *Porter v Moore* [1904] 2 Ch 367 (Ch) 374–75.
130 [1919] 1 KB 623 (KB).

Avory J simply cited *Whitechurch v Cavanagh* as the basis of his decision that no such estoppel arose against the defendant railway. In contrast, Lush J held that no estoppel arose against the defendant railway because the clerk had made no representation that he was authorised to act contrary to the statute (a notice of which was posted at the railway), the defendant had not revealed to him all the material facts (in particular the value of the goods) and because even were an estoppel established, it could not be used to give the clerk authority he was not permitted by statute to have. The latter strand of reasoning relates to estoppel being used to subvert a statute, to which we return further below. His Lordship concluded by stating: 'The truth here is that the mistake was caused entirely by the acts and omissions of the [claimant].'

It is not clear whether what is being complained of in these cases is that the defendant induced the representation[131] or that, given the defendant's role and knowledge as to the information (or lack therof) that the claimant was operating under, it was unreasonable for the defendant to rely on the claimant's representation (or even that the defendant did not rely on the representation at all).[132] Therefore, they are not strong authority in favour of the *Larner* approach to fault on the part of the defendant. In contrast, *Simm v Anglo-American Telegraph Company* suffers from no such ambiguity, it there being accepted that the defendant was unaware that the transfer of shares was forged.

However, the authorities on this question do not all run the same way. In particular, Robert Goff J expressly held in *Amalgamated Investment and Property Co Ltd (In Liquidation) v Texas Commerce International Bank Ltd*,[133] in a passage subsequently approved by Mustill J in *The 'Leila'*[134] and in a number of Australian estoppel by convention authorities,[135] that the defendant bank in that case could rely on an estoppel by convention, notwithstanding that the origins of its assumption (shared with the other party) lay in its own error. In that case, the defendant bank assumed that the claimant's guarantee was binding because of an internal error, not derived from anything said or done by the claimant but from persons within, or documents held within the bank. Notwithstanding this, Robert Goff J found that the claimants' course of conduct influenced the bank, in the sense that it operated to confirm and reinforce the bank's mistaken belief. It made no difference to this finding that the origin of the mistake lay within the bank's own

[131] The cases have even been cited as examples of fraudulent inducement: Feltham, Hochberg and Leech, above n 12, at 110.

[132] Wilken, above n 8, at 204. The same twin analyses can be made of *National Westminster Bank Ltd v Barclays Bank International Ltd* [1975] QB 654 (QB) 676–77 (Kerr J).

[133] [1982] QB 84 (CA and QB) 100–01 (Robert Goff J).

[134] *Government of Swaziland Central Transport Administration and Alfko Aussenhandels GmbH v Leila Maritime Co Ltd and Mediterranean Shipping Co SA (the 'Leila')* [1985] 2 Lloyd's R 172 (QB (Comm Ct)) 179.

[135] *Coghlan v S H Lock (Australia) Ltd* (1985) 4 NSWLR 158 (New South Wales Supreme Court) 166, 167 (Samuels JA, Hope JA agreeing); *Eslea Holdings Ltd v Butts* (1986) 6 NSWLR 175 (New South Wales Supreme Court) 185; *Santos v Delhi Petroleum Pty Ltd* [2002] SASC 272 (South Australian Supreme Court) [460]–[61] and [502] (Lander J) [690]–[701] (Besanko J); *Whitehouse v BHP Steel Limited* [2004] NSWCA 428 (New South Wales Court of Appeal) [35]–[44], [56]–[58] (Tobias JA, Giles and McColl JJA concurring).

organisation. This decision was upheld on appeal. Denning MR held that the fact that the defendant's mistake was internally generated could not prevent an estoppel from arising.[136] How can these two seemingly inconsistent approaches to fault on the part of the defendant be reconciled?

One answer lies in the nature of the estoppel in issue in *Amalgamated Investment* and subsequent authorities approving that decision. Estoppel by convention is founded not on a representation made by the claimant on which a defendant detrimentally relies, but on an agreed state of affairs the truth of which is assumed by the parties as the basis of the dealings with each other.[137] This difference might be thought to indicate that there is no need for any kind of inducement, or causal link between the claimant's acts and the defendant's change of position: it is enough that the defendant changed his position in reliance on a mistaken assumption shared by the claimant, even though the claimant had no role in inducing the assumption on which the defendant acted. However, as Kerr LJ explained in *The August Leonhardt*:

> All estoppels must involve some statement of conduct by the party alleged to be estopped on which the alleged representee was entitled to rely and did so rely. In this sense all estoppels may be regarded as requiring some manifest representation which crosses the line between representor and representee, either by statement or conduct . . . [I]n cases of . . . estoppels by convention, there must be some mutually manifest conduct by the parties which is based on a common but mistaken assumption. The alleged representor's participation in this conduct can then be relied upon by the representee as a basis for this form of estoppel.[138]

Closer inspection of the reasoning in *Amalgamated Investment* reveals that the court was concerned precisely with this question of causation—a question which was not regarded as in issue in *Larner*. In *Amalgamated Investments*, both parties were independently mistaken and so the question was whether the representations of the claimant caused, in any relevant sense, the defendant to make the assumption on which it subsequently relied. That Robert Goff J saw the issue as one of causation, rather than fault, is made clear by his emphasis that a representation can be said to have influenced a defendant where it simply strengthened a pre-existing belief. And it is this causal aspect of Robert Goff J's reasoning that Denning MR expressly approves on appeal.[139]

[136] *Amalgamated Investment and Property Co Ltd (In Liquidation) v Texas Commerce International Bank Ltd* [1982] QB 84 (CA and QB) 120.

[137] eg A Turner (ed), above n 12, adopted in *Amalgamated Investment and Property Co Ltd (In Liquidation) v Texas Commerce International Bank Ltd* [1982] QB 84 (CA and QB): on appeal (HL) 126 (Everleigh J) 130 (Brandon LJ). Also *Con-Stan Industries of Australia Pty Ltd v Norwich Winterthur Insurance (Australia) Ltd* (1986) 160 CLR 226 (High Court of Australia) 244.

[138] *K Lokumal & Sons (London) Ltd v Lotte Shipping Co Pte Ltd (The 'August Leonhardt')* [1985] 2 Lloyd's Rep 28 (CA) 34–35. See also: *Grundt v Great Boulder Pty Gold Mines Ltd* (1937) 59 CLR 641 (High Court of Australia) 675–76 (Dixon J). For a detailed examination of the authorities on the nature of the link required in this form of estoppel, endorsing Kerr LJ's approach, see R Derham, 'Estoppel by Convention-Part II' (1997) 71 *Australian L J* 976, 976–80.

[139] *Amalgamated Investment and Property Co Ltd (In Liquidation) v Texas Commerce International Bank Ltd* [1982] QB 84 (CA and QB) 120, referring to Robert Goff J's judgment at 108B.

Notwithstanding the support for this analysis in the judgments, it may be asked whether the distinction between causation and fault in the sense being used in this section withstands scrutiny. It is at least arguable that the very reason why the role of the defendant in inducing the representation of the claimant may be relevant as a bar to the defence of estoppel by representation is that, having induced the representation or assumption in the first place, the defendant should be left to bear the consequences. This comes close to echoing the same question of causation at the heart of *Amalgamated Investment.* If that is right, then it does seem that *Amalgamated Investment* undermines the authority of *Larner.*

However, there is a means of reconciling the two approaches to fault, again focusing on the difference between the two kinds of estoppels under consideration. Derham argues that because the essence of estoppel by convention is the agreement or consensus between the parties, the essence of the task before the court is to interpret the alleged convention. In that context, it may not be fatal that the defendant might have been the source of the mistake which resulted in the parties adopting the shared assumption.[140] Although Derham does not expand on this point, the reason for this distinction is presumably because it is not the mistake that is the basis of the estoppel by convention, but the common assumption on which the parties subsequently rely.[141] In that context, the fact that the assumption originated in the mistake of the party seeking to raise the estoppel (the defendant) is not normatively relevant as a bar to the defence: it is enough that the claimant encouraged or strengthened the assumption on which the defendant relied. In contrast, in cases of estoppel by representation, the mistake is at the heart of the defendant's complaint: that the claimant's representation induced the mistaken assumption on which the defendant then relied. It is for this reason that the defendant's earlier responsibility for the content of the representation is relevant. It almost provides a counter-estoppel against the defendant: the claimant relied on the defendant's misrepresentation in making her representation to the defendant and for the defendant now to resile from that representation would cause the claimant detriment.

If these cases of estoppel by convention can be distinguished from those of estoppel by representation in this way, it seems at least arguable that the view taken by the Court of Appeal in *Larner v London County Council*[142] that innocent inducers may be debarred from the estoppel by representation defence remains good law.

What lessons can be drawn from this analysis for the change of position defence? This chapter has demonstrated that, in estoppel, the defendant must have reasonably relied on the claimant's representation. In the change of position defence, in cases where the defendant instigated his change of position, the chapter has shown

[140] Derham, above n 138, at 976, 977

[141] *Cf Santos v Delhi Petroleum Pty Ltd* [2002] SASC 272 (South Australian Supreme Court) 502 (Lander J): 'It does not matter whether both parties were mistaken. What matters is whether there was a common assumption.'

[142] [1949] 2 KB 683 (CA) 688–89.

that there may be grounds for saying that he must have done so in reasonable reliance on his receipt. If this is correct, then the defendant's reliance on his receipt in cases of defendant-instigated changes of position is central to the change of position defence, in the same kind of way that the defendant's reliance on the claimant's representation is central to estoppel. This further suggests that, in both defences, it may be normatively important that the defendant's autonomy in decision-making has been affected (by his receipt, or the representation). However, if the defendant has in part caused his own receipt (or the claimant's representation) then, in doing so, he has interfered with the claimant's autonomy. Reciprocity thus suggests that the defendant's role in inducing the claimant's decision to transfer the benefit to him undermines his own right to protection. These considerations support the view that the fault of the defendant in inducing his receipt may operate as a bar to the change of position defence.

(2) Defendant in Breach of Duty

The circumstances in which a defendant will be precluded from relying on estoppel by representation where he has been guilty of some breach of duty are difficult to determine. There is, however, clear authority that a defendant who has induced the claimant's representation through his fraudulent misrepresentation will not be permitted to rely on the defence.[143]

It is also said that a claimant who makes a representation as a result of duress will not be estopped from resiling from the representation,[144] even where the defendant was an innocent third party, unassociated with the duress.[145] Duress is not a tort per se,[146] so the question must be asked why this class of transaction attracts special treatment. The answer given in *Debs v Sibec Developments Ltd*[147] by Simon Brown J is that where the representation has been made under duress, it is not 'voluntary' in the sense required to found an estoppel. His Lordship drew support from authority relating to the application of the defence of *non est factum*.[148] However, there is an obvious difference between duress and *non est factum*: duress does not operate so as to vitiate entirely the claimant's intention.[149] That is why

[143] Examples include *Carlton v Bowcock* (1885) 51 LT 659 (QB) 661 (Cave J) and *Fitzgerald & Fitzgerald v R* [1936] QSR 335 (Queensland Supreme Court). See also: Turner (ed), above n 12, at 137–38.

[144] *D & C Builders Ltd v Rees* [1996] 2 QB 617 (CA) 625 (Lord Denning MR) 626 (Danckwertz LJ).

[145] Turner (ed), above n 12, at 138; Wilken, above n 8, at 204.

[146] *Universe Tankships Inc of Monrovia v International Transport Workers Federation* [1983] 1 AC 366 (HL) 385 (Lord Diplock), cited with approval in *Dimskal Shipping Co SA v International Transport Workers Federation* [1992] 2 AC 152 (HL) 166 (Lord Goff).

[147] [1990] RTR 91 (QB) 97–98.

[148] Feltham, Hochberg and Leech, above n 12, at 109–10 draws the same analogy.

[149] P Atiyah, 'Economic Duress and the "Overborne Will"' (1982) 98 *LQR* 197, 200; *Director of Public Prosecutions for Northern Ireland v Lynch* [1975] AC 653 (HL); endorsed by McHugh JA in *Crescendo Management Pty Ltd v Westpac Banking Corporation* (1988) 19 NSWLR 40 (New South Wales Supreme Court) 45–46; in turn approved in *Dimskal Shipping Co SA v International Transport Workers Federation* [1992] 2 AC 152 (HL) 165–166 (Lord Goff).

transactions entered into under duress are voidable, not void.[150] Representations made under duress are therefore better analogised to representations made under a mistake and there is no suggestion that those representations should not be capable of giving rise to an estoppel.

In *Debs v Sibec Developments Ltd*, a third party forced the claimant at gunpoint to sign a false receipt evidencing a sale of the claimant's title to his car to the third party. The third party then stole the claimant's car and sold it to the defendant, a good faith purchaser. Later, the claimant brought an action in conversion against the defendant. The claimant sought to resile from the representation inherent in the receipt that he had sold his title to the car to the third party. The defendant was innocent of any association with the robbery of the car. For that reason, it cannot be the case that he was precluded from raising the estoppel because of his role in inducing the representation, an argument we considered previously and that would have been available against the coercing party.[151] However, the decision may still be correct. In receiving the car, the defendant committed the tort of conversion. In that context, to allow the defence arguably would stultify the reason against the law's strict liability prohibition of the tortious act. In other words, the defence was properly barred on grounds of public policy.

Alternatively, could it be argued that to allow the defence would effectively sanction pressure that the law has identified as illegitimate? The difficulty with this alternative analysis is that the defendant in this case was not personally involved in the duress. In that context, it is unclear that allowing him the defence would sanction the illegitimate pressure applied by the third party. This can be contrasted with cases where the defendant himself is the party responsible for the duress. In *D & C Builders Ltd v Rees*,[152] for example, the defendant used economic duress to extract from the claimant a receipt purportedly in satisfaction of an outstanding debt owed by the defendant to the claimant. The defendant subsequently attempted to estop the claimant from seeking the balance of the outstanding debt, relying on the receipt. The court held that no such estoppel could arise, given the genesis of the receipt. Although not explained, one obvious basis for the decision is that to allow the defendant to set up the estoppel relying on the receipt would entirely subvert the claimant's right to recovery of the outstanding amount arising as a result of the defendant's duress. We return to this kind of public policy argument in the next section below.

It is not every breach of duty that will preclude a defendant from relying on an estoppel. There is a significant body of case law, commonly considered under the terminology of 'waiver' or 'promissory estoppel', which relates precisely to the circumstances in which an estoppel will operate to preclude a claimant from relying on her rights. Most commonly, these are cases where a party has promised not to rely on her contractual rights to performance by the defendant. It is a commonplace in

[150] *Universe Tankships Inc of Monrovia v International Transport Workers Federation* [1983] 1 AC 366 (HL) 384 (Lord Diplock).

[151] An argument that would have been available in *D & C Builders Ltd v Rees* [1996] 2 QB 617 (CA).

[152] [1996] 2 QB 617 (CA).

such cases that were the estoppel not to apply, the defendant would be liable for having breached his contractual duty towards the claimant. Wilken argues that this form of estoppel (which he labels 'equitable forbearance') is closely related to, but analytically distinct from estoppel by representation.[153] The chief difference lies in the nature of the representation. In cases of equitable forbearance, the representation is as to the future and therefore promissory in nature. As such it may be the source of legal obligations. Estoppel by representation, being a mere rule of evidence, however, cannot.

Assuming, without conceding that is so, it remains undoubtedly the case that the slightest variation in emphasis could change a statement from 'I promise I will not enforce my rights' to 'I hereby waive or forego my rights'. It is not obvious why the difference in terminology should lead to different results, particularly given, as Wilken concedes, that the other requirements for equitable forbearance are identical to estoppel by representation. This is not an argument advocating fusion of the two estoppels: it is simply noting that there is no obvious reason why the defendant in breach of duty in one case, who is permitted to raise an estoppel, should not likewise be permitted in the other.

If, as is submitted, the nature of the estoppel itself is not a ground for distinguishing the treatment of this category of wrongdoer, a further explanation must be found as to why this class of defendant should be permitted to raise an estoppel against the claimant. The most obvious is that in the cases of fraudulent misrepresentation and conversion considered above, allowing the defence would stultify the reason for the law's prohibition. In contrast, in cases of equitable forbearance, there is no such stultification. This is because contractual rights are consensually created and, absent some overriding policy consideration, there is no reason why a party cannot consent to forego those rights. The same respect for the parties' autonomy in decision-making that supports recognition of the legally binding effect of contracts applies with equal force where a party chooses not to enforce those rights.

On this reasoning, where the effect of recognising the forbearance would be to stultify the law's prohibition, the estoppel should fail, notwithstanding that all the other elements of equitable forbearance are established. Therefore, a minor should not be estopped from resiling from her representation that she will forego, or has given up the protection offered by a statute. The very reasons why the statute protects the minor—her assumed immaturity of judgment—would also bite on the purported waiver of those rights.

In summary, the circumstances in which a defendant will be precluded from raising an estoppel on the grounds of breach of duty are difficult to identify. It is probably correct to say that where a claimant's representation was induced through the defendant's breach of duty (as in cases of fraudulent misrepresentation) or duress, the defendant will be precluded from relying on the representation as a basis of estoppel. However, this does not take us much further than the

[153] Above n 8, ch 7. *Cf* AJ Phipps, 'Resurrecting the Doctrine of Common Law Forebearance' (2007) 123 *LQR* 286.

previous section. It is also possible to say that where the benefit which was the subject of the claim was obtained as a result of duress or breach of duty (not necessarily the defendant's) *and* that recognising the estoppel would undermine, or stultify, the reason behind the law's prohibition, then the defendant will also be barred from raising an estoppel against the claimant. However, there are circumstances where the status of the defendant as wrongdoer is irrelevant to the defence. These are cases where to allow the defence would not stultify the reason behind the law's prohibition. Further than these fairly broad guidelines, however, it is difficult to go.

(3) Illegality

In contrast to the considerable uncertainty surrounding the bars considered above, it is undoubtedly the case that estoppel cannot be used to undermine the effect of a statute.[154] Another way of putting this is that an estoppel cannot be raised where to do so would stultify the law.[155] Framed in this way, the rule is but one example of a wider bar (some examples of which were discussed in the previous section) which prohibits an estoppel from arising where to permit it would stultify either a prohibition imposed by, or for the protection of a particular class granted by, the law. Therefore, estoppel cannot be used to prevent a minor from asserting the invalidity of a contract,[156] nor can it be raised where to do so would affect, contrary to their statutory rights, the position of creditors in a bankruptcy.[157]

The examples of this bar in play are too numerous—and uncontentious-to mention. Suffice to say that they point to a very real limitation on the circumstances in which estoppel and, perhaps, the change of position defence, should be available. In particular, so far as the latter is concerned, in every case where the 'unjust factor' giving rise to the claimant's primary right to restitution is based on public policy (such as minority, illegality, mental incapacity or reversal of judgment restitution) the question must be asked whether recognition of the defence would stultify the reason behind the law's grant of restitution. If it would, then the estoppel case law suggests that the defence must be denied.

D Conclusion

This chapter's examination of estoppel by representation has yielded a number of important insights relevant to the disputed features of the change of position defence.

[154] Turner (ed), above n 12, at 138–42; Wilken, above n 8, at 205–06.
[155] Wilken, *ibid*, at 163.
[156] Turner (ed), above n 12, at 146; Feltham, Hochberg and Leech, above n 12, at 171.
[157] Turner, *ibid*, at 147; Feltham, Hochberg and Leech, above n 12, at 171–72.

It has demonstrated that reliance is a causal concept that would have a legitimate role to play in change of position cases, where the change of position has been brought about through the defendant's act or omission (for example, purchasing a meal at a restaurant). Further, if reliance is adopted, the causal test to be applied at both stages of the reliance enquiry should be that the receipt must be a factor in the defendant making or maintaining an assumption and that the assumption be a factor in the defendant's decision to change his position. This is because problems of overdetermination, endemic forensic uncertainty and indeterminacy in decision-making have a tendency to render application of the 'but for' and NESS tests of causation inappropriate. By contrast, in cases where the benefit itself has independently altered, or has been changed through the intervention of a third party or natural event, the 'but for' test is always satisfied and creates no difficulties. For example, where a benefit has been stolen by a thief, it must be the case that but for the receipt of the benefit, the thief would not have stolen the benefit. The receipt of the benefit clearly is a 'but for' cause of its loss at the hands of the thief. The same is the case where a benefit is destroyed by fire or spontaneously devalues. But for the receipt of the benefit, it would not have been burnt or devalued. This causal analysis notably provides a means of reconciling the 'broad' (but for) and and 'narrow' (reliance) versions of the change of position defence. Both versions have a role to play, depending on the nature of the causal links between receipt and change of position that must be established.

Further, the analysis raised the question whether reliance on a receipt for the purposes of the change of position defence must be reasonable. It demonstrated that the reasonableness requirement in estoppel goes beyond a mere evidential tool and operates as a substantive limit on the protection otherwise afforded to the defendant. Further, the reasonableness requirement provides a means of determining the application of the estoppel defence in cases where a defendant suspected, but did not actually know, of the vitiating factor that affected the claimant's decision to transfer. Finally, the analysis suggests that a reasonable reliance requirement renders redundant, or subsumes, any separate requirement of 'good faith' on the part of a defendant. These are all aspects of adopting a reasonableness requirement which merit consideration in the context of the change of position defence.

The estoppel case law further raises the question whether the detrimental change of position that supports the change of position defence should be assessed not at the time of the original change of position, but when the claimant seeks restitution of the benefit transferred to the defendant. At this point, the estoppel case law suggests that the question becomes whether the change is readily reversible either in money or in kind. The change may be non-pecuniary in nature and may arise from an omission to act, or a decision to forego an opportunity.

The final lessons to be derived from the estoppel case law relate to the role of the defendant's fault as a bar to the defence. The analysis in this chapter demonstrates that it is at least premature to dismiss the defendant's role in inducing the impugned transaction as irrelevant to the change of position defence. Further, the estoppel case law demonstrates that the position of defendants who have acted in breach of duty, or have induced the representation through duress, is not straightforward. Of primary importance in determining whether such defendants are debarred from raising an estoppel is the question whether recognising the defence will stultify the reason behind the law's prohibition of the relevant conduct.

This approach effectively mirrors that taken in cases where statutory policies and provisions are in play. In such cases, the question is not whether the defendant is a wrongdoer, or whether the impugned transaction was illegal, but whether recognising the defence would stultify the policy behind the law's prohibition. This analysis suggests that any potential bar arising out of the breach of duty by a defendant in the context of the change of position defence should likewise be considered to see whether grant of the defence would offend the policy behind the law's prohibition.

3

Lessons from the Defence of Payment Over by an Agent

A Introduction

IT WAS IN 1966 that Goff and Jones first postulated that the law of agency provided an isolated example of what should be a more general defence of change of position.[1] However, it was not until the seminal decision of *Lipkin Gorman (a firm) v Karpnale Ltd*[2] that the relationship between agency law and the change of position defence came under serious scrutiny by other restitution scholars.[3] In that case, Lord Goff of Chieveley referred to an existing group of cases that could,

> arguably be said to rest upon change of position: (1) where an agent can defeat a claim to restitution on the ground that, before learning of the plaintiff's claim, he has paid the money over to his principal or otherwise altered his position in relation to his principal on the faith of the payment . . .[4]

Since this decision, restitution scholars have exposed a significant degree of confusion in the case law as to the purpose of the agency defence referred to by Lord Goff and its constituent elements. In essence, the cases support two different agency defences. The first, which was identified by Lord Goff, has two key elements:

[1] R Goff and GH Jones, *The Law of Restitution* (Sweet & Maxwell, London, 1966). The authors now consider the defences to be separate: G Jones (ed), *Goff and Jones The Law of Restitution* 7th edn (Sweet & Maxwell, London, 2007) [40-027].

[2] [1991] 2 AC 548 (HL), 578.

[3] W Swadling, 'The Nature of Ministerial Receipt' in P Birks (ed), *Laundering and Tracing* (Clarendon Press, Oxford, 1995) ch 9; P Birks, 'Overview: Tracing, Claiming and Defences' in Birks (ed), *Laundering and Tracing, ibid*, ch 11; M Bryan, 'Recovering Misdirected Money from Banks: Ministerial Receipt at Law and in Equity' in FD Rose (ed), *Restitution and Banking Law* (Mansfield Press, Oxford, 1998) ch 10; P Birks, 'The Burden on the Bank' in FD Rose (ed), *ibid*, ch 11; J Moore, *Restitution from Banks* (D Phil book, University of Oxford, 2000), summarised and adopted by C Mitchell, 'Assistance' in P Birks and A Pretto (eds), *Breach of Trust* (Hart Publishing, Oxford, 2002) 184–87; AS Burrows, *The Law of Restitution* 2nd edn (Butterworths, London, 2002) 597–608; R Stevens, 'Why do agents "drop out"?' [2005] *LMCLQ* 101.

[4] *Lipkin Gorman (a firm) v Karpnale Ltd* [1991] 2 AC 548 (HL) 578.

- The agent must have received the benefit in his capacity as agent.
- The agent must have paid the benefit over to his principal before receiving notice of the transferor's claim to restitution of the benefit or its value.

The defence also requires that the agency be disclosed.[5] This element clearly has no analogue in the change of position defence. It cannot, therefore, be expected to yield any insights for the change of position defence and, accordingly, will not be addressed in this chapter. It may, however, be relevant to determining the ongoing relationship between the two defences, a matter that will be addressed briefly in the final chapter.[6]

This agency defence accepts that a defendant agent may be enriched by his receipt from the claimant even though he received the benefit solely in his capacity as agent for his principal. It also accepts the principle that a payment to a known agent constitutes a payment to his principal for the purpose of any subsequent claim for restitution of the value of the payment.[7] The consequence is that unless the agent has paid over the benefit to his principal without notice of the claim for restitution, the claimant will have a choice of defendants: the agent or his principal. As the essence of this agency defence is that the defendant has paid over the benefit without notice of the claim, it is here labelled the 'payment over defence' to distinguish it from the second agency defence.

The second kind of agency defence goes significantly further than the payment over defence. It treats as paramount the principle that a transfer of benefit to a known agent constitutes a transfer of benefit to the principal for the purpose of any subsequent claim for restitution of the transferred benefit.[8] Applying that principle with full rigour, the defence stipulates that where a transfer has been made to a known agent, the proper defendant to any claim for restitution is the principal. Therefore, in contrast to the payment over defence, the broad version of the agency defence applies whether or not the agent has paid the benefit over to his principal. Effectively, it states that an agent who receives ministerially (that is, solely in his capacity as agent) is not the proper defendant to proceedings to recover the transferred benefit, even if the benefit is retained in the agent's hands. For that reason, this version of the agency defence will be labelled 'ministerial receipt' in this book, to underline the central importance to the defence of the capacity in which the defendant receives the benefit.

Given that it regards any payment over by the agent as irrelevant, the defence of ministerial receipt must have a different rationale or rationales (and thus

[5] *Sadler v Evans* (1766) 4 Burr 1984, 98 ER 34.

[6] At 230–34.

[7] *Edgell v Day* (1865) Law Rep 1 CP 80 (CCP), 84 (Erle CJ): 'The general principle of law is, that a payment of money to an agent is payment to the principal'. *Portman Building Society v Hamlyn Taylor Neck (a firm)* [1998] 4 All ER 202 (CA) 207 (Millett LJ). Different considerations apply where the agent is a tortfeasor, or is the defendant to a claim for breach of a contract to which the agent was a signatory: Stevens, above n 3.

[8] *Edgell v Day, ibid*; *Portman Building Society v Hamlyn Taylor Neck (a firm)* [1998] 4 All ER 202 (CA) 207 (Millett LJ).

elements) from the change of position defence.[9] For that reason, this chapter will confine its examination to the payment over defence. Notably, the existence of a defence of ministerial receipt does not detract from the fact that there also exists an established defence of payment over that can usefully be examined for the purpose of comparison with the change of position defence. Indeed, even if the payment over defence were eventually to be rendered redundant by a defence of ministerial receipt, that would not change the fact that, historically, the payment over defence operated in response to much the same sorts of claims and answered the same sorts of questions as the change of position defence now does: what difference should it make in a claim for restitution of a received benefit that a defendant has changed his position following receipt of the benefit; of what relevance is the fact that the defendant received notice of the claim for restitution before changing his position; what difference should the fault of the defendant make to the availability of any defence? It makes sense in that context to examine the payment over defence to see whether it has any lessons to offer for resolution of the disputed features of the change of position defence. This is particularly so given that Lord Goff's formulation of the change of position defence in *Lipkin Gorman* was seemingly formulated with features of the payment over defence in mind.

This chapter will show that the payment over defence has significant lessons for the defence of change of position in three areas: first, the kinds of changes that potentially count for the purpose of the defence; secondly, the significance of notice in the defence; and thirdly, the potential bars to the defence arising from the defendant's conduct. The chapter examines each of these elements in turn, commencing with the lessons that arise from the requirement of 'payment over'.

B The Requirement of Payment Over

It has been a matter of significant controversy as to what constitutes an effective payment over for the purpose of the payment over defence. That controversy has tended to revolve around cases where an agent has not physically paid money over to his principal, but rather has made a credit entry in the principal's account, or has set off the amount to be paid to the principal against an amount owing from him to the agent. The question arises whether these kinds of changes count for the purpose of the defence and if not, why not. Three cases have traditionally been central to this enquiry.

The first is the leading common law case of *Buller v Harrison*.[10] In that case, the claimant insurer mistakenly paid out on an insurance policy to the insured's agent.

[9] The defence, its rationale and relation to change of position are examined in ch 10, at 233. The authorities supporting the defence are further explored in ch 10 and in Burrows, above n 3, at 600–01; Moore, above n 3, at 250–53; J Edelman and E Bant, *Unjust Enrichment in Australia* (OUP, Melbourne, 2006) 362–63. *Cf* Stevens, above n 3.

[10] (1777) 2 Cowp 565, 98 ER 1243.

Instead of physically paying the amount over to his principal, the agent recorded the amount in his books as offsetting the debt owed to him by his principal. When the claimant subsequently discovered his mistake, he sought recovery of the amount from the agent. The agent sought to rely on the payment over defence. Effectively, the agent argued that he should be treated as if he had paid the money over to his principal, then received it back for the purpose of settling the outstanding account (a 'constructive' payment over). His defence failed. Lord Mansfield stated:

> In this case, there was no new credit, no acceptance of fresh bills, no fresh goods bought or money advanced. In short, no alteration in the situation in which the defendant and his principals stood towards each other . . ..[11]

A strict approach to what constitutes payment over was confirmed in the subsequent case of *Cox v Prentice*.[12] In that case, an agent was mistakenly overpaid for the purchase of a silver bar. When the purchaser sought to recover the amount of the overpayment, the agent argued that he had sent an account to his principal which included an allowance for the full amount of the sale price received and that this satisfied the requirement of payment over. Again, the defence failed. Lord Ellenborough stated:

> I take it to be clear, that an agent who receives money for his principal is as liable as a principal so long as he stands in his original situation; and until there has been a change of circumstances by his having paid over the money to his principal, or done something equivalent to it. Here it is admitted that no money has been paid over by the defendant to his principal, nor has there been any other thing done by him to create a change of circumstances. The only question then is, whether the action lies against the defendant, considering it as if it were an action against the principal.[13]

Le Blanc J agreed:

> The circumstances of the account between the defendant and his principal being still open without new credit given, does, I think according to *Buller v Harrison*, dispose of the objection.[14]

The final case in the trilogy is *Holland v Russell*.[15] The facts are very similar to *Buller v Harrison*. An insurer made a mistaken payment to the defendant agent, who acted for the insured. The agent paid over most of the amount to his principal but retained two small sums, one of which was by way of satisfaction of a debt owed by the principal to the agent. The other was paid to a third party at the direction of the principal. Unlike *Buller v Harrison*, in this case the agent succeeded in his defence, even in relation to the amount he had retained by way of set off to the debt owed to him by the principal.

[11] *Buller v Harrison* (1777) 2 Cowp 565, 568; 98 ER 1243, 1244.
[12] (1815) 3 M & S 344, 105 ER 641.
[13] *Cox v Prentice* (1815) 3 M & S 344, 348; 105 ER 641, 643.
[14] *Ibid*, at 644.
[15] (1863) 4 B & S 14, 122 ER 365 (Exch) approving *Holland v Russell* (1861) 1 B & S 424, 121 ER 773 (QB).

How can the results and reasoning in these cases be reconciled? The most obvious way is not to focus on whether the purported payment over was physically made or not—such a distinction cannot survive *Holland v Russell*. Nor does the notion of a 'constructive payment over' assist: that label simply signals the conclusion that the relevant change of position counts notwithstanding the lack of physical payment. Rather, the key to understanding the cases lies in the concept of reversibility. As Cockburn CJ explained in the first appeal in *Holland v Russell*,[16] in *Buller v Harrison*, the account between principal and agent was still open and so the entry in it concerning the disputed receipt could be reversed (in the event the agent was required to repay the amount) without causing harm to either principal or agent. The reversal would simply restore the parties to the position they occupied prior to the original receipt. The result would have been different had there been 'new credit . . . acceptance of fresh bills, . . . fresh goods bought or money advanced' as a result of the entry. Then any order for restitution would leave the defendant in a worse position than that occupied prior to the original receipt, because the subsequent change in his position could not be reversed without causing him detriment.

The same reasoning underlies the other two cases. In *Cox v Prentice*, the issued account did not materially alter the position between agent and principal; or if it did, such a change could easily be reversed by issuing a fresh account without any resultant harm to either principal or agent. In contrast, in *Holland v Russell*, the account between principal and agent had been settled and could not be unilaterally reversed by the agent.[17] This is because the settling of an account operates as a novation, substituting a new contract for former debts. Further, were the defendant required to make restitution of the amount received from the claimant, he might not have been able to recover the amount of the payment from his principal because it related to an amount the subject of the settlement of account.[18] And if he was permitted to recover, the principal would be in the invidious position of having effectively paid the amount of the receipt twice to the defendant.

On this analysis, the concept of a detrimental change of position—detrimental in the sense that the change cannot be reversed without placing the defendant in a worse position than he occupied prior to his receipt—underpins the defence of payment over. This rationalisation of the cases, as based on the reversibility or otherwise of the pleaded change of position, gains support from numerous subsequent cases concerning the effectiveness of a purported payment over.[19] However,

[16] (1861) 1 B & S 424, 435; 121 ER 773, 777.

[17] *Holland v Russell* (1861) 1 B & S 424, 435; 121 ER 773, 777 (QB) (Cockburn CJ); *Holland v Russell* (1863) 4 B & S 14, 16; 122 ER 365, 366 (Exch) (Erle CJ): 'all the money has been accounted for in a settlement of account approved by the foreign principal'.

[18] On disputing a settled account, see below, at 74.

[19] *Colonial Bank v Exchange Bank of Yarmouth, Nova Scotia* (1885) 11 App Cas 84 (PC) 88–89 (Lord Hobhouse); *Bavins Junior & Sims v London & South Western Bank Ltd* [1900] 1 QB 270 (CA) 277 (Collins LJ) 275–76 (AL Smith LJ) 278 (Vaughan Williams LJ); *Continental Caoutchouc & Gutta Percha Co v Kleinwort Sons & Co* (1904) 90 LTR 474 (CA) 476 (Collins MR); *Kleinwort, Sons & Co v Dunlop Rubber Co* (1907) 97 LT 263 (HL) 264 (Lord Loreburn LC, Lord James concurring) 265 (Lord Atkinson); *Kerrison v Glyn, Mills, Currie & Co* (1911) 81 LJKB 465 (HL) 472 (Lord Mersey); *Jaffer v Commonwealth Bank of Australia Ltd* [2001] SASC 191 (South Australian Supreme Court) [63] (Perry J).

it cannot conclusively be accepted without considering the High Court of Australia's unanimous decision in *Australia and New Zealand Banking Group Ltd v Westpac Banking Corporation*.[20] In that case, ANZ mistakenly transferred $114,000 to the Westpac account of its customer's creditor, Jakes Meats Pty Ltd ('Jakes'), instead of $14,000 as instructed by its customer. When the mistake was discovered three days later, ANZ notified Westpac and asked for contact details for Jakes so that it could deal directly with it on the matter. ANZ provided the details and Westpac subsequently contacted and reached an agreement with Jakes for the amount to be repaid by instalments. Only a very small amount ($2500) was received before Jakes went into liquidation. ANZ then demanded repayment of the balance from Westpac, who refused. Before the High Court, Westpac's defence was that before it received notice of the mistake, it had already applied (in honouring cheques drawn on the account) all but a small amount of the received payment on behalf of Jakes.

Any analysis of the High Court's decision is rendered difficult by the number of important and debatable concessions made by Westpac during the course of the litigation.[21] However, a point that has been repeatedly derived from the case by commentators is that the High Court rejected any need for an additional element of detriment to the defendant above the requirement of payment over.[22] That is, a payment over can be effective even where it can be reversed without detriment to the defendant. If that is correct, it would pose a significant challenge to the foregoing analysis.

On close inspection, however, the case does not support such an analysis. The High Court noted that the requirement of payment over will not normally be satisfied where the defendant has made a 'mere book entry' on the faith of his receipt 'which has not been communicated to the third party or which can be reversed without affecting the substance of transactions or relationships . . .'.[23] In the former case, a defendant may be estopped from reversing his change where the third party has altered his position in reliance on his receipt,[24] which may render the entry irreversible. The latter example is a more straightforward one of a situation where a change has become irreversible.

One of Westpac's key concessions was that the court should not take into account the application of any amount of the mistaken payment in extinguishment of the debt owed to itself or any provisional inter-bank credits arising from

[20] (1988) 164 CLR 662 (High Court of Australia).

[21] Westpac conceded that the initial contact by ANZ constituted the equivalent of a formal demand for repayment, so that only changes that took place between the date of receipt and the date of giving of notice could be relevant to the defence: (1988) 164 CLR 662, 669. It also conceded prima facie liability (671) and that it bore the onus of making out the defence (675), concessions that excluded consideration of a strong defence of ministerial receipt by the court (675). Nonetheless, the court clearly had sympathy for such an approach.

[22] This forms a central plank in the thesis of Dr Moore: Moore, above n 3, at 115–28. Also: Swadling, above n 3, at 256; Birks, 'Overview: Tracing, Claiming and Defences' in Birks (ed), above n 3, at 344. Against is Burrows, above n 3, at 606–07.

[23] *Australia and New Zealand Banking Group Ltd v Westpac Banking Corporation* (1988) 164 CLR 662 (High Court of Australia) 674.

[24] *United Overseas Bank v Jiwani* [1976] 1 WLR 964 (QB).

cheques that could have still been dishonoured at the time it received notice of the mistake from ANZ.[25] That is, it was conceded that any change that was reversible at the time the defendant received notice of the mistake could not be pleaded by way of defence. The correctness of this concession was called into question by the High Court. However, it is important to emphasise that the doubt cast on the concession did not relate to whether reversibility was an important feature of the payment over defence[26]; rather, it related to whether the defendant came under an obligation at the time of receiving notice of the mistake to take steps unilaterally to reverse the changes of position already made in reliance on its receipt. In casting doubt on the existence of any such obligation, the High Court commented,

> one is led to speculate about what Westpac's position vis-à-vis Jakes would have been if it had, of its own initiative, dishonoured those cheques and reversed those entries and provisional credits. Certainly, its position would have been a difficult one if it had subsequently turned out that ANZ's claim for repayment could be met by a good defence on the part of Jakes.[27]

To those comments, it might be added that, depending on the terms of the contract governing the overdraft facility, unilaterally to dishonour the cheques might well expose Westpac to claims by Jakes for breach of contract. These factors strongly militate against imposing a duty on a defendant at the time of receiving notice of the mistake to reverse unilaterally changes already made in reliance on its receipt. It does not suggest that the question whether the changes were irreversible is irrelevant to the defence on which the defendant subsequently relies.

Indeed, the basis on which the High Court then proceeded was to consider whether, even taking into account all of Westpac's concessions, all but $17,021.68 had been 'irrevocably' paid out by Westpac by the time it received notice of the mistake.[28] In that respect, the High Court regretted the lack of opportunity arising from Westpac's concessions to consider whether any part of the overpayment had been 'effectively and *irrevocably* applied to eliminating [Westpac's] pre-existing indebtedness'.[29] It is clear that the court considered the reversibility of any change made on the faith of the mistaken payment to be at the core of the payment over requirement.

This is emphasised in a subsequent passage in which the High Court considered ANZ's argument that, in order for the payment over defence to apply, there must be some additional detriment over and above the requirement of payment over. ANZ argued that it was necessary to assess Westpac's detriment by comparing two distinct positions. The first was the position Westpac would have been in had it not received the mistaken payment at all, in which case the upper limit of the

[25] *Australia and New Zealand Banking Group Ltd v Westpac Banking Corporation* (1988) 164 CLR 662 (High Court of Australia) 677–78.

[26] As argued by Bryan, above n 3, at 178–79.

[27] *Australia and New Zealand Banking Group Ltd v Westpac Banking Corporation* (1988) 164 CLR 662 (High Court of Australia) 678.

[28] *Ibid.*

[29] *Ibid*, at 680 (emphasis added).

agreed overdraft on Jake's account would likely have been reached, with the consequence that a number of cheques subsequently drawn on the account would likely have been dishonoured. The second was the position Westpac would have been in had it immediately repaid the amount of the mistaken payment on receiving notice of the claim, debited Jakes' account in that amount and dishonoured all the cheques that it might then have dishonoured.

The High Court rejected this analysis. Although not entirely clear, its primary reason for doing so seems to lie in the view that it was not relevant to compare, on the one hand, the position the defendant might have been in but for its receipt and on the other, the defendant's position had it unilaterally reversed the transaction at the time of receiving notice of the mistake. Echoing perhaps the same distrust of hypothetical scenarios we saw earlier in the context of estoppel,[30] the High Court stated that, rather, the question was what Westpac actually did in reliance on its receipt. It is at this point and in relation to these facts only, that the question of irreversibility arises and must be answered. It is in that context that the High Court noted that 'the payment by the agent to the principal of the money which he has received on the principal's behalf, of itself constitutes the relevant detriment or change of position.'[31] It then expanded on that proposition by reference to *Buller v Harrison* and *Cox v Prentice*, among others, which cases were considered earlier in this section and were raised by ANZ in support of its submission. The High Court emphasised that at the heart of those cases was the reversibility of the pleaded change.[32] The court concluded by finding that, Westpac having 'irretrievably'[33] paid out $82,978.32 in cheques on the faith of its receipt, its defence must succeed to that extent.

In closing this discussion of *ANZ v Westpac*, it might be asked what would have been the result had the agreed overdraft limit on Jakes' account been such that Westpac would have honoured the cheques drawn on the account, whether or not the mistaken payment had been received. Initially, this might seem to be a question going to the issue of detriment: if the financial position of Westpac would have been the same whether or not the mistaken payment had been received, it should not be able to succeed in its defence because there had been no detrimental change of position. However, the better approach is to view the example as involving a question of causation. In the supposed circumstances, Westpac's change of position would not have been caused by its receipt, because the mistaken payment would have formed no part of Westpac's decision to honour the cheques. The existence of the pre-agreed overdraft demonstrates that the decision to honour cheques up to that limit had already been made, prior to (and without reference to) the receipt of the mistaken payment. In those circumstances, there was no reliance on the mistaken payment. We return to this requirement of reliance in part C below.

[30] Ch 2, at 34–35, 40.

[31] *Australia and New Zealand Banking Group Ltd v Westpac Banking Corporation* (1988) 164 CLR 662 (High Court of Australia) 681.

[32] *Ibid*, at 682–83.

[33] *Ibid*, at 684.

In contrast, if in reliance on its receipt, the bank extended fresh credit to the customer, for example by granting an overdraft facility that had not previously existed, the result might well have been different. In those circumstances, the causation element would be satisfied and the question would then be whether that change (granting the overdraft facility) could be reversed without detriment to the bank. As we have seen, as a matter of authority, *Buller v Harrison*[34] would suggest that granting fresh credit would count as a relevant change of position. Certainly as a matter of principle, if the bank paid out on cheques in accordance with the overdraft facility, if it would be in breach of the terms of the overdraft facility to dishonour cheques coming within its limits and if its client subsequently went into liquidation, it would appear at least arguable that the change was irreversible.

In conclusion, the case law concerning the payment over defence overwhelmingly supports the view that the essential characteristic of a 'payment over' is that it must be irreversible. It is this characteristic that makes the change made on the faith of the receipt operate to the detriment of the defendant in the event he is required to make restitution or restitution in full. We saw the same concept of detrimental change of position operating in the context of estoppel in chapter two. Given the close relationship between both defences and the change of position defence (and indeed, between estoppel and ministerial receipt)[35] it is at least arguable that the same approach should underpin the change of position defence. That is, a change of position should only count for the purpose of the defence if it is irreversible.

Precisely how difficult must it be, however, for a defendant to reverse the change? The agency cases provide some, albeit limited, guidance on this score. At one end of the scale is the case where a defendant agent can unilaterally reverse a credit entry in his books of account, thereby restoring the parties to the *status quo ante*. As we have seen, the agency cases are unanimous in saying that such a change of position will not satisfy the defence. It follows that other steps a defendant can take unilaterally, such as selling an asset purchased with the moneys received should, at least prima facie, be considered reversible. The defendant would need to demonstrate circumstances which rendered reversing the change difficult or impossible, such as the market for the asset having since disappeared or the asset having since depreciated or been destroyed, in order for the defence to succeed.

At the other end of the scale are cases such as where the defendant agent is estopped from reversing the credit entry[36] or has entered into new contractual obligations on the strength of the receipt.[37] In such cases, the change is irreversible (or not reversible without causing the defendant to breach a duty) and any requirement that the defendant agent must make restitution must operate to the prejudice of the defendant.

[34] (1777) 2 Cowp 565, 98 ER 1243 discussed above, at 67–69; also *Cox v Prentice* (1815) 3 M & S 344, 349; 105 ER 641, 643 (Le Blanc J).

[35] Swadling, above n 3, argues that the agency defence is a species of estoppel.

[36] *United Overseas Bank v Jiwani* [1976] 1 WLR 964 (QB).

[37] *Buller v Harrison* (1777) 2 Cowp 565, 98 ER 1243 568 (Lord Mansfield).

What the agency cases do not appear to consider is what arguably could be regarded as middle ground: cases where the defendant has changed his position but may be able to reverse the change by bringing an action to reverse or recover the change made in reliance on his receipt. Consider the case where a defendant has paid over an amount received from the claimant to a third party on the instructions of his principal, which amount is subsequently the subject of a successful claim for mistake.[38] The defendant may be able to bring an action against that third party for recovery of the amount, the likely ground for restitution being mistake. Likewise, where the amount received was applied by the agent in final settlement of a debt owed to him by his principal, it is not impossible (although unusual) for the settled account to be re-opened on proof of it having been drawn up under a mistake.[39] Even where the amount has been physically paid to the principal, it is not impossible for the agent to seek reimbursement for expenses incurred and indemnity from liabilities arising from claims made against the agent by the claimant for restitution of the amount originally received.[40] In all these cases, the change made by the defendant agent may (depending, for example, on whether the third party or principal has any defences or bars arising with respect to the action) be reversible with varying degrees of effort and expense.

The assumption underlying the agency cases' treatment of these instances seems to be that such changes are sufficiently irreversible for the purpose of the payment over defence. In turn, this suggests that a generous approach is taken by the courts to the question whether a change is irreversible. The defence is only precluded where the change is unilaterally or readily reversible by the defendant. From a policy perspective, this generosity of approach makes a degree of sense. It cannot be desirable for defendants to be required to instigate time-consuming, costly litigation which may not in the end prove to be successful in order to make out the payment over defence. Nor is it desirable that defendants be left to pursue against their principals or third parties whatever legal avenues of redress are open to them if it is uncertain that they will be successful in their pursuit. This approach to the issue of reversibility is further supported by the comment of the High Court of Australia in *ANZ v Westpac* that it is far from self-evident that an agent should be required to take steps to recover money paid over to his principal once the agent becomes aware of the claimant's mistake.[41] This suggests that the agent should be entitled to leave out of account any right that he might have to recover back his payment over.[42]

The agency cases suggest that any reversibility requirement imposed pursuant to the change of position defence should likewise not be too stringent: a defendant should not be required to pursue time-consuming and costly litigation as a

[38] As in *Holland v Russell* (1863) 4 B & S 14, 122 ER 365.

[39] F Reynolds, *Bowstead and Reynolds on Agency* (Sweet & Maxwell, London, 2006) 242.

[40] *Ibid*, at 301–05.

[41] *Australia and New Zealand Banking Group Ltd v Westpac Banking Corporation* (1988) 164 CLR 662 (High Court of Australia) 677–78.

[42] Birks, 'The Burden on the Bank' in FD Rose (ed), above n 3, at 213.

prerequisite to obtaining the protection of the defence. On the other hand, where, for example, a change can be reversed by the defendant selling an object purchased as a result of his initial receipt, or through a cheap and quick refund process available through a government department, the change should prima facie be sufficiently reversible not to count as a detrimental change of position. The defendant will need to bring evidence as to the legal or practical hurdles to reversing the change in order for the defence to succeed.

C Notice

It is a key component of the payment over defence that the defendant agent must have no notice of the claim for restitution at the time he changes his position. Notice does not mean that the defendant agent must know that the claim is good: it is enough that the agent knows of the claim. If the agent is not sure whether or not the claim is good, or whether he ought to proceed with payment over to his principal, the traditional view is that he should interplead rather than change his position by paying the amount over to his principal, knowing that there is a risk that the amount might have to be returned.[43]

It is likely that the notice requirement in the payment over cases reflects an underlying requirement of reasonable reliance.[44] We saw in the chapter two on estoppel that the reliance requirement in the context of that defence is necessary to establish the causal link between the representation and the defendant's subsequent change of position.[45] We also saw that a defendant who changes his position knowing that the representation on which he purports to base his actions is incorrect, cannot be said to have relied on the representation. Rather, the defendant takes a conscious risk in changing his position that the claimant will not resile from her representation.[46]

The reliance requirement arguably carries a similar causal function in the payment over defence. As Professor Birks explained:

> The question whether the agent has honoured his obligation to pay over to the principal turns on whether in making a later payment, or entry into an account that later became binding, the agent acted because of the payment in. It is a causal question, and the index of causation is intentional reliance.[47]

Although not usually expressed in these terms, the agency cases are consistent with an underlying requirement of reliance. For example, in *Holland v Russell*, it was

[43] *Portman Building Society v Hamlyn Taylor Neck (a firm)* [1998] 4 All ER 202 (CA) 207 (Millett LJ).
[44] All the payment over cases concern defendant-instigated changes of position: see discussion in ch 2, at 30–31, 41–42.
[45] Ch 2, commencing at 30.
[46] Ch 2, at 28–30.
[47] Birks, 'The Burden on the Bank' in FD Rose (ed), above n 3, at 213.

held that when the agent paid over he had to have 'full belief in the validity of the transaction'.[48] In *Edwards v Hodding*,[49] an auctioneer, who was also solicitor for the vendors, was aware of ongoing purchaser's inquiries concerning the title to the land the subject of sale. While the vendors were still in the process of investigating and answering those enquiries, the agent paid over the deposit to the vendors. Although the court found that he was liable because he had what was 'equivalent to express notice' from the purchaser that he should not pay over the deposit, the simpler explanation of the result is that the agent took an active risk in making the payment over knowing that his receipt was insecure. As Chambre J stated, the defendant received the deposit, knowing the condition of retaining it was that there should be a good title to the property.[50] The logical conclusion must be that in those circumstances he did not rely on his receipt, but rather took a risk either that the title enquiries would be satisfied, or that the claimant would not seek or succeed in recovering the amount of the deposit. Finally, in the important decision of *Lipkin Gorman (a firm) v Karpnale Ltd*,[51] we saw Lord Goff expressly describe the defence as requiring an alteration in position 'on the faith of the receipt'.

As explained earlier, pursuant to the notice requirement of the payment over defence, it is unnecessary for the defendant agent to know that the claim in respect of the received amount is good. It is enough that he is aware of, or suspects, the existence of a claim. Faced with that knowledge or suspicion, the traditional view is that the defendant should interplead rather than risk making a payment over. This suggests that the same 'reasonableness' requirement that informs estoppel also underpins the payment over defence. On this approach, a defendant agent who is notified of a claim relating to his receipt but who nonetheless pays the amount over, has not reasonably relied on his receipt but has taken a calculated risk in making the payment over to his principal.

If this is correct then where a defendant agent is aware of facts that would put a reasonable agent on enquiry, and the agent does not make such enquiries, the agent should lose the benefit of the defence. This is because the known facts which form the basis on which the defendant acts do not support the actions taken. That is, the requirement of reliance is a requirement of reasonable reliance.

As with estoppel, the question arises as to the function of a reasonableness requirement. We saw in chapter three that it has some evidential role, going to the issue of reliance.[52] It is often difficult to prove directly the effect of a receipt on a defendant's decision to change his position. It thus makes sense for courts to adopt an objective approach in determining the question whether this agent relied on his receipt, by asking whether the receipt is of the kind that a reasonable agent would rely on in making a payment over. If it is, then courts will more likely be prepared to infer that this particular defendant relied on his receipt. In this role, the concept

[48] *Holland v Russell* (1863) 4 B & S 14, 17; 122 ER 365, 366 (Erle CJ).
[49] (1814) 5 Taunt 815, 128 ER 913.
[50] *Ibid*, at 915.
[51] [1991] 2 AC 548 (HL) 578; the full extract appears at text to n 4.
[52] At 39–40, 46.

of reasonableness assists in determining whether the representation caused the defendant to change his position.

However, this evidential role need not be the only part played by a reasonableness requirement. As with estoppel, a court may find through circumstantial evidence that a defendant agent did in fact rely on a receipt, although no reasonable person would have done. In that context, the application of a reasonableness requirement operates as a substantive restriction on the protection otherwise offered by the defence. The reasonableness requirement therefore changes what was solely a factual causal inquiry into a mixed causal and normative one.

It is submitted that recognising a reasonableness requirement in the payment over defence has much to commend it. In particular, it is difficult to see why a defendant agent who had no reasonable basis for making a payment over should be permitted to rely on that payment over by way of defence. This is particularly so given the strong normative claim the claimant has for recovery of the payment made pursuant to, for example, a mistake. However, in practice, the question will not usually arise (which may explain its absence from express discussion in the authorities)[53] because it usually will be reasonable for a defendant agent who has no actual notice of a claim to make a payment over, even if he has knowledge of some facts that, if investigated further, might have revealed the existence of a claim. This is because the nature of the agent's business as agent will often preclude him from having any real or sensible opportunity to follow up the security of the basis of every payment received. This is highlighted by the Australian case of *Port of Brisbane Corp v ANZ Securities.*[54] The facts of that case and its procedural history are complicated but for present purposes can be summarised as follows. The defendant stockbroker received the proceeds of a cheque as agent for its client, Windermere. At the time of receiving the payment it honestly believed that the payment had been made by its client for the purpose of investment. Unbeknown to it, its client was the vehicle for a massive fraud that had been perpetrated on the claimant, on whose account the cheque had been fraudulently drawn. At first instance,[55] the trial judge found that, in acting on its receipt, the defendant stockbroker had changed its position on the basis of an unreasonable belief as to the source of the funds and thus could not rely on the change of position defence. In particular, he found that the defendant should have made enquiries as to the identity of the drawer of the cheque, which enquiries might have revealed the existence of the fraud.

This factual finding was not challenged on appeal.[56] Nonetheless, McPherson JA of the Queensland Court of Appeal noted that requiring, in effect, that a defendant

[53] An exception is *Jaffer v Commonwealth Bank of Australia Ltd* [2001] SASC 191 (South Australian Supreme Court) [69] (Perry J), where the defendants reliance was found to be reasonable.

[54] [2002] QCA 158, [2003] 2 Qd R 661 (Queensland Court of Appeal).

[55] *Port of Brisbane Corporation v ANZ Securities Limited* [2001] QSC 466 (Queensland Supreme Court) [39]–[69].

[56] *Port of Brisbane Corp v ANZ Securities* [2002] QCA 158, [2003] 2 Qd R 661 (Queensland Court of Appeal) [21].

must be sure that the purported payee held good title to the benefit transferred before allowing the change of position defence to succeed,

> . . . would involve the recipient in such an extensive a range of enquiries (to many of which would probably receive only inconclusive answers) about the source of the money as to make it virtually impossible for commerce to be carried on at all. A stockbroker who refused to receive or to deal with money from his client without first checking the client's title to it would soon find himself out of business. He is, after all, conducting a stock-broking business, not a detective agency. The same is true of a host of other activities, including the practice of accountants, solicitors and estate agents, in which funds are constantly being received from clients on trust to be applied for particular purposes. In many instances, the exigencies of the contemplated transaction would not permit a thorough, or indeed any, investigation as to the original source of the funds or their true ownership at the time of their receipt.[57]

Consistent with this approach, his Honour later went on to note that constructive notice should be rejected as a basis for denying a defendant the defence in commercial transactions and should be limited to cases involving dealings with land and estates.[58]

If this approach to reasonable reliance is adopted, it should often be reasonable for an agent to perform his duty of paying over the amount to his principal in the absence of clear notice of the existence of a claim, or knowledge of facts that of themselves suggest that the basis of his receipt is insecure (as in *Edwards v Hodding*).

This section has concluded by arguing that the notice requirement in the payment over defence is consistent with a broader, underlying requirement of reasonable reliance. Reliance in this context provides the crucial causal link between the agent's receipt and his subsequent change of position. If that is correct, and reliance is a causal concept equally applicable to the change of position defence, then the question arises whether the notice requirement should also be adopted in that context. On this approach, a defendant who has notice of a mistake or other vitiating factor at the time he changes his position would not be able to rely on the change of position defence. This is not because he has necessarily acted in bad faith, but simply because in changing his position knowing that his receipt is insecure, he cannot be said to have reasonably relied on his receipt.

[57] *Ibid*, at[17].

[58] *Port of Brisbane Corp v ANZ Securities* [2002] QCA 158, [2003] 2 Qd R 661 (Queensland Court of Appeal) [22]. On this point, the trial judge and the Court of Appeal appear not to be so far apart: *Port of Brisbane Corporation v ANZ Securities Limited* [2001] QSC 466 (Queensland Supreme Court) [53] (Chesterman J) citing P Birks, 'Change of Position: The Nature of the Defence and its Relationship to other Restitutionary Defences' in M McInnes (ed), *Restitution: Developments in Unjust Enrichment* (LBC Information Services, North Ryde, 1996) 58. The difference in result lay in the trial judge's finding (on receiving expert evidence as to reasonable commercial practice) that the defendant's failure to make enquiries on the facts known to it was unreasonable.

D Bars to the Defence

The previous sections have argued that the payment over defence requires a defendant agent to have irreversibly changed his position in reasonable reliance on his receipt. A defendant who has notice of the claim, or who can unilaterally reverse the change made in reliance on the receipt, does not gain the protection of the defence.

The question raised in this section is whether there are any independent bars to the payment over defence. This is particularly pertinent for the change of position defence, as Lord Goff appeared to have the payment over defence in mind when he noted in *Lipkin Gorman (a firm) v Karpnale Ltd* that a 'wrongdoer' would not be entitled to the defence of change of position.[59] However, examination of the payment over authorities reveals that the use of the word 'wrongdoer' is as problematic in that context, as has proven to be the case with the change of position defence.

The primary authority for the view that a wrongdoer cannot avail himself of the payment over defence is *Snowdon v Davis*.[60] In that case, a sheriff issued two warrants relating to the recovery of arrears of taxes owed by the inhabitants of New Windsor. The bailiff levied the entire amounts against the claimant, an inhabitant of New Windsor, under threat of distraining his goods. These acts were not authorised by the warrants. The bailiff gave evidence that he had paid the sums acquired under the first warrant over to the sheriff, who in turn had paid it over to the exchequer. He had also paid the amounts acquired under the second warrant to the under-sheriff before the action had been brought.

Sir James Mansfield CJ delivered the judgment of the court. His Lordship referred to a series of cases in which money was paid to an agent for the express purpose of it being handed over to his principal and in which the agent was held not to be personally liable to repay. Mansfield CJ then asked:

> Can it in this case be said with any propriety, that the money was paid to the bailiff for the purpose of paying it to the sheriff, or to the intent that the sheriff might pay it into the exchequer? The Plaintiff pays it under the terror of process, to redeem his goods, not with the intent that it should be delivered over to any one in particular. To make the argument the more curious, if it had appeared that the Plaintiff had looked at the warrant, he could not have paid the money with a view that it should be paid over to the sheriff; for there he would have seen an authority to levy 4l. 1s. 6d. only. He clearly then paid the money under the terror of a distress. With respect to the other writ, the circumstances are the same.[61]

[59] *Lipkin Gorman (a firm) v Karpnale Ltd* [1991] 2 AC 548 (HL) 580. In *Mercedes-Benz (NSW) Pty Ltd v National Mutual Royal Savings Bank Limited* (New South Wales Court of Appeal 27 February 1996)[23]–[27] Sheller JA, with whom Priestly and Clarke JJA agreed, approved the comments of Palmer AJ at first instance that '. . . it was no doubt to this line of authority that Lord Goff in Lipkin Gorman . . . [was] referring'.

[60] (1808) 1 Taunt 359, 127 ER 872.

[61] *Snowdon v Davis* (1808) 1 Taunt 359, 363; 127 ER 872, 874.

A long line of cases have followed *Snowdon v Davis* in holding that a defendant agent who has exerted duress on the claimant to obtain his receipt cannot rely on the payment over defence.[62] However, Goff and Jones have noted that the explanation offered by Lord Mansfield is not convincing: in particular, it is inconsistent with other cases where a defendant received money paid under duress and in which the agent's defence applied.[63] For example, in *D Owen & Co v Cronk*,[64] a defendant received money paid by the claimant acting under the duress of a third party. The defendant, unaware of the duress, paid the money over to his principal. The defence of payment over was held to apply. In rationalising the results of the two cases, Goff and Jones analyse *Snowdon v Davis* as authority for the proposition that where 'the money comes into the agent's hands as a consequence of some wrongdoing to which he was a party or of which he had some knowledge, he cannot take advantage of the defence'.[65] The same approach is endorsed by the leading agency text, *Bowstead and Reynolds on Agency*.[66]

The wrongdoing analysis suffers from the obvious difficulty that it is far removed from the language and reasoning actually employed in the judgment. Taking this point, Swadling[67] argues that the actual reasoning is consistent with an estoppel analysis of the agency defence. However, Swadling rationalises the bar on the basis that the transfers in these cases are not truly consensual. It is now well accepted that duress does not operate so as to entirely vitiate the claimant's intention.[68] That is why transactions entered into under duress are voidable, not void.[69] Further, were the claimant's vitiated intention the basis for precluding the defence, it should likewise be precluded in cases where the claimant has transferred the benefit pursuant to a mistake. That clearly is not the case.

[62] *Miller v Aris* (1800) 3 Esp 231, 170 ER 598; *Smith v Sleap* (1844) 12 M & W 585, 152 ER 1332; *Wakefield v Newbon* (1844) 6 QB 276, 155 ER 1502; *Parker v The Bristol and Exeter Railway Company* (1851) 6 Ex 702, 155 ER 726; *Oates v Hudson* (1851) 6 Ex 346, 155 ER 576; *Steele v Williams* (1853) 8 Ex 625, 155 ER 1502; *TD Keegan Ltd v Palmer* [1961] 2 Lloyds Rep 449 (QB).

[63] G Jones (ed), above n 1, at [40-031].

[64] [1985] 1 QB 265 (CA). A separate line of cases involving claims for recovery of payments against excise officers seems to have afforded the defendant protection against claims for restitution on public policy grounds peculiar to the defendant's position, namely the disruption to public finances, coupled with the duty on the officer (enforced by penalty) to pay over the amount received to the treasury: *Bannatyne & Co v Carter* (1900) 19 NZLR 482 (New Zealand Supreme Court), following *Whitbread v Brooksbank* (1774) 1 Cowp 66, 972; 29 ER 970, 972 (Lord Mansfield): '. . . it might be of great inconvenience, if this case should hereafter be made a precedent, that an action for money had and received, will lie against an officer of revenue for an overpayment'. Also *Greenway v Hurd* (1792) 4 TR 553, 555; 100 ER 1171, 1172 (Lord Kenyon CJ): 'If the defendant [excise officer] had not paid the money over, he would have subjected himself to punishment . . .'.

[65] G Jones (ed), above n 1, at [40-031].

[66] Reynolds, above n 39, at 569.

[67] Above n 3, at 251 and 258–59.

[68] P Atiyah, 'Economic Duress and the Overborne Will' (1982) 98 *LQR* 197, 200; *Director of Public Prosecutions for Northern Ireland v Lynch* [1975] AC 653 (HL); endorsed in *Crescendo Management Pty Ltd v Westpac Banking Corporation* (1988) 19 NSWLR 40 (New South Wales Supreme Court) 45–46 (McHugh JA); in turn approved in *Dimskal Shipping Co SA v International Transport Workers Federation* [1992] 2 AC 152 (HL) 165–66 (Lord Goff).

[69] *Universe Tankships Inc of Monrovia v International Transport Workers Federation* [1983] 1 AC 366 (HL) 384 (Lord Diplock).

Even if one were to accept Goff and Jones' wrongdoing analysis as consistent with the results of the cases, much is left unclear. Duress is not a tort per se,[70] so in what sense does it involve wrongdoing? The label cannot have been intended to indicate lack of good faith or dishonesty. Duress may be applied in all good faith, the party applying the pressure believing (wrongly) that the pressure being applied is legitimate. For example, in *Snowdon v Davis* itself there is no hint that the bailiff was not acting in good faith throughout. The same may be said of other duress cases where the payment over defence was denied.[71] In any event, as we saw in the previous section, there is no need for an independent requirement of good faith where there is already a reliance requirement: any 'bad faith' change of position made knowing of the vitiating factor will not, in any event, have been made in reliance on the receipt.

Many cases of duress involve independently tortious acts. For example, the defendant bailiff in *Snowdon v Davis* committed the tort of conversion when he detained the claimant's goods without authorisation. In that sense, the defendant was a 'wrongdoer', although not sued in that capacity. However, many cases of duress involve acts that are not independently tortious but nonetheless are sufficiently illegitimate to give rise to actionable duress.[72] These cases of 'lawful act duress' give rise to claims for restitution of the value of benefits conferred as a result of the illegitimate pressure, even though the defendant cannot be regarded as having committed an independently unlawful act. On one view, it would seem rather strange if the law were to permit such defendants to rely on the payment over defence while not allowing it in the case of independently tortious defendants, when the crux of the claimant's action is the duress, not any tort that might, or might not, have been committed. For that reason, it might be thought that the defence should or should not apply whatever the particular kind of illegitimate pressure that is applied.

On the other hand, where the tort itself underpins the reason why the defendant's act constitutes duress, and was the very means by which the defendant obtained his receipt, it could be argued that to allow the defence would stultify the reason against the law's prohibition of the tortious act. In other words, the defence is barred on grounds of public policy. Another, similar 'stultification' explanation is that if the defence were to be made available, the policy behind rendering the pressure illegitimate for the purposes of the doctrine of duress would be stultified. Both these arguments rest on the same kind of reasoning that lies behind denying the defence where parties have engaged in an illegal act, reasoning to which we will return further below.

However, it must be questioned whether the case for precluding access to the payment over defence on the grounds of public policy is as strong in cases of

[70] *Ibid*, at 385 (Lord Diplock), cited with approval in *Dimskal Shipping Co SA v International Transport Workers Federation* [1992] 2 AC 152 (HL) 166 (Lord Goff).

[71] eg *Miller v Aris* (1800) 3 Esp 231, 170 ER 598; *Oates v Hudson* (1851) 6 Ex 346, 155 ER 576.

[72] eg *Williams v Bayley* (1866) LR 1 HL 200 (HL); *Unwin v Leaper* (1840) 1 Man & G 747, 133 ER 533; *Smith v Cuff* (1817) 6 M & S 160, 105 ER 1203.

duress as in cases of illegality. As noted earlier, a defendant may have applied duress unwittingly, not realising the illegitimacy of the pressure being applied and may have acted entirely lawfully in the process of applying the pressure. Indeed, in many cases, the defendant's intention in applying the pressure will be as impaired as that of the claimant in succumbing to it. So it is unclear that the case for excluding such defendants on the grounds of public policy is as strong in duress cases as in the case of illegal transactions.

The final possibility is that where a defendant has actively exercised the illegitimate pressure in question, he is a wrongdoer in a very attenuated sense, being at fault in having induced the claimant's impaired decision (impaired, because made under illegitimate pressure) to transfer the benefit. If this last analysis is correct, it raises the possibility that a defendant's fault in having innocently induced a *mistake* which impairs a claimant's decision to transfer a benefit to the defendant, or having *unduly influenced* a claimant's decision to transfer a benefit to the defendant, ought also operate to deny the defendant the defence. Although one could label such defendants 'wrongdoers', we have seen that label is highly ambiguous. A better label, in keeping with the analysis in the previous chapter, is that the defendant is an 'inducer'.

Although *Snowdon v Davis* is itself a very difficult case, subsequent cases have helped to provide examples of instances in which a defendant's 'wrongdoing', in all its many varieties discussed above, has operated to preclude an agent from relying on the payment over defence.

In *Sharland v Mildon*,[73] the widow of a testator employed the defendant agent (Hewish) to collect some of the debts due to the testator's estate. Hewish did so, believing that the widow was the administratrix. The widow then died intestate and without having obtained the necessary letters of administration. As Sir James Wigram V-C stated, it followed without doubt that the widow was an executor *de son tort*. The question was, what about Hewish?

Reluctantly, the Vice-Chancellor concluded that Hewish was personally liable for the amount he had collected, notwithstanding that he had paid it over to the widow. It was 'admitted or well-established'[74] that had Hewish retained the money in his hands, he would have been liable as executor *de son tort*.[75] That being so, Hewish could not discharge himself except by paying the money that he had received over to the legal personal representative of the testator. Further, Wigram V-C held that the 'authorities clearly show that the doctrine that the possession of an agent is the possession of a principal has no application in the case of a wrongdoer.'[76]

As authority for this latter proposition, two cases were cited. The second was *Snowdon v Davis*, which one might be excused from thinking did not 'clearly show'

[73] (1846) 5 Hare 469, 67 ER 997.

[74] *Sharland v Mildon* (1846) 5 Hare 469, 473; 67 ER 997, 999.

[75] Relying on *Padget v Priest* (1787) 2 TR 97, 200; 100 ER 53, 55. There, Buller J was similarly reluctant to find a servant an executor *de son tort*, but was unable to avoid that conclusion as at the time of the plea pleaded he had money of the intestate's in his hands.

[76] *Sharland v Mildon* (1846) 5 Hare 469, 473; 67 ER 997, 999.

a great deal beyond the limited context of duress. The first was *Stephens v Elwall*.[77] In that case, a clerk received property on behalf of his principal that had been purchased from bankrupts. He sent the goods on to his principal in America. Ellenborough CJ found that it was no defence to an action against the clerk for conversion that he had solely received the goods in his capacity as agent. This case does confirm the general proposition that it is no answer to a claim in tort, that the tort was committed by an agent authorised to so act by his principal. But it is less clear it applies to the different question whether, when a claim is brought not on the basis of the tort, but on an independent cause of action such as duress, the fact that the defendant agent is also a wrongdoer should operate to bar the payment over defence. As we have seen in the earlier discussion of *Snowdon v Davis*, it is arguable that where the defendant agent received the benefit as a result of the commission of the breach of duty, the payment over defence should be precluded as a matter of public policy and in particular to prevent the stultification of the law's prohibition of the tortious act. However, that rationale was not considered in *Stephens v Elwall* and there is no sign in *Sharland v Mildon* that Wigram V-C appreciated that the case is distinguishable as being based on the tort of conversion, rather than on a claim in duress.

Notwithstanding that the authorities are not as clear as Wigram V-C considered, what is clear is that an executor *de son tort* may properly be labelled a wrongdoer and, having received the benefit in that capacity, may be denied the defence for the public policy reasons discussed above. Other cases are less easy to so rationalise. *Ex parte Edwards, In Re Chapman*[78] is often taken as a leading authority for the proposition that an agent wrongdoer cannot rely on the payment over defence. On closer inspection, however, the case is less convincing, displaying a degree of confusion with the notice requirement considered in the previous section of this chapter. In that case, John Storey presented a bankruptcy petition against James Chapman. The act of bankruptcy on which the petition was founded was the failure of Chapman to comply with a debtor's summons which Storey had previously served on him for an outstanding debt. Thomas Edwards acted as solicitor for Storey in the matter of the summons and also in the petition. The hearing of the petition was adjourned on three occasions, Chapman each time paying considerable sums to Storey in consideration of the postponement. Those amounts were received by Edwards as agent for Storey. While the bankruptcy petition was still pending, Edwards paid over the amounts received from Chapman to Storey. Subsequently, the petition was heard and Chapman was adjudicated a bankrupt. The trustee in bankruptcy then sought to recover the amounts from Edwards.

Baggallay LJ noted that Chapman,

> knew perfectly well that, if an adjudication of bankruptcy was made on the petition, the title of the trustee in bankruptcy would relate back to the act of bankruptcy, and that all of the property which would otherwise have belonged to the bankrupt would be the

[77] (1815) 4 Mau & Sel, 105 ER 830.
[78] (1884) 13 QBD 747 (CA).

> property of the trustee as from the date of the act of bankruptcy. Knowing this, Edwards handed over the money to Storey. It is sufficient to state the facts in order to shew that, having regard to the relation between the parties, the payments made by Edwards to Storey cannot possibly stand as against the trustee.[79]

On the face of it, this reasoning resembles that discussed in the previous section relating to notice. Chapman knew about the petition and its potential effects and thus knew that the security of his receipt was tenuous. He could not be said therefore to have reasonably relied on his receipt in making the payment over.

Likewise, Lindley LJ based his decision on the fact that Edwards knew of the act of bankruptcy and knew that, were the petition to be granted,

> the person who paid the money to him would have no right to pay it, and that the person for whom he received it would have no right to retain it. Under these circumstances Edwards was not justified in paying over the money to Storey.[80]

Both Lindley and Baggallay LLJ however went on to rely on *Sharland v Mildon* as support for their conclusion. There was, of course, a clear distinction between that case and this. As we saw earlier, in *Sharland v Mildon* the agent had no idea that the widow was not the executrix. So that case could not have been being cited in support for the notice argument considered in the previous section. However, as we also saw previously, *Sharland v Mildon* did contain statements concerning the inability of a wrongdoer to rely on the agency defence. So, in theory, it is possible that Lindley and Baggallay LLJ drew on it as authority for excluding a wrongdoer from the defence and thus, by inference, that they considered the defendant agent in the instant case a wrongdoer.

Lindley LJ did not explain why he considered *Sharland v Mildon* on point, simply stating that it was 'very like' the instant case.[81] However, Baggallay LJ did cite it as authority for the proposition that,

> if a person is employed as agent to do a particular thing, and receives money for his principal in the course of his agency, still if the person who employs him has no right to the money, the agent is not entitled to hand it over to him, and is liable to the true owner if he does so hand it over.[82]

Although this reflects part of the reasoning, and certainly the result in *Sharland v Mildon*, it omits the important point that, in that case, the defendant became a trustee *de son tort* as a result of his receipt and therefore a wrongdoer. In contrast, it is not clear that the solicitor in *ex parte Edwards* was a wrongdoer in an equivalent sense.

In contrast, Cotton LJ's approach was more clearly based on a wrongdoing analysis. His Lordship's view was that Storey could not both seek to have an adjudication on his petition of bankruptcy while simultaneously purporting to receive

[79] (1884) 13 QBD 747 (CA), at 750–51.
[80] *Ibid*, at 752.
[81] *Ibid*.
[82] *Ibid*, at 751.

and retain money which, were he to succeed on his petition, would have been applicable rateably among all Chapman's creditors. In that context, the payment by Edwards to Storey was a 'wrongful act' and for that reason the defence of payment over could not apply.[83] However, Cotton LJ also noted that had the petition been dismissed, Edwards could have handed over the money safely at that point, provided he had no notice of another act of bankruptcy. Cotton LJ concluded: 'Of course, if he had had notice of another act of bankruptcy, he would have stood in the same position as that in which he now stands.'[84] It seems, therefore, that even on Cotton LJ's approach, the notice of bankruptcy was enough to disqualify Edwards from the payment over defence, without the further need to identify a separate wrongdoing on his part.

The same confusion between the concepts of notice and wrongdoing is apparent in *Holland v Russell.*[85] In that case, the defendant agent innocently failed to disclose a letter to an insurer which would have entitled the insurer to avoid the policy. He made that decision in the belief that non-communication of the letter would not avoid the policy. Erle CJ accepted that the 'non-disclosure of the contents of that letter is a wrong thus far, that under such circumstances the insurer may avoid the policy if he chooses . . . it is not a wrong as between him and the agent by whom it was effected'.[86] Given the policy was voidable only, the defendant was entitled to demand payment on it, and on receiving the amount, pay it over to his principal. Erle CJ explained that:

> Had the agent known the insurer intended to dispute his right to receive the money, and hastened to pay it over to his principal to avoid that claim, or did anything else to shew that the money was not paid over by him in the full belief of the validity of the transaction, it would have been a fraudulent act.[87]

However, in those circumstances, the defendant would have had notice of the claim and would therefore have been precluded from relying on the defence in any event. Labelling the defendant a wrongdoer in that context adds little to our understanding of the circumstances in which wrongdoing separate from notice of a claim will operate as a bar to the defence.

Finally, there exists a line of agency cases that involve payments made to agents (usually parish officers) pursuant to illegal contracts for the maintenance of illegitimate children.[88] The leading authority for the purposes of the payment over defence is *Townson v Wilson.*[89] In that case, a man paid £40 to the defendant officers of a parish for the maintenance of his illegitimate child, in consideration of being released from all liability for the child. When the child died after only

[83] *Ibid*, at 752.

[84] *Ibid.*

[85] (1863) 4 B & S 14, 122 ER 365. We considered that case earlier in this chapter in the context of examining the payment over requirement, at 68–69.

[86] *Holland v Russell* (1863) 4 B & S 14, 16–17; 122 ER 365, 366.

[87] *Holland v Russell* (1863) 4 B & S 14, 17; 122 ER 365, 366.

[88] eg *Chappell v Poles* (1837) 2 M & W 867, 150 ER 101 and the authorities cited therein.

[89] (1808) 1 Camp 396, 170 ER 997.

11 weeks, the man sought the recovery of the full amount paid to the defendants. Lord Ellenborough explained that the agreement was illegal on the grounds of public policy, because 'it gave the parish an interest in abridging the life of the child'.[90] However, his Lordship also noted that at the time of making the payment, the man was arrested and thus subject to duress to make the payment. It followed that the parties were not *in pari delicto* and the man could recover the amount of the payment, less an amount by way of set-off for 'so much as the defendants expended on the lying-in of the mother, and the maintenance of the infant'.[91] It was no defence that the officers had received the payment in their public capacity and had since paid the money over to their successors in title. 'If any person gets money into his hands illegally, he cannot discharge himself by paying it over to another . . .'[92]

It is interesting to ask why the amount spent in supporting the mother and child was permitted to be offset against the full amount received when it too could be caught by the illegality bar. One possibility, supported by the characterisation of the amount as operating by way of set-off, is that Lord Ellenborough envisaged it as a counterclaim for recovery of the benefit conferred on the man by the parish officers in discharging expenses which otherwise the man would have incurred in supporting the mother and child. Although the man might have argued that he would have refused to maintain the wife and child for the relevant period, it may be that Lord Ellenborough considered him under a moral, if not legal obligation to maintain the mother and child and recognised the validity of the counterclaim on that basis. The policy against the maintenance agreement (protecting the child) would in no way be stultified by permitting this claim, which reflected payments made in support of the child's wellbeing. In contrast, allowing the officers to rely on the payment over defence so far as it related to handing the money over to their successors in office, might be seen as undermining the stringency of the prohibition on this kind of maintenance agreement, with the result that the defence should be denied.

In conclusion, and although not without difficulty, the agency case law does shed considerable light on the circumstances in which a defendant is considered a 'wrongdoer' such as to deny him the benefit of the payment over defence and, by analogy, the defence of change of position. The first is where the defendant has committed a tort or other breach of duty in obtaining the benefit from the claimant. In those circumstances, it is arguable that the defendant should be barred from relying on the defence of payment over where to do so would undermine or stultify the reason for the law's prohibition. The second is based on similar grounds: where the defendant was involved in an illegal act in obtaining the benefit from the defendant and recognising the payment over defence would stultify the reason behind the law's prohibition of the illegal act. The third, and most contentious, is where the defendant was at fault in inducing the claimant's impaired decision to transfer the benefit to the defendant, as where the defendant induced the claimant to transfer the benefit as a result of duress. Acceptance of this

[90] *Townson v Wilson* (1808) 1 Camp 396, 397; 170 ER 997, 998.
[91] *Ibid.*
[92] *Ibid.*

third category of case is dependent on accepting that, in duress cases, it will not always be possible to identify the defendant as having carried out independently unlawful conduct such that he can be labelled a wrongdoer. Nor will it always be the case that the defendant will have acted in bad faith, or pursuant to an illegal transaction. If defendants in cases of duress are generally to be denied the defence, the rationale for that prohibition must lie in their role in inducing the impaired decision to transfer in the first place.

E Conclusion

This chapter has demonstrated that the payment over defence suggests answers to a number of questions posed by the change of position defence: what difference should it make in a claim for restitution of a received benefit that a defendant has changed his position following receipt of the benefit; of what relevance is the fact that the defendant received notice of the claim for restitution before changing his position; what difference should the fault of the defendant make to the availability of any defence?

This chapter has proceeded on the basis that the answers to those questions should at least be taken into account in considering the disputed features of the change of position defence. In this regard, the chapter has demonstrated that the payment over defence requires a defendant agent to have irreversibly changed his position in reasonable reliance on his receipt. A defendant who has notice of the claim, or who can unilaterally reverse the change made in reliance on the receipt, does not gain the protection of the defence. There is no separate requirement that the defendant must have acted bona fide in the belief that he was entitled to deal with his receipt in the manner in which he did: the concept of good faith is implicit or subsumed in the reasonable reliance requirement.

In terms of bars to the defence, there are clearly a number of cases in which defendants who can be labelled 'wrongdoers' are precluded from relying on the payment over defence. Tortfeasors and those who engage in illegal acts may be barred from the defence, as well as those who have been directly involved in procuring the transfer of the benefit as a result of duress. However, the reasons for those prohibitions are less obvious, particularly in the case of defendants involved in duress. This chapter has concluded that it is possible that the duress cases support the view that a defendant's role in inducing the claimant's impaired decision to transfer a benefit may properly be a ground for denying the defendant the defence of payment over.

4

Lessons from Rescission

A Introduction

THIS CHAPTER WILL explore the rationale, elements and operation of the requirement of *restitutio in integrum* as applied in the context of the restitutionary process of rescission. It will demonstrate that the traditional rescission case law contains a number of important insights relevant to the disputed features of the change of position defence.[1] This is because in applying the requirement of *restitutio in integrum*, courts have long been forced to consider the legal ramifications which should flow from alterations in a party's circumstances following receipt of a benefit, which benefit should now prima facie be restored. The rescission case law reveals a nascent concern with those same matters that lie at the heart of the change of position defence.

As with chapters two and three, this chapter proceeds on the assumption that it is highly desirable that the change of position defence develops in a manner consistent with the existing law and its underlying policy concerns as a whole. It demonstrates that there is a close relationship between the defence and the concept of *restitutio in integrum*. It follows that the considerations underpinning the requirement of *restitutio in integrum* should be taken into account when considering the disputed rationale, elements and operation of the change of position defence. To this end, this chapter concludes by identifying and exploring the insights that can be drawn from the rescission case law for the disputed features of the change of position defence.

B *Restitutio in Integrum*

(1) Rescission and the Requirement of *Restitutio in Integrum*

Rescission refers to the process of undoing or reversing a transaction *ab initio* so as to restore the parties to the *status quo ante*. Used in this sense, rescission does

[1] This chapter seeks to identify the principles and policies underlying the common law and equitable case law on rescission. For this reason, it will not examine the operation of statutes such as the Misrepresentation Act 1967, which may reflect different considerations.

not encompass cases in which a claimant terminates a contract, for example, on the ground of a repudiatory breach.[2] In such cases, the contract is only 'rescinded' in so far as it is executory and the accrued rights and liabilities of the parties remain unaffected.[3]

Rescission in the sense employed in this chapter has two aspects. The first relates to the right or power to rescind that arises both at common law and in equity, in response to certain classes of legally significant event. As explained in chapter one, this book adopts the taxonomy of the law proposed by Professor Birks, in which legal and equitable rights are analysed as being generated by legally significant events such as consent, wrongs and unjust enrichment.[4] A right to rescind a contract arises at common law in cases of fraudulent misrepresentation and duress and, in equity, in cases of non-fraudulent misrepresentation and undue influence. A right to rescind also arises in cases of gifts brought about as a result of a claimant's vitiated intention.[5] Although the facts supporting such claims may also give rise to a right to rescind arising from a breach of duty, it is broadly accepted that they are capable of analysis as claims in unjust enrichment. That is, a right to rescind a transaction arises in cases of mistake,[6] undue influence and duress and thus, on the established 'unjust factors' approach to claims in unjust enrichment,[7] is generated by the event of unjust enrichment.

The second aspect of rescission lies in the effect of exercising the power to rescind. The purpose of the remedy (in the sense of a court order) of restitution is to reverse transfers of value, so as to restore the parties to the *status quo ante*.[8] Given the dominant analysis of rescission as an act of the rescinding party, in which the order of the court merely confirms the valid exercise of the power to rescind and its consequences,[9] rescission is not a restitutionary remedy in this same sense.[10] However, once exercised, rescission does effect restitutionary relief,

[2] eg *Hunt v Silk* (1804) 5 East 449, 102 ER 1142.

[3] *Johnson v Agnew* [1980] AC 367 (HL) 393 (Lord Wilberforce).

[4] P Birks, 'Definition and Division: A Meditation on Institutes 3.13' in P Birks (ed) *The Classification of Obligations* (Clarendon Press, Oxford 1997).

[5] eg *Allcard v Skinner* (1887) 36 Ch D 145 (CA); *Quek v Beggs* (1990) 5 BPR 11,766 (New South Wales Supreme Court); *Louth v Diprose* (1992) 175 CLR 621 (High Court of Australia).

[6] It is uncertain whether rescission arises in cases of gift with respect to spontaneous, as opposed to induced mistake. Although the author takes the view that, as a matter of principle, it should, the resolution of this controversy is not necessary to this book.

[7] *Deutsche Morgan Grenfell Group Plc v Commissioners of Inland Revenue* [2006] UKHL 49, [2007] 1 AC 558 [21] (Lord Hoffmann); ch 1, at 11.

[8] Ch 1, at 13.

[9] D O'Sullivan, S Elliot and R Zakrzewski, *The Law of Rescission* (OUP, Oxford 2008) regard rescission at common law and in equity as distinct processes, the ramifications of which are considered in ch 10, at 235–36. The conclusions there drawn apply with equal force to a third view that rescission both at law and in equity operates (or should operate) by court order: see eg J O'Sullivan, 'Rescission as a Self-Help Remedy: A Critical Analysis' (2000) 59 *CLJ* 509 and M Bryan, 'Rescission, Restitution and Contractual Ordering: The Role of Plaintiff Election' in A Robertson (ed) *The Law of Obligations: Connections and Boundaries* (UCL Press, London 2003).

[10] *Cf Whittaker v Campbell* [1983] 3 All ER 582 (DC) 586 (Robert Goff LJ): 'The remedy of rescission, by which the unjust enrichment of the representor is prevented . . . is a straightforward remedy in restitution subject to limits which are characteristic of that branch of the law.'

in the sense of enabling or effecting[11] the return of the benefit[12] received at the expense of the claimant.[13]

Although he accepts that rescission of executed and partly-executed contracts is restitutionary in nature, Professor Burrows argues that rescission of executory contracts is non-restitutionary.[14] He argues that contractual rights in and of themselves do not constitute benefits that can be the subject of a claim for restitution. However, that conclusion is difficult to reconcile with the law's long-standing acceptance that contractual rights against banks that arise from the deposit of money in an account are valuable benefits for the purpose of claims in unjust enrichment.[15] The law has also long recognised that releasing a defendant from contractual duties may be beneficial for the purpose of the law of unjust enrichment. If the law accepts that contractual rights and the release from contractual duties constitute benefits for the purposes of claims in unjust enrichment, then there seems little reason to distinguish between rescission of executed and executory contracts.

It could also be argued that in the case of executory contracts, rescission involves the destruction, rather than the giving back (restitution) of contractual rights. However, even assuming this is so it is not impossible to describe rescission in this context as operating to reverse (in the sense of undo) the benefit conferred on the defendant so as to restore the parties to the *status quo ante.* Overall, the distinction between restitution and rescission seems too fine to be of significant practical or theoretical relevance.

On this analysis, the relationship between rescission for unjust enrichment and restitution for unjust enrichment is extremely close. For this reason, if no other, the requirement of *restitutio in integrum* calls for close scrutiny. Rationality in the law demands that like cases are treated alike. If the right to rescind and the right to restitution arise in response to the same sort of claim, and the effect of exercising the right to rescind is predominantly restitutionary in nature, then the considerations underpinning the requirement of *restitutio in integrum* in cases of rescission for unjust enrichment should be taken into account in cases of restitution for unjust enrichment.

[11] On the effects of rescission, see B Häcker, 'Rescission and Third Party Rights' [2006] *Restitution L Rev* 21, 23–25 and B Häcker, 'Rescission of Contract and Revesting of Title: a Reply to Mr Swadling' [2006] *Restitution L Rev* 106. For a critical view of the proprietary consequences of rescission at common law, see W Swadling, 'Rescission, Property, and the Common Law' (2005) 121 *LQR* 123.

[12] The right to rescind often incorporates a proprietary power to revest title to the thing passed to the defendant, but need not do so (as in the case of rescission of personal contractual rights under an executory contract): see further J Edelman and E Bant, *Unjust Enrichment in Australia* (OUP, Melbourne 2006) 67–69. Further, with the increasing recognition of 'pecuniary rescission' as an alternative to proprietary relief (discussed below, at 107), it is clear that the historical perception of rescission as solely concerned with effecting restitution *in specie* is suspect.

[13] P Birks, *An Introduction to the Law of Restitution* (revised edn, Clarendon Press, Oxford 1989) 163; O'Sullivan, Elliot and Zakrzewski, above n 9, at [205].

[14] AS Burrows, *The Law of Restitution* (2nd edn, Butterworths, London 2002) 57–58; G Virgo, *The Principles of the Law of Restitution* (2 edn, OUP, Oxford 2006) 29.

[15] NY Nahan, 'Rescission: A Case for Rejecting the Classical Model?' (1997) 27 (1) *U Western Australia L Rev* 66, 72–73; Edelman and Bant, above n 12, at 102.

That being said, it is not altogether easy to identify the precise ambit and operation of the requirement of *restitutio in integrum*. Its basic role seems straightforward enough. Consistent with the underlying purpose of rescission to restore the parties to the *status quo ante*, a claimant's right to rescind a contract or other transaction both at common law and in equity[16] and obtain restitution of any benefits[17] conferred pursuant to that contract or transaction, is conditional on '*restitutio in integrum*' being possible.[18] That label reflects a concept of rescission as a bipartite process, requiring an unwinding of the transaction on both sides so that the parties are restored to an equivalent position to that which they occupied prior to the impugned transaction.[19] Where *restitutio in integrum* is no longer possible, the claimant's primary claim to restitution of benefits conferred on the defendant is denied.[20]

However, beyond this basic description, the precise requirements of *restitutio in intergum* become less clear. It has tended to be equated with counter-restitution.[21] The latter is usually described as the requirement that if a claimant is to obtain restitution of a benefit transferred to a defendant, she must be prepared to make counter-restitution to the defendant of any benefits received from the defendant. On this view, the concept of *restitutio in integrum* is concerned only with alterations in a party's position that involve conferral of a benefit on the other party.

While there is no doubt that the requirement of counter-restitution in this limited sense forms a core component of the concept of *restitutio in integrum*, it is less obvious that it comprises the whole. A key issue in examining the relationship between the requirement of *restitutio in integrum* and the change of position defence is whether the former concept extends to other changes made or suffered by a party as a consequence of entering into a transaction which cannot now be undone, so that it is no longer possible to return the affected party to the *status quo ante*. If it does, the requirement of *restitutio in integrum* is not limited to counter-restitution in the restricted sense described above, but is better translated as a right to restoration of position, which incorporates consideration of both parties'

[16] The different approaches of the two jurisdictions to satisfying the requirement are dealt with below, at 104–07.

[17] Including any contractual rights conferred pursuant to the transaction.

[18] Discussed at length in *Halpern v Halpern* [2007] EWCA Civ 291, [2007] 2 All ER (Comm) 330 [55]–[75] (Carnwath LJ, Sedley and Waller LJJ concurring).

[19] *Newbigging v Adam* (1886) 34 Ch D 582 (CA) 595 (Bowen LJ); *Abram Steamship Co Ltd v Westville Shipping Co Ltd* [1923] AC 773 (HL) 781 (Lord Atkinson); *Spence v Crawford* [1939] 3 All ER 271 (HL) 289 (Lord Wright). *Cf* O'Sullivan, Elliot and Zakrzewski, above n 9, at [18.03].

[20] *Clarke v Dickson* (1858) EB & E 148, 120 ER 463.

[21] eg Nahan, above n 15; Burrows, above n 14, at 177. Professor Virgo does not refer to *restitutio in integrum* as a bar to rescission at all, but only to cases where restitution and counter-restitution are impossible: Virgo, above n 14, at 31–33. *Cf* P Hellwege, 'Unwinding mutual contracts: *restitutio in integrum* v. the defence of change of position' in D Johnston and R Zimmerman (eds) *Unjustified Enrichment: Key Issues in Comparative Perspective* (CUP, Cambridge 2002). A recent judicial example is *Halpern v Halpern* [2007] EWCA Civ 291, [2007] 2 All ER (Comm) 330 [54]–[75] (Carnwath LJ, Sedley and Waller LJJ concurring).

changes of position beyond their mutual exchange of benefits.[22] On this model, because rescission operates *ab initio*, changes of position of both parties that were unremarkable prior to the exercise of the power to rescind subsequently become relevant for the purpose of determining whether the parties can be returned to the *status quo ante.*

One indicator that the requirement of *restitutio in integrum* may be broader than the limited conception of counter-restitution discussed above is the existence of the traditional bar to rescission where third party rights have intervened. This is usually discussed as a separate bar to rescission, independent of the requirement of *restitutio in integrum.*[23] However, the bar does exemplify one kind of change that can render it impossible to return the parties to the *status quo ante.* On the other hand, in many if not all cases,[24] this will be because the intervention of third-party rights has rendered restitution of the benefit *in specie* impossible (because, for example, the benefit has been sold to a third party bona fide purchaser).[25] To that extent, the concern with third party rights overlaps with the requirement of counter-restitution.

Given the uncertain ambit of the concept of *restitutio in integrum*, the safest starting point for consideration of its rationale, elements and operation lies in the accepted core requirement of counter-restitution, to which we now turn.

(2) The Requirement of Counter-restitution

(a) Rationale

It is relatively clear that the rationale of the requirement of counter-restitution is to prevent the unjust enrichment of the rescinding party (the 'claimant'). As Lord Wright explained in *Spence v Crawford*: 'Though the defendant has been fraudulent,

[22] P Watts, 'Rescission of Guarantees for Misrepresentation and Actionable Non-Disclosure' (2002) 61(2) CLJ 301, 303. *Cf* O'Sullivan, Elliot and Zakrzewski, above n 9, at [18.02], [18.03], [18.07] [18.103]–[18.117] who consider that courts may go beyond counter-restitution to other 'prejudicial changes of circumstance' that may make *restitutio in integrum* impossible. However, apart from noting that any change must be irreversible, the learned authors concentrate their analysis on the fault of the parties rather than the nature of those other prejudicial changes in circumstances. The authors elsewhere deny that the bar is an example of change of position on the basis that change of position is assumed to be solely concerned with disenrichment, as to which see further, at ch 5, 126–38.

[23] eg P Birks, 'Unjust Factors and Wrongs: Pecuniary Rescission for Undue Influence' [1997] *Restitution L Rev* 72, 72; Burrows, above n 14, at 175; W Peel (ed), *Treitel The Law of Contract* (12th edn Sweet & Maxwell, London 2007) [9-104]–[9-105]; Virgo, above n 14, at 33 simply refers to it as the bona fide purchaser bar.

[24] It has been suggested to apply where a third party has extended credit to a defendant in reliance on his apparent entitlement to an asset: *Clarke v Dickson* (1858) EB & E 148, 120 ER 463 or where third parties have entered into insurance contracts on the basis that the rescinding parties were members of the insurance association: *Lloyds v Leighs* [1997] CLC 1398 (CA (Civ)).

[25] To this extent, the bar may be significantly affected by acceptance of the availability of pecuniary rescission: discussed below, at 107. For a recent examination of the bar in the light of possible pecuniary rescission, see Häcker, 'Rescission and Third Party Rights' above n 11.

he must not be robbed, nor must the plaintiff be unjustly enriched, as he would be if he both got back what he had parted with and kept what he had received in return.'[26]

(b) Elements and Operation

Lord Wright's rationalisation suggests that the requirement of counter-restitution may be fruitfully analysed not merely as imposing a condition of rescission on a claimant, but as reflecting the defendant's right to counterclaim for restitution of the value of the benefit conferred on the claimant.[27] As Burrows explains, where a benefit is transferred by the defendant to the claimant on the basis of the impugned transaction, that basis fails once rescission occurs.[28] Viewed from this (reverse) perspective, the requirement of counter-restitution sees the claimant become the defendant to a counterclaim by way of set-off in unjust enrichment for restitution of the benefit received, the unjust factor being failure of consideration.

If this is correct, then the requirement of counter-restitution is potentially broader than has been generally assumed. On the above analysis, it naturally raises the same sort of question that underpins the change of position defence: namely, when a party is faced with a claim for (counter-) restitution, what legal significance attaches to her changes of position? This question is not limited to mutual changes by exchange with the other party to the transaction: it extends to other changes that might affect her ability to be restored to her former position. In that context, broader change of position considerations might legitimately be expected to inform and operate as a limit on the requirement of counter-restitution.[29] Indeed, if rescission involves mutual cross-claims in restitution as this analysis suggests, it is arguable that change of position considerations should be taken into account in determining the claimant's liability to make counter-restitution. To conclude otherwise would be to tolerate a core inconsistency in the treatment of near-identical forms of claim.[30]

This conclusion might be doubted on the ground that any set-off against the claimant will be based on failure of consideration. As we will see in chapter seven, in many cases of failure of consideration, the recipient will have changed her position knowing that her receipt was conditional and that the condition was not satisfied at the time of her change of position. Knowing her receipt to be insecure, she

[26] *Spence v Crawford* [1939] 3 All ER 271 (HL) 288–89 (Lord Wright).

[27] *Cf* O'Sullivan, Elliot and Zakrzewski, above n 9, at [14.02], [14.45], [15.60], [15.51], [15.57], discussed in ch 10, at 236.

[28] Burrows, above n 14, at 176, 539. It follows that limitations periods should rarely be in issue. *Cf Kleinwort Benson Ltd v Sandwell Borough Council* [1994] 4 All ER 890 (QB), where the contract was void rather than voidable and so limitation periods were in issue.

[29] Nahan, above n 15, at 82–85. *Cf* Hellwege, above n 21, at 283–86.

[30] Whether the mutual nature of rescission supports a different approach to change of position issues is explored below, at 100.

cannot be said to have relied on her receipt.[31] Similarly, it could be argued that in cases of rescission, the claimant's receipt is only ever conditional on there being no mistake, undue influence or other factor that could give rise to her right to rescind the contract. In those circumstances, it might be argued that the sorts of considerations that underpin the change of position defence are automatically precluded in claims for counter-restitution. However, this is counteracted by the fact that a rescinding claimant will normally be unaware of her mistake, or subject to the effects of the influence or duress at the time of changing her position. In those circumstances, she cannot be said to have taken the risk that her receipt was insecure in changing her position.

The foregoing analysis has concluded that change of position considerations may properly inform a claimant's liability to make counter-restitution. Conversely, it follows from the accepted principle that *restitutio in integrum* applies to both the claimant and the defendant,[32] that a *defendant's* change of position may also legitimately inform the extent of his restitutionary liability with respect to the claimant's primary claim, at least where the claimant's ground for rescission is based in unjust enrichment.[33] On this approach to rescission, the claimant's primary claim and the defendant's counterclaim mirror each other exactly and result in a complete undoing of the impugned transaction, so as to restore the parties to the *status quo ante*. It is inherent in this analysis that the reversibility of the parties' changes of position (whether it is possible to restore them to the *status quo ante*) is assessed at the time of the exercise of the power to rescind, rather than at the time of the original changes of position.[34] In this context, the role of any change of position defence will be to protect the parties in circumstances where, due to their change of position, it is no longer possible to return them to the *status quo ante*.[35]

If this analysis is correct, we should expect detailed examination of the rescission case law to reveal that courts do take into account the respective parties' changes of position in reducing or eliminating their mutual restitutionary liabilities. That enquiry should also reveal the kinds of factors that courts have considered relevant to that process. More specifically, given the demonstrated affinity between rescission and restitution for unjust enrichment, a close enquiry into the rescission case law may reveal principles or policy concerns that, by analogy, should be taken into

[31] The operation of the change of position defence in cases of failure of consideration is considered in ch 7, at 197–98, and ch 10, at 244–49.

[32] *Spence v Crawford* [1939] 3 All ER 271 (HL) 289 (Lord Wright).

[33] Many of the rescission cases can be alternatively analysed as based on breach of duty, eg, fraudulent misrepresentation. Where the basis of the claim is wrongdoing, rather than unjust enrichment, there may be reasons why the change of position defence ought never to apply: discussed below, at 106–07.

[34] Assuming the correctness of the self-help model of rescission, an interesting question is whether changes of position that occur after the power to rescind has been exercised should be taken into account: considered in ch 6, at 188–91.

[35] *Cf* P Birks, 'Change of Position and Surviving Enrichment' in W Swadling (ed) *The Limits of Restitutionary Claims: A Comparative Analysis* (The United Kingdom Committee of Comparative Law, Glasgow 1997) 40 (considering 'reciprocity' as a possible rationale of the defence), discussed further below, at 118–19.

account for the purposes of determining the disputed features of the change of position defence.

This proposed approach to unpacking the change of position implications of the requirement of *restitutio in integrum* is both founded on Lord Wright's seminal analysis of the requirement of counter-restitution and seems sound from the perspective of broader restitutionary principle. However, before proceeding with that analysis, it is necessary to address what at first sight appears to be a strong contrary authority. In *Kleinwort Benson Ltd v Sandwell Borough Council*,[36] a bank and local council entered into an interest rate 'swaps' contract, pursuant to which one party paid the other fixed interest on a notional lump sum, while the other paid interest pursuant to a variable rate. By the time the transaction came to its conclusion, the bank was the 'loser', having paid to the local council more than the council had paid to it. Subsequently, it was discovered that interest rate swap contracts were ultra vires local councils and thus void. The bank sought to recover the amount of its net payment to the council.

Hobhouse J held that because the bank had received all that it bargained for pursuant to the terms of the contract, no claim based on the conventional 'unjust factor' of failure of consideration could succeed. Commentators have since demonstrated that it would have been possible to find that there was a total failure of consideration with respect to each of the payments made by the bank. This is because the council was always entitled to restitution of its payments (for reasons of policy) and thus the bank was never in a position to have gained from the swap.[37] This chance of 'winning' surely formed a basis on which the bank made its payments? However, without the benefit of that analysis before him, Hobhouse J determined that the ground of restitution was that the contract was void. This is a 'juristic reasons' style approach to liability that, as we saw in chapter one, has yet to gain acceptance in English law. For this reason, if no other, the authority of this decision must be treated with caution outside the very particular factual circumstances in which it arose.

Although Hobhouse J was able to find for the bank as a matter of general analysis, a further problem for the bank was that three of its payments were made more than six years prior to the commencement of its action. Those payments thus appeared to be statute-barred, if one took the view (as did counsel for both sides) that each payment by the bank (and council) gave rise to a separate claim (or counterclaim) in unjust enrichment. However, Hobhouse J overcame this difficulty by viewing the requirement of counter-restitution as going to identify the *net sum* by which a defendant has been enriched for the purposes of the claimant's claim in unjust enrichment, rather than as constituting a full counterclaim by way of set-off in unjust enrichment on the part of the defendant. It followed that the bank's claim was for the net amount which was only conclusively determined at the date of the last payment—well within the limitations period.

36 *Kleinwort Benson Ltd v Sandwell Borough Council* [1994] 4 All ER 890 (QB) 941.
37 B McFarlane and R Stevens, 'In Defence of Sumpter v Hedges' (2002) 118 *LQR* 569, 576–77.

As Burrows notes, the consequence of Hobhouse J's approach is that, contrary to the analysis suggested in this section, the defendant to a claim of rescission need not establish each element of the counterclaim in unjust enrichment and a defence of change of position may not apply. The practical difference between the two approaches can be marked. Suppose a claimant purchases title to a car from the defendant as a result of the defendant's innocent misrepresentation that the car has never been involved in an accident.[38] The claimant pays £1000 for title to a car worth £800 (had the truth about the car's history been known). The claimant later crashes the car for a reason unrelated to the original misrepresentation. She subsequently discovers the misrepresentation and seeks to rescind the contract of sale, demanding back the full cost of the purchase price. Assuming for the moment that pecuniary rescission is possible, so that the claimant could in theory return to the defendant the full value of the title to the car originally received, what is the consequence of the car's accidental destruction? On the set-off approach advocated in this book, the claimant may be entitled to claim a change of position defence to the extent to which her car has diminished in value as a result of the crash.[39] That means that if the car is a complete write-off, she may be able to recover the full measure of the purchase price without being required to make counter-restitution of the car's original value. In contrast, if the 'net balance' approach is applied, she can only recover the difference between the value of what she originally paid and received, that is £200. The subsequent destruction of the car is effectively ignored.

There is no doubt that Hobhouse J's decision presents quite a different approach to the role and structure of counter-restitution than is suggested in this book. However, it is not an insurmountable authority, for a number of reasons.

First, it is arguable that the net benefit approach adopted by Hobhouse J was both novel and unnecessary to the outcome of that case. As the bank itself argued, there was another way of reaching the same result, arguably by a more traditional method. On the bank's analysis, it claimed for the full amount paid to the council. In response, the council pleaded limitation in respect of the bank's first three payments and counterclaimed for all the payments that it, the council, had made to the bank. In response to this counterclaim, the bank was entitled to plead by way of defence (presumably, change of position) all its own payments, including the first three. Hobhouse J rejected this approach as 'overly complicated' and 'contrary to principle'. Yet it reached effectively the same result, without the necessity of changing the usual approach to the unjust enrichment enquiry, accepted by both parties to the action, that each payment received gave rise to a separate cause of action.

[38] A common example in German scholarship: R Zimmerman and J Du Plessis, 'Basic Features of the German Law of Unjustified Enrichment' [1994] *Restitution L Rev* 14, 41–42; BS Markesinis, W Lorenz and G Dannemann, *The German Law of Obligations* (Clarendon Press, Oxford 1997) 765; T Krebs, *Restitution at the Crossroads: a comparative study* (Cavendish Publishing Limited, London 2001) 102–04.

[39] This will depend on a variety of factors, including any role fault may play in the defence.

Secondly, the support garnered from comparative law for Hobhouse J's approach is ambivalent. Birks welcomed Hobhouse J's net benefit approach, noting by way of endorsement that a similar approach is generally taken in German law pursuant to the *saldo* theory.[40] This approach effectively restricts the claimant's primary action in cases of bilaterally executed contracts voidable under German law for fraudulent misrepresentation, duress and certain types of mistake, to the net balance of benefits transferred between the parties.[41] However, there are five reasons why the *saldo* theory should not be relied on as a model for endorsement of Hobhouse J's net benefit approach.

The first, and most important, is that the *saldo* theory has to be seen in the light of the overall approach of German law to claims in unjust enrichment. Professor Dawson has remarked that the search for the net balance of surviving gain is a major feature of that jurisdiction's unjust enrichment jurisprudence.[42] Certainly, it is commonly understood that paragraph 818(3) BGB (which contains the German change of position defence) reduces every claim to the value surviving in the hands of the defendant, rather than the value received.[43] That is, paragraph 818(3) does not simply contain a defence, but lays down the very measure of restitution.[44] In that context, the net balance approach of the *saldo* theory is consistent (at least to that extent)[45] with the broader concerns of that jurisdiction's law of unjust enrichment.[46] In contrast, as explained in chapter one, the English and Australian approach to the law of unjust enrichment is that the primary claim is for the full amount initially received, subject to defences now recognised as including the change of position defence.[47] The English approach therefore is not to reduce all claims to what Birks called 'abstractly surviving enrichment'.[48] One should therefore be cautious in drawing strength from the dominant German approach to counter-restitution, which may reflect a different approach from the role of the law of unjust enrichment in general.

A similar difficulty arises out of the different approaches taken in German and English law to the question of when it will be 'unjust' for a defendant to retain his enrichment. On the German approach, the court looks to the surviving enrichment in the hands of the defendant and asks whether there is any juristic reason for retention of that enrichment, such as a contract or gift. As explained in chapter one, this

[40] P Birks, *Unjust Enrichment* (2nd edn, OUP, Oxford 2005) 225–26.

[41] See generally: Zimmerman and Du Plessis, above n 38, at 40–42; Markesinis, Lorenz and Dannemann, above n 38, at 764–65; Krebs, above n 38, at 101–04.

[42] J Dawson, 'Erasable Enrichment in German Law' (1981) 61 *Boston U L Rev* 217, 295.

[43] P Birks, 'Change of Position and Surviving Enrichment' in W Swadling (ed) *The Limits of Restitutionary Claims: A Comparative Analysis*, above n 35, at 58–59.

[44] Zimmerman and Du Plessis, above n 38, at 38–39; Krebs, above n 38, at 280.

[45] On the inherent contradictions in the German position, see below, at 100.

[46] Dawson, above n 42, at 217, 295.

[47] At 17–18; also *Sempra Metals Limited v Commissioners of Inland Revenue* [2007] UKHL 34, [2008] 1 AC 561 [23] (Lord Hope) [153] (Lord Scott) [233] (Lord Mance).

[48] Birks, 'Change of Position and Surviving Enrichment' in W Swadling (ed) *The Limits of Restitutionary Claims: A Comparative Analysis* above n 35, at 58–60.

can be described as a juristic reasons approach.[49] Certainly, it seem that a juristic reasons approach underpins Hobhouse J's decision,[50] which in turn would explain his Lordship's ready adoption of the net benefit approach to enrichment. However, as was also explained in chapter one, this book does not accept that a juristic reasons approach has been adopted in English law. Indeed, rescission itself offers a good example of an area of English law that is very difficult to reconcile with a juristic reasons approach. Cases of rescission in the common law tradition proceed on the assumption that there *is* an existing, juristic reason for retention, which the claimant is trying to set aside. That is the whole point of the exercise. This difficulty simply highlights the lack of 'fit' between the German law relating to when a party may avoid a contract and the established English rescission case law.

The second reason for viewing the *saldo* theory with caution is that it is not the only approach historically or presently active in German law. On the contrary, the original approach to cases of counter-restitution, which is still operative in German law, assumes that each party has an independent enrichment claim against the other (the *zweinkondiktionentheorie* or 'two claims' theory). Under the two claims approach, each party can rely on the change of position defence.[51] Therefore, the two common law models of counter-restitution contemplated above, that is the full counterclaim by way of set-off and net balance theories, also find expression in German law. Indeed, in some cases, for example those involving fraudulent defendants or claimants who are minors, the two claims theory is still preferred in German law.[52]

This leads us to the third reason for viewing the *saldo* theory with caution. There is by no means unanimous support for the *saldo* theory in German law.[53] It was developed in response to the perceived injustices of the two claims theory, in particular, the perceived injustice in allowing the risk of destruction of an object over which he could not exercise control to rest with the party claiming counter-restitution, as exemplified in the car crash example given above.[54] In contrast with the two claims theory, the *saldo* theory places the risk of deterioration or destruction of the received object on the shoulders of the person who is capable of exercising control over the object—that is, the person in possession at the time the asset deteriorates or is destroyed.

This concern seems remarkable, given that the accidental destruction, or inherent deterioration of a benefit received in a simple unilateral claim for restitution (for example, a claim to recover a mistaken payment) forms the paradigm example of disenrichment that attracts the application of the German change of position defence. Suppose a defendant receives a mistaken payment which is held

[49] At 10.

[50] *Kleinwort Benson Ltd v Sandwell Borough Council* [1994] 4 All ER 890 (QB) 955, 956.

[51] Zimmerman and Du Plessis, above n 38, at 41; Markesinis, Lorenz and Dannemann, above n 38, at 764–65; Krebs, above n 38, at 101–03.

[52] Markesinis, Lorenz and Dannemann, above n 38, at 765.

[53] Dawson, above n 42, at 217, 295–300; Krebs, above n 38, at 102–03.

[54] Zimmerman and Du Plessis, above n 38, at 42–43.

by his agent on his behalf. The agent subsequently steals the money and cannot be found. Or suppose the payment is received at a time of hyper-inflation and the defendant fails to invest the payment to protect its real value. In such cases, the German change of position defence will clearly apply.[55] There is no perceived injustice in that context in allowing the claimant (who after all, has a strong normative claim for restitution) to bear the risk of the accidental, or even negligent destruction of the benefit in the hands of the defendant. In that context, it seems very strange that the position should be regarded as so wholly different when the benefit is conferred pursuant to a contract avoided for innocently-induced mistake. Commentators have picked up on the inconsistency, which is also present in relation to contracts terminated, for example, due to an inherent defect.[56]

Fourthly, it is highly undesirable that entirely different approaches should apply to the unjust enrichment enquiry depending on whether the claim is for rescission *ab initio* of a contract for mistake, or for restitution of a unilateral mistaken payment. As discussed previously, the right to rescind both at common law and in equity is generated by claims in unjust enrichment and, once exercised, enables or effects restitution of the benefit conferred pursuant to the transaction. Given this affinity between restitution for unjust enrichment and rescission for unjust enrichment, it is highly undesirable that entirely different approaches to liability apply depending on the precise nature of the restitutionary relief sought. But that would be the consequence of adopting a net benefit approach and automatically losing what would otherwise be the primary unjust enrichment defence as soon as rescission is in play. Such a deviation from the normal structure of the unjust enrichment enquiry requires clear justification. In this regard, German commentators have highlighted the mutual and interdependent nature of contractual performances as being the feature of the failed contracts cases that demands special treatment.[57] However, on that reasoning, the change of position defence should never be available in cases of failure of consideration where the defendant has also transferred a benefit to the claimant, even where the failure occurs subsequent to the transfers of value taking place and was utterly unforeseen, as in cases of frustration.[58] This is a highly unsatisfactory result, with no clear justification.

Finally, there is highly persuasive authority in favour of adopting a two claims approach to the requirement of counter-restitution from another jurisdiction. The High Court of Australia clearly adopted the view in *David Securities Pty Ltd v Commonwealth Bank of Australia*[59] that the defence of failure of consideration

[55] Discussed in Dawson, above n 42, at 217, 279–80; see also: Krebs, above n 38, at 281.

[56] Although the law on termination underwent substantial reform in 2002, including the provisions addressing the restitutionary consequences of termination, problems remain with the chosen method of addressing the problem of risk allocation consequential on change of position: R Zimmerman, 'Restitution After Termination for Breach' in AS Burrows and Lord Rodger of Earlsferry (eds) *Mapping the Law: Essays in Memory of Peter Birks* (OUP, Oxford 2006) 328–36. For criticism of the earlier provision, see eg the criticisms of Lorenz, discussed in Krebs, above n 38, at 102–03.

[57] Krebs, *ibid*, 91.

[58] Discussed further in ch 7, at 197.

[59] *David Securities Pty Ltd v Commonwealth Bank of Australia* (1992) 127 CLR 353 (High Court of Australia) 380 (Mason CJ, Deane, Toohey, Gaudron and McHugh JJ).

(from the claimant's perspective, a defence of counter-restitution required) operated as a counterclaim by way of set-off to the primary claim.[60] Likewise, in the recent decision of *Ovidio Carrideo Nominees Pty Ltd v The Dog Depot Pty Ltd*,[61] the Supreme Court of Victoria Court of Appeal held that a tenant's claim for restitution of rent paid to a landlord by mistake failed, inter alia, because the landlord had a defence (again labelled 'good consideration') in the shape of a counterclaim for restitution of the benefit of quiet occupation of the premises transferred to the tenant.[62] Given this characterisation of the counterclaim of failure of consideration, a change of position defence should be in theory available to the claimant.

In summary, adopting a two claims approach to rescission is consistent both with Lord Wright's rationalisation of the requirement of counter-restitution and with existing principles of English unjust enrichment law. Further, it recognises and articulates the affinity between restitution and rescission for unjust enrichment. This is not to say that the answer to when prima facie liability arises, or whether a change of position defence applies, will not differ according to the context. A contract for value, for example, will generally only be able to be rescinded where the defendant was aware of, or induced the vitiating factor.[63] This means that in many (although not all)[64] rescission cases a defendant will automatically be excluded from any change of position defence because, knowing of the vitiating factor, she often[65] will not have changed her position 'in good faith'. Further, the role a defendant plays in inducing a claimant to enter into a contract might not only be a pre-condition to the right to rescind arising, but also mean that a change of position defence is rarely available, compared to cases of unilateral transfer.[66] Notably, this sensitivity to context does not alter the basic structure of the unjust enrichment enquiry.

The analysis suggests that any concern about who should bear the risk of loss of transferred benefits is capable of being addressed within the usual unjust enrichment enquiry, in particular, by developing a nuanced change of position defence that can accommodate the concerns with risk allocation that lie behind the development of the *saldo* and two claims theories. In that regard, it is notable that one of main responses German authors have had to difficulties associated with

[60] *Ibid*, at 382 (Mason CJ, Deane, Toohey, Gaudron and McHugh JJ) 400 (Brennan J).

[61] *Ovidio Carrideo Nominees Pty Ltd v The Dog Depot Pty Ltd* [2006] VSCA 6, [2006] V ConvR 54-713 (Victorian Supreme Court of Appeal); applied in *R & Z Mazzei Nominees Pty Ltd v Aegean Food Import Export Pty Ltd* [2006] VSC 210 (Victorian Supreme Court) and followed in *Ragi Pty Ltd v Kiwi Munchies Pty Ltd* [2007] NSWADT (New South Wales Administrative Decisions Tribunal).

[62] The value of the counterclaim was 'broadly equal' to the amount of the rent paid: *Ovidio Carrideo Nominees Pty Ltd v The Dog Depot Pty Ltd* [2006] VSCA 6, [2006] V ConvR 54-713 (Victorian Supreme Court of Appeal) [22] (Chernov J) [50] (Nettle J) (Ashley JA concurring with both judgments).

[63] Edelman and Bant, above n 12, at 183–88 (mistake), 212–14 (duress), 229–31 (undue influence).

[64] Cases of gift and contracts of guarantee, both of which may also be the subject of claims for rescission, are treated differently: Edelman and Bant, *ibid*, at 188–91 (mistake), 213–14 (duress), 231–33 (undue influence).

[65] Again not always: eg *National Bank of New Zealand Ltd v Waitaki International Processing (NI) Ltd* [1992] 2 NZLR 211 (New Zealand Court of Appeal) (defendant knew of mistake and invested benefit in good faith).

application of the two claims theory has been to reintroduce notions of fault into the change of position defence.[67] This supports the view that the problem lies in the formulation of the change of position defence, rather than being inherent in the two claims approach.

(c) Application of the Two Claims Approach to Rescission Cases

This chapter commenced by noting that courts considering cases of rescission are obliged by the requirement of *restitutio in integrum* to determine the legal significance of the parties' respective changes of position in determining whether it is possible for the parties to be returned to the *status quo ante*. This raised the possibility that, in applying the requirement of *restitutio in integrum*, courts may have been considering the kind of question at the heart of the change of position defence: namely, when faced with a claim in restitution, what legal significance attaches to the defendant's changes of position? The preceding section then demonstrated that it is possible for rescission to be viewed as a bilateral process of claim and set-off (a two claims approach), in which the sorts of considerations underpinning the change of position defence could in theory have a role to play. The balance of this chapter explores this proposition by applying a two claims analysis to the traditional case law on rescission. The purpose of this analysis is to see the extent to which courts applying the requirement of *restitutio in integrum* can be seen to have been taking into account the respective parties' changes of position in reducing or eliminating their restitutionary liabilities and the kinds of factors that courts have considered relevant to that process. The expectation is that given the demonstrated affinity between rescission and restitution for unjust enrichment, the enquiry may reveal principles or policy concerns that, by analogy, should be taken into account for the purposes of determining the disputed features of the change of position defence.

For the purpose of this analysis, the types of possible alterations that may flow from an impugned transfer of benefit are divided into three broad types. Looking first to the defendant's side of the transaction, the defendant may change his position by conferring a benefit on the claimant (a change by exchange). Secondly, the benefit he received from the claimant may independently alter in nature or deteriorate (an independent change in the received benefit). Thirdly, the defendant may alter his position by actively changing the received benefit, or by acting or omitting to act in some way that does not directly impinge on the received benefit (a defendant-instigated change of position). Clearly, a change by exchange also constitutes a defendant-instigated change of position. However, it is singular in its characteristic of conferring a benefit on the claimant. As this characteristic may attract different considerations from those that attach to other defendant-instigated changes, it is given its own label for the purposes of the following analysis.

[66] Discussed below, at 109–14.

[67] Markesinis, Lorenz and Dannemann, above n 38, at 765.

Turning to the other side of the ledger, the claimant too may change her position as a result of the receipt of a benefit from the defendant. There may be an independent change in the received benefit, or the claimant may instigate a change in her position as a result of her receipt. These changes are in addition to the conferral of benefit on the defendant which is the subject of the exercise of the power to rescind.

The varieties of change can be illustrated by reference to the example given earlier in the context of the discussion of the *saldo* theory. It will be recalled in that example that a claimant purchases title to a car for £1000 as a result of the innocent misrepresentation of the defendant. The defendant conveys title to the car to the claimant (a change by exchange). Suppose further that the defendant invests the proceeds of sale in shares that drop in value (a defendant-instigated change). The car meanwhile depreciates in value (an independent change in the claimant's received benefit), before the claimant crashes it (a change instigated by the claimant). The claimant subsequently discovers the misrepresentation and purports to rescind the transaction, seeking recovery of the purchase price.

The balance of this chapter will seek to identify the legal significance of the kinds of change of position evidenced in the core example. It will first consider the significance of changes in the defendant's circumstances, before turning to consider the position of the claimant.

(3) The Defendant's Changes of Position

(a) Change by Exchange

The first category of change of position to be considered is where the defendant has made a change by exchange. As we have seen in the previous section, in general, both common law and equity respond to this category of change by requiring the claimant to make counter-restitution to the defendant of the received benefit. The requirement of *restitutio in integrum* traditionally demands that any changes made by the claimant (claimant-instigated changes of position) with respect to the benefit received from the defendant (the defendant's change by exchange) be assessed in order to determine whether counter-restitution *in specie* of that benefit remains possible.[68] If the claimant-instigated changes of position are so significant as to change the nature of the received benefit, so that it cannot be restored, in general, the result is that the claimant is denied restitution completely. Therefore, if a purchaser of a cow slaughters it he is not entitled to rescind the sale transaction on

[68] The call for pecuniary rescission to be accepted as an alternative to rescission *in specie* is a recent development, considered below, at 107. However, given that the historical model required rescission *in specie*, any analysis of that model must proceed on that basis: see immediately below.

[69] *Clarke v Dickson* (1858) EB & E 148, 120 ER 463 at 155, 466 (Crompton J).

offering the defendant the carcass.[69] Nor can a claimant rescind a contract for the purchase of shares where the company to which the shares related has since been reformed or changed in nature.[70] Nor can a claimant rescind where he has purchased a mine under the impugned contract and has since worked it out.[71] Similarly, if the claimant in the core example writes off the car so that it is effectively destroyed, counter-restitution of the car to the defendant will be impossible and her claim for rescission and restitution of the £1000 will be denied completely.

However, from the perspective of the 'two claims' analysis of the counterclaim in unjust enrichment, this approach, sometimes described as a defence of 'counter-restitution impossible,' seems anomalous.[72] From that analysis, one might have expected that any changes brought about in respect of the benefit received by the claimant would operate to protect the claimant from the defendant's counterclaim in unjust enrichment. That is, if the car in the core example has been effectively destroyed in the accident, the two claims analysis suggests that the claimant has a defence of change of position. But the case law is clear that far from operating to protect the claimant from the defendant's counterclaim for restitution, the legal effect of the claimant's change of position is to deny her any restitutionary relief at all. The claimant's change of position operates to protect the defendant, the party seeking counter-restitution against the claimant. What can account for this result?

The answer commonly given by unjust enrichment commentators has been that the defence simply reflects the common law courts' blunt unwillingness or procedural inability to value non-monetary benefits conferred so as to allow the return of the benefit received not *in specie*, but in its monetary equivalent.[73] The common law required precise *restitutio in integrum*, which meant that it was a defence to an action for rescission if benefits in kind or benefits conferred through services could not be returned *in specie*.

In contrast, equity has always been far more willing and able to effect substantial (if not precise) *restitutio in integrum*. In the leading Australian case of *Alati v Kruger*,[74] the respondent purchased a business from the appellant in reliance on the appellant's fraudulent misrepresentations about the weekly takings of the business. The respondent went into possession and for reasons unrelated to the misrepresentations the business deteriorated. Therefore, it was not possible to return the business to the appellant precisely in the same condition in which it had been transferred. Nor could the use by the respondent of the premises be returned *in*

[70] *Western Bank of Scotland v Addie* (1866–69) LR 1 Sc 145, 159; *Capcorn Holding Plc v Edwards* [2007] EWHC 2662 (Ch); *cf Spence v Crawford* [1939] 3 All ER 271 (HL) discussed below, at 110–11.

[71] *Clarke v Dickson* (1858) EB & E 148, 120 ER 463; *cf Erlanger v The New Sombrero Phosphate Company* (1878) 3 App Cas 1218 (HL); *Lagunas Nitrate Co v Lagunas Syndicate* [1899] 2 Ch 392 (CA).

[72] The incongruity is noted by Professor Worthington but regarded as an 'fortuitous accident' rather than a reasoned response: S Worthington, 'The Proprietary Consequences of Rescission' [2002] *Restitution L Rev* 28, 58.

[73] Burrows, above n 14, at 176–78; Worthington, *ibid.*

[74] *Alati v Kruger* (1955) 94 CLR 216 (High Court of Australia), discussed further in ch 6, at 189–90.

specie. In a joint judgment, Dixon CJ, Webb, Kitto and Taylor JJ observed that either of these points might have meant that under the common law approach to rescission, the appellant was not entitled to rescind. Nonetheless, the appellant was regarded as entitled to rescind on proper terms, the High Court ordering, among other things, that an account be taken to determine the value of those benefits received by the appellant that could not be returned *in specie*. As the majority explained:

> The difference between the legal and the equitable rules on the subject simply was that equity, having means which the common law lacked to ascertain and provide for the adjustments necessary to be made between the parties in cases where a simple handing back of property or repayment of money would not put them in as good a position as before they entered into their transaction, was able to see the possibility of restitutio in integrum and therefore to concede the right of a defrauded party to rescind, in a much wider variety of cases than those which the common law could recognise as admitting of rescission.[75]

This historical difference between the procedural abilities of the two jurisdictions is well established. However, even with its superior machinery at hand, equity notably still required there to be a substantial identity between benefits to be restored and that originally received by the claimant for *restitutio in integrum* to be possible.[76] In the core case, destruction of the car would traditionally preclude rescission as effectively in equity as at common law. It is therefore necessary, for the moment, to accept that both jurisdictions worked on the basis that the defendant was prima facie entitled to return of certain benefits *in specie*. Why then did the destruction, deterioration or depreciation of such a benefit not simply operate to defeat the counterclaim? Why did the fundamental alteration in the nature of the benefit instead operate to protect the defendant and to defeat the claimant's right to rescind?

The answer discernible in the authorities is that when counter-restitution *in specie* was impossible, *the defendant's* change by exchange in conferring the benefit (in our example, the car) on the claimant became irreversible. In this light, the defence of counter-restitution impossible can be viewed as simply a blunt and somewhat unwieldy early version of a change of position defence, designed to protect defendants to claims for rescission. If that is correct, it would seem that a concept analogous to a change of position defence was present both at common law and in equity long before the advent of *Lipkin Gorman (a firm) v Karpnale Ltd*,[77] at least to the extent of any change by exchange.

This analysis is supported by the approach taken in equity to the question of deterioration or depreciation of benefits conferred on a claimant, where the benefit the subject of the counterclaim has been altered, but its identity remains in

[75] *Alati v Kruger* (1955) 94 CLR 216 (High Court of Australia) 224 (Dixon CJ, Webb, Kitto and Taylor JJ); *Erlanger v The New Sombrero Phosphate Company* (1878) 3 App Cas 1218 (HL) 1278 (Lord Blackburn).

[76] *Spence v Crawford* [1939] 3 All ER 271 (HL) 279 (Lord Thankerton). Nahan, above n 15, at 68–69.

[77] *Lipkin Gorman (a firm) v Karpnale Ltd* [1991] 2 AC 548 (HL).

substance the same. The basic principle was set out in *Erlanger v The New Sombrero Phosphate Company*[78] by Lord Blackburn:

> It would be obviously unjust that a person who has been in possession of property under the contract which he seeks to repudiate should be allowed to throw that back on the other party's hands without accounting for any benefit he may have derived from the use of the property, or if the property, though not destroyed, has been in the interval deteriorated, without making compensation for that deterioration.

On equity's more flexible approach to the requirement of *restitutio in integrum*, the claimant makes sufficient counter-restitution to the defendant of the benefit originally conferred by returning the benefit *in specie*, albeit in its altered state, together with a payment reflecting the value of its deterioration. So, in our core example, if the car was not totally destroyed but merely damaged, the claimant could make counter-restitution by tendering the car (albeit in a damaged state), together with an amount for its deterioration arising from the accident.[79] This counter-restitution has the consequence that the defendant's change by exchange is in substance reversed. It follows that subject to the defendant having any other defence, or the right to rescission being barred on another ground, the claimant's right to restitution of the benefits transferred on the defendant pursuant to the primary transaction may succeed. The process implicitly accepts that were it not possible for counter-restitution to be rendered substantially possible in this manner, the defendant would have a complete defence to the claimant's claim for restitution.[80]

Equity's willingness to award an amount for deterioration to effect full reversal of the defendant's change by exchange is subject to a number of exceptions. Most significantly for present purposes,[81] the defendant's own role in the transaction may preclude him from complaining of the depreciation of the asset transferred to the claimant. Suppose, for example, the defendant in our core example had fraudulently induced the claimant to purchase the car. Could he still complain that, the car having deteriorated in value by £200 as a result of the accident, counter-restitution was no longer possible unless compensation was made? In *Armstrong v Jackson*,[82] a broker sold his shares in a company to his client in breach of his fiduciary duty and as a result of various fraudulent misrepresentations. By the time the client found out and sought to rescind the contract of purchase, the shares had depreciated to a fraction of their original value. The question arose whether *restitutio in integrum* was still possible. In holding that it was, McCardie J emphasised that the shares could still be returned *in specie* and that it did not lie in the defendant's mouth, having fraudulently induced the claimant to purchase his shares, to

[78] *Erlanger v The New Sombrero Phosphate Company* (1878) 3 App Cas 1218 (HL) 1278, cited with approval in *Alati v Kruger* (1955) 94 CLR 216 (High Court of Australia) 223–24 (Dixon CJ, Webb, Kitto and Taylor JJ).

[79] Its inherent deterioration prior to the accident is considered separately below, at 115.

[80] *Lagunas Nitrate Co v Lagunas Syndicate* [1899] 2 Ch 392 (CA) 457 (Rigby LJ).

[81] It was also restricted where the claimant had not been at fault: see below, at 114–15.

[82] *Armstrong v Jackson* [1917] 2 KB 822 (KB).

complain that if the contract be set aside, he would be left in a worse position than if the contract had never been entered into.[83] In other words, the defendant's fault operated to bar him from the full protection otherwise afforded by the defence of counter-restitution impossible.

The foregoing analysis of the defence of counter-restitution impossible has proceeded on the basis that both the common law and equity historically required counter-restitution of benefits in kind to be *in specie*. There is now a significant chorus of calls for that requirement to be abandoned and for pecuniary rescission to be accepted as a normal and acceptable alternative.[84] These calls should be heeded. There is now no reason for such a blunt instrument to be used to protect a defendant's right to restitution of a benefit conferred on a claimant. Provided the claimant is prepared to reach into her pocket, counter-restitution should always be possible.

In concluding this discussion, it should be noted that recognition of the possibility of pecuniary counter-restitution does not diminish the significance of the defence of counter-restitution impossible. The defence reveals that the requirement of *restitutio in integrum* reflects judicial concern both to avoid the unjust enrichment of the claimant, and to protect a defendant from what has become an irreversible change of position in conferring the benefit on the claimant. Notably, there remain other forms of changes, not constituting a change by exchange, that might also be the subject of special consideration pursuant to the requirement of *restitutio in integrum*, to which we will now turn.

(b) Independent Changes in the Received Benefit

Suppose, reversing the facts in our core example, that it was the claimant who sold her title to a car to the defendant as a result of the innocent misrepresentation of the defendant. By the time the claimant realises her mistake and purports to rescind the transaction, the car has naturally depreciated to one half of its original value. Who bears the loss of value arising from the deterioration of the car?

It is generally accepted that a defendant will not be held liable to pay an amount to the claimant for the inherent depreciation of a benefit not due to the fault of the

[83] *Armstrong v Jackson* [1917] 2 KB 822 (KB) 829–30; also *Northern Bank Finance Corporation Limited v Charlton* [1979] ECC 7 (Supreme Court (Ireland)) 18 (O'Higgins CJ. Butler J concurring, both dissenting on whether *restitutio in integrum* possible); *Cheese v Thomas* [1994] 1 WLR 129 (CA) 136 (Nicholls V-C). *Cf Alati v Kruger* (1955) 94 CLR 216 (High Court of Australia), discussed above, at 104–05.

[84] eg Nahan, above n 15; Burrows, above n 14, at 541–42; Edelman and Bant, above n 12, at 348–50; Häcker, 'Rescission and Third Party Rights', above n 11, at 21. Indeed, Swadling argues that the question is why pecuniary rescission is not the rule: see Swadling, above n 11. For case examples, see *Hartigan v International Society for Krishna Consciousness Incorporated* [2002] NSWSC 810 (New South Wales Supreme Court); *Mahoney v Purnell* [1996] 3 All ER 61 (QBD) and *McKenzie v McDonald* [1927] VLR 134 (Victorian Supreme Court). Other strategies include making an order for proprietary restitution subject to a charge in favour of the defendant in the amount of the benefit transferred on the claimant: *Winefield v Clarke* [2008] NSWSC 882 (New South Wales Supreme Court).

defendant. This rule operates much like a change of position defence. As a matter of practice, however, the concern rarely arises in cases of rescission.[85] As Lord Wright commented in *Spence v Crawford*,[86] the 'plaintiff who seeks to set aside the contract will generally be reasonable in the standard of restitution he requires'.

Lord Wright added that in cases of deterioration in which the defendant has been fraudulent, the court may order 'compensation to make good the change of position'.[87] That is, where the defendant is fraudulent he cannot rely on the alteration in his position in diminution of his liability to return in substance the original benefit received.

(c) Defendant-instigated Changes of Position

The previous two sections demonstrated that the rescission case law reveals a consistent judicial concern to limit a defendant's liability to make restitution to the claimant where the defendant's position has changed as a result of transferring a benefit to the claimant in exchange, or where the benefit the subject of the primary claim has independently devalued. However, commentators have argued that courts do not look further to any defendant-instigated loss in determining whether *restitutio in integrum* is possible. The requirement 'does not have as its aim the avoidance of loss on the part of the defendant'.[88] In our core example, this would mean that the defendant's change of position in investing the purchase price of the car in depreciating shares would not operate to reduce his liability to make restitution to the claimant. If this proposition is correct, it suggests that the differences between the operation of the requirement of *restitutio in integrum* and the change of position defence are so significant that any attempt to draw analogies between them must be of very limited value only.

The primary authority for this proposition is *MacKenzie v Royal Bank of Canada*.[89] In that case, a bank induced a wife to grant a guarantee in its favour by an innocent misrepresentation. The bank subsequently provided financial assistance to her husband's business in good faith and purporting to rely on the guarantee. In advising that the guarantee should be rescinded, the Privy Council commented that there was 'no difficulty as to restitutio in integrum. The mere fact that the party making the representation has treated the contract as binding and has acted on it does not preclude relief'.[90]

[85] Worthington, above n 72, at 56, fn 173.

[86] *Spence v Crawford* [1939] 3 All ER 271 (HL) 289.

[87] *Spence v Crawford* [1939] 3 All ER 271 (HL), 89, citing *Lagunas Nitrate Co v Lagunas Syndicate* [1899] 2 Ch 392 (CA).

[88] E McKendrick, 'Total Failure of Consideration and Counter-Restitution: Two Issues or One?' in P Birks (ed) *Laundering and Tracing* (OUP, Oxford 1995) 63; also Burrows, above n 14, at 177–78; Peel (ed), above n 23, at [9-098].

[89] *MacKenzie v Royal Bank of Canada* [1934] AC 468 (PC).

[90] *Ibid*, at 476.

There is, however, another explanation for the court's decision. That is, that relief was denied because the bank had been responsible for inducing the wife's entry into the contract in the first place. This role precluded the bank from raising its subsequent change of position by way of defence, even though made in good faith. This analysis leaves open the possibility that in other rescission cases, as where the claimant has spontaneously entered into the transaction,[91] the defendant may be able to rely on self-instigated changes of position by way of defence to an action for rescission.

There are a number of other classes of case where the courts' failure to consider defendants' clear changes of position could be thought to indicate a more general bar to the defence in cases of defendant-instigated changes of position. For example, banks have not been able to rely on their good faith change of position in cases involving contracts of suretyship avoided because of mistake (even if spontaneous), duress or undue influence (usually arising from the primary debtor).[92] However, the undoubted exclusion of the defence in this group of cases does not necessarily support the inference of a wider bar. There are two likely reasons for the exclusion of the defence in the suretyship cases. The primary reason said to be applicable in England, is that to permit the change of position defence would subvert the policy of protecting certain vulnerable groups, here domestic sureties.[93] A second reason, arising out of the Australian case law, is that banks are only liable in the first place if they are aware of the risk that the surety's intention might be impaired through mistake, duress or undue influence. In those circumstances, they cannot be said to have reasonably relied on their receipt so as to attract the operation of the reliance version of the defence, unless they have taken proper steps to reduce the level of risk to a point where it is proper to proceed.[94] While reflecting the position in Australia, in England this explanation may not withstand Lord Nicholls' counsel of caution to banks dealing with any sureties that stand in a non-commercial relationship to the primary debtor, that prima facie liability may arise even where there is no knowledge of a risk of vitiated intention, provided the bank is aware of the non-commercial relationship.[95] An alternative analysis of his Lordship's approach, that would accommodate the second explanation, is that Lord Nicholls took the view that banks should always be aware of a risk of vitiated intention in cases of non-commercial sureties. Notably, this analysis also imports a reasonableness requirement.[96] On either of these approaches, the courts' failure

[91] Examples in the context of undue influence are considered further below, at 112–14.

[92] eg *Garcia v National Australia Bank* (1998) 194 CLR 395 (High Court of Australia) (mistake); *Barclays Bank Plc v O'Brien* [1994] 1 AC 180 (HL) (undue influence); *Governor and Company of the Bank of Scotland v Bennett* [1998] EWCA 1965 (illegitimate pressure).

[93] P Birks, 'The Burden on the Bank' in FD Rose (ed) *Restitution and Banking Law* (Mansfield Press, Oxford 1998) 195–201; M Chen-Wishart, 'Unjust Factors and the Restitutionary Response' (2000) 20 OJLS 557, 562–64.

[94] Edelman and Bant, above n 12, at 188–91 (mistake), 213–14 (duress), 231–33 (undue influence).

[95] In *Royal Bank of Scotland Plc v Etridge (No 2)* [2001] UKHL 44, [2002] 2 AC 773795.

[96] As to which see ch 2, at 43–47, ch 3, at 76–78 and ch 5, at 151–55.

to take into account defendant-instigated changes of position should not be taken as indicative of a broader bar to any defence arising from that change of position.

In contrast with those rescission cases that appear to exclude consideration of good faith changes of position instigated by the defendant, there exists a number of cases in which the defendant's change of position has been expressly considered. In *Morrison v Universal Marine Insurance Co*,[97] the claimant had innocently failed to disclose a relevant fact in obtaining his insurance contract with the defendants, a failure that gave rise to a right in the defendants to rescind the contract. In delivering the judgment of the court, Honyman J considered in *obiter dicta* that the claimant would have been able to resist the claim for rescission by the defendant insurers if, prior to the act of rescission, he had changed his position by refraining to take insurance elsewhere. In *AH MacDonald & Co Pty Ltd v Wells*,[98] the High Court of Australia unanimously held that a claimant was not entitled to rescind a transaction entered into as a result of the defendant's innocent misrepresentation because the defendant had 'unalterably changed his position' in reliance on the transaction by entering into an agreement with a third party for the purchase of certain patents.

More detailed consideration of this issue was undertaken in the House of Lords decision in *Spence v Crawford*[99] In that case, the defendant induced the claimant to sell to him the claimant's shares in a company by misrepresenting (understating) the financial position of the company. On the claimant seeking rescission, the defendant argued that he had changed his position by (among other things) first, altering the share holdings in the company and secondly, by selling certain stock at a loss as required under the contract. As to the first, Lord Thankerton, with whom Lords Atkin and Russell concurred, said that the defendant was not entitled 'in bar of restitution' to rely on his dealings with the subject purchased, which he was enabled by his fraud to carry out.[100] Lord Thankerton left open the question whether a defendant guilty only of innocent misrepresentation might be entitled to rely on the change as a bar to restitution.[101] As to the second pleaded change, Lord Thankerton said that the court would be doing what was practically just by making it a condition of restitution that the defendant be compensated for the difference between the market value of the stocks at the time of entering into the rescinded transaction and the price when they were sold.[102] The result was similar to that which would be achieved by applying a change of position defence in favour of the defendant.

How his Lordship was able to distinguish between the first and second situations is not clear, given that both changes were the result of the defendant's fraud-

[97] *Morrison v Universal Marine Insurance Co* (1873) LR 8 Exch 197 (Exch) 205.

[98] *A H McDonald & Co Pty Ltd v Wells* (1931) 45 CLR 506 (High Court of Australia) 512–13 (Rich, Starke and Dixon JJ).

[99] *Spence v Crawford* [1939] 3 All ER 271 (HL).

[100] *Ibid*, at 281.

[101] *Ibid*, at 282–83.

[102] *Spence v Crawford* [1939] 3 All ER 271 (HL)

ulent activities. This concern was openly expressed by Lord Wright.[103] However, his Lordship found it unnecessary finally to decide on these matters because the parties had agreed on a form of order should the court agree that the contract should be rescinded and there should be restitution. It is this last point which probably explains how Lord Thankerton was able to reconcile the different results between the two otherwise similar changes of position.

Like Lord Thankerton, Lord Wright drew a distinction between cases of innocent and fraudulent misrepresentation, His Lordship said that a

> court will be less ready to pull a transaction to pieces where the defendant is innocent, whereas in the case of fraud the court will exercise its powers to the full in order, if possible, to prevent the defendant from enjoying the benefit of his fraud at the expense of the innocent claimant.[104]

Given that once the issue whether the defendant was guilty of fraudulent misrepresentation was resolved, the main issue before the court was the relevance of the defendant's changes of position, the clear inference is that a defendant who has innocently misled the claimant may be able to rely on those changes by way of defence, while the fraudulent defendant cannot.

The court's concerted effort in *Spence v Crawford* to leave open the position of innocent misrepresentors stands in stark contrast with *MacKenzie v Royal Bank of Canada*,[105] a case which certainly did not involve fraudulent misrepresentation by the defendant bank.[106] Nor is the position of 'innocent inducers' clarified by turning to the analogous cases of undue influence. There is now a significant line of cases that together demonstrate equity's willingness to take into account good faith changes of position instigated by the defendant in cases of presumed undue influence. This may appear to give considerable support to the extension of a defence to innocent wrongdoers.

However, the nature of undue influence is deeply controversial. One key debate is whether undue influence is concerned with the impaired intention of the claimant or the breach of a duty by the defendant not to exploit the claimant.[107] In the context of presumed undue influence cases, this debate resolves down to the question whether the fact presumed is that the defendant's influence interfered with the claimant's decision to transfer, or that the defendant exploited the claimant. As we will see below, there certainly exist cases where a claimant was presumed to have entered into a transaction as a result of undue influence,

[103] *Spence v Crawford* [1939] 3 All ER 271 (HL) 290.

[104] *Spence v Crawford* [1939] 3 All ER 271 (HL)

[105] *MacKenzie v Royal Bank of Canada* [1934] AC 468 (PC); Watts, above n 22, at 303–07.

[106] It is possible that the bank in that case could be considered to have acted negligently, in which case fault was potentially once again in issue.

[107] eg P Birks and N Chin, 'On the Nature of Undue Influence' in J Beatson and D Friedman (eds) *Good Faith and Fault in Contract Law* (OUP, Oxford 1995); R Bigwood, 'Undue Influence: 'Impaired Consent' or 'Wicked Exploitation'' (1996) 16 *OJLS* 503; Edelman and Bant, above n 12, ch 10. There are other views of its rationale, such as that the claim is concerned with both vitiation of intention and exploitation, or that it is an area concerned with public policy: eg Virgo, above n 14, ch 10.

notwithstanding that her decision was spontaneous and unprompted by the defendant.[108] This tends to suggest that the basis of the claim in undue influence cannot be founded on any active wrongdoing (in the sense of breach of duty) by the defendant. However, the cases do not entirely exclude the possibility that the claim may be based on wrongdoing. It has been argued that a defendant in a position of influence may be under a fiduciary-like duty not to accept a benefit, for example.[109] If that is correct, it may be possible to breach the duty simply by accepting a benefit in circumstances where the defendant has not taken positive action to ensure that the claimant was free of the defendant's influence at the time of entering into the transaction. It is not possible in the context of this book to resolve this debate. It is sufficient to note that given this controversy, and in the absence of a clear case where influence was found to be actively exercised and nonetheless the defence should apply, the position of innocent influencers remains ambiguous.

With this caveat in mind, it remains to consider the line of cases that together demonstrate equity's willingness to take into account good faith changes of position instigated by a defendant in cases of presumed undue influence. Although determined on the basis of the equitable doctrine of *laches* or delay, the seminal case of *Allcard v Skinner*[110] contains one of the earliest examples of recognition (*obiter dicta*) that a defendant's change of position may be relevant to reduce, or indeed extinguish, the prima facie liability of the defendant.[111] In the course of his judgment, Lindley LJ stated that even if restitution had been given it would have been reduced:

> I cannot come to the conclusion that nothing has been done on the faith of the money being the property of the sisterhood. It is contrary to human nature to suppose that the Claimant's money was not for years regarded as the money of the sisterhood, and that the sisterhood did not act on that assumption and make their arrangements accordingly.[112]

In that case, the claimant gave all her assets to the religious order of which she was a member. Although the claimant was required by the order to undertake vows of chastity, poverty and obedience, there was no evidence that her choice of the order as donee was either required or suggested by it. It is thus unclear whether the

[108] *Smith v Smith* (New South Wales Supreme Court 12 July 1996); *Reid v Reid* (New South Wales Supreme Court 30 November 1998); *Hartigan v International Society for Krishna Consciousness Incorporated* [2002] NSWSC 810 (New South Wales Supreme Court).

[109] P Finn, 'The Fiduciary Principle' in T Youdan (ed) *Equity, Fiduciaries and Trusts* (The Law Book Co, Carswell 1989); Bigwood, above n 107; Chen-Wishart, above n 93; L Ho, 'Undue Influence and Equitable Compensation' in P Birks and FD Rose (eds) *Restitution and Equity: Resulting Trusts and Equitable Compensation* (Mansfield Press, Hong Kong 2000) 200–01.

[110] *Allcard v Skinner* (1887) 36 Ch D 145 (CA). The judges were divided as to the nature of the claimant's right to restitution arising from the undue influence, in particular, whether it was in the nature of a proprietary restitutionary power (Lindley LJ, with whom Bowen LJ in essence agreed), or a vested proprietary interest pursuant to a trust (Cotton LJ). This distinction is explored further in ch 7, at 206–09.

[111] M Chen-Wishart, 'Loss Sharing, Undue Influence and Manifest Disadvantage' (1994) 110 *LQR* 173. Chen-Wishart also identifies *Cheese v Thomas* [1994] 1 WLR 129 (CA) as an example of an intuitive application of a change of position defence.

[112] *Allcard v Skinner* (1887) 36 Ch D 145 (CA) 188–89.

discussion of change of position extended to cases where the defendant had innocently induced the gift, or was only intended to apply to cases where the gift was 'spontaneous'.[113]

In contrast, in the Australian case of *Quek v Beggs*,[114] it is clear that the claimant spontaneously determined to give the vast majority of her considerable estate to her pastor and his wife. The professed aim of the gifts was to ensure that her teenage children (with whom she had fallen out) would be denied any significant share in her estate in the event of her (anticipated) death. After she died, the children discovered the gifts and sought to rescind them on the ground of presumed undue influence. While the court held that the larger gifts should indeed be set aside, some of the defendants' actions made in reliance on the gifts were considered and accepted as a basis for reducing the extent of their liability. In particular, and acting entirely in good faith, the defendants had taken out a mortgage over one of the given properties and used that money to improve the property of a third party. The defendants later discharged the mortgage through the sale of another of the given properties. McLelland J held that it would be inequitable to make the defendants account for the sums used in improving the third party's property, as they would be unable to be restored to their original position. His Honour also considered whether the defendants should be allowed the amount of any income tax paid by them in respect of the properties conveyed to them by Mrs Quek and concluded that it depended on the extent to which any tax was recoverable from the respective taxation authorities. This is entirely consistent with an application of a change of position defence.

Finally, in another Australian case, *Hartigan v International Society for Krishna Consciousness Incorporated*,[115] the claimant gave her only major asset, her house, to the defendant corporation under the misguided belief that it was required by the teachings of the Hari Krishna religious movement. The defendant was a holding company that, in any event, had no role in the teachings of the movement. Bryson J nonetheless found that the gift should be set aside on the ground of undue influence. The defendant sought to defend itself by claiming that it was no longer possible to achieve *restitutio in integrum*, because the property in question had been sold and the proceeds applied to discharge debts. Bryson J rejected the

[113] *Cf Winefield v Clarke* [2008] NSWSC 882 (New South Wales Supreme Court), a case where an unrebutted presumption of undue influence had arisen between an elderly mother and her carer daughter. Although it is not entirely clear, it is likely that the suggestion that the mother transfer her property into their joint names was initiated by the defendant daughter, albeit with the selfless intention of protecting her mother from being removed unwillingly from her home. By the time of the hearing, the daughter had discharged the balance of the mortgage over the property the subject of the claim and Barrett J stood the matter over to receive submissions on how that change should be accounted for in the declaration of relief. Although this initially resembles an intuitive application of a change of position defence, it is perhaps better analysed as involving a counterclaim by way of set-off for restitution of the benefit (discharge of mortgage) conferred on the claimant: see above, at 94–95, 103–07.

[114] *Quek v Beggs* (1990) 5 BPR 11,766 (New South Wales Supreme Court), discussed in Nahan, above n 15, at 83.

[115] *Hartigan v International Society for Krishna Consciousness Incorporated* [2002] NSWSC 810 (New South Wales Supreme Court).

defence only because the defendant had received a considerable financial benefit by discharging the debt early so that it would not be inequitable for it to be returned to the 'relative position of indebtedness which it would have been in had it not received the proceeds of the sale'.[116]

These cases together demonstrate equity's willingness to take into account good faith changes of position instigated by a defendant in determining the extent of the defendant's liability to make restitution. What is unclear, however, is the extent to which the defendant's role in inducing the impugned transaction affects his right to rely on those changes. As *Quek v Beggs* and *Hartigan* demonstrate, a claimant may be presumed to have entered into a transaction as a result of undue influence, even where her decision was spontaneous and unprompted by the defendant. If that is correct, then in the absence of a clear finding that influence has been exercised and nonetheless the defence should apply, the position of innocent inducers remains ambiguous.

(4) The Claimant's Changes of Position

The previous section demonstrated that the requirement of *restitutio in integrum* has operated to protect defendants who have in good faith changed their position as a result of their receipt. This section considers indications in the rescission case law that, in some circumstances, courts will protect *claimants* who have changed their position as a result of their receipt of a benefit from the defendant. The analysis highlights the inherent tension that can arise in cases of mutual cross-claims in unjust enrichment, where both parties may have conflicting claims to protection arising from their changes of position.

(a) Independent Changes in the Received Benefit

We saw earlier that claimants purporting to rescind a transaction would sometimes be required to pay an amount to the defendant for the deterioration or depreciation of the benefit the subject of a successful claim in counter-restitution. This was to enable the reversal of the impugned transfer and reflected judicial concern with the defendant's change by exchange. However, the claimant's obligation to pay for the deterioration of a received asset was not absolute. As the majority of the High Court of Australia explained in *Alati v Kruger*,[117] even at common law, the claimant did not have to pay where the deterioration was due to no fault on the part of the claimant, as where deterioration was inherent in the nature of the asset.[118]

[116] *Hartigan v International Society for Krishna Consciousness Incorporated* [2002] NSWSC 810 (New South Wales Supreme Court) [98]; also *McCulloch v Fern* [2001] NSWSC 406 (New South Wales Supreme Court) [89]–[113].

[117] *Alati v Kruger* (1955) 94 CLR 216 (High Court of Australia) 225 (Dixon CJ, Webb, Kitto and Taylor JJ).

[118] *Cf Newbigging v Adam* (1886) 34 Ch D 582 (CA) 582; *Adam v Newbigging* (1888) LR 13 App Cas 308 (HL) 330.

Therefore, returning to our core example, the claimant would be entitled to return the car to the defendant by way of counter-restitution, without being required to pay an amount for its inherent depreciation since the date of purchase. The defence of counter-restitution impossible does not appear to apply in this case.

The case law is generally silent on why this should be so.[119] The claimant's good faith cannot be a relevant ground for denying the defendant his right to protection arising from his change by exchange. Arguably, the only answer is that the rule reflects judicial concern to provide *the claimant* with a *pro tanto* change of position defence.[120] This is not entirely surprising; indeed, as we saw earlier in this chapter, it is what might be expected from the application of a 'two claims' approach to the requirement of counter-restitution. On that approach, the defendant's counterclaim in unjust enrichment for the benefit conferred on a claimant should be subject to the usual defences, including the change of position defence. The much more difficult question is how the claimant's right to protection can be reconciled with the countervailing right of the defendant to protection arising from his change by exchange. We return to this question further below.

(b) Claimant-instigated Changes of Position

The change of position defence analysis is further supported by suggestions in the rescission case law that the claimant should in some cases be protected from changes of position instigated by her on receipt of a benefit from the defendant. In *Head v Tattersall*,[121] the claimant purchased a horse warranted (incorrectly) to have been hunted with the Bicester hounds. On its way back to the claimant's stables, the horse suffered an accident which depreciated its value. When the claimant returned the horse and sought recovery of the purchase price, the defendant argued that *restitutio in integrum* was no longer possible. The court unanimously held that the claimant was entitled to rescind the transaction and recover the full purchase price on return to the defendant of the seriously injured animal. Although the reasoning of the members of the court differed, the proposition for which the case is generally taken to stand was advanced by Bramwell B:

> The buyer must return the horse in the same condition as when he bought it, but subject to any of those incidents to which the horse may be liable, either from its inherent nature, or *in the course of the exercise by the buyer of those rights over it which the contract gave.*[122] (emphasis added)

[119] One exception is the discussion of Cleasby B in *Head v Tattersall* (1871–72) LR 7 Ex 7 (Exch) 13–14 (risk of depreciation should lie with eventual owner). However, the original premise is unsupported by authority and assumes the very issue in question.

[120] Chen-Wishart, above n 93, at 562; Worthington, above n 72, at 55.

[121] *Head v Tattersall* (1871–72) LR 7 Ex 7 (Exch).

[122] *Head v Tattersall* (1871–72) LR 7 Ex 7 (Exch) 12. The highlighted phrase is cited with approval in *Alati v Kruger* (1955) 94 CLR 216 (High Court of Australia) 225 (Dixon CJ, Webb, Kitto and Taylor JJ).

Each member of the court emphasised that a crucial factor in their decision was that the horse was not injured as a result of the negligence or fault of the claimant.

The case is difficult for a number of reasons. First, the contract of sale contained a provision entitling the purchaser to return the horse within a certain period of time if the warranty was inaccurate. In that context, the focus of much of the court's discussion was on whether the contract required precise *restitutio in integrum* as a condition to return of the purchase price and whether the claimant had been at fault so as to affect his contractual entitlement to return. It is thus unclear whether the more general statements of principle contained in the judgments should apply outside that strictly contractual context. Secondly, and on the assumption that the court's observations were meant to apply more broadly,[123] they are difficult to reconcile with the defence of counter-restitution impossible. The established examples of where that defence applied, as where a claimant slaughtered a purchased cow or worked out a purchased mine, or indeed crashed her newly-bought car, would also constitute examples of where a claimant was exercising rights pursuant to the impugned contract. Unless the highlighted test is interpreted very narrowly, to restrict the protection afforded to the claimant to changes incurred in reliance on, or as a direct consequence of the particular misrepresentation (the horse bolted precisely because it did not have the warranted experience, or the car crashed for a reason directly related to the misrepresentation), *Head v Tattersall* seems to afford the claimant a broad defence of change of position at the expense of the defendant's countervailing right to protection arising from his change by exchange. We return to this problem in the section immediately below.

In addition to *Head v Tattersall*, there is also some support for the view that a claimant should be entitled to protection (usually labelled damages) where she has incurred expenses in reliance on an impugned contract.[124] For example, in *Alati v Kruger*,[125] the High Court of Australia took into account the claimant's change of position in incurring transaction costs and paying stamp duty on the basis of a fraudulently induced transaction in determining the extent of his liability to make counter-restitution to the defendant. This resembles the result that would flow from application of a defence of change of position in favour of the claimant. Similarly, in *Whittington v Seale-Hayne*,[126] the claimant purchased a lease of land and a residence for the purpose of running a poultry business. The defendant innocently represented that the premises were sanitary and fit for habitation when that was not the case. The court considered that the rents, rates and repairs carried by the claimant under the contract should be taken into account in rescinding the

[123] Clearly the basis of the citation in *Alati v Kruger* (1955) 94 CLR 216 (High Court of Australia). *Cf* W Peel (ed), above n 23, at [9-096].

[124] This reflects the position in German law: Dawson, above n 42, at 217, 287. *Cf Fibrosa Spolka Akcyjna v Fairbairn Lawson Combe Barbour Ltd* [1943] AC 32 (HL) 49 (Viscount Simon LC); *Horsler v Zorro* [1975] Ch 302 (Ch).

[125] *Alati v Kruger* (1955) 94 CLR 216 (High Court of Australia).

[126] *Whittington v Seale-Hayne* (1900) 82 LT 49 (Ch).

agreement. However, the claimant had also suffered significant consequential losses arising from the unsanitary conditions and sought an indemnity from the defendant.[127] This claim with respect to the consequential losses was denied, Farwell J emphasising that it effectively sought compensation consequent on entering into the contract, a positive claim for relief that went far beyond what was required by the concept of *restitutio in integrum.*[128]

(c) An Irreconcilable Tension?

The preceding analysis suggests that a claimant may be entitled to rely on a change of position defence to defeat in whole or in part the defendant's right to counter-restitution. But this highlights the apparently intractable tension that arises from dual characterisation of a defendant's change by exchange as both supporting a counterclaim for restitution *and* constituting a change of position (by the defendant) requiring protection.[129] The former characterisation permits the claimant to raise any good faith changes of position by way of defence to the counterclaim. The latter characterisation demands that any change in the claimant's position be ignored so that the defendant's change of position is given full protection.

There are several ways in which this dilemma could be resolved. The first would be to deny the claimant any right to rely on her change of position to reduce her liability to make counter-restitution and, if she attempted to do so, to deny her right to restitution pursuant to the primary claim. Effectively, this is the outcome of the traditional defence of counter-restitution impossible. However, this first approach is highly arbitrary. It does not explain why the defendant's right to protection from the primary claim to restitution should trump the claimant's right to protection from the defendant's counterclaim. The injustice of the approach is particularly apparent where the defendant is a wrongdoer.

Secondly, one could give full force to the two claims approach to counter-restitution and say that the defendant's change of position in conferring a benefit on the claimant (his change by exchange) is protected *through* affording to the defendant a counterclaim for restitution of the benefit. On this approach, the protection given to the defendant's change by exchange extends only so far as the counterclaim is successful. In general, the counterclaim should not be defeated if counter-restitution *in specie* is impossible: pecuniary restitution should be an accepted alternative. However, where a claimant has changed her position in such a way as to satisfy the change of position defence (as by crashing the transferred car without fault), the defendant's counterclaim (and with it the protection afforded to his change of position arising from his change by exchange) is defeated to the extent of the claimant's change.

[127] Relying on *Newbigging v Adam* (1886) 34 Ch D 582 (CA).

[128] *Whittington v Seale-Hayne* (1900) 82 LT 49 (Ch) 50–51.

[129] The standard response is simply to retreat to the defence of counter-restitution impossible: eg *Standard Bank London Ltd v Canara Bank* [2002] EWHC 1574 (QB (Comm Ct)) [86] (Moore-Bick J).

On this two claims approach, as with the first option considered, even the fraudulent defendant's change of position is protected by recognition of a counterclaim in unjust enrichment. This is justified by the need to ensure that the claimant is not unjustly enriched. However, the protection afforded to the defendant extends only as far as the counterclaim succeeds. This removes the possibility found in the counter-restitution impossible defence, that a wrongdoing defendant can rely on the claimant's change of position to defeat the claimant's action in its entirety.

Finally, one could adopt an entirely different approach to liability in the case of mutual cross-claims in unjust enrichment, such as exemplified by the German *saldo* theory. However, that option remains undesirable for all the reasons discussed earlier in this chapter. On balance, the second of the three options seems best as a matter of principle, precedent and practice.

C Conclusion

This chapter's analysis of the requirement of *restitutio in integrum* has revealed a number of insights that bear on the rationale, elements and operation of the change of position defence.

(1) Rationale

The analysis demonstrates that the requirement of *restitutio in integrum* is broader than simple counter-restitution and requires consideration of other changes to the parties' positions that may prevent them from being returned to the *status quo ante*. This suggests that a prime rationale for the change of position defence (whether in the context of rescission or restitution for unjust enrichment) may be reciprocity: if the claimant wants to be restored to the *status quo ante*, then the defendant must be able to be so restored as well.[130] Where that is no longer possible because of the defendant's change of position, restitution must be denied to the extent that the defendant's position can no longer be restored.

While this insight provokes interesting questions concerning the correlative nature of claims in unjust enrichment, it is a very high-level rationale that does not directly shed much light on the contested features of the change of position defence. For example, it does not of itself indicate whether reliance should or should not be an element of the defence or whether the fault of the defendant should operate as a bar to the defence. This indicates that there must be a more specific rationale or rationales underpinning both rescission case law and the change of position defence.

[130] *Cf* P Birks, 'Change of Position and Surviving Enrichment' in W Swadling (ed) *The Limits of Restitutionary Claims: A Comparative Analysis*, above n 35, at 40.

The most obvious contender, linked to the overriding requirement that the parties be returned to the *status quo ante*, is that the doctrine seeks to protect the parties from the harm that would otherwise arise from their changes of position were the parties now to be required to make restitution of their receipts. The concept of harm in play is broad: it includes not only situations where a party would be left bearing a financial loss, but where the party would be left in a substantially different (whatever the financial ramifications) position from that he originally occupied.[131] The law's refusal to force a party to adopt a position he never originally occupied and thus never chose must reflect, at least in part, a concern to protect the party's autonomy in decision-making. It is also consistent with a policy of protecting the parties' respective interests in the security of their receipts (although, clearly, an additional policy of protecting the parties' interest in the security of their bargain is often present in cases of rescission).

(2) Elements

Consistent with the preceding discussion, there is no indication in the rescission case law that the protection provided by the concept of *restitutio in integrum* is limited to 'disenriching' changes of position. Rather, the focus of the rescission case law is on whether any changes of position made by the parties are in substance reversible, so that the parties can be returned to the *status quo ante.* Importantly, this question of reversibility is assessed at the time of rescission, rather than the original changes of position. In that context, to ask whether the changes were inherently pecuniary in nature, or disenriching at the time they originally took place, is misguided.[132]

This analysis suggests that, rather than asking whether the defendant's change of position was disenriching, a better way of phrasing the change of position defence enquiry is to ask whether, as at the date of the hearing[133] the defendant's change of position has become irreversible. This recasting of the defence would help to remove a number of anomalies that otherwise appear to arise on the 'disenrichment' approach to the defence. In particular, it would help to explain why a defendant who might originally have been benefited by his change of position[134] might nonetheless be entitled to rely on the defence.[135]

On the other hand, the rescission case law consistently suggests that the independent depreciation of a received benefit should limit an innocent receiver's liability to make restitution. This seems to suggest that a defendant does not need

[131] Evident, for example, from cases where the company to which transferred shares related has since been reformed or changed in nature: above, at 104.

[132] An interesting analogy arises with the timing for assessment of the detrimental change of position required for estoppel: *Grundt v Great Boulder Pty Gold Mines Ltd* (1937) 59 CLR 641 (High Court of Australia) 674–75 (Dixon J) discussed in ch 2, at 48–49.

[133] Or the time the defendant became aware of the unjust factor.

[134] As where the defendant chose to have his hair cut, or take a world cruise, all of which would be considered actionable benefits for the purposes of the primary claim in unjust enrichment.

[135] Discussed further in ch 5, commencing at 127.

to demonstrate that he has changed his position in reliance on the security of his receipt in order to attract protection, unless reliance is satisfied by a defendant's decision simply to receive or retain an asset.[136] Alternatively (and consistent with the analysis derived from the estoppel case law),[137] it may suggest that independent changes in the received benefit should be treated differently from defendant-instigated changes of position. Protection of the defendant's security of receipt should generally[138] be extended where the very benefit received has independently depreciated or been destroyed. In contrast, where the change has arisen through the defendant's own actions, the defendant must have relied on his receipt in order for the defence to apply. This second analysis notably presents a means of reconciling the 'broad' and 'narrow' versions of the change of position defence.

More broadly, the rescission case law supports Lord Goff's prediction that the change of position defence will only rarely be available.[139] Often, it will be automatically precluded by the preconditions necessary for the right to rescind to arise, as in cases of contracts for value where the defendant must be shown to have known of or induced the vitiating factor for the right to rescind to arise. However, even where the preconditions to rescission are not so strict, as in cases of gift, there exist a number of bars to the defence.

First, with one notable exception, defendants who fraudulently induce entry into a transaction are not generally permitted to plead any subsequent changes of position in reduction of their liability. The historical exception is where the defendant's change of position involved the conferral of a benefit on the claimant, which benefit can no longer be recovered ('counter-restitution impossible'). However, that exception has been shown to have its own peculiar operation and rationale and should not be taken in support of recognising a more general extension of the change of position defence to fraudulent defendants.

Secondly, there are suggestions in the rescission case law that any change of position defence should be denied where the defendant induced, albeit innocently, the claimant's entry into the transaction. However, the cases are by no means unanimous on this point, with a number contemplating that innocent inducers may be entitled to plead their change of position by way of defence. More controversially, *Head v Tattersall*[140] suggests that the fault or negligence of the defendant may be relevant where the received benefit has been damaged, lost or destroyed while in the defendant's control.

Although the role of the defendant's fault has not yet been finally resolved, when taken together with the estoppel and payment over case law, the rescission case law certainly supports the view that 'the recent rejection by the Privy Council in *Dextra*

[136] Professor Birks took such a wide view of reliance: P Birks, 'Change of Position and Surviving Enrichment' in W Swadling (ed) *The Limits of Restitutionary Claims: A Comparative Analysis*, above n 35, at 50–51.

[137] Ch 2, at 41–42.

[138] Subject to bars such as may arise from the defendant's fault.

[139] *Lipkin Gorman (a firm) v Karpnale Ltd* [1991] 2 AC 548 (HL) 580.

[140] *Head v Tattersall* (1871–72) LR 7 Ex 7 (Exch).

Bank & Trust Co Ltd v Bank of Jamaica,[141] of the relevance of fault to the defence of change of position in an action to recover a mistaken payment, may be simplistic'.[142]

(3) Ambit of Operation

The ambiguity noted earlier as to whether 'innocent inducers' may be entitled to the defence will have particular relevance in cases arising out of innocent misrepresentation and undue influence. To this extent, the rescission case law confirms rather than clarifies the uncertainty as to which claims in unjust enrichment the change of position defence applies.

On the other hand, given its historical emphasis on the right of the parties to restitution *in specie*, the rescission case law does leave open the possibility that the change of position defence should apply to proprietary claims in unjust enrichment.

Finally, the courts' prevarication over the position of innocent misrepresentors may appear to suggest that where a defendant is a wrongdoer pursuant to a strict liability tort and is innocent of any deliberate wrongdoing (such as may occur in cases of conversion, or breach of fiduciary duty) there may be some room for the change of position defence to apply. However, there is a wide gulf between a person who innocently misrepresents a fact and in doing so commits no breach of duty (although other legal consequences may apply as a consequence of that misrepresentation) and a person who breaches a duty, albeit unwittingly or in good faith. The rescission case law therefore provides little support for extension of the change of position defence beyond the law of unjust enrichment to innocent wrongdoers sued in that capacity.

In concluding this part, part one of this book has demonstrated that the modern change of position defence has not developed against a vacant backdrop. The seeds of the change of position defence were already present in the doctrines of rescission and estoppel and in the defence of payment over. This is because in these areas, as with the change of position defence, courts are regularly required to consider whether the fact that a defendant had changed his position as a result of his receipt should affect his prima facie liability to make restitution to the claimant. Given the apparent similarity in the change of position issues before the courts, this part has argued that the courts' approaches to these issues in the context of rescission, estoppel and payment over may also provide insights for the disputed features of the change of position defence. At the very least, rationality in the law demands that they be taken into account when considering the elements, ambit of operation and rationale of the modern change of position defence.

Part two of the book builds on part one by taking into account its lessons as part of the process of clarifying the disputed features of the change of position defence. Chapter five addresses the primary elements of the change of position defence.

[141] *Dextra Bank and Trust Co Ltd v Bank of Jamaica* [2002] 1 All ER (Comm) 193 (PC).
[142] Watts, above n 22, at 306–07 (citation added).

Chapter six examines the role of the defendant's fault as a bar to the defence. Chapter seven considers the ambit of operation of the change of position defence. Chapter eight then returns to examine the rationale(s) of the change of position defence, considered in light of the identified elements of, bars to and ambit of operation of the defence.

Part Two

Definition

5

Primary Elements

A Introduction

THE MODERN STARTING point for determining the primary elements of the change of position defence is *Lipkin Gorman (a firm) v Karpnale Ltd*,[1] in which the defence was first expressly recognised in English law. In that case, Lord Goff stated that the change of position defence should be available 'where an innocent defendant's position is so changed that he will suffer an injustice if called upon to repay or repay in full'[2] and, later:

> At present, I do not wish to state the principle any less broadly than this: that the defence is available to a person whose position has so changed that it would be inequitable in all the circumstances to require him to make restitution, or alternatively to make restitution in full.[3]

As Lord Goff intended, these very general statements left identification of the detailed elements of the defence to be worked out on a case by case basis.[4] This chapter demonstrates that much of the difficult detail has indeed been worked out in subsequent cases, subject to two persisting areas of uncertainty, foreshadowed in chapter one. The first area of controversy is what kinds of change count for the purpose of the defence, in particular, whether the defence is limited to disenriching changes of position. The second is the 'reliance issue', namely whether reliance is a necessary element of the defence (the 'narrow' version of the defence) or whether it is sufficient to establish that the defendant's good faith change of position was caused by his receipt (the 'broad' version).

The aim of this chapter is to demonstrate that these disputed features of the defence can be settled by drawing on the lessons learnt from the doctrines that were the subject of part one, together with consideration of current authority, legal principle and issues of policy raised in relation to the defence. Through the combination of these methods, the primary elements of the change of position defence become clear.

1 *Lipkin Gorman (a firm) v Karpnale Ltd* [1991] 2 AC 548 (HL).
2 *Ibid*, at 579.
3 *Lipkin Gorman (a firm) v Karpnale Ltd* [1991] 2 AC 548 (HL) 580.
4 *Ibid*.

B Elements

(1) A Detrimental Change of Position

In *David Securities Pty Ltd v Commonwealth Bank of Australia*, the High Court of Australia identified as the core requirement of the change of position defence the fact that 'the defendant has acted to his or her detriment on the faith of the receipt'.[5] Putting to one side for the moment the issue of reliance, the definition invites the question, what counts as a detrimental change of position?

(a) *Detriment as 'Disenrichment'*

Professor Birks consistently argued that the core underlying concept[6] of the change of position defence is 'disenrichment'.[7] That is, only changes of position that lead to the loss of all or part of the value of the benefit received will count for the purpose of the defence. It is this loss of 'net' enrichment which makes it 'inequitable',[8] 'unconscionable'[9] or 'unjust'[10] to require restitution or restitution in full. For example, on Birks' approach, if I receive a mistaken payment and deposit it in my account at the bank, the change of position consisting in the deposit does not count for the purposes of the defence because I remain enriched to the full extent of my receipt. In contrast, if I use (as in the core example given in chapter one) the money to purchase an ephemeral benefit that does not increase my net assets, such as a meal, my net assets have decreased by the amount of my purchase. Assuming the other elements of the defence are satisfied, my change of position defence should succeed.[11]

Birks' enrichment-based analysis has been welcomed by courts[12] and commentators[13] concerned by the open-ended and discretionary nature of competing

[5] *David Securities Pty Ltd v Commonwealth Bank of Australia* (1992) 127 CLR 353 (High Court of Australia) 385 (Mason CJ, Deane, Toohey, Gaudron and McHugh JJ) (emphasis in original omitted).

[6] Birks did not entirely discount the possibility of an 'unjust-related' change of position defence: see P Birks, *Unjust Enrichment* (2nd edn, OUP, Oxford 2005) 209, 258 and further below, at n 57.

[7] *Ibid*, at 208–12.

[8] *Lipkin Gorman (a firm) v Karpnale Ltd* [1991] 2 AC 548 (HL) 579 (Lord Goff).

[9] *Niru Battery Manufacturing Co v Milestone Trading Ltd* [2003] EWCA Civ 1446, [2004] QB 985 [149] Clarke LJ.

[10] *David Securities Pty Ltd v Commonwealth Bank of Australia* (1992) 127 CLR 353 (High Court of Australia) 385 (Mason CJ, Deane, Toohey, Gaudron and McHugh JJ).

[11] The question whether I would have purchased the benefit in any event is a question of causation: see below, commencing at 143.

[12] eg *Dextra Bank and Trust Co Ltd v Bank of Jamaica* [2002] 1 All ER (Comm) 193 (PC).

[13] eg R Grantham and C Rickett, 'Change of Position in New Zealand' [1999] *New Zealand Business L Q* 77, 77–78; R Grantham and C Rickett, 'Change of Position and Balancing the Equities' [1999] 7 *Restitution L Rev* 162, 162–63; AS Burrows, *The Law of Restitution* (2nd edn, Butterworths, London 2002) 510; G Virgo, 'Change of Position: the importance of being principled' [2005] *Restitution L Rev* 34, 35–37; J Palmer, 'Chasing a Will-o-the Wisp? Making Sense of Bad Faith and Wrongdoers in Change of Position' [2005] *Restitution L Rev* 53, 55–58.

versions of the defence. In particular, the New Zealand statutory versions of the defence (which have greatly influenced the development of their common law counterpart)[14] compare the fault of the parties in determining the level of protection to be afforded to the defendant. This approach has been condemned as 'hopelessly unstable'.[15] A similar reaction has greeted recent English Court of Appeal decisions which have suggested that the touchstone of the defence is 'inequitability'.[16] In comparison to these approaches, a strict disenrichment version of the defence appears attractive because it leaves little room for arbitrary judicial discretion. The value of the defendant's expenditures is offset against the value of the initial receipt. The claimant's remedy of restitution is limited to any remaining amount.

Notwithstanding these attractions, there is some difficulty with understanding the change of position defence as concerned solely, or even primarily, with disenrichment. Pivotal to Birks' characterisation of the defence was that it must be understood as counteracting an element of the primary claim in unjust enrichment, either: (1) that there is an enrichment of the defendant; (2) that the enrichment comes at the expense of the claimant; or (3) that it is 'unjust' for the defendant to retain the benefit. Birks saw the defence of change of position as counteracting the enrichment element of the primary claim in unjust enrichment. Assuming for the moment[17] that it is useful to conceptualise the defence as operating to counter elements of the primary claim in this manner,[18] it should follow that the concepts of enrichment for the purpose of the primary claim and disenrichment in the context of the defence, will mirror each other.

However, the concept of disenrichment as used by Birks in the context of the defence does not sit easily with the concept of enrichment which applies for the purposes of establishing the primary claim in unjust enrichment.[19] In particular, it is generally accepted that a benefit that is chosen or desired by the defendant may be regarded as enriching for the purposes of the primary claim, notwithstanding that the benefit is inherently ephemeral in nature and non wealth-enhancing, such

[14] *National Bank of New Zealand Ltd v Waitaki International Processing (NI) Ltd* [1999] 2 NZLR 211 (New Zealand Court of Appeal); *cf Saunders & Co v Hague* [2004] 2 NZLR 475 (New Zealand High Court) 491, where Chisolm J considered himself, arguably incorrectly, as bound by the Privy Council decision in *Dextra Bank and Trust Co Ltd v Bank of Jamaica* [2002] 1 All ER (Comm) 193 (PC) to ignore considerations of relative fault.

[15] *Dextra Bank and Trust Co Ltd v Bank of Jamaica* [2002] 1 All ER (Comm) 193 (PC) [45], adopting the arguments of P Birks, 'Change of Position and Surviving Enrichment' in W Swadling (ed) *The Limits of Restitutionary Claims: A Comparative Analysis* (The United Kingdom Committee of Comparative Law, Glasgow 1997) 41. The role of fault is considered in ch 6.

[16] *Niru Battery Manufacturing Co v Milestone Trading Ltd* [2003] EWCA Civ 1446, [2004] QB 985 and *Commerzbank Ag v Price-Jones* [2003] EWCA Civ 1663, (2003) 147 SJLB 1397, criticised by AS Burrows, 'Clouding the Issues on Change of Position' [2004] *CLJ* 276, 279.

[17] An alternative approach of analysing the defence as linked to the nature and purpose of the relief sought is considered in ch 6, at 171.

[18] Not all commentators accept the utility of this analysis: eg G Virgo, *The Principles of the Law of Restitution* (2 edn, OUP, Oxford 2006) 692.

[19] Other misalignments are considered below, at 132–6.

as a provision of a meal, haircut or a holiday.[20] This is because the chief obstacle to accepting any benefit with market value as enriching for the purposes of the primary claim in unjust enrichment is the law's concern to protect defendants' freedom of choice.[21] Where a party has chosen a benefit, that concern is by definition eliminated.[22] Consistent with this approach, a defendant who chose to purchase a fine meal in reliance on his receipt of a mistaken payment should not be able to rely on the change of position defence because he chose the benefit and thus was enriched by the pleaded change. But the cases show that it is precisely this kind of 'wasted' expenditure that typically counts towards establishing the change of position defence. For example, in *Philip Collins Ltd v Davis*,[23] musicians used royalties mistakenly paid to them by the claimant to fund a bohemian lifestyle that they clearly chose, desired and enjoyed. Notwithstanding the fact that the musicians had obtained undisputed (albeit ephemeral) benefits as a result of the royalty payments, their claimed change of position defences succeeded.

Birks answered this concern by turning to the principle of subjective devaluation.[24] Drawing an analogy with that principle, Birks argued that a defendant should be able to argue that, although initially the chosen benefit was of value to him, once aware of the claim against him, he no longer valued the benefit. This is because had the defendant known of the true state of affairs, he would not have changed his position by purchasing the new benefit. In this way, the defendant's intention was as much impaired as the claimant's and equally deserving of protection.[25]

However, as Nolan notes, a defendant may be entitled to devalue subjectively a benefit thrust on him, but why should he be able to devalue subjectively a benefit chosen by him, albeit chosen on an incorrect assumption?[26] So far as the primary claim in unjust enrichment is concerned, a defendant would not be able to resist a claim for restitution of a received benefit on the basis that, although he requested and received the claimant's services, he did so under the mistaken belief that they were required when, in fact, he could have done without them. And, although it is

[20] The converse proposition, that receipt of a money benefit that was neither chosen nor desired by a defendant is not enriching, was considered and rejected with reluctance in *Perpetual Trustees Victoria Limited v Ford* [2008] NSWSC 29 (New South Wales Supreme Court).

[21] eg M McInnes, 'Enrichment Revisited' in J Neyers, M McInnes and P S (eds) *Understanding Unjust Enrichment* (Hart, Oxford 2004); Birks, *Unjust Enrichment* 2nd edn, above n 6, at 54; J Edelman and E Bant, *Unjust Enrichment in Australia* (OUP, Melbourne 2006) 107–08; G Virgo, *The Principles of the Law of Restitution* 2 edn, above n 18, at 68. Against are J Beatson, *The Use and Abuse of Unjust Enrichment: essays on the law of restitution* (Clarendon Press, Oxford 1991) and R Grantham and C Rickett, *Enrichment and Restitution in New Zealand* (Hart Publishing, Oxford 2000) 20–21 and 60–61, both criticised in Edelman and Bant, *ibid*, at 100–01.

[22] eg *Brenner v First Artists' Management Pty Ltd* [1993] VR 221 (Victorian Supreme Court) (defendant's choice of management services demonstrated that he was enriched by their receipt).

[23] *Philip Collins Ltd v Davis* [2000] 3 All ER 808 (Ch) 829–30 (Jonathan Parker J).

[24] P Birks, *An Introduction to the Law of Restitution* (revised edn, Clarendon Press, Oxford 1989) 413–14; P Birks, 'Overview: Tracing, Claiming and Defences' in P Birks (ed) *Laundering and Tracing* (Clarendon Press, Oxford 1995) 331–32.

[25] Developing this argument is McInnes, above n 21.

[26] R Nolan, 'Change of Position' in P Birks (ed) *Laundering and Tracing* (Clarendon Press, Oxford 1995) 140.

outside the scope of this book, it is uncertain that a defendant's subjective belief as to the value of a chosen benefit counts, once it is proven that the defendant chose the benefit. Benefits generally are valued according to their market value, not according to the subjective beliefs of the defendant.[27]

A further difficulty with accepting the subjective devaluation approach is that the very fact that the defendant's intention was impaired at the time he changed his position may mean that the defendant has a claim against the third party for recovery of the value of that change of position. Suppose a defendant changes his position by making a gift of a received benefit to his brother. In the event he is required to make restitution of the benefit to the claimant, he may have a claim against the brother for restitution of the gift (based on mistake). As we will see later in this chapter, the existence of this claim may have the consequence that the gift, being reversible, does not count as a relevant change for the purpose of the defence.[28] In that context, it seems odd if the very vitiation of the defendant's intention, said by Birks to underpin the right to devalue subjectively the change of position, can operate to defeat that pleaded change. It suggests at the very least a lack of 'fit' between the disenrichment analysis and the change of position defence.

Finally, the recent House of Lords decision in *Sempra Metal Limited v Commissioners of Inland Revenue*[29] casts further doubt on Birks' subjective devaluation approach to the defence. In that case, *Sempra* paid tax earlier than it would otherwise have done, pursuant to what subsequently turned out to be invalid taxation legislation. The majority accepted that, in so doing, *Sempra* had conferred a benefit on the government in the form of the use value (interest) of the early payments.[30] The pertinent question before the House of Lords for the purpose of this book was how that benefit should be valued. A majority accepted that the starting position must be the objective value of the benefit: that is, the reasonable cost of borrowing the money paid early to the government.[31] However, should that objective approach be modified or abandoned if the government (or a defendant in a similar position) could demonstrate that the defendant had not actually employed the early payment so as to obtain its reasonable use-value? What if, for example, the defendant had paid it into a non-interest-bearing account, or (as a personal defendant) had hidden it under his bed?[32]

27 *Sempra Metals Limited v Commissioners of Inland Revenue* [2007] UKHL 34, [2008] 1 AC 561 discussed immediately below. The question is considered in detail in Edelman and Bant, above n 21, at 107–08, 117–20.

28 At 139–43.

29 *Sempra Metals Limited v Commissioners of Inland Revenue* [2007] UKHL 34, [2008] 1 AC 561.

30 The payments themselves had been subject to a set-off before the matter came to court and thus were no longer in dispute.

31 *Sempra Metals Limited v Commissioners of Inland Revenue* [2007] UKHL 34, [2008] 1 AC 561 [13], [33], [42]–[49] (Lord Hope) [103], [116]–[19] (Lord Nicholls) [154] (Lord Walker, concurring generally with Lords Hope and Nicholls); dissenting were Lord Scott at [132], [145]–[47] and Lord Mance at [230]–[34].

32 *Sempra Metals Limited v Commissioners of Inland Revenue* [2007] UKHL 34, [2008] 1 AC 561 [119] (Lord Nicholls) [233] (Lord Mance).

Lord Nicholls, in the majority, suggested that in such circumstances courts could depart from the objective market value of the benefit pursuant to the concept of 'subjective devaluation'.[33] However, arguably, Lord Nicholls is not employing that label in the same sense as Birks, notwithstanding his attribution of the concept to Birks. There is, for example, no suggestion in the majority speeches that the defendant's subjective views of the value of the benefit are of any relevance to its valuation by the court. Rather, what is regarded as relevant is what the defendant actually did, or omitted to do, in reliance on his receipt. The features of Lord Nicholls' approach to resolving this problem, as with the 'equitable defence' mentioned by Lord Hope,[34] are as follows: (1) the onus of demonstrating the response of the defendant to his receipt lies on the defendant; (2) it will apply where the defendant shares the claimant's mistake or, presumably, is otherwise unaware of the vitiating factor; and (3) it extends to a case where a defendant has omitted to invest reasonably in reliance on his receipt. Taken together, these features are suggestive of a change of position defence, a point recognised but left open by Lord Nicholls. If this analysis is correct, then the proper approach to such claims is to recognise that they give rise to a personal right to restitution of the objective value of the use of the money, but subject to the change of position defence.

A slightly different argument that supports a disenrichment approach to the defence has been made by Nolan. He argues that once a defendant becomes aware of the claimant's claim for restitution, he is entitled to 'revalue' any changes he made as a result of the receipt.[35] However, if we accept that the defendant was initially enriched by his chosen expenditure, then his regret at that decision after the event should not change his liability: mere disappointment that he will have to repay the amount is not enough.[36] Nolan is closer to the mark, however, when he goes on to consider whether a defendant who retains a readily realisable benefit as a result of his change of position is entitled subjectively to revalue his change of position.[37] Nolan concludes that he is not because a defendant in such circumstances arguably remains enriched. Another explanation, however, is that the relevant change is easily reversible, a subtly different approach, to which we now turn.

(b) Detriment as 'Irreversibility'

We saw in chapters two, three and four of part one that irreversibility is a core component of the concept of 'change of position' at work in the law relating to estoppel, the defence of payment over and rescission. Could this concept provide

[33] *Sempra Metals Limited v Commissioners of Inland Revenue* [2007] UKHL 34, [2008] 1 AC 561 [119] (Lord Nicholls) [233] (Lord Mance), at [118]–[19].

[34] *Ibid*, at [23]–[24], [48].

[35] Nolan, above n 26, at 139–43.

[36] *Scottish Equitable Plc v Derby* [2001] EWCA Civ 369, [2001] 3 All ER 818 [34] (Robert Walker LJ); *Mahme Trust Reg v Tayeb* [2002] EWHC 1543 (Ch), [2003] WTLR 21 [143] (Rimer J).

[37] Nolan, above n 26, at 141–42.

a more satisfactory test of what counts as a relevant change of position than the concept of 'disenrichment'?

Until recently, there has been relatively little express discussion in the change of position case law or commentaries of any requirement that the change must be irreversible for the change of position defence to operate.[38] There is now a line of English and Australian decisions involving defendants who claimed to have changed their position by paying tax on their receipt.[39] In these cases, the courts recognised that, in order for the defence to apply, the defendant must show that the tax was irrecoverable from the taxing authority. Outside the taxation context, *Scottish Equitable Plc v Derby*[40] also provides support for the existence of a reversibility requirement. In that case, Mr Derby received an overpayment through the carelessness of his life assurance company and spent some of it on small improvements to his daily lifestyle. In rejecting Mr Derby's pleaded change of position defence, Robert Walker LJ (Simon Brown and Keene LJJ concurring) endorsed as critical the trial judge's findings that the improvements were 'very modest and not irreversible'. Finally, in the recent Western Australian Supreme Court of Appeal decision in *Alpha Wealth Financial Services Pty Ltd v Frankland River Olive Company Ltd*,[41] Buss JA, with whom Steytler P concurred, stated that in order for the defence to apply, 'the recipient must have changed his or her position, and the change must be legally or practically irreversible or there must be significant difficulties in reversing the change'.

The irreversibility approach is consistent with courts' approaches to the question of what constitutes a relevant change of position.[42] Suppose I receive a

[38] E Bant and P Creighton, 'The Australian Change of Position Defence' (2002) 30 (2) *U Western Australia L Rev* 208, 212–13; McInnes, above n 21, at 165, 197–98; Edelman and Bant, above n 21, at 323–25. The irreversibility requirement is also present in United States cases: H Dagan, *The Law and Ethics of Restitution* (Cambridge University Press, Cambridge 2004) 48–49, 68–70.

[39] *Hillsdown Holdings Plc v Pensions Ombudsman* [1997] 1 All ER 862 (QB) 904 (Knox J); *Hinckley and Bosworth BC v Shaw* (1999) 1 LGLR 385 (QB); *K & S Corp Ltd v Sportingbet Australia Pty Ltd* [2003] SASC 96, (2003) 86 SASR 313 (South Australian Supreme Court); *Fazzolari v Couchouron* [2003] VCAT 503, (2003) V Conv R 58-572 (Victorian Civil and Administrative Tribunal). *Cf Lokan v Defence Force Retirement and Death Benefits Authority* [2007] AATA 1652 (Administrative Appeals Tribunal of Australia) [14]–[15] (Deputy President PE Hack SC).

[40] *Scottish Equitable Plc v Derby* [2001] EWCA Civ 369, [2001] 3 All ER 818 [34] (Robert Walker LJ). See also: *Eden Productions Pty Ltd v Southern Star Group Ltd* [2002] NSWSC 1166 (New South Wales Supreme Court) [226] (Gzell J) (trustee with enforceable indemnity was protected from any detriment arising from his change of position); *Day v Day* [2005] EWHC 1455 (Ch) [49] (Mr L Henderson QC) (payments found to constitute change of position defence were 'irrevocable').

[41] *Alpha Wealth Financial Services Pty Ltd v Frankland River Olive Company Ltd* [2008] WASCA 119 (Western Australia Supreme Court of Appeal) [202]; see also: *Fitzsimons v Minister for Liquor Gaming and Racing for the State of New South Wales* [2008] NSWSC 782 (New South Wales Supreme Court) [128]–[29] (McDougall J).

[42] eg *Boscawen v Bajwa* [1996] 1 WLR 328 (CA) 341 (Millett LJ) (defendant who has changed position by discharging a mortgage should be expected to obtain a fresh advance); *Gertsch v Atsas* [1999] NSWSC 898, (1999) 10 BPR 18 431 (New South Wales Supreme Court) (court accepted as relevant change of position, the defendant's act of repaying mortgage on evidence that that no lender was now willing to advance loan to defendant on security of her property); *Credit-Suisse (Monaco) SA v Attar* [2004] EWHC 374 (QB (Comm Ct)) (defence denied to defendant who had purchased shares in reliance on his receipt and sold them by the time of the action).

mistaken payment and, as in the core case, change my position by purchasing and consuming a meal. No claim in unjust enrichment generally will lie against the third party restaurant to recover the value of the payment because it was made pursuant to a valid contract and no grounds exist for setting it aside.[43] Further, given the ephemeral nature of the benefit received in exchange for my payment to the third party, I cannot reverse the change to fund my restitutionary liability through a sale of the benefit received in exchange. The same would be true if I purchased a holiday or a haircut in reliance on my receipt. Changes of this sort by their very nature tend to be irreversible and so automatically qualify for the purposes of the defence.

We saw from part one that underpinning the reversibility requirement in the context of rescission is the aim of reversing or unwinding the transitions so as to return the parties as near as possible to the *status quo ante*. In undertaking that process, we saw that courts can and should be able to make financial adjustments to any orders for restitution.[44] Returning to the example given earlier of me depositing the amount of my receipt in my bank account, my change in that case is readily reversible: barring disaster such as the supervening insolvency of the bank, I can easily withdraw the amount if required to do so, without thereby suffering any prejudice. If there are bank charges associated with the withdrawal, these can be taken into account by allowing me to deduct the amount of the charges from my restitutionary liability. The reversibility approach explains equally as well as the disenrichment approach why the defendant in that case cannot rely on the change of position defence.

The irreversibility approach closely resembles a 'disenrichment' approach, in that both ultimately reduce the effect of the pleaded change to monetary terms. However, there are subtle differences between the two. The irreversibility approach does not commence by asking whether the pleaded change itself is inherently disenriching. Rather, it asks whether the pleaded change is irreversible and then values the identified (irreversible) change in order to set it off against the value of the claimant's right to restitution. Although the two approaches look very similar, they differ in a number of respects.[45] The most significant is that the irreversibility approach would allow the change of position defence where the pleaded change is not inherently pecuniary in nature.

Suppose a defendant receives a payment of £100,000 from a lottery. Overjoyed at his good fortune, he and his wife decide to start a family. After they have conceived a child, they are notified that the payment was made to them by mistake. Does the conception of the child count as a relevant change of position? Birks pointed out that children have financial consequences.[46] But can the conception of a child itself be regarded as a 'disenrichment' without doing at least some

[43] A unilateral mistake is not enough to give rise to a right to rescind a contract. The reversibility of payments through litigation is further considered below, at 141–43.

[44] At 105, 107.

[45] Other differences are explored, at 135–38 and 146.

[46] P Birks, 'Change of Position: The Two Central Questions' (2004) 120 *LQR* 373, 375: the decision to have children has an 'unacknowledged foundation in disenrichment'.

violence to that concept? Birks himself noted that so far as the primary claim in unjust enrichment is concerned, the concept of an 'enrichment' should exclude things like children, who cannot really be assessed as material gains.[47] If 'disenrichment' for the purposes of the defence of change of position is meant (as Birks argued) to mirror the concept of 'enrichment' at play in the primary claim, then this category of case ought to be excluded.

The debate over whether things like children can be regarded in purely pecuniary terms is not, of course, unfamiliar to the law. In torts law, for example, recent cases in England[48] and Australia[49] have debated and split on this very issue. The conclusion in England is that it simply is not possible, nor appropriate, to view the advent of a child in balance sheet terms: weighing up the (intangible) benefits of a new addition to the family against its inherent (financial, emotional and physical) costs.

If we accept that children are not inherently disenriching in balance-sheet terms, what is the consequence? On the above analysis, it is difficult to see how the decision to have a child can satisfy the disenrichment approach to the change of position defence. In contrast, in a recent proprietary estoppel case in Australia,[50] Handley JA accepted that a decision by the defendant to have further children in reliance on her brother's representation would have counted as a relevant detriment had it been proven. Seen in terms of reversibility, rather than disenrichment, this makes sense. His Honour's approach was subsequently adopted unanimously by the Victorian Supreme Court of Appeal in *Donis v Donis*.[51] In that case, a woman changed her position by, inter alia, marrying and conceiving a child in reliance on representations that she held, or would hold, a quarter-share interest in a property. In finding the element of detriment established, Nettle JA (Maxwell ACJ and Ashley JA concurring) emphasised that 'the detriment suffered is of a kind and extent that involves life-changing decisions with irreversible consequences of a profoundly personal nature'.

The conception of a child generally constitutes an irreversible change of position.[52] In the usual case, on the irreversibility approach, the law then attempts to place a value on any irreversible change, in order to set it off against the claimant's primary right to restitution. It does so because it must attempt to draw up an account of the parties' positions that will enable their return as near as possible to the *status quo ante*. On the one hand, there is the claimant's prima facie right to restitution; on the other, there is the defendant's irreversible change of position. In order to bring the latter into account, courts must try to place some value on the irreversible change. In cases (such as the decision to have children) where the

[47] Birks, *Unjust Enrichment* 2nd edn, above n 6, at 51.

[48] *Rees v Darlington Memorial Hospital NHS Trust* [2003] UKHL 52, [2004] 1 AC 309 (HL).

[49] *Cattanach v Melchior* [2003] HCA 38, (2003) 215 CLR 1 (High Court of Australia).

[50] *Sullivan v Sullivan* [2006] NSWCA 312 (New South Wales Court of Appeal).

[51] *Donis v Donis* [2007] VSCA 89 (Victorian Supreme Court of Appeal).

[52] *Cf* Lord Scott as to the difference between the case of an unwanted foal as opposed to an unwanted human pregnancy: *Rees v Darlington Memorial Hospital NHS Trust* [2003] UKHL 52, [2004] 1 AC 309 (HL) [134]–[39].

irreversible change of position is very significant and impossible to value, and no amount of money can restore the defendant to anything like his former position, the most likely consequence on the irreversibility approach to the defence is that the defence will operate to defeat entirely the claimant's prima facie right to restitution.[53]

(c) The Irreversibility Approach is to be Preferred

Of the two approaches to what constitutes a detrimental change of positon, which is to be preferred? In most cases, either approach will achieve the same result. This is because most pleaded changes of position will be inherently pecuniary in nature. An irreversible pecuniary change of position will usually satisfy the disenrichment approach to the defence and vice versa. Therefore, in most cases it will not matter which analysis applies.

Notwithstanding the closeness between the two approaches, the irreversibility approach is to be preferred for six reasons. First, as the previous section demonstrates, it allows that there may be changes on which it is intrinsically very difficult, or indeed impossible, to place a monetary value and would not qualify as enriching for the purpose of the primary claim in unjust enrichment, but which should qualify as relevant to the defence. In *Commerzbank Ag v Price-Jones*,[54] Munby J cited a decision on the part of a defendant to forgo the opportunity to improve his wealth[55] and a decision to enter into a divorce as examples of changes that, in his Lordship's view, would count for the defence.[56] To those examples could be added a decision to marry or to have a child. The fact that such changes are difficult or even impossible to value does not make them irrelevant for the purpose of the defence.[57] As suggested earlier, where the change is very significant and irreversible, the most likely result is that the defence will simply operate as a complete bar to the claim.[58]

Secondly, the irreversibility requirement explains when the defence may be available and why, in cases where the defendant ostensibly remains enriched by his pleaded change of position.[59] In the Canadian case of *RBC Dominion Securities Inc*

[53] As in *Kinlan v Crimmin* [2006] EWHC 779, (Ch (Companies Ct)). See also the approach taken in rescission to cases where rescission would leave a party in an entirely different position from that which he occupied prior to the transaction: ch 4, at 103–04, 119.

[54] *Commerzbank Ag v Price-Jones* [2003] EWCA Civ 1663, (2003) 147 SJLB 1397.

[55] *Commerzbank Ag v Price-Jones* [2003] EWCA Civ 1663, (2003) 147 SJLB 1397 [65]–[72]. Ch 2 noted that loss of opportunity has long been accepted as constituting a relevant detriment for the purpose of the defence of estoppel, at 50–51.

[56] *Commerzbank Ag v Price-Jones* [2003] EWCA Civ 1663, (2003) 147 SJLB 1397 [68].

[57] In Birks, *Unjust Enrichment* 2nd edn, above n 6, at 258, Birks suggests the fact that a contract has been fully performed as a 'plausible example of a non-disenriching change of circumstances'.

[58] As in *Kinlan v Crimmin* [2006] EWHC 779, (Ch (Companies Ct)).

[59] Other examples include: *New England Mutual Life v Hastings* 733 F Supp 516 (DRI 1990) (United States District Court-Rhode Island) 520–21 (radical and irreversible change in lifestyle supported the change of position defence, notwithstanding the continued enrichment of the defendant) and *Gertsch v Atsas* [1999] NSWSC 898, (1999) 10 BPR 18 431 (New South Wales Supreme Court), the latter discussed further below, at 138. Cf *Equuscorp Pty Ltd v Bassat* [2007] VSC 553 (Victorian Supreme Court) [136] (Byrne J).

v Dawson,[60] the defendant (Mrs Dawson) received a mistaken payment, on the faith of which she replaced some of her existing household furnishings and furniture with new items and refurbished some existing furniture. The troublesome aspect of the case has always been that the Newfoundland Court of Appeal accepted that Mrs Dawson remained enriched following the change of position, at least by the difference between the value of the old furnishings and the new.[61] Notwithstanding this, it held that the change of position defence applied completely.

Although the case can be explained on the disenrichment approach to the defence by applying Birks' subjective devaluation or Nolan's subjective revaluation analyses, we saw above that those analyses are not free from difficulty. In contrast, the irreversibility approach is comparatively simple to apply and has relatively few theoretical difficulties. On that approach, the difficulties facing Mrs Dawson in reversing her changes (including finding equivalent and acceptable secondhand furniture to that which she initially replaced and reversing the refurbishing work carried out on retained furniture) were sufficiently significant to require the full protection of the defence. In this regard, there is no doubt that the onus lay on Mrs Dawson to establish that her position had irreversibly changed. However, as discussed further below, the court may have been prepared to accept that the existence of significant practical hurdles to reversing the changes sufficed.[62]

Thirdly, the irreversibility approach to the change of position defence emphasises that, as with estoppel, payment over and rescission, the detriment must be assessed at the time the claimant seeks restitution of the benefit received by the defendant, rather than at the time of the original change of position.[63] In contrast, the 'disenriching' approach to the defence has a tendency to imply that what needs to be established is that the change of position was disenriching at the time the original change occurred.[64] As we saw above, that arguably is not so. If a defendant chooses a meal and consumes it, he is thereby enriched by his chosen benefit. It is only subsequently, when required to make restitution of the value of the amount spent on the meal that the purchase of the meal operates to his prejudice. This was the same point made by Dixon J in relation to the requirement of a detrimental change of position in estoppel[65]: in estoppel, it is often only when the claimant seeks to resile from her representation that a change of position

[60] *RBC Dominion Securities Inc v Dawson* (1994) 111 DLR (4th) 230 (Newfoundland Court of Appeal).

[61] *RBC Dominion Securities Inc v Dawson* (1994) 111 DLR (4th) 230 (Newfoundland Court of Appeal) 240.

[62] *Cf Saunders & Co v Hague* [2004] 2 NZLR 475 (New Zealand High Court) 495–96 (Chisholm J) (defendant pleaded hurdles to selling house, not established on the facts).

[63] Explored further immediately below.

[64] Underpinning this assumption is probably a tacit acceptance of reliance as a necessary element of the defence in cases of defendant-instigated change of position. A very broad disenrichment defence in which reliance plays no role may not suffer from this problem.

[65] *Grundt v Great Boulder Pty Gold Mines Ltd* (1937) 59 CLR 641 (High Court of Australia) 674–75, discussed in ch 2, at 48–51.

made by a defendant will operate to her detriment. The same is true of change of position. It is only when the defendant is required to make restitution that it will become clear whether the change of position will operate to his detriment. And the key question in that context is whether the change can be reversed without the defendant thereby suffering prejudice.

Fourthly, the focus of the reversibility requirement on the position of the defendant at the time of the hearing explains why questions of remoteness are irrelevant to the change of position defence. Professor Burrows, adopting a 'dis-enrichment' approach to the defence, argues that it may be necessary to employ notions of remoteness to limit the extent of the defence.[66] But that only appears to be necessary because Burrows is focusing overly on the instant of the original change of position, rather than the reversibility of the change of position at the time the claimant seeks restitution of the benefit. It is at the later date that the court must determine whether the change of position can be reversed without detriment to the defendant. Provided that the change has been caused by the original receipt (the requirements for which are explored in the next section of this chapter), subsequent changes of position that have flowed from the original change must be taken into account.

For this reason, it does not matter that the reason why the defendant's original change of position becomes irreversible is because of some act or event independent of the defendant. For example, in the Australian case of *Corporate Management Services (Australia) Pty Ltd v Abi-Arraj*,[67] the defendant changed his position by embarking on extensions and renovations of the family home in reliance on a compensation award that was subsequently varied. The court found that the work done on the home had since deteriorated and there was no prospect of it being finished. In the circumstances, the court found that the defendant should be fully protected from any order for restitution. Similarly, in *Gertsch v Atsas*,[68] the court accepted that the second defendant had relevantly changed his position by purchasing a luxury car which was uninsured and later stolen. In the hypothetical example given earlier of me depositing the amount of a mistaken payment in my account, that change of position will count if, in the intervening period between deposit and the claim for restitution, the bank unexpectedly fails and the money is lost. In these cases, the change of position has become irreversible by the time of the claim and it is irrelevant that the change became irreversible because of entirely unforeseeable events.

Fifthly, the shift of focus from disenriching to irreversible changes of position makes it clear that changes brought about as a result of a defendant's decision not

[66] Burrows, *The Law of Restitution* 2nd edn, above n 13, at 515; Nolan, above n 26, at 135, 149–51.

[67] *Corporate Management Services (Australia) Pty Ltd v Abi-Arraj* [2000] NSWSC 361 (New South Wales Supreme Court).

[68] *Gertsch v Atsas* [1999] NSWSC 898, (1999) 10 BPR 18 431 (New South Wales Supreme Court).

to act[69] or to forgo a benefit,[70] fall within the scope of the defence, even though they do not entail positive acts of expenditure. Again, this is entirely consistent with the approach taken in estoppel case law.[71] Although these kinds of changes can be incorporated sensibly within the disenrichment approach to the defence, the apparent focus of that approach on the need to identify an outflow of wealth can, and has, caused confusion.[72] No such confusion arises on the irreversibility approach.

Finally, the irreversibility approach to the change of position defence does not lead to the feared breadth of judicial discretion that has been said to so greatly favour adoption of the disenrichment analysis of the defence. On the irreversibility approach, once the defence is made out, the court undertakes a valuation of the (irreversible) changes to the defendant's position and offsets that amount against what would otherwise be the full measure of restitution.[73] In terms of both process and result, therefore, it is often much like the disenrichment approach to the defence, with the difference that the changes to be valued need not be intrinsically financial in nature (and as we have seen, are generally valued as at the date the claimant sought restitution, rather than the time of the initial change of position). It is notable that courts have not shied away from difficult issues of valuation of detriment in other, analogous, areas[74] and do not often seem to find the exercise

[69] *City of Sydney v Burns Philp Trustee Co (In liquidation)* (New South Wales Supreme Court 13 November 1992) (change constituted by council's failure to obtain a private valuation of commercial property); *Gertsch v Atsas* [1999] NSWSC 898, (1999) 10 BPR 18 431 (New South Wales Supreme Court) (changes included the defendant's decision not to exercise her proven earning capacity); *Eastbourne Borough Council v Foster* (QB 20 December 2000) (change included failure to look for work elsewhere, failure to consider suing his legal advisors and failure to bargain for redundancy package), appealed on another point *Eastbourne Borough Council v Foster* [2001] EWCA Civ 1091; *Gilsan (International) Ltd v Optus Networks Pty Ltd* [2004] NSWSC 1077 (New South Wales Supreme Court) [260] (McDougall J) (change included failure to withhold amounts by way of provisions or reserve to protect its position in the event of claim for recovery of overpayments), approved on this point on appeal in *Optus Networks Pty Ltd v Gilsan (International) Ltd* [2006] NSWCA 171 (New South Wales Court of Appeal) [79] (Hodgson JA, Beasley and McColl JJA concurring). The recent example given in *Sempra Metals Limited v Commissioners of Inland Revenue* [2007] UKHL 34, [2008] 1 AC 561 [233] (Lord Mance) of a defendant hiding a mistaken payment under her bed, and thus omitting to invest the money so as to obtain commercial rates of interest for its use, also would constitute a good example of this category of change.

[70] *Kilham v Banque Nationale de Paris* (Victorian Supreme Court 28 June 1995) [50] (giving up of a security); *Palmer v Blue Circle Southern Cement Ltd* [1999] NSWSC 697, (1999) 48 NSWLR 318 (New South Wales Supreme Court) (decision not to apply for social security benefits); *Scottish Equitable Plc v Derby* [2001] EWCA Civ 369, [2001] 3 All ER 818 [32]–[33] (Robert Walker LJ) (giving up a job where there is little chance of re-employment); *Commerzbank AG v Price-Jones* [2003] EWCA Civ 1663, (2003) 147 SJLB 1397 [71]–[72] (Munby J) (decision not to seek employment elsewhere); *Ethnic Earth Pty Ltd v Quoin Technology Pty Ltd (in liq) (No 3)* [2006] SASC 7, (2006) SASR 103 (South Australian Supreme Court) [86] (Bleby J) (giving up opportunities to claim forfeiture of money from claimant); *Kinlan v Crimmin* [2006] EWHC 779, (Ch (Companies Ct)) (decision to give up control of company).

[71] Examined in ch 2, at 50–51.

[72] *National Westminster Bank Plc v Somer International (UK) Ltd* [2001] EWCA Civ 970, [2002] QB 1286 [47] (Potter LJ).

[73] The process is further considered below, at 138–43.

[74] As is often required in proprietary estoppel: ch 2, at 50–51.

problematic in practice. In *Gertsch v Atsas*,[75] for example, the third defendant decided not to exercise her proven earning capacity in favour of becoming a full-time student, in reliance on a distribution from a will. Foster AJ held that this 'radical' change in lifestyle gave rise to a relevant change of position for the purposes of the defence. His Honour measured the extent of the change by reference to the value of the earning potential the third defendant had relinquished as a result of the change.

(d) Proving the Irreversible Change of Position

The previous section established that the defendant must be able to demonstrate both that he has changed his position and that the change is irreversible. Courts have been generous when it comes to the weight of proof required for changes of position that comprise positive expenditure. As the court explained in *RBC Dominion Securities Inc v Dawson*,[76]

> to require that a private individual, who believed she was spending her own money, prove her expenditures as if she were claiming damages in an action for negligence would be most unfair. It was the plaintiff's error that put her in the funds in the first place and led her to believe that the funds were hers to spend without having to account to anyone for her expenditures.

In such circumstances, the court would be 'satisfied with reasonable approximations'.[77]

As we saw in the case of estoppel, when the pleaded change of position comprises a decision to forego an opportunity, courts will require cogent evidence both of the intrinsic value of the lost opportunity and the likelihood that it would have been realised.[78] Proof requires more than a bald assertion by the defendant, particularly since realisation of a lost opportunity may have been dependent on the decisions of third parties.[79] In *Commerzbank Ag v Price-Jones*,[80] the majority of the English Court of Appeal rejected the defendant's pleaded change of position because the fact that, but for his receipt, the defendant 'would have decided to seek similar employment elsewhere [was] not sufficiently significant, precise or substantial in extent to be treated as a change of his position'.[81] While the majority did

[75] *Gertsch v Atsas* [1999] NSWSC 898, (1999) 10 BPR 18 431 (New South Wales Supreme Court).

[76] *RBC Dominion Securities Inc v Dawson* (1994) 111 DLR (4th) 230 (Newfoundland Court of Appeal) 240 (Cameron JA, giving the judgment of the court).

[77] *RBC Dominion Securities Inc v Dawson* (1994) 111 DLR (4th) 230 (Newfoundland Court of Appeal) 240 (Cameron JA, giving the judgment of the court). See also: *Philip Collins Ltd v Davis* [2000] 3 All ER 808 (Ch) 827 (Jonathan Parker J); *Scottish Equitable Plc v Derby* [2001] EWCA Civ 369, [2001] 3 All ER 818 [33] (Robert Walker LJ); *Fea v Roberts* [2005] All ER (D) 69 (Ch) [111]–[12] (Hazel Williamson QC).

[78] Ch 2, at 40.

[79] H Liu, 'Changing the Shape of Change of Position' (2004) 15 *Kings College LJ* 301, 306–10, 312–13.

[80] *Commerzbank AG v Price-Jones* [2003] EWCA Civ 1663, (2003) 147 SJLB 1397.

[81] *Commerzbank AG v Price-Jones* [2003] EWCA Civ 1663, (2003) 147 SJLB 1397 [40] (Mummery LJ).

not elaborate further, there are two likely explanations for the court's rejection of this aspect of the defendant's case. First, it appears that there was little independent evidence before the court as to the likelihood that the defendant would have obtained better employment conditions elsewhere (for example, a better wage, job stability or career prospects).[82] Given its very speculative nature, the value of the alleged lost opportunity was nil. Secondly, had the defendant merely demonstrated a good chance of obtaining 'similar' employment elsewhere, the value of any change would have been nil. Either way, the pleaded change was not demonstrated to be of such a nature that it would be inequitable for the defendant to be required to make restitution in full.

It is not enough that the defendant proves that he changed his position: the change must also be irreversible. We saw in chapters two and three that it is not always easy to determine when a change is sufficiently irreversible for the purposes of the estoppel and payment over defences. The conclusion reached in both chapters was that the change must be readily reversible, in the sense of being able to be reversed without undue time, cost or effort by the defendant. The same question as to the required degree of reversibility arises in respect of the change of position defence.

In many cases, the issue of reversibility will be relatively straightforward and easy for a defendant to prove. For example, in *Palmer v Blue Circle Southern Cement Ltd*[83] the defendant changed his position in reliance on his receipt of a certain level of workers' compensation by deciding not to apply for social security benefits. By the time the claimant's mistake came to light, the defendant was no longer entitled to apply. An example to opposite effect is *Scottish Equitable Plc v Derby.*[84] It will be recalled that Mr Derby received an overpayment through the carelessness of his life assurance company. He used a portion of the payment to purchase a pension from an insurance company. The uncontested evidence was that the insurance company was prepared to 'unwind' the policy and refund the purchase price, with the consequence that the defendant had not irreversibly changed his position.

In other cases, the requirement of irreversibility is more contentious. Where a defendant purchases an asset in reliance on his receipt, courts have generally regarded such a change as reversible (at least in part) because the asset can be sold.[85] The value of any defence will usually be limited to any proven depreciation

[82] Mummery LJ drew a contrast with the situation where a defendant has turned down a firm offer of a better paid job, which may well qualify as a relevant change: *Commerzbank AG v Price-Jones* [2003] EWCA Civ 1663, (2003) 147 SJLB 1397 [39].

[83] *Palmer v Blue Circle Southern Cement Ltd* [1999] NSWSC 697, (1999) 48 NSWLR 318 (New South Wales Supreme Court).

[84] *Scottish Equitable Plc v Derby* [2001] EWCA Civ 369, [2001] 3 All ER 818.

[85] *Lipkin Gorman (a firm) v Karpnale Ltd* [1991] 2 AC 548 (HL) 560 (Lord Templeman); *Credit-Suisse (Monaco) SA v Attar* [2004] EWHC 374 (QB (Comm Ct)) [98], discussed by C Mitchell, 'Change of Position: the developing law' [2005] *Lloyd's Maritime and Commercial L Q* 168, 173; see also: McInnes, above n 21, at 165, 197–98, citing *Sullivan v Lee* (1994) 95 BCLR (2d) 195 (British Columbia Supreme Court); *Empire Life Insurance Co v Neufeld Estate* (1998) 4 CCLI (3d) 278 (British Columbia Supreme Court). McInnes cites *RBC Dominion Securities Inc v Dawson* (1994) 111 DLR (4th) 230 (Newfoundland Court of Appeal) as authority to the contrary.

of the asset.[86] It has not been fatal to the question of reversibility that there may be some costs and time consumed in the process of reversing the change, as may be the case, for example, in the sale of land.[87] The same approach can be seen in cases where a defendant has discharged a debt in reliance on his receipt. In general, courts will assume that a lender will be able to be found on similar terms as previously existed, so as to return the defendant to his position of former indebtedness.[88] Cogent evidence will need to be brought that no willing lender now exists.[89] Even where a lender does not exist, there will usually need to be some other changes of position consequent on discharging the debt in order for the defence to succeed, given that the effect of the court's order will be to impose a judgment debt in favour of the claimant where formerly there was a debt in the same amount, but to another party. It must be recalled in this context that lying behind the reversibility requirement is the overall aim to restore the parties to the *status quo ante*: where that prior status involved debt, return to that state of relative indebtness involves relatively little hardship to the defendant.[90]

In general, the change of position cases that consider the reversibility issue appear more flexible than their counterparts in estoppel and payment over where, as we saw, courts were reluctant to require a defendant to reverse a change made in reliance on his receipt unless that reversal could be readily effected without undue cost, time or effort on the part of the defendant. As has been emphasised previously, there is a strong argument for consistency between the change of position defence and related areas such as estoppel and payment over. Any deviation must be clearly justified. However, the comparative willingness of courts to require changes made in reliance on a receipt to be reversed for the purpose of the change of position defence may be justified as reflecting a greater familiarity with, and welcome acceptance of the possibility of ordering fine monetary adjustments between the parties as part of the process of undoing the impugned transaction or

[86] *Lipkin Gorman v Karpnale Ltd* [1991] 2 AC 548 (HL) at 560 (Lord Templeman). *Cf Sullivan v Lee* (1994) 95 BCLR (2d) 195 (British Columbia Supreme Court), where the court ordered the defendant to convey to the claimant the motor home and electrical goods purchased as a result of her receipt.

[87] *Campden Hill v Chakrani* [2005] EWHC 911 (Ch) [87] (Hart J).

[88] *Boscawen v Bajwa* [1996] 1 WLR 328 (CA) 341 (Millett LJ); *Pearce v Lloyds TSB Bank Plc* [2001] EWCA Civ 1907; *National Bank of Egypt International Limited v Oman Housing Bank SAOC* [2002] EWHC 1760 (QB (Comm Ct)); *Hartigan v International Society for Krishna Consciousness Incorporated* [2002] NSWSC 810 (New South Wales Supreme Court) [98] (Bryson J). By the same process of reasoning, it should be difficult for the Revenue to prove an irreversible change of position, as its expenditure of received revenue should be recoverable through imposition of new (and valid) taxes: cf *Test Claimants in the FII Litigation v Revenue and Customs Commissioner* [2008] EWHC 2893 (Ch) discussed in ch 6, at 168–70, 187 and ch 7, at 203–04.

[89] As in *Gertsch v Atsas* [1999] NSWSC 898, (1999) 10 BPR 18 431 (New South Wales Supreme Court) [88], [95] (Foster AJ).

[90] *Hartigan v International Society for Krishna Consciousness Incorporated* [2002] NSWSC 810 (New South Wales Supreme Court) [98] (Bryson J). Depending on the circumstances, it may be necessary to make orders scheduling the time for repayment, to ensure that the defendant has sufficient time to make alternative arrangements, as in *Gertsch v Atsas* [1999] NSWSC 898, (1999) 10 BPR 18 431 (New South Wales Supreme Court).

making restitution on terms.[91] For example, a defendant who is required to sell land or obtain a mortgage to replace one that has been discharged, should be entitled to retain an amount to offset the costs of the exercise (ie reversing the change of position), so that he is not left in a worse position as a result of the requirement to make restitution. In those cases where the costs equal or outweigh the value of the benefit received, and the other elements of the defence are satisfied, the defendant should be afforded a complete defence.

This same flexibility in approach should theoretically apply where the defendant can show that there are not merely costs, but other significant difficulties in reversing a pleaded change of position. For example, the defence may apply where the market for an asset purchased by way of change of position is negligible, or extensive modifications have been made to the asset which render it less likely to be sold, or where there are other, consequential difficulties in returning the defendant to his former position.[92] In theory, a value can be placed on those difficulties (the extent to which the asset resists reversing), that amount being offset against the primary claim to restitution. Where the difficulties are insurmountable, as where the market for the asset has disappeared since its purchase and is unlikely to return within a reasonable period of time, the most likely result is that the defence will operate completely.

Even with such a flexible approach, cases where the defendant may be able to reverse his change of position through litigation remain particularly contentious.[93] Suppose a defendant pleads that he has changed his position by making a gift to a third party. If a court is to undertake a full evaluation of the reversibility of the gift, a number of questions must be answered. Does an action lie against the third party? What is the likelihood that the third party will refuse to return the benefit (in whole or in part)? What are the chances of success in any disputed action? Will that third party, in turn, be able to rely on a change of position defence? What will be the costs of pursuing that third party?

We saw in chapters two and three that in the areas of estoppel and payment over, courts clearly considered that a change that could only be reversed through litigation constituted a detrimental change of position, to the full extent of the pleaded change.[94] They did not engage in questions as to the likelihood of success and costs of pursuing such claims. In support of applying this generous approach in the change of position context is Lord Goff's speech in *Lipkin Gorman v Karpnale*.[95] In that case, Lord Goff instanced a gift to a charity as being a leading example of the kind of change of position that would give rise to the change of

[91] As in *Gertsch v Atsas* [1999] NSWSC 898, (1999) 10 BPR 18 431 (New South Wales Supreme Court), discussed by Mitchell, above n 85, at 172–73. In theory, of course, this flexibility should be capable of feeding back into those areas, as has arguably happened in rescission: ch 4, at 104–07.

[92] Mitchell, *ibid*, at 168. *Cf Saunders & Co v Hague* [2004] 2 NZLR 475 (New Zealand High Court) (hurdles to sale of house pleaded as part of change of position, not established on the facts).

[93] *Cf* Nolan, who regards the problem simply as one requiring a choice between legal versus factual (dis)enrichment: Nolan, above n 26, at 170–72.

[94] Ch 2, at 52–53; ch 3, at 74–75.

[95] *Lipkin Gorman (a firm) v Karpnale Ltd* [1991] 2 AC 548 (HL) 580.

position defence. From this it could be inferred that although the defendant may have a claim against the charity, that possibility was irrelevant to characterisation of the gift as an operative change of position.

However, as we saw at the start of this chapter, Lord Goff was not purporting to provide a complete guide to the circumstances in which the defence would and would not be available. So it is possible that his Lordship was not precluding the view that the change had to be irreversible to count for the purposes of the change of position defence. Further, since *Lipkin Gorman*, there has developed a clear line of authority in the change of position case law that a defendant who has changed his position by making payment to a taxing authority should be required to bring evidence that the payments cannot be recovered from the taxing authority.[96]

So, as a matter of precedent, it is not clear whether a change of position will count for the purpose of the defence where it is potentially reversible through litigation. The change of position case law generally suggests that a defendant will not discharge his burden of proving an irreversible change of position except by demonstrating the existence of significant practical or legal hurdles to recovery,[97] but does not unequivocally indicate how high the bar must be set. However, as a matter of policy, acceptance of a reversibility requirement clearly does not entail that a defendant proves that he has already fully exhausted any claims he may have against a third party in order for his change of position defence to succeed. Nor does it require that the defendant proves on the balance of probabilities that he is unlikely to be able to recover the amount of the payment from a third party through court proceedings. This is because, unless the third party is joined in the proceedings, with resultant escalation in costs and court time, courts are extremely badly equipped to evaluate the risks and likelihood of success in litigation involving third parties. Further, litigation is a notoriously uncertain, expensive and time-consuming process. There is a real issue as to how much time, effort and expense an innocent defendant should be required to invest in attempting to reverse (or investigate the reversibility of) a change made in reliance on his receipt. In that context, it is arguable that proof by the defendant that any claim will be contested will be enough to show a sufficient hurdle to recovery to satisfy the requirements of the defence.

Although this approach is generally consistent with the estoppel and payment over case law, it might be argued that it is too generous to the defendant and is in stark contrast with the relatively demanding approach taken by the courts in cases

[96] *Hillsdown Holdings Plc v Pensions Ombudsman* [1997] 1 All ER 862 (QB) 904 (Knox J); *Hinckley and Bosworth BC v Shaw* (1999) 1 LGLR 385 (QB); *K & S Corp Ltd v Sportingbet Australia Pty Ltd* [2003] SASC 96, (2003) 86 SASR 313 (South Australian Supreme Court); *Fazzolari v Couchouron* [2003] VCAT 503, (2003) V Conv R 58-572 (Victorian Civil and Administrative Tribunal). *Cf Lokan v Defence Force Retirement and Death Benefits Authority* [2007] AATA 1652 (Administrative Appeals Tribunal of Australia) [14]–[15] (Deputy President PE Hack SC).

[97] See in particular: *Alpha Wealth Financial Services Pty Ltd v Frankland River Olive Company Ltd* [2008] WASCA 119 (Western Australia Supreme Court of Appeal) [202], considered above, at 131. Also: *Fitzsimons v Minister for Liquor Gaming and Racing for the State of New South Wales* [2008] NSWSC 782 (New South Wales Supreme Court) [128]–[29] (McDougall J).

of reversing changes of position involving sales of assets. However, unlike the case of sale of an asset, the reversibility of the impugned enrichment in the case of litigation is in large measure out of the hands of the defendant. In those circumstances, and assuming the defendant changed his position in reliance on his receipt, there is no reason to burden the defendant with pursuing a course of action which may or may not prove to be successful and will undoubtedly come at considerable cost to the defendant, both financial and personal.

This approach to litigation still requires that the defendant must bring some evidence before the court that a demand for return of the mistaken payment has been made and refused, or that the third party has indicated that in the event the defendant is required to make restitution, the third party will resist any attempt to recover the value of that amount from the third party. It also invites some sensitivity to context. Where, for example, the third party is a government department with a simple internal administrative recovery procedure for mistaken payment claims, the defendant may be expected to furnish some evidence that this normal procedure is not going to proceed before the change of position defence can succeed.[98] On the other hand, where the third party is a charity, submission of a statement by the charity that it has applied the funds to its charitable purposes, or will resist any attempt to recover the funds from it, should be enough to satisfy the irreversibility requirement. This approach should not be unduly time-consuming or costly to the defendant and is already used in practice elsewhere in the law.[99]

(2) Causation

(a) Introduction

One of the most significant controversies surrounding the change of position defence has been whether the defendant must be shown to have relied on his receipt (the 'narrow' version) or whether it is sufficient to demonstrate that the defendant's change of position was caused by his receipt, usually in a 'but for' sense (the 'broad' version). This was described in chapter one as the 'reliance' issue. A key example of where the reliance issue is said to matter is where the change of position arises through a supervening act or event independent of the defendant, such as where the benefit received by the defendant is immediately stolen or destroyed by a third party before the defendant has had the opportunity to act in reliance on his receipt. While the change will count for the purpose of the broad version of the defence, it generally will not count for the purposes of the narrow version because the change was not made by the defendant in reliance on his receipt. This statement is subject to the important caveat, raised in the

[98] An approach implicit in the taxation cases: above, at 131.

[99] Notably in estoppel: *Deutsche Bank (London Agency) v Beriro and Co Ltd* [1895–99] All ER Rep 1164 (CA), discussed in ch 2, at 52–53. The practice has also been seen in cases involving unauthorised distributions from trust estates: *Attorney General for New South Wales v Fulham* [2002] NSWSC 629 (New South Wales Supreme Court).

preceding part of this chapter, that where a defendant has changed his position in reliance on his receipt it does not matter that the change becomes irreversible through a supervening act.[100]

Although there has been considerable judicial[101] and academic[102] support for the broad version of the defence, it remains true that in the vast majority of cases, both in England[103] and Australia,[104] the test that has been applied is whether the defendant relied on his receipt. In general, the underlying assumption evidenced by both courts and commentators engaged in this debate has been that one approach must be adopted to the exclusion of the other.[105]

In contrast, this section argues that both approaches have a role to play within the one change of position defence, once the causal role of reliance is properly under-

[100] As in *Gertsch v Atsas* [1999] NSWSC 898, (1999) 10 BPR 18 431 (New South Wales Supreme Court) and *Corporate Management Services (Australia) Pty Ltd v Abi-Arraj* [2000] NSWSC 361 (New South Wales Supreme Court), discussed above, at 136.

[101] *Lipkin Gorman (a firm) v Karpnale Ltd* [1991] 2 AC 548 (HL) 580–81 (Lord Goff); *Dextra Bank and Trust Co Ltd v Bank of Jamaica* [2002] 1 All ER (Comm) 193 (PC); *Scottish Equitable Plc v Derby* [2001] EWCA Civ 369, [2001] 3 All ER 818 [30] (Robert Walker LJ); *Commerzbank AG v Price-Jones* [2003] EWCA Civ 1663, (2003) 147 SJLB 1397 [53] (Munby J); *Test Claimants in the FII Group Ligitation v Revenue and Customs Commissioners* [2008] EWHC 2893 (Ch) [235], [343] (Henderson J).

[102] P Key, 'Change of Position' (1995) 58 *Modern L R* 505, 513; Nolan, above n 26, at 145–47; Burrows, *The Law of Restitution* 2nd edn, above n 13, at 512–17; Mitchell, above n 85, at 179–80.

[103] *Streiner v Bank Leumi (UK) Plc* (QB 31 October 1985); *Euroactividade AG v Moeller* (CA 1 February 1995); *Eastbourne Borough Council v Foster* (QB 20 December 2000) appealed on another point in *Eastbourne Borough Council v Foster* [2001] EWCA Civ 1091; *National Bank of Egypt International Limited v Oman Housing Bank SAOC* [2002] EWHC 1760 (QB (Comm Ct)) [29] (Steele J); *Rose v AIB Group (UK) plc* [2003] EWHC 1737 (Ch (Companies Ct)), [2003] 1 WLR 2791 [55] (Nicholas Warren QC); *Cressman v Coys of Kensington (Sales) Ltd* [2004] EWCA Civ 47, [2004] 1 WLR 2775 [41] (Mance LJ, Thorpe and Wilson LJJ concurring); *Credit-Suisse (Monaco) SA v Attar* [2004] EWHC 374 (QB (Comm Ct)) [98] (Gross J); *Day v Day* [2005] EWHC 1455 (Ch) [49] (L Henderson QC); *Fea v Roberts* [2005] All ER (D) 69 (Ch) [85]–[112] (Hazel Williamson QC); *Kinlan v Crimmin* [2006] EWHC 779, (Ch (Companies Ct)) [60] (Mr Philip Sales).

[104] The requirement has been described interchangeably as 'reliance', or acting 'on the faith of' the receipt: *David Securities Pty Ltd v Commonwealth Bank of Australia* (1992) 127 CLR 353 (High Court of Australia) 385–86 (Mason CJ, Deane, Toohey, Gaudron and McHugh JJ); *State Bank of New South Wales Ltd v Swiss Bank Corporation* (1995) 39 NSWLR 350 (New South Wales Court of Appeal) 356 (the court); *Mercedes-Benz (NSW) Pty Ltd v National Mutual Royal Savings Bank Limited* (New South Wales Court of Appeal 15 April 1996) [17]–[18] (Sheller JA, Clarke and Priestly JJA concurring); *Gertsch v Atsas* [1999] NSWSC 898, (1999) 10 BPR 18 431 (New South Wales Supreme Court) [60] (Foster AJ); *Rogers v Kabriel* [1999] NSWSC 368 (New South Wales Supreme Court) [67] (Young J); *Corporate Management Services (Australia) Pty Ltd v Abi-Arraj* [2000] NSWSC 361 (New South Wales Supreme Court) [13]–[21] (James J); *Sanwa Australia Finance Ltd v Finchill Pty Ltd* [2001] NSWCA 466 (New South Wales Court of Appeal) [26]–[30] (Davies AJA, Beazley and Heydon JJA concurring); *Port of Brisbane Corp v ANZ Securities* [2002] QCA 158, [2003] 2 Qd R 661 (Queensland Court of Appeal) [13] (McPherson JA, Davies JA and Mullins J concurring); *Goodman v Product Action Inc* [2003] SAIRC 5 (South Australian Industrial Relations Commission) [30] (Industrial Magistrate Ardle); *Ethnic Earth Pty Ltd v Quoin Technology Pty Ltd (in liq) (No 3)* [2006] SASC 7, 94 SASR 103 (South Australian Supreme Court) [85] (Bleby J); *Lokan v Defence Force Retirement and Death Benefits Authority* [2007] AATA 1652 (Administrative Appeals Tribunal of Australia) [16] (Deputy President PE Hack SC); *Alpha Wealth Financial Services Pty Ltd v Frankland River Olive Company Ltd* [2008] WASCA 119 (Western Australia Supreme Court of Appeal) [20]–[21] (Pullin JA) [202] (Buss JA, Steytler P concurring).

[105] Although see *Rose v AIB Group (UK) plc* [2003] EWHC 1737 (Ch (Companies Ct)), [2003] 1 WLR 2791 [49] (Nicholas Warren QC); *Commerzbank AG v Price-Jones* [2003] EWCA Civ 1663, (2003) 147 SJLB 1397 [53] (Munby J) and Virgo, *The Principles of the Law of Restitution* 2 edn, above n 18, at 693–703.

stood. An examination of the causation requirement in the context of the different classes of change of position to which it must apply explains the existing case law, brings the change of position defence into line with the approaches to causation reflected in the rescission case law, as well as of estoppel and payment over and provides a principled basis for choosing between the different approaches to the defence.

(b) But-for Causation in Cases of Independent Changes of Position

In chapters two and four, a distinction was drawn between independent changes of position, in which the precise benefit received from the claimant independently devalues or is destroyed or lost by an act or event independent of the defendant, and defendant-instigated changes of position, where the change is brought about as a result of the defendant's decision to act or forebear to act. We saw in chapter four that the rescission case law strongly suggested that in the case of independent changes of position reliance should not be a prerequisite in order for a change of position defence to apply. Chapter two suggested a reason for that approach: where a change occurs independently to a received benefit, there is no difficulty in applying a but-for test of causation.[106] By definition, the original receipt of the benefit in those cases must be a relevant cause of the subsequent change of position. Therefore, if a received benefit is destroyed by fire, or stolen by a thief, the change of position defence should apply: but for the receipt of the benefit, it would not have been destroyed or stolen. This can be contrasted with defendant-instigated changes of position where the applicable causal concept is reliance and where it can be problematic and arguably inappropriate to apply a 'but for' test of causation because of the particular difficulties of overdetermination, endemic forensic uncertainty and indeterminacy that characterise many cases of decision-making.

There are supporting considerations from other areas of the law for applying the defence to independent changes of position. In particular, it is well-settled that the law does not force people to accept gifts of money or chattels. The recipient of such a gift is entitled to disclaim it within a reasonable time of becoming aware of the gift.[107] It follows that where a defendant has done nothing at all following receipt of a benefit, or was not even aware of his receipt and the benefit has since been stolen or destroyed, he should still be in a position retrospectively to disclaim the benefit.[108]

On the other hand, this approach does seem to introduce an inconsistency in the policy approach to allocation of risk following receipt, in cases where a

[106] Ch 2, at 42; see also Virgo, *ibid*, at 695.

[107] On disclaimer generally, see N Crago, 'Principles of Disclaimer of Gifts' (1999) 28 *U Western Australia L Rev* 65.

[108] *National Commercial Banking Corporation of Australia v Batty* (1986) 160 CLR 251 (High Court of Australia), followed in *Micro Minerals Pty Ltd v Grossberg* [1998] FCA 1795 (Federal Court of Australia) and applied as a defence in *Custom Coaches (Sales) Pty Ltd v Frankish* [2002] NSWSC 795 (New South Wales Supreme Court), discussed in Edelman and Bant, above n 21, at 104, 327.

benefit received by a defendant has independently increased in value, as opposed to decreased in value. In general, benefits for the purposes of a primary personal claim in unjust enrichment are valued as at the date of receipt.[109] The consequence is that a claimant can only obtain restitution of the independently increased value of a received benefit if she brings a claim *in rem*.[110] This means that so far as personal claims are concerned, the defendant enjoys the benefit of any independent increase in the value of the received benefit. On the approach suggested in this book, the defendant does not, however, bear the converse risk of any independent decrease in the value of the asset. This difference in treatment may seem unfair. However, the reason for it lies in the distinction drawn earlier between the change of position defence and the concept of enrichment adopted for the purpose of the primary claim in unjust enrichment. If (as this book says) the change of position defence is not concerned with rebutting the element of enrichment, there is no obvious reason why it should be concerned with, or mirror, increases in the value of a received benefit. If it is rather concerned with protecting the defendant from detriment arising from irreversible changes of position, then issues of who should profit from increases in the value of the benefit are irrelevant.

Finally, it has been argued that a policy reason in favour of allowing a defendant to bear the risk of the independent loss or destruction of the received benefit is that the defendant is in possession or control of the asset and thus is in the best position to guard against its loss or destruction.[111] However, as Nolan has observed, were the defence to be excluded in cases of independent changes of position, the defendant would be made not only to bear the risk of independent loss or destruction, but the risk of a claim in restitution for recovery of the lost or destroyed asset.[112] Absent some other factor, such as the defendant's fault,[113] there remains no obvious reason of principle or policy for excluding independent changes of position from the change of position defence.

(c) Good Faith in Cases of Independent Changes of Position

The previous section demonstrated that a defendant will be able to rely on the change of position defence in cases of independent changes of position, where his receipt was a 'but for' cause of his change of position. It will be recalled that the

[109] Any other position would run directly into conflict with the separate existence of the change of position defence. On timing of valuation, see: *Cressman v Coys of Kensington (Sales) Ltd* [2004] EWCA Civ 47, [2004] 1 WLR 2775; *Dowell v Custombuilt Homes Pty Ltd* [2004] WASCA 171 (Western Australia Supreme Court of Appeal) [98] (Murray J).

[110] The position is different where a defendant has instigated a change of position, such as by purchasing shares that rise in value and then subsequently selling those shares for the increased price: there, the relevant 'receipt' is the second substituted asset, that is the proceeds of the sale: Edelman and Bant, above n 21, at 120–21, discussing *Trustee of the Property of FC Jones & Sons v Jones* [1997] Ch 159 (CA) 168 (Millett LJ).

[111] Edelman and Bant, *ibid*, at 326–27.

[112] Nolan, above n 26, at 150–51.

[113] Considered in ch 6.

broad version of the change of position defence posited by commentators requires only a good faith change of position on the part of the defendant that was caused by his receipt in a 'but for' sense. This raises the question whether, in order to rely on the defence in cases of independent changes of position, the defendant must additionally demonstrate 'good faith'.

In principle, it is difficult to see why dishonesty on the part of the defendant in receiving a benefit should be relevant to the defence in cases of independent changes of position, where the change suffered by the defendant has come about independently of that dishonesty. Where the defendant's dishonesty was irrelevant to what happened subsequent to his receipt then, provided it does not support an independent bar to relief,[114] it should be irrelevant to establishing the prima facie defence.

A separate question is whether the dishonesty of the defendant may become relevant because of how the defendant treats the received benefit. Suppose a claimant mistakenly delivers a valuable painting to the defendant's front door. The defendant realises that there must be a mistake. He leaves the painting on the front porch where it is stolen by thieves. Assuming the defendant is enriched by his receipt,[115] the question arises whether the defendant's conduct in leaving the enrichment exposed in this way should deprive him of the defence. Although initially this looks like a question of good faith, it is submitted that it is better analysed as a case where the defendant's carelessness subsequent to his receipt should be relevant as a bar to his defence and is addressed in that context in chapter six.[116]

(d) Reliance in Cases of Defendant-instigated Changes of Position

We saw in chapters two and three that reliance plays an important causal role in both estoppel and payment over.[117] It can, and arguably must play the same role in the change of position defence in cases of defendant-instigated changes of position. In this context, the causal links that must be established are between the fact of receipt of the benefit, the assumption induced by that receipt and the defendant's decision to change his position. As with estoppel, there is significant difficulty in determining the extent to which a defendant's change of position has been caused by his receipt. Where the change comes about as a result of the defendant's act or omission, the same problems of overdetermination, forensic uncertainty and indeterminacy in human decision-making that were discussed in the estoppel context again makes the 'but for' or 'NESS' tests of causation

[114] The defendant's fault as a bar to the defence is addressed in ch 6.

[115] Not an easy task. As he may have done nothing to 'accept' the benefit, he is not precluded from disclaiming it. Provided acceptance is established, enrichment may be identified where the painting is a 'readily returnable benefit': *Cressman v Coys of Kensington (Sales) Ltd* [2004] EWCA Civ 47, [2004] 1 WLR 2775.

[116] At 187–91.

[117] Ch 2, commencing at 28 and ch 3, at 75–76.

generally inappropriate. In contrast, the concept of reliance, employing the 'a factor' test at each stage of the enquiry, offers a useful causal test between receipt and the defendant's change of position.

This analysis demonstrates that the debate about adopting 'broad' and 'narrow' versions of the defence is founded on a false dichotomy. Both versions contain the need for the defendant's change of position to be caused by his receipt. There is thus no great division between them. It is just that that in cases of defendant-instigated changes of position, reliance is the relevant causal concept. And in that decision-making context, the frequency with which problems of overdetermination, endemic forensic uncertainty and indeterminacy arise favours adoption of an 'a factor' test over the usual 'but for' test of causation. In contrast, we have seen that there is no great difficulty with applying a 'but for' test of causation in the case of independent changes of position.

What precisely is the required mental state for reliance in the context of the change of position defence? The receipt must have caused the defendant to make an assumption as to the basis or terms of his receipt, and that assumption must inform his decision to act. This suggests that (again, as with reliance in estoppel) a reliance requirement incorporates or subsumes a requirement of good faith.[118] Certainly, there is no such thing as bad faith reliance in this context. A defendant who receives a benefit knowing that it is paid pursuant to a mistake, for example, and then changes his position in the hope that the claimant will not become aware of the mistake, does not act in reliance on his receipt in the relevant sense. On the other hand, we also saw from estoppel that it is possible for a defendant to act in honest reliance on (in the case of estoppel) a representation, even though he harbours doubts about its truth. This might be because he trusts the representor's judgment more than his own, or because he has independently checked the veracity of the representation, or for other reasons. The question then becomes whether that reliance is reasonable. Likewise, there may be cases where a defendant genuinely acts in reliance on his receipt for the purposes of the change of position defence, yet has some lingering doubts over the basis of his receipt, or knows that there are some risks associated with acting in reliance on his receipt. Here too, the question becomes whether the defendant's reliance is reasonable. We return to the question of reasonableness below.[119]

Returning to reliance simpliciter, the preceding discussion suggests it will usually be difficult for a defendant to demonstrate that he relied on his receipt where he had knowledge of the operative unjust factor affecting the claimant's decision to transfer. However, exceptionally, a defendant will have relied on his receipt notwithstanding that he understood his receipt was insecure. This is possible where the defendant intended to act, and did act, consistently with the known (or understood) basis of his receipt. Suppose, for example, a defendant receives a large amount of money knowing that it was conferred pursuant to a mistake. Suppose

[118] Ch 2, at 28–30, 45.

[119] At 151.

further that consistent with that knowledge, the defendant places the money with a financial institution for safekeeping pending its return to the claimant (who is currently refusing to be repaid).[120] If the institution then fails before the defendant can return the benefit, the change of position defence should still apply. The defendant intended to act, and did act, consistently with the known basis of his receipt and thus relied on it. The same analysis applies where a defendant receives a benefit that he understands to be payable to a third party and acts in accordance with that understanding.[121] Provided that the defendant's decision to act is consistent with and follows the known or understood basis of his receipt, he has acted in reliance on it.

The discussion to date concerns the principled role of reliance as a causal concept. Reliance may have a further role, beyond this causal function. As chapter two noted, reliance is also normatively significant: it signals that the autonomous decision-making of the defendant has been affected by (in the case of the change of position defence) the receipt of the benefit.[122] In itself, this provides a good reason for protecting changes brought about as a result of that decision-making process.[123]

In addition to these considerations of principle and policy that favour adoption of a reliance element in cases of defendant-instigated changes of position, the balance of precedent clearly favours a reliance version of the defence.[124] This is not surprising given that the vast majority of them involve defendant-instigated changes of position.[125] Indeed, recent English Court of Appeal decisions that purport to apply the broad version of the change of position defence, on closer analysis apply a narrow, reliance model.[126] In *Commerzbank AG v Price-Jones*,[127] for example, a defendant investment banker changed his position by remaining in his current employment and not seeking out alternative employment in reliance on his mistaken understanding of the contents of a letter sent to him by his employer bank. His mistaken expectation was subsequently fulfilled when the

[120] *Cf National Bank of New Zealand Ltd v Waitaki International Processing (NI) Ltd* [1992] 2 NZLR 211 (New Zealand Court of Appeal). In that case, the statutory defence required that the defendant had relied on the *validity* of the payment, so reliance was not made out. Further, the defendant was regarded as at fault in his choice of investment: see further in ch 6, at 188–91 and ch 10, at 251–52, 253–54.

[121] As in *Thomas v Houston Corbett* [1969] NZLR 151 (New Zealand Court of Appeal); *State Bank of New South Wales Ltd v Swiss Bank Corporation* (1995) 39 NSWLR 350 (New South Wales Court of Appeal); *Dextra Bank and Trust Co Ltd v Bank of Jamaica* [2002] 1 All ER (Comm) 193 (PC); *Orix Australia Corp Ltd v M Wright Hotel Refrigeration Pty Ltd* (2000) 155 FLR 267 (South Australian Supreme Court).

[122] At 40–41.

[123] Concern to protect the defendant's autonomy is one of the prime rationales suggested for the defence: see further ch 8, at 212–14.

[124] Above n 103 and n 104.

[125] The fault lies in assuming that reliance must thus also be required in cases of independent changes of position, as in *Streiner v Bank Leumi (UK) Plc* (QB 31 October 1985); *Euroactividade AG v Moeller* (CA 1 February 1995), discussed by Mitchell, above n 85, at 178–79.

[126] See also: *Niru Battery Manufacturing Co v Milestone Trading Ltd* [2003] EWCA Civ 1446, [2004] QB 985 discussed below, at 153–54.

[127] *Commerzbank AG v Price-Jones* [2003] EWCA Civ 1663, (2003) 147 SJLB 1397.

bank, pursuant to an independent mistake, paid him an amount that corresponded with that expectation.[128]

Mummery LJ (with whom Sedley LJ agreed) noted that there must be a sufficient causal link between the defendant's change of position and the actual payment received by him. His Lordship found the defendant's assumption that he was entitled to the amount of the mistaken payment, and his decision to stay at the bank on that basis, was not relevantly caused by the payment (or promise to pay).[129] Put into the language of reliance, the bank's payment (or promise to pay) played no part in the defendant's decision to change his position. Munby J agreed, citing[130] with approval (as did Mummery LJ before him) the statement of Jonathan Parker J in *Philip Collins Ltd v Davis* that the 'change of position . . . must, on the evidence, be referable in some way to the payment of the money'.[131] On the facts, the defendant acted on the basis of his mistaken belief to which the bank had in no way contributed. It followed that the change of position defence could not succeed. Although Munby J declared himself to be applying the broad version of the defence,[132] it is clear that both judges were applying a concept of reliance.

This decision can nonetheless be criticised for having applied an overly narrow concept of reliance that is not tailored to the characteristics of the change of position defence. There is no doubt that the causal question was complicated by the fact that the case involved an anticipatory change of position. Perhaps reflecting this, the court at times appeared to consider that the causal question was whether the bank's letter (ie its representation) had caused the defendant's mistaken assumption, an enquiry which echoes the causal question in estoppel. However, in the context of change of position, the causal question is slightly different: has the defendant acted in reliance on his receipt? Of course, a reasonable defendant can be expected to construe the basis on which a payment is received from the circumstances of the payment. If the defendant then acts on that assumed basis, he has relied on his receipt. Any representations (explicit or implicit) made by the claimant will often play a role in informing the defendant's assumption as to the basis of his receipt. But, unlike estoppel, the change of position defence does not require the defendant to prove that the claimant was responsible for the defendant's assumption as to the basis of his receipt. Subject to one caveat, to which we return below, it is only necessary to show that the defendant relied on his receipt of the benefit. The required link with the claimant is that the benefit was received at the claimant's expense and that, by definition, has already been satisfied in establishing the primary claim.

That it is unnecessary for the purposes of the change of position defence to show that the claimant must have induced the defendant's assumption is clear from the

[128] The peculiar case of anticipatory changes of position is considered further below, at 155–57.
[129] *Commerzbank AG v Price-Jones* [2003] EWCA Civ 1663, (2003) 147 SJLB 1397 [43]–[44].
[130] *Commerzbank AG v Price-Jones* [2003] EWCA Civ 1663, (2003) 147 SJLB 1397 [58]–[59].
[131] *Philip Collins Ltd v Davis* [2000] 3 All ER 808 (Ch) 827.
[132] *Commerzbank AG v Price-Jones* [2003] EWCA Civ 1663, (2003) 147 SJLB 1397 [54].

significant number of change of position cases from a variety of common law jurisdictions where the defendant's assumption as to the basis of his receipt was formed as a result of the fraud of a third party.[133] In accepting that a change of position defence applies in such cases, courts have accepted that it does not matter that the chief source of the defendant's mistaken assumption as to the basis of his receipt derived from a third party, not the claimant. Subject to one important caveat, it follows that it should prove no bar to the defence that the main source of the defendant's assumption lay in his own error.

(e) Reliance must be Reasonable

The caveat is that, as with estoppel and payment over, it is arguable that the defendant's reliance on his receipt must be reasonable.[134] More precisely, there must be a reasonable basis for the defendant's adoption of a particular assumption as to the basis of his receipt and further, that assumption must be one on which a reasonable defendant would rely.

As with estoppel and payment over, the reason for adopting the requirement of reasonable reliance is one of policy: namely, to restrict the protection granted to the defendant in cases of defendant-instigated changes of position to cases where he has acted in reasonable reliance on his receipt. As Birks noted, there is no very strong case for protecting defendants who fail to take reasonable precautions to protect themselves, such as by making enquiries as to the nature of a received payment.[135] Further, a reasonable reliance requirement encourages parties to take steps to avoid the costs of mistakes.[136] However, as Birks went on to say, the standard of enquiry set by a reasonable person may not be very exacting and should be applied carefully in the context of commercial practice. This echoes the same concerns discussed in the context of both estoppel[137] and the payment over defence.[138] In particular, the applicable standard of care must be assessed having regard to the defendant's subjective characteristics. The same standard of care will not apply to a personal defendant of little education and financial experience as applies with respect to a major financial institution. Further, the realistic opportunities for a defendant to check the provenance of his receipt must be viewed against, for example, the exigencies of his legitimate business and

[133] *Thomas v Houston Corbett* [1969] NZLR 151 (New Zealand Court of Appeal); *Lipkin Gorman (a firm) v Karpnale Ltd* [1991] 2 AC 548 (HL); *State Bank of New South Wales Ltd v Swiss Bank Corporation* (1995) 39 NSWLR 350 (New South Wales Court of Appeal) (defence refused on another ground, see below, at 152–53); *Dextra Bank and Trust Co Ltd v Bank of Jamaica* [2002] 1 All ER (Comm) 193 (PC); *Orix Australia Corp Ltd v M Wright Hotel Refrigeration Pty Ltd* (2000) 155 FLR 267 (South Australian Supreme Court).

[134] Ch 2, at 43–47; ch 3, at 76–78.

[135] P Birks, 'Overview: Tracing, Claiming and Defences' in P Birks (ed), above n 24, at 325.

[136] See also: ch 6, at 78–79. On the economic arguments, see J Beatson and W Bishop, 'Mistaken Payments in the Law of Restitution' (1986) 30 *U Toronto L J* 149 and H Dagan, above n 38, at 46–60.

[137] At 45.

[138] At 77–78.

the consequences of making exhaustive enquiries to his ability to operate in a commercially practical way.[139] In this way, Birks' warning only serves to highlight the familiarity of the wider law with the task of assessing the reasonableness of a party's conduct and the relevance of that concept in determining the scope of legal liability.[140]

The requirement that a defendant's reliance must be reasonable in order for the change of position defence to apply has been accepted in a number of jurisdictions.[141] In the Australian case of *Orix Australia Corp Ltd v M Wright Hotel Refrigeration Pty Ltd*,[142] the defendant received a cheque from the claimant. The circumstances surrounding the payment of the cheque, together with the acts of a fraudulent third party, induced the defendant to believe that the funds had been advanced by the claimant to finance the purchase of equipment for the third party. As the defendant could no longer supply the equipment, the defendant paid the sum to the third party. The defence of change of position succeeded, the court noting that the defendant's belief was 'not unreasonable'[143] in the circumstances of the case.

In contrast, in *State Bank of New South Wales Ltd v Swiss Bank Corporation*,[144] the defence failed because the defendant had not acted consistently with the terms on which it received the payment.[145] There, the claimant bank paid $20m to the defendant bank to be credited to a customer's account, but failed to indicate the relevant customer. The defendant credited the $20m to a particular customer on

[139] *Australia and New Zealand Banking Group Ltd v Westpac Banking Corporation* (1988) 164 CLR 662 (High Court of Australia), discussed in ch 4, at 70–71; see also 77–78.

[140] See also: Nolan, above n 26, at 149–51.

[141] Scots law requires reasonable reliance. *Credit Lyonnais v George Stevenson & Co Ltd* [1901] 9 SLT 93 (OH) 95 (Lord Kyllachy): '. . . the defenders, in order to establish such a defence, would require to show (1) that they had reasonable grounds for believing that the money was theirs; and (2) that having that reasonable belief, they acted upon it in such manner as to make repetition unjust.' Also *Royal Bank of Scotland v Watt* 1991 SC 48 (IH (2 Div)) 57 (Lord Murray). In New Zealand, see *Thomas v Houston Corbett* [1969] NZLR 151 (New Zealand Court of Appeal); *ASB Securities Limited v Geurts* [2005] 1 NZLR 484 (New Zealand High Court). Even in Germany, often regarded as the offering the paradigmatic 'broad' version of the defence, defendants who have changed their position on the basis of 'grossly negligent' assumptions as to the basis of their receipt have been denied the defence: M Jewell, 'The Boundaries of Change of Position—A Comparative Study' [1999] *Restitution L R* 1.

[142] *Orix Australia Corp Ltd v M Wright Hotel Refrigeration Pty Ltd* (2000) 155 FLR 267 (South Australian Supreme Court).

[143] *Ibid*, at 271.

[144] *State Bank of New South Wales Ltd v Swiss Bank Corporation* (1995) 39 NSWLR 350 (New South Wales Court of Appeal); also *Sanwa Australia Finance Ltd v Finchill Pty Ltd* [2001] NSWCA 466 (New South Wales Court of Appeal) [29]–[30] (Davies AJA, Beazley and Heydon JJA concurring). *State Bank* has also been analysed as resting on failure of basis, providing another reason for denying the defence: *Saba Yachts Limited v Fish Pacific Ltd* [2006] NZHC 1452 (New Zealand High Court) [59]–[62] (Winkelmann J). For discussion of the interaction between failure of basis and the change of position defence, see ch 7, at 197–98 and ch 10, at 244–50.

[145] *Port of Brisbane Corp v ANZ Securities* [2002] QCA 158, [2003] 2 Qd R 661 (Queensland Court of Appeal) [15] (McPherson JA, Davies JA and Mullins J concurring), discussed in ch 3, at 77–78. In that case, the Court of Appeal found that the instruction was received by the true payer and so the issue in *Swiss Bank* did not arise: at [16]–[17] and [21]–[23]. *Cf Port of Brisbane Corporation v ANZ Securities Limited* [2001] QSC 466 (Queensland Supreme Court) [39]–[69] (Chesterman J).

the advice of a third party.[146] In the circumstances, only the payer could have identified the intended payee. On appeal, the New South Wales Court of Appeal expressed its conclusions in terms of 'good faith'. However, this is difficult to square with the fact that the defendant honestly, albeit unreasonably, believed the instructions of the third party. The better explanation is that given the circumstances of the payment, the defendant had not acted in reasonable reliance on its receipt.

A requirement of reasonable reliance also underpins a number of English decisions,[147] although the reasoning again tends to be obscured under the label of 'good faith'.[148] For example, in *Commerzbank* itself, the reasonableness of the defendant's assumption as to the basis of his receipt was identified by Mummery LJ as crucial to the failure of the defence in that case.[149] Central to his Lordship's findings was the view that the defendant's mistaken belief was not one that could have been held by a reasonable person in his position. The defendant was an investment banker of some sophistication. Yet he had made no enquiries of his employer to check that the payment was correct and intended and his interpretation of the crucial letter was not based on the 'plain' wording of the letter, but on what the defendant subjectively (and mistakenly) believed the bank intended to do. Factually, the case contrasts nicely with the earlier Court of Appeal decision in *Scottish Equitable Plc v Derby*,[150] where a pensioner received a significant overpayment from his insurance company. The size of the overpayment was such that almost any other person could be expected to realise that it must have been a mistake. However, given his inexperience in financial matters and his action in checking that the amount of the payment was correct, the pensioner's reliance on the overpayment was entirely reasonable. It is notable that the courts' findings in both these cases support a requirement of reasonable reliance in the change of position defence—notwithstanding that both[151] express support for the broad version of the change of position defence.

The same is true of *Niru Battery Manufacturing Co v Milestone Trading Limited.*[152] In that case, the Court of Appeal held that the change of position defence was excluded not only where the defendant acted dishonestly in the restricted sense then apparently required by the House of Lords decision in *Twinsectra v Yardley.*[153]

146 *Cf Bank Tejarat v Hong Kong and Shanghai Banking Corporation Ltd* [1995] 1 Lloyd's Rep 239 (QB (Comm Ct)) 246, where in the circumstances it was reasonable for the defendant to believe the instructions related to and came from its client, notwithstanding the misdescription of its name.

147 eg in *Rose v AIB Group (UK) plc* [2003] EWHC 1737 (Ch (Companies Ct)), [2003] 1 WLR 2791, where Nicholas Warren QC applied an objective approach to reliance. Cf *Maersk Air Ltd v Expeditors International (UK) Ltd* [2003] 1 Lloyd's Rep 491 (QB (Merc)).

148 eg *Fea v Roberts* [2005] All ER (D) 69 (Ch) [104] (Hazel Williamson QC) comparing good faith with reasonable reliance.

149 *Commerzbank AG v Price-Jones* [2003] EWCA Civ 1663, (2003) 147 SJLB 1397 [79]–[82].

150 *Scottish Equitable Plc v Derby* [2001] EWCA Civ 369, [2001] 3 All ER 818.

151 *Scottish Equitable Plc v Derby* [2001] EWCA Civ 369, [2001] 3 All ER 818 [30] (Robert Walker LJ); *Commerzbank AG v Price-Jones* [2003] EWCA Civ 1663, (2003) 147 SJLB 1397 [54] (Munby J).

152 *Niru Battery Manufacturing Co v Milestone Trading Ltd* [2003] EWCA Civ 1446, [2004] QB 985, discussed with insight as to a reasonable reliance requirement by AM Tettenborn, 'Change of Position—More Obfuscation?' [2005] *Restitution L R* 155.

Rather, the touchstone was whether it was 'inequitable' or 'unconscionable' for the defendant to retain the benefit.[154] The court held that the concept of 'inequitability' extended to cases where a defendant had failed to act in good faith, as where a defendant had acted in such a way as constituted 'a failure to act in a commercially acceptable way and sharp practice'.[155]

In that case, the defendant changed its position knowing or suspecting that the payment received from the claimant was made by mistake. The Court of Appeal spent much time considering the extent to which the concept of 'dishonesty' overlapped with 'good faith', whether good faith incorporated an objective element and whether an unreasonable failure to make enquiries where the defendant suspected a mistake constituted good faith or not. Ultimately, the court decided that, in failing to make further enquiries, the defendant had failed to act in good faith such that it would be inequitable for the defendant to retain the benefit.

However, as the court also noted (in preferring to frame its decision in terms of broad 'inequitability' or 'unconscionability' rather than dishonesty),[156] this is a very attenuated notion of good faith, which captures a defendant who knows the facts giving rise to the claimant's right to restitution but genuinely does not realise that they require him to make restitution.[157] This puts considerable strain on the concept of good faith.[158] A better way of understanding the court's approach, and one which gives content to the concept of 'inequitability,'[159] is that it imposes a requirement of objective, or reasonable reliance. If a defendant changes his position knowing facts that would not, objectively speaking, support the assumption on which the defendant acts, it suggests that any subsequent reliance is not reasonable.

Before leaving this section, it is important to emphasise that recognising a requirement of reasonable reliance does not mean that the defence will always be precluded where a defendant knows that there is a risk that the basis on which he acts is incorrect. The reasonableness standard is not absolute and is sensitive to context. A defendant may be aware, for example, that there is a chance that his understanding may be incorrect but has taken steps to minimise that risk to the point where it is reasonable to proceed. For example, the pensioner in *Derby*[160] checked the amount of his payment with the paying institution—an institution moreover which he was entitled to think was reasonably competent in its calcula-

[153] *Twinsectra v Yardley* [2002] UKHL 12, [2002] 2 AC 164, which must now be read subject to its subsequent clarification in *Barlow Clowes v Eurotrust International* [2005] UKPC 37, [2006] 1 WLR 1476 .

[154] *Niru Battery Manufacturing Co v Milestone Trading Ltd* [2003] EWCA Civ 1446, [2004] QB 985 [147]–[52] (Mummery LJ) [181]–[85] (Sedley LJ).

[155] *Ibid*, at [164] (Clarke LJ, Butler-Sloss P concurring).

[156] *Ibid*, at [148] (Clarke LJ) [183] (Sedley LJ).

[157] An example given by Lord Goff in *Lipkin Gorman (a firm) v Karpnale Ltd* [1991] 2 AC 548 (HL) 580.

[158] A point noted in *Rose v AIB Group (UK) plc* [2003] EWHC 1737 (Ch (Companies Ct)), [2003] 1 WLR 2791 [44] (Nicholas Warren QC). See also *Charter plc v City Index Ltd (Gawler & Ors)* [2007] EWCA Civ 1382, [2008] Ch 313 [44] (Carnwath LJ, Mummery LJ concurring).

[159] Criticised in Burrows, 'Clouding the Issues on Change of Position', above n 16.

[160] *Scottish Equitable Plc v Derby* [2001] EWCA Civ 369,[2001] 3 All ER 818.

tions. Even had he retained some lingering doubts as to his entitlement, it was entirely proper for him to proceed on his assumption that his receipt was secure.

We saw in chapter four[161] that the same approach to risk-taking arguably underpins the cases concerning rescission of mortgages and guarantees given by wives and other domestic sureties pursuant to a mistake, undue influence or duress.[162] In those cases, defendant banks and similar financial institutions have usually changed their position in reliance on their receipt of a guarantee or mortgage from the domestic surety by extending credit to a third party borrower. It is well known that in order to defend any claim for rescission in such cases, a financier must demonstrate that it took reasonable steps to eliminate any risk that the domestic surety entered the transaction pursuant to a mistake, undue influence or duress. It is not, however, necessary for financiers to show that these steps have been successful. Rather, as Lord Bingham stated in his concurring speech in *Royal Bank of Scotland v Etridge (No 2)*:

> If these requirements are met the risk that a wife has been misled by her husband as to the facts of a proposed transaction should be eliminated or virtually so. The risk that a wife has been overborne or coerced by her husband will not be eliminated but will be reduced to a level which makes it proper for the lender to proceed.[163]

(f) Anticipatory Changes of Position

Clearly, on the foregoing analysis of causation, anticipatory changes of position pose something of a problem for the change of position defence. As a matter of logic, it is not possible to say that a prior change is caused by a later receipt, either on the 'but for' or reliance approaches to causation. For this reason, the Privy Council's opinion in *Dextra Bank & Trust Co Ltd v Bank of Jamaica*[164] that it is 'surely no misuse of language' to say that, in such cases, the defendant may have relied on the payment for the purposes of the change of position defence, is open to doubt.[165]

As the earlier analysis of the Court of Appeal in *Commerzbank* demonstrated, in cases of anticipatory change of position, the trigger for the defendant's change of position is never his receipt, but his assumption or expectation that is in turn based on some other act or matter. For this reason, Clarke J's view in *South Tyneside MBC v Svenska International plc*[166] that a change of position made in

[161] At 109–10.

[162] eg *Garcia v National Australia Bank* (1998) 194 CLR 395 (High Court of Australia) (mistake); *Barclays Bank Plc v O'Brien* [1994] 1 AC 180 (HL) (undue influence); *Governor and Company of the Bank of Scotland v Bennett* [1998] EWCA 1965 (illegitimate pressure). The leading case in England is *Royal Bank of Scotland Plc v Etridge (No 2)* [2001] UKHL 44, [2002] 2 AC 773. In Australia, see *Garcia v National Australia Bank* (1998) 194 CLR 395 (High Court of Australia).

[163] *Royal Bank of Scotland Plc v Etridge (No 2)* [2001] UKHL 44, [2002] 2 AC 773.

[164] *Dextra Bank and Trust Co Ltd v Bank of Jamaica* [2002] 1 All ER (Comm) 193 (PC) [38]. Other offenders include Edelman and Bant, above n 21, at 328.

[165] *Cf* Nolan, above n 26, at 163, arguing long before *Dextra* that the distinction between reliance on a receipt and reliance on an anticipated receipt is 'not mere linguistic pedantry'.

[166] *South Tyneside MBC v Svenska International plc* [1995] 1 All ER 545 (QB) 565–67.

reliance on the assumed validity of a transaction subsequently discovered to be void does not count for the purpose of the change of position defence is entirely defensible. In such a case, the defendant has received nothing on which to rely: the contract being void, not even contractual rights have been received by the defendant at the time he changes his position.

Notwithstanding its position as a matter of principle, as a matter of practice, the distinction between anticipatory and subsequent changes of position has increasingly been rejected. There is now a significant number of cases which have expressly refused to distinguish between the two.[167] There is a further number that implicitly appear not to have drawn the distinction, when it would have been relevant on the facts of the case.[168]

This judicial acceptance of anticipatory changes of position has clear attractions as a matter of practice. It removes the need to make invidious distinctions in cases involving series of payments, where the defendant may have changed his position sometimes before and sometimes after receipt, in the expectation of the continuing and regular receipt of benefits from the claimant.[169] Further, there are no strong considerations of policy against the extension. The law is not being asked to enforce the defendant's expectations, thereby usurping the role of contract.[170] This is because the defence will only be available where the anticipated benefit is ultimately received and thus the defendant's expectations have already been met.

Therefore, the acceptance of anticipatory changes of position can be supported as a matter of practice and policy, as an exception to the normal causation requirements of the change of position defence. However, it is important that this exception is kept within the limits tolerated by the considerations of practice and policy discussed earlier. In particular, the policy considerations suggest that it is important that the anticipated benefit is the one actually received. That is the only way of avoiding the charge that the defence obliquely enforces a defendant's expectations, rather than protecting his security of receipt. In this respect, one senses that underpinning the unease evidently felt by the Court of Appeal in *Commerzbank*, was that the payment received by the defendant was not the bonus he mistakenly expected, but a quite coincidental mistaken payment made by the claimant bank. In those circumstances, there was simply no link, whether causal or transactional, between

[167] *Philip Collins Ltd v Davis* [2000] 3 All ER 808 (Ch) 385 (Jonathan Parker J); *Dextra Bank and Trust Co Ltd v Bank of Jamaica* [2002] 1 All ER (Comm) 193 (PC) [38]; *Commerzbank AG v Price-Jones* [2003] EWCA Civ 1663, (2003) 147 SJLB 1397 [36]–[38] (Mummery LJ) [60]–[64] (Munby J). *Cf Lokan v Defence Force Retirement and Death Benefits Authority* [2007] AATA 1652 (Administrative Appeals Tribunal of Australia) [16] (Deputy President PE Hack SC); *Alpha Wealth Financial Services Pty Ltd v Frankland River Olive Company Ltd* [2008] WASCA 119 (Western Australia Supreme Court of Appeal) [204] (Buss JA, Steytler P concurring); *Fitzsimons v Minister for Liquor Gaming and Racing for the State of New South Wales* [2008] NSWSC 782 (New South Wales Supreme Court) [125] (McDougall J).

[168] *Thomas v Houston Corbett* [1969] NZLR 151 (New Zealand Court of Appeal); *Lipkin Gorman (a firm) v Karpnale Ltd* [1991] 2 AC 548 (HL).

[169] As in *Philip Collins Ltd v Davis* [2000] 3 All ER 808 (Ch).

[170] A concern expressed by AS Burrows, *The Law of Restitution* (1st edn, Butterworths, London 1993) 425, but withdrawn in Burrows, *The Law of Restitution* 2nd edn, above n 13, at 517–19.

the defendant's expectation, change of position and subsequent receipt, sufficient to support the defence.

(g) Proving Causation

As an intrinsic element of the defence, the onus of proving causation falls naturally on the defendant.[171] Indeed, as the reliance requirement focuses on the effect of a receipt on a defendant's decision to change his position, it is entirely appropriate that the defendant be required to prove on the balance of probabilities what lies most completely within his own sphere of evidence. In *Standard Bank London Ltd v Canara*[172] Moore-Bick J put it thus:

> [I]n order to establish a change of position by voluntarily parting with or disposing of the money it will normally be necessary for the payee to be able to show that the receipt of the money operated on his mind and caused him to act as he did.

In that case, Canara pleaded that it had changed its position in reliance on the security of cash deposits made by the claimant, by opening various letters of credit in favour of a third party. However, it was unable to bring any cogent evidence to support that claim: the recollection of the only witness on the point was faulty or non-existent and the contemporaneous documents that accompanied the decisions to open the letters of credit made no mention of the cash deposits. Moore-Bick J concluded that in the circumstances, he was unable to find that the existence of the cash deposits played 'any' role in Canara's decision to change its position.[173] Accordingly, Canara's change of position defence failed.

Although it is unnecessary for a defendant to prove 'but for' causation to rely on the change of position defence, it will often be relevant for a defendant to show that following receipt of the benefit, he deviated from a usual pattern of behaviour. Although this often resembles (and is described as[174]) an application of but-for causation, it need not be so regarded. This sort of evidence is relevant to proving reliance because the natural inference to draw from that evidence is that the receipt caused the defendant to alter his position.

Conversely, where a defendant cannot demonstrate any alteration in his usual habits, it will be very difficult, although not impossible,[175] to prove reliance. Again, this is often assumed to be because 'but for' causation cannot be satisfied. However, it is equally consistent with the fact that the onus lies on the defendant

171 *Scottish Equitable Plc v Derby* [2001] EWCA Civ 369, [2001] 3 All ER 818 [31] (Robert Walker LJ); *National Bank of Egypt International Ltd v Oman Housing Bank SAOC* [2002] EWHC 1760 (QB (Comm Ct)), [2003] 1 All ER (Comm) 246 [29] (David Steel J).

172 *Standard Bank London Ltd v Canara Bank* [2002] EWHC 1574 (QB (Comm Ct)) [104], citing *Philip Collins Ltd v Davis* [2000] 3 All ER 808 (Ch) and *Scottish Equitable Plc v Derby* [2001] EWCA Civ 369, [2001] 3 All ER 818 in support.

173 *Standard Bank London Ltd v Canara Bank* [2002] EWHC 1574 (QB (Comm Ct)) [119].

174 As in *Scottish Equitable Plc v Derby* [2001] EWCA Civ 369, [2001] 3 All ER 818.

175 As in *Eastbourne Borough Council v Foster* (QB 20 December 2000), appealed on another point in *Eastbourne Borough Council v Foster* [2001] EWCA Civ 1091.

to prove reliance. In the absence of any change in a well-established pattern of behaviour, it will be open to the court to infer that the receipt of the benefit had no impact (was not even 'a factor') in the defendant's decision to continue on that course of conduct. For example, in *Scottish Equitable v Derby*,[176] Mr Derby was unable to point to any significant, irreversible changes to his normal (frugal) spending habits. His defence accordingly failed. While the court expressed its findings in terms of the 'but for' test of causation, it would have been equally correct to state that the payment played no part in Mr Derby's decision to continue his usual pattern of behaviour.

This process of inferring causation (or lack thereof) in decision-making from other proven facts is well known to the law.[177] We saw numerous examples in the context of estoppel.[178] It usually requires the court to consider what a reasonable person would or would not do in reliance on his receipt. If the defendant has acted as a reasonable person would have done and a reasonable person would have done so in reliance on his receipt, the court may infer reliance. For example, if a defendant who is in receipt of compensation payments fails to apply for social security within the stipulated time period,[179] it will be open to a court to infer that he failed to do so in reliance on his receipt.

Finally, we saw earlier that reliance has two components: the assumption induced by the receipt and the acts or omissions taken on the basis of that assumption. The defendant bears the onus of proving both components. Even if (contrary to the view taken in this book) good faith is a discrete element of the defence, the onus must lie on the defendant to prove good faith.[180] It follows that there should be no 'assumption' of good faith. If good faith is seen as a component of reliance (as this book advocates), it becomes even clearer that any inconsistency in the burden of proving the elements of the defence cannot be tolerated.

Nonetheless, occasionally, there appears a tendency on the part of courts to assume good faith, unless proven to the contrary (ie by the claimant). Not only is this unacceptable as a matter of principle, it can have significant effects on the result of the case. A good example is *Abou-Rahmah v Abacha*,[181] a case that also highlights the benefits of adopting a requirement of reasonable reliance rather

[176] *Scottish Equitable Plc v Derby* [2001] EWCA Civ 369, [2001] 3 All ER 818.

[177] eg *Barton v Armstrong* [1976] AC 104 (PC) 118 (Lord Cross), discussed in *Gould v Vaggelas* (1985) 157 CLR 215 (High Court of Australia) 237 (Wilson J).

[178] Ch 2, at 39–40.

[179] As in *Palmer v Blue Circle Southern Cement Ltd* [1999] NSWSC 697, (1999) 48 NSWLR 318 (New South Wales Supreme Court).

[180] In *Lipkin Gorman (a firm) v Karpnale Ltd* [1991] 2 AC 548 (HL), Lord Goff referred to it both as part of the positive defence and also identified 'bad faith' as a bar to the defence. However, cases since *Lipkin Gorman* generally have proceeded on the basis that it forms part of the positive defence and that the onus of proof thus rests with the defendant: *Philip Collins Ltd v Davis* [2000] 3 All ER 808 (Ch) 827 (Jonathan Parker J); *Scottish Equitable Plc v Derby* [2001] EWCA Civ 369, [2001] 3 All ER 818; *Cressman v Coys of Kensington (Sales) Ltd* [2004] EWCA Civ 47, [2004] 1 WLR 2775. In Australia, there is no doubt that the onus of proving any good faith requirement rests with the defendant: *Alpha Wealth Financial Services Pty Ltd v Frankland River Olive Company Ltd* [2008] WASCA 119 (Western Australia Supreme Court of Appeal), discussed below, at 160.

than struggling to manage solely with the concept of good faith. In that case, the defendant bank had opened an account for a client notwithstanding its suspicions that the client might be involved in money-laundering. It subsequently received a payment from the claimant to the account of its client. The bank paid over the amount of the deposit to a third party, in accordance with its client's instructions. It later transpired that the claimant had been the victim of a fraud to which the bank's client was a party. The claimant brought an action against the bank for recovery of the amount of the payment on the basis that it had been paid pursuant to a mistake. The bank pleaded the change of position defence.

The Court of Appeal struggled to determine whether the bank had acted in good faith, even in the extended sense of 'commercially acceptable conduct' employed in *Niru Battery Manufacturing Co v Milestone Trading Limited.*[182] Ultimately, the court divided on the issue. Arden LJ (with whom Pill LJ concurred in a separate judgment)[183] held that, in order for the defendant not to have acted in good faith (or 'inequitably'), it must have particular suspicions relating to the specific transactions in question.[184] Further, Arden LJ took the view that the bank could not be said to have acted other than in good faith: it had complied with the relevant requirements of Nigerian law in opening the account and in the absence of suspicions relating to the specific transactions in question, no more was required.

However, the court had already found that the defendant bank suspected that its client would use its account to launder funds. In that context, the onus lay on the defendant to show that, notwithstanding this finding, it had changed its position in reliance on its receipt (or 'in good faith', as the Court of Appeal considered). More specifically, given the earlier finding, the defendant had to show that it changed its position in reliance on the assumption that the receipt of the money was unimpeachable. One way of doing this would have been for the defendant to show that it had specific evidence relating to the particular impugned transactions that showed that, in these instances at least, the payments were without taint and thus that the defendant had acted in good faith.[185] However, the majority arguably reversed this requirement in finding that the defendant had no notice of anything suspicious in relation to the particular, impugned transactions and could not therefore be said to have acted other than in good faith.

Rix LJ, dissenting, took a different view of what was required to show 'commercially acceptable conduct' in the context of the case and concluded that the bank, on the facts, had failed to act in accordance with an objective standard of good faith.[186] Rix LJ held that the bank's general suspicion as to the use of the

[181] *Abou-Rahmah v Abacha* [2006] EWCA Civ 1492, [2007] 1 All ER (Comm) 827.

[182] *Niru Battery Manufacturing Co v Milestone Trading Ltd* [2003] EWCA Civ 1446, [2004] QB 985, discussed earlier, at 153–54.

[183] *Abou-Rahmah v Abacha* [2006] EWCA Civ 1492, [2007] 1 All ER (Comm) 827 [99]–[103].

[184] *Ibid*, at [81], [84], [87].

[185] As done in *ASB Securities Limited v Geurts* [2005] 1 NZLR 484 (New Zealand High Court). Contrast the situation, discussed in ch 2, at 29–30, 45, where a defendant is reassured by a claimant payer that the defendant is entitled to his receipt.

[186] *Abou-Rahmah v Abacha* [2006] EWCA Civ 1492, [2007] 1 All ER (Comm) 827 [50]–[52], [58].

client's account must attach to each and every transaction and precluded the defendant from relying on the change of position defence.[187] It is submitted that, when attention is refocused on a requirement of reasonable reliance, Rix LJ's approach is clearly to be preferred. As soon as the defendant bank admitted that it had suspicions that the account might be being used to launder money, it must have been aware of the risk that its receipt of any moneys through that account was insecure. In those circumstances, and in the absence of some good reason for believing the particular impugned transactions were clean, the bank could not be said to have reasonably relied on its receipt.[188]

A contrary example, in which the onus of proof issues were clearly appreciated by the appellate court, is the Western Australian case of *Alpha Wealth Financial Services Pty Ltd v Franklin River Olive Company Ltd.*[189] In that case, the judge at first instance held that a recipient of a mistaken payment had changed his position so as to attract both the common law and applicable statutory change of position defences.[190] In so doing, his Honour found: 'There is no evidence that the defendant had acted other than in good faith.'[191] On appeal, the Western Australian Supreme Court of Appeal held that the judge had fallen into error: the onus of establishing good faith[192] or reliance[193] under both the common law and statutory defences lay on the defendant. It followed that the defendant's failure to adduce sufficient evidence as to his state of mind at the time of changing his position redounded to his disadvantage, not to the disadvantage of the claimant.

(3) The Impact of Third Parties

The final factor to consider as potentially informing the elements of the change of position defence involves the role of third parties. There are a number of ways in which third parties may have an impact on a defendant's claimed change of position defence. We have seen already in this chapter that a defendant may have changed his position in reliance on his receipt by conferring a benefit on a third party. The success of his defence will depend on the extent to which he can demonstrate that this change is irreversible. In turn, that may depend on what the third

[187] *Ibid*, at [53]–[55], [58].

[188] *Maersk Air Ltd v Expeditors International (UK) Ltd* [2003] 1 Lloyd's Rep 491 (QB (Merc)) [47]–[49] (Alton J); *ASB Securities Limited v Geurts* [2005] 1 NZLR 484 (New Zealand High Court) [63]–[64].

[189] *Alpha Wealth Financial Services Pty Ltd v Frankland River Olive Company Ltd* [2006] WASC 70, 199 FLR 91 (Western Australian Supreme Court); *Alpha Wealth Financial Services Pty Ltd v Franklin River Olive Company Ltd* [2008] WASCA 119 (Western Australia Supreme Court of Appeal).

[190] Under s 125 Property Law Act 1969 (WA), the terms of which are set out in ch 10, at 250. The Australian statutory defences are considered further in ch 10, at 244–54.

[191] *Alpha Wealth Financial Services Pty Ltd v Frankland River Olive Company Ltd* [2006] WASC 70, 199 FLR 91 (Western Australian Supreme Court) [86] (Commissioner Sanderson).

[192] *Alpha Wealth Financial Services Pty Ltd v Frankland River Olive Company Ltd* [2008] WASCA 119 (Western Australia Supreme Court of Appeal) [39] (Pullin JA).

[193] *Ibid*, at [210]–[12] (Buss JA, with whom Steytler P concurred).

party has done as a result of her receipt. To this extent, the impact on third parties of a defendant's change of position is incorporated into the defence.

What remains unclear is whether third parties' interests should be taken into account beyond their impact on the irreversibility requirement. Third parties may not have relied on any benefit transferred to them by the defendant, for example, but rather on the apparent financial position of the defendant in advancing credit to the defendant, or by otherwise organising their affairs on the basis of the defendant's apparent financial position. In that context, they may be prejudiced by an order for restitution made against the defendant, notwithstanding that the defendant's change of position is (so far as he is concerned) reversible.

In many statutory versions of the defence, these kinds of consideration would be regarded as relevant in determining whether the defence applied.[194] This is because they direct the court to consider the effect that an order for restitution would have on third parties. For example, in *Alpha Wealth Financial Services Pty Ltd v Franklin River Olive Company Ltd*,[195] Commissioner Sanderson of the Western Australian Supreme Court was required to consider the application of a statutory change of position defence contained in section 125 Property Law Act 1969 (WA).[196] This directs a court considering whether to grant the statutory defence to '. . . hav[e] regard to all possible implications in respect of the parties (other than the plaintiff or claimant) to the payment and of other persons acquiring rights or interests through them . . .'. Commissioner Sanderson noted that if the defendant was ordered to make restitution there was a real prospect that the investment scheme in which the claimant, defendant and third parties were involved would be forced to come to an end. He concluded that the interests of those third parties strongly supported the application of the statutory change of position defence.

To date, there has been little discussion in either the case law or commentaries regarding the broader relevance of third party interests to the common law change of position defence. In *Lipkin Gorman (a firm) v Karpnale*,[197] Lord Goff expressed the defence only in terms of having regard to the position of the defendant. However, looking beyond the change of position case law, the law is not entirely

[194] eg s 50AA(2)(c) Trustee Act (Northern Territory); *s* 24(2)(c) Perpetuities and Accumulations Act 1992 (Tasmania); s 125 Property Law Act 1969 (Western Australia); s 65(8) Trustees Act 1962 (Western Australia). The statutory defences are further considered in ch 10, at 244–54.

[195] *Alpha Wealth Financial Services Pty Ltd v Frankland River Olive Company Ltd* [2006] WASC 70, 199 FLR 91 (Western Australian Supreme Court); reversed on other grounds in *Alpha Wealth Financial Services Pty Ltd v Frankland River Olive Company Ltd* [2008] WASCA 119 (Western Australia Supreme Court of Appeal).

[196] See also ch 10, at 250, 253. The provision is considered in detail in E Bant and P Creighton, 'The Statutory Change of Position Defences in Western Australia' (2003) 31 *U Western Australia L Rev* 47.

[197] *Lipkin Gorman (a firm) v Karpnale Ltd* [1991] 2 AC 548 (HL) 580. In *Alpha Wealth Financial Services Pty Ltd v Franklin River Olive Company Ltd* [2006] WASC 70, 199 FLR 91 (Western Australian Supreme Court) [83], Commissioner Sanderson expressly accepted that the chief difference between statutory and common law versions of the defence law lay in their treatment of third party interests: reversed on other grounds in *Alpha Wealth Financial Services Pty Ltd v Franklin River Olive Company Ltd* [2008] WASCA 119 (Western Australia Supreme Court of Appeal).

indifferent to third party interests. We saw in chapter four, for example, that a traditional bar to rescission is that third party interests have intervened.[198] And the position of third parties has always been accepted as relevant in cases where equitable relief such as specific performance or an injunction is sought. These pockets of the law demonstrate that it would not be impossible as a matter of process for courts to take third party interests into account in the change of position defence were that thought appropriate.

That said, the existence of a separate third party bar to rescission is now under serious attack.[199] Further, there is a real difference between taking into account third-party interests for the purposes of exercising a discretion to award specific performance or an injunction, knowing that damages in lieu can be awarded to protect the claimant's position and taking into account third party interests as a factor in recognising or denying a change of position defence where no financial compensation to the affected party will be forthcoming if those interests prove to be determinative. Finally, were the position of third-party interests capable of giving rise to a change of position defence even where the defendant's position was not itself irreversible, or could lead to the denial of the defence where the defendant's change of position was reversible, it is arguable that an entirely new form of defence would be born.[200] On balance, therefore, and on the current state of the general (non-statutory) law, it must be concluded that there is little support for taking into account third-party interests as an element of establishing the change of position defence.

C Conclusion

This chapter has demonstrated that the disputed elements of the change of position defence can be settled by drawing on the lessons learnt from the doctrines the subject of part one, taken together with the modern change of position case law and arguments of principle and policy. This analysis reveals the following elements of the defence:

- The defendant must have suffered a detrimental change of position. The requirement of detriment does not demand that the change of position be necessarily pecuniary in nature. Rather, the change must be prejudicial to the defendant in the sense that, as at the date the claimant seeks restitution of the benefit, to require the defendant to make restitution or restitution in full would leave him in a worse (here including utterly different)[201] position than he

[198] Ch 4, at 93.

[199] B Häcker, 'Rescission and Third Party Rights' [2006] *Restitution L Rev* 21; NY Nahan, 'Rescission: A Case for Rejecting the Classical Model?' (1997) 27 (1) *U Western Australia L Rev* 66.

[200] Such a defence would be squarely distributive in focus, rather than addressing the interests and rights of the parties *inter se*.

[201] As where a defendant has conceived a child: above, at 132–34.

occupied prior to his original receipt. The key to determining this issue will be whether the defendant's change of position can to be reversed by the defendant as at the date the claimant seeks restitution of the benefit, and reversed without excessive cost, effort or expense. If the defendant's change of position is not reversible in part or in full, then (assuming the other elements of the defence are satisfied), the defence must succeed to the extent of the irreversible change.

- Subject to the exceptional cases of anticipatory changes of position, the irreversible change of position must have been caused by the defendant's receipt of the enrichment the subject of the primary claim (the 'causation' requirement). The analysis demonstrates that the appropriate test of causation will depend on the nature of the pleaded change of position.
- Where there has been an independent change to the received benefit, the but-for test of causation will generally be satisfied. Where, however, the pleaded change of position is defendant-instigated, the change must have been made by the defendant in reliance on his receipt. Further, in establishing the two limbs of reliance (namely: (1) that the receipt caused the adoption of an assumption; and (2) the assumption caused the defendant's decision to act) the but-for test should be abandoned in favour of an 'a factor' test of causation.
- Where reliance is required, it must be reasonable.
- In general, there is no separate requirement of good faith on the part of the defendant: this is because good faith is subsumed in the reasonable reliance requirement and is generally irrelevant in cases of independent changes of position.

This last point, however, is subject to the caveat that the defendant's conduct must not be such as to disentitle him from relying on the defence. It is to this question of applicable bars to the defence that we now turn.

6

Fault as a Bar to the Defence

A Introduction

CHAPTER FIVE IDENTIFIED the primary elements of the change of position defence. Once a defendant proves those elements, he prima facie makes good his defence. The onus then falls on the claimant to demonstrate reasons why the defendant should be excluded from the defence to which he is otherwise entitled.

This chapter identifies the situations in which a defendant who otherwise satisfies the primary elements of the defence may be denied the defence in whole or in part due to his fault in receiving the benefit or changing his position (the 'fault' bar). The chapter also demonstrates that it is important to keep constantly in mind the primary elements of the defence in considering whether a particular category of defendant may successfully raise the defence: the requirement of reasonable reliance will often determine that question, long before questions of fault operating as a bar to the defence come into play.

We saw in chapter one that the concept of fault can be usefully divided into six issues: (1) the role of 'good faith' in the operation of the defence; (2) the position of 'wrongdoers'; (3) the position of defendants to claims based on duress or undue influence; (4) the position of defendants who have been involved in illegal conduct; (5) the position of defendants who have induced the claimant's impaired decision to enter into the transaction; and (6) the carelessness of the defendant in changing his position.

Chapter five addressed the role of good faith as a primary element of the defence. It showed that the good faith of the defendant is generally irrelevant to independent changes of position. It also demonstrated that good faith is an inherent ingredient of reasonable reliance. Reasonable reliance aside, the defendant's bad faith may also be relevant as supporting an independent bar to the defence (for example, the defendant committed a wrong involving dishonesty, such as the tort of deceit). The balance of this chapter addresses the relevance of good or bad faith solely in that context. The chapter considers the possible bars to the defence by reference to each of the remaining categories of fault, commencing with the position of wrongdoers.

B Wrongdoers

In *Lipkin Gorman (a firm) v Karpnale*,[1] Lord Goff noted that it was 'commonly accepted' that the change of position defence would not avail wrongdoers.[2] We saw in chapter one that a 'wrong' is defined in this book as a breach of legal or equitable duty[3] and thus 'wrongdoers' are those who have breached a legal or equitable duty owed to the claimant. On that basis, there remain two kinds of cases in which the question whether wrongdoers are and should be denied the defence arises.

The first is where, although having committed a wrong, the defendant is not sued on that basis but in an independent claim in unjust enrichment. In these cases, the defendant could be described as an 'incidental' wrongdoer, the wrong being incidental to the claim the wrongdoer must defend. For example, suppose a defendant deliberately misleads a claimant into believing that she owes the defendant money. The claimant will have a choice of actions: she can seek to recover the payment relying on the tort of deceit, or she can decide to pursue a claim in unjust enrichment based on the facts that her (induced) mistake caused the transfer to the defendant. Where the claimant brings her action based not on the tort, but on the vitiated decision to transfer, should the defendant be able to raise the change of position defence?

As a starting point, it is notable that the law generally allows claimants to pick and choose between alternative actions arising from the one set of facts. An accepted incident of that choice is that one action may prove more favourable to the claimant than another. Factors such as evidential difficulties, limitation periods, choice of law issues and available defences will all impact on the claimant's choice. She is entitled to make that choice with only her own self-interests in mind. Having made her choice, however, and having proven the particular claim, there must be some principled reason for denying the incidental wrongdoer a defence that would otherwise be available with respect to the claim.

For example, assuming the change of position defence is not available to claims in deceit, the unavailability of that defence will be one reason for a claimant to choose to bring and prove that kind of claim. If the claimant chooses not to pursue that route because of difficulties of proof, however, and instead relies on a simple mistake claim, should the defendant be entitled to raise the change of position defence? Of course, a defendant who is incidentally revealed in the course of proceedings to have fraudulently induced a transfer will struggle to prove reliance (in the case of a defendant-instigated change of position) because, having inten-

[1] *Lipkin Gorman (a firm) v Karpnale Ltd* [1991] 2 AC 548 (HL) 580.

[2] Commentators note that the passage leaves open the question whether Lord Goff accepted that view: AS Burrows, *The Law of Restitution* (2nd edn, Butterworths, London 2002) 525; G Virgo, *The Principles of the Law of Restitution* (2 edn, OUP, Oxford 2006) 705.

[3] At 5.

tionally induced the mistake, he knew his receipt was insecure. His defence will thus likely fail in any event. If the requirement that reliance must be reasonable is accepted, as chapter five argued it should be, the same result will often follow in cases of negligent misrepresentation. Where a defendant has negligently induced the claimant to transfer a benefit to the defendant, then any subsequent reliance is unlikely to be reasonable. It follows that the defence is unlikely to apply in such cases where the pleaded change of position was defendant-instigated.

On the other hand, chapter five showed that in cases of independent changes of position, a defendant does not need to prove reasonable reliance. It is enough that the received benefit independently devalued or was lost or destroyed for reasons independent of the defendant. Is it arguable that the fraudulent or negligent inducer in this class of case should still be able to rely on the defence?

We saw in the context of estoppel,[4] the payment over defence[5] and (in general) rescission[6] that there was little support in the authorities for extending protection to incidental wrongdoers. However, it was often unclear whether the instant court appreciated the difference between the defendant being sued on the basis of unjust enrichment, or on the tort itself. The courts' responses might thus not be determinative of the issue.

Assuming for the moment that the courts were alive to this distinction, we saw that one rationale for excluding the defence in such cases might be that to allow it would undermine the law's prohibition of the tortious behaviour revealed, albeit incidentally, on the proven facts of the case. So, in cases where the defendant fraudulently (or negligently) induced the claimant to transfer the benefit to the defendant, it might undermine the law's prohibition of the defendant's tortious behaviour to allow the defendant later to raise the independent change to the received benefit by way of defence.

Importantly, it would be necessary on this approach to evaluate in each category of case whether permitting the change of position defence would undermine the policy behind the law's prohibition of the (incidental) wrong. And one factor weighing against excluding the defence will be that the claimant herself chose to bring a claim in unjust enrichment, to which the defence prima facie applies. Also weighing against the exclusion of the defence are the kinds of policy considerations that underline cases of illegality, which will be addressed in section E below.[7] In particular, it is arguable that where the law already supplies a regime in one context for addressing wrongful behaviour, courts should only deny a defence applicable outside that context where it is clearly necessary to protect the policy underlying the law's existing prohibition. In that regard, it will again be necessary to determine whether the existing policy or prohibition conflicts with and overrides the defendant's right to protection. These are difficult questions that, once more, must be answered by reference to each category of wrongful behaviour.

[4] At 59–62.
[5] At 79–85.
[6] At 106–07, 108, 110–11.
[7] Commencing at 184.

Alternatively, courts could take the view that the defence should be denied in such cases simply because the defendant induced the transfer in the first place. That is, wrongdoing apart, courts will not permit the defence where the defendant has been at fault in a very broad sense, in inducing the claimant's vitiated decision to transfer the benefit (an 'innocent inducer'). We return to this basis for excluding the defence in section D below.

Turning to the change of position case law on the point, there is some support in the authorities for disallowing the defence in cases where the claimant transferred the benefit to the defendant in reliance on the defendant's incidentally-revealed misrepresentation. In *Saronic Shipping Co Ltd v Huron Liberian Co*,[8] the defendant had presented false invoices to the claimant that, in turn, triggered the claimant's mistaken payment. Mocatta J found that these facts supported a right to restitution of the mistaken payment, based on the unjust factor of mistake. The defendant in turn sought to rely on the change of position defence as then articulated by Goff and Jones.[9] In rejecting that defence, Mocatta J applied by analogy Lord Denning's judgment in *Larner v London County Council*[10] that the defendant should be denied the defence where it was 'at fault' in either having innocently misrepresented the position to the claimant or having breached a duty to the claimant. However, the findings of fact in the case are ambiguous as to the state of knowledge of the defendant in presenting the false invoices. They suggest both that the defendant knew there was no basis in the agreement between the parties for the invoices and that he had a complete misunderstanding as to legal position between the parties.[11] The case thus leaves open the precise basis for Mocatta J's rejection of the defence, being consistent both with an incidentally-revealed breach of duty bar or innocent inducement analysis.

By contrast, in *Test Claimants in the FII Group Litigation v Revenue and Customs Commissioner*,[12] Henderson J was clear that the change of position defence should be open to an incidental wrongdoer. In that case, payments were made to the Revenue pursuant to unlawful taxation regimes. The claimants sought restitution of the payments on the ground that they were made under a mistaken belief as to the validity of the applicable tax.[13] Henderson J considered that the wrongdoer bar applies only to cases where the cause of action to which the defence is raised involves the commission of some legal wrong. As mistake-based claims in unjust enrichment are not dependent on any wrongdoing by the defendant, the wrongdoer bar cannot apply.[14]

[8] *Saronic Shopping Co Ltd v Huron Liberian Co* [1979] 1 Lloyd's Rep 341 (QB (Comm Ct)).

[9] *Ibid*, at 366.

[10] *Larner v London County Council* [1949] 2 KB 683 (CA) 689, discussed in ch 2, at 54.

[11] *Saronic Shopping Co Ltd v Huron Liberian Co* [1979] 1 Lloyd's Rep 341 (QB (Comm Ct)) 365, 366.

[12] *Test Claimants in the FII Litigation v Revenue and Customs Commissioner* [2008] EWHC 2893 (Ch).

[13] An alternative 'Woolwich'-style claim was also available on the facts but faced a limitation period problem.

[14] *Ibid*, [320], [337]. The alternative claim on the facts was a 'Woolwich' style claim, after *Woolwich Equitable Building Society v IRC* [1992] 3 All ER 737 (HL), see below at 187. It is debatable whether this form of claim necessarily rests on wrongdoing either, discussed in E Bant, 'Restitution from the Revenue and Change of Position', [2009] *Lloyds Maritime Commercial LQ* (forthcoming).

Henderson J regarded this conclusion as particularly apposite given that the claimants' motive for pleading their claims in mistake (as opposed to basing them on the specific wrong) was to take advantage of a more generous limitation period.[15] This reasoning reflects the view, discussed earlier,[16] that if a claimant has chosen a particular class of claim in order to obtain an associated benefit, there must be some principled reason for denying the incidental wrongdoer a defence that would otherwise be available with respect to the claim. Henderson J considered that there was no such reason and so applied the change of position defence.

We saw earlier, however, that an important countervailing consideration or principle in play in these cases is the danger that the application of the defence will undermine the policy behind the law's prohibition of the (incidental) wrong.[17] In that context, it is regrettable that Henderson J did not go on to consider the public policy issues that were arguably at the core of the *FII* case. In particular, there is a longstanding and vital public interest in ensuring that the Revenue only collects taxes to which it is entitled under valid legislation. The claimants mistakenly assumed that the applicable taxation regimes were lawful and it was this mistake that caused their mistaken payments. In these circumstances, there is a clear danger that applying the defence to their mistake claims wholly undermines the strong policy reasons supporting restitution from the Revenue.[18]

Given the current state of the authorities, the position of incidental wrongdoers remains uncertain. In principle, the main reason for denying the change of position defence to this category of defendant is that it may undermine a policy underlying the law's prohibition of the defendant's tortious behaviour. An important countervailing factor in favour of its application will be that the claimant herself chose to bring a claim in unjust enrichment, to which the defence prima facie applies. Further, where the law already supplies a regime in one context for addressing wrongful behaviour, courts should only deny a defence applicable outside that context where it is clearly necessary to protect the policy underlying the law's existing prohibition. Notwithstanding these factors in favour of permitting the defence, in many cases of incidental wrongdoing the defendant will have induced the impugned transaction on which he subsequently seeks to rely. As we will see in section D below, this appears to provide an additional reason for denying relief. On balance, therefore, it seems that incidental wrongdoers will often struggle to avail themselves of the change of position defence.

The second class of case involving wrongdoers is where a defendant has committed a wrong against (breached a duty to) the claimant and is sued by the claimant on that basis. As we noted earlier, many wrongs (such as deceit) involve dishonest conduct that will itself often provide a basis for denying the defendant the defence. However, this is not always the case: there exist many wrongs of strict

[15] *Ibid*, [341].
[16] Above at 166.
[17] Above at 167.
[18] See below at 187.

liability. In that context, the main question is whether the 'innocent' defendant guilty of a breach of duty to the claimant may or should be entitled, in response to a claim for restitution of a benefit received as a result of that breach, to rely on the change of position defence.

It has been suggested, for example, that an innocent converter should be entitled to rely on the change of position defence to reduce his restitutionary liability in conversion.[19] The same argument has been made with respect to innocent breaches of fiduciary duties (an equitable wrong).[20] However, we saw in part one that there is even less support in the estoppel,[21] payment over[22] and rescission[23] case law for extending the defence to these categories of claim than there is in the case of incidental wrongdoers. The recent decision of Henderson J in *Test Claimants in the FII Group Litigation v Revenue and Customs Commissioner*[24] reinforces this conclusion. It will be recalled that, in that case, Henderson J held that the wrongdoer bar to the change of position defence applies only to cases where a defendant is sued on the basis of the commission of a legal wrong. In reaching this view, Henderson J considered that the 'wrongdoing' that Lord Goff had in mind in *Lipkin Gorman* was the conversion by the defendant of a banker's draft.[25] If correct, there must now be considerable force in the view that the change of position defence will not apply to so-called 'innocent wrongdoers'.

Further, Nolan's argument that the law already takes into account changes of position of breaching fiduciaries, and that this pocket of the law could support a wider extension of the defence to other innocent wrongdoers, breaks down on closer analysis.[26] Suppose a defendant in breach of fiduciary duty uses his considerable business acumen to obtain a huge personal profit. His principal also profits from the breach. Later, the principal brings an action for breach of fiduciary duty, seeking an account of profits in respect of the breach. The allowances granted in such cases focus on the 'reasonable value' of the defendant's services.[27] In contrast, the change of position defence focuses on the value of the defendant's irreversible change of position, which more often will look to the irrecoverable cost to the defendant of providing the services. The allowance cases thus appear designed to prevent the unjust enrichment of the claimant, not address the defendant's change of position. The same analysis applies to cases where allowances for improvements

[19] *Kuwait Airways Corp v Iraqi Airways Co (Nos 4 and 5)* [2002] UKHL 19, [2002] 2 AC 883 [79] (Lord Nicholls); R Nolan, 'Change of Position' in P Birks (ed) *Laundering and Tracing* (Clarendon Press, Oxford 1995) 154; Burrows, *The Law of Restitution* 2nd edn, above n 2, at 524–27; G Jones (ed), *Goff and Jones The Law of Restitution* (7th edn Sweet & Maxwell, London 2007) [40-016].

[20] Nolan, *ibid*, at 154.

[21] At 59.

[22] At 81–83.

[23] At 107, 108, 110–11.

[24] *Test Claimants in the FII Litigation v Revenue and Customs Commissioner* [2008] EWHC 2893 (Ch), discussed above at 168–69.

[25] *Ibid*, [320].

[26] Nolan, above n 19, at 154.

[27] eg *Boardman v Phipps* [1967] 2 AC 46 (HL); *O'Sullivan v Management Agency and Music Ltd* [1985] QB 428 (CA).

have been made in favour of innocent converters.[28] In so far as courts have focused on the value of the services to the claimant, the cases more closely resemble counterclaims by way of set-off for restitution of the benefit conferred on the claimant than examples of the change of position defence.

As a matter of precedent then, there is little to support the extension of the change of position defence to claims based on wrongdoing. As a matter of principle, the position is more open to argument. We have seen that in cases of defendant-instigated changes of position, the change of position defence operates to protect a defendant from a claim for restitution where he has irreversibly changed his position in reliance on his receipt. It prevents the defendant from being put in a worse (including entirely different) position than he occupied prior to his receipt. In this way, the defence supports and reflects the restricted aims of restitution. Restitution does not aim to impose loss on a defendant, to punish him or to require him to disgorge profits. Its aim is limited to reversing transfers of value so as to restore the parties to the status quo ante. In that context, the defence operates to ensure that, in circumstances where a defendant's position has irreversibly changed, restitution does not operate contrary to its underlying purpose.[29] Seen in this light, and subject to any overriding policy considerations, there is no reason in principle why the defence should not apply to claims for restitution arising from a strict liability wrong or, for that matter, a claim for restitution made to vindicate a claimant's continuing proprietary interest in a benefit transferred to a defendant.

Indeed, the entire rescission case law arguably offers implicit support for this view. We saw in chapter four that the concept of *restitutio in integrum* automatically applies with respect to rescission. The doctrine is a logical corollary of the aim of rescission reverse or unwind the transaction so as to restore the parties to the *status quo ante.* The concept, therefore, applies across all classes of rescission case, whether the right to rescind arises in response to a claim in unjust enrichment (as must be the case, for example, with respect to not-wrongs such as innocent misrepresentation) or in respect of a wrong such as fraudulent misrepresentation. We saw that the doctrine may operate to more limited effect with respect to wrongdoers. However, there was no suggestion in any of the cases that it was irrelevant to consider the application of the doctrine of *restitutio in integrum* to every class of rescission case.

We have noted the similarities between the remedies of rescission and restitution[30] and between the concepts of *restitutio in integrum* and the change of position defence. The obvious inference to draw from the rescission case law for the purposes of change of position is that the defence is inextricably linked with the remedy of restitution, because of the purpose of that remedy to reverse the transfer of value so as to restore the parties to the *status quo ante.*

[28] *Munro v Willmott* [1949] KB 295 (KB); *Greenwood v Bennett* [1973] 1 QB 195 (CA).

[29] P Hellwege, 'The Scope of Application of Change of Position: A Comparative Study' [1999] *Restitution L R* 92, 96–100.

[30] Ch 4, at 90–91.

The question remains, however, whether an extension of the defence to wrongs-based claims for restitution would be acceptable as a matter of policy. As we have seen in the first part of this book, policy looms large in the question of determining the ambit of operation of the change of position defence. Unfortunately, it is not a question capable of general reply. Each wrong must be individually addressed to see whether recognition of a change of position defence would undermine the law's prohibition. Certainly, the position taken by the law to date in respect of innocent converters and breaching fiduciaries has indicated that it will. This is most likely because permitting the defence is seen to undermine the protection of claimants' proprietary rights in the first case[31] and because of the overriding need to deter breaches of fiduciary duty in the second.[32] In the end, it would require a significant change in judicial attitude to those policy considerations to support an extension of the defence to such wrongdoers.

C Duress and Undue Influence

We saw in part one that, in general, there is little support in the estoppel, payment over and rescission case law for the general application of a change of position defence in cases of duress and undue influence.[33] However, we also saw that duress is not a tort per se and it is highly controversial whether undue influence necessarily involves wrongful behaviour.[34] It follows that the basis for excluding the defence cannot rest on the characterisation of these claims as involving the commission of a legal or equitable wrong. Of course, it may be that a defendant to a claim in duress or undue influence will be incidentally demonstrated to have committed a wrong, such as intimidation in a case of duress, or breach of fiduciary duty in a case of undue influence. If that is the case, the analysis in the previous section will apply. However, in order for there to be a general bar to the defence in cases of duress and undue influence, another rationale must be found.

Chapter five suggested a reason why the defence may not often be available in claims of duress or undue influence: where the evidence shows, for example, that the pressure applied by a defendant was obviously illegitimate or the defendant knowingly exploited his influence over the claimant, the defendant will be unable to demonstrate that he relied, or relied reasonably on his receipt. However, that still leaves open three classes of case: first, cases where the pressure or influence came from a third party rather than the defendant; secondly, cases where the defendant deliberately exerted pressure or influence over the defendant but did so

[31] Considered further in ch 7, at 204–09.

[32] G Virgo, *The Principles of the Law of Restitution* 2 edn, above n 2, at 705.

[33] Ch 2, at 59–60, ch 3, at 79–82, and ch 4, at 109, cf 111–14.

[34] On duress, see: *Universe Tankships Inc of Monrovia v International Transport Workers Federation* [1983] 1 AC 366 (HL) 385 (Lord Diplock), cited with approval in *Dimskal Shipping Co SA v International Transport Workers Federation* [1992] 2 AC 152 (HL) 166 (Lord Goff). On undue influence: *Niersman v Pesticcio* [2004] EWCA Civ 372, [2004] WTLR 699 [20] (Mummery LJ) and discussion in ch 4, at 111–12.

with the best of intentions (for example, believing it to be in the best interests of the claimant); and thirdly, cases of undue influence where the claimant formed her intention to benefit the defendant without prompting from the defendant (a 'spontaneous' decision to benefit the defendant).

We saw from part one that there are some limited examples of defendants being afforded protection similar to that provided by the change of position defence in the first and third category of case.[35] A good example in the context of undue influence is *Hartigan v International Society for Krishna Consciousness Incorporated*.[36] In that case, the claimant transferred title to the family home (and surrounding farm) to the defendant association, which held property for the Krishna Consciousness Movement. The claimant was a devotee of the movement and the property was virtually her only material asset. At the time of making the transfer, she had two small children and was expecting another. In the circumstances, Bryson J of New South Wales Supreme Court found that a presumption of undue influence arose that was not rebutted by the defendant.

The defendant sought to defend the claim on the ground that it had changed its position by selling the property and applying the proceeds to reduce its debt. The defendant was in no way involved in the teachings of the movement and thus was not the party in the position of influence vis-à-vis the claimant. In any event, there was evidence that the claimant had made the transfer on the basis of her mistaken understanding of the requirements of her religion. The case therefore straddles categories (1) and (3), being open to interpretation both as a case where the relationship of excessive influence was with a third party (the movement) and a case where the decision was spontaneous, because resulting from the claimant's mistaken appreciation of her religious duties.

Bryson J rejected the defence only because the defendant had received a considerable financial benefit by discharging the debt early and to return it to the 'relative position of indebtedness which it would have been in had it not received the proceeds of sale' would be no great hardship.[37] Although not expressed in terms of the change of position defence, his Honour's findings are entirely consistent with that defence and in particular, the core requirement that any change of position must be irreversible. Had the defendant changed its position in a manner that was irreversible, for example by exhausting the proceeds of sale on funding for an international religious conference, then it is arguable that the defence may have succeeded.[38]

[35] For duress, see: *D Owen & Co v Cronk* [1985] 1 QB 265 (CA). For undue influence, see: *Allcard v Skinner* (1887) 36 Ch D 145 (CA); *Quek v Beggs* (1990) 5 BPR 11,766 (New South Wales Supreme Court); *Hartigan v International Society for Krishna Consciousness Incorporated* [2002] NSWSC 810 (New South Wales Supreme Court); *Cheese v Thomas* [1994] 1 WLR 129 (CA) discussed in ch 4, at 112–14.

[36] *Hartigan v International Society for Krishna Consciousness Incorporated* [2002] NSWSC 810 (New South Wales Supreme Court). A good example of the first category of case in the duress context is *D Owen & Co v Cronk* [1985] 1 QB 265 (CA), discussed in ch 3, at 80 and below, at 174–5.

[37] *Hartigan v International Society for Krishna Consciousness Incorporated* [2002] NSWSC 810 (New South Wales Supreme Court) [98].

[38] Subject again to the caveat that the other elements of the defence were satisfied and no other bar applied.

Part one concluded that, in categories (1) and (3), the only basis for excluding the defence would be to prevent the law's prohibition of duress and undue influence from being undermined. We will see in section E below that this is a form of policy reasoning that arguably reflects an independent 'stultification' bar to the change of position defence. An example of a duress case where such policy considerations were present is *Williams v Bayley*.[39] This case arguably comes within category (2) (a case where a defendant actively exercised duress albeit with the best of intentions), but reflects the kind of policy reasoning that might affect the availability of the change of position defence in categories (1) and (3). In that case, a father gave various securities to bankers under their implied threat that, if he did not interfere to save his son, the latter would be liable to be reported to the authorities for numerous forgeries to which the bankers had fallen victim. The probable consequence was that the son would be prosecuted for forgery and transported for life. The House of Lords accepted that the bankers acted in good faith throughout: nonetheless the securities were 'avoided' for illegitimate pressure.

For the purpose of this discussion, it is notable that the bankers had changed their position by proceeding with the settlement (which failed when the son absconded), yet no adjustment was made to reflect that reliance. Lord Westbury in particular dwelt on the public policy aspects of the case, specifically the 'soundest considerations of policy and morality, that you shall not make a trade of a felony'.[40] In this particular case, permitting a change of position defence would arguably undermine or stultify the policy of the law to prohibit agreements that compromise criminal prosecutions. As Lord Westbury observed, if 'such transactions existed to any considerable extent, [they] would be found productive of great injury and mischief to the community'.[41]

In this case, considerations of policy fell against admitting a defence of change of position. But that will not always be so: the policy of each category of claim must be independently considered. For example, we considered in chapter three the case of *D Owen v Cronk*.[42] In that case, the claimant transferred a benefit to the defendant because of duress to his goods imposed by a third party. This was therefore a category (1) case. The defendant was unaware of the circumstances of duress and was permitted to rely on the defence of payment over. As a matter of general observation, any deterrent objectives underlying the prohibition of duress to goods must be weakened where, as in a category (1) type case, the defendant was not involved or implicated in the illegitimate pressure. In *D Owen v Cronk* itself, the defendant did not carry out the prohibited behaviour, nor arguably was he part of the class of person whom the law is seeking to deter from future acts of duress to goods. In those circumstances, it is arguable that the policy underlying the law's

[39] *Williams v Bayley* (1866) LR 1 HL 200.

[40] *Ibid*, at 220.

[41] *Ibid*, at 221. The change of position may itself have been independently unlawful, because it involved the bankers desisting from reporting the son to the authorities: see further below, at 186.

[42] *D Owen & Co v Cronk* [1985] 1 QB 265 (CA), discussed in ch 3, at 80.

prohibition of duress to goods was not undermined by recognising a defence in favour of the defendant.

That conclusion might not be open in every category (1) duress case. Returning to *Williams v Bayley*, suppose that a defendant had received a benefit from the father as a result of the bankers' duress. Suppose further that, unaware of the circumstances of duress, he irreversibly changed his position in reasonable reliance on his receipt. In that scenario, the policy of the law discussed by Lord Westbury may well demand the exclusion of the defence, notwithstanding that the defendant was an innocent and passive recipient of the benefit of the banker's agreement. This is because of the very strong public interest in prohibiting agreements to compromise criminal prosecutions and the consequential need to deny them any legal effect.

This discussion demonstrates that public policy considerations must be closely scrutinised to determine the application of the defence to category (1) and (3) duress cases. Turning to the related doctrine of undue influence, this enquiry becomes highly problematic because, as we have seen previously, the rationale and thus the relevant public policy considerations applicable in this class of claim are hopelessly unclear.[43] The application of the change of position defence will be highly dependent on the proper characterisation of the rationale and nature of the doctrine. If, for example, the doctrine is concerned to protect claimants against transferring benefits pursuant to an impaired intention (an autonomy-based rationale) then this purpose may not be unduly undermined by permitting the defence in either category (1) or (3) cases. Although the claimant's impaired autonomy is a basis for obtaining restitution of the transferred benefit, her right may not be absolute. By drawing an analogy with the cases of spontaneous mistake, we can say that the defendant's change of position should be taken into account in determining his level of restitutionary liability. This sort of analysis would support the conclusion reached in *Hartigan* and those other cases of undue influence in which the defendant's change of position was taken into account in determining the defendant's level of restitutionary liability.

If, on the other hand, the policy of the law is to prevent any defendant in a position of influence vis-à-vis a claimant from retaining benefits from that claimant unless they have taken reasonable steps to emancipate her from the influence, then a much stronger case exists for imposing a blanket ban of the defence in category (3) cases. There is also support for this sort of analysis in the authorities. For example, in the classic Australian case of *Johnson v Buttress*,[44] the deceased (Mr Buttress) had become highly dependent on Mrs Johnson for support in almost all aspects of his life. He spontaneously[45] determined to transfer his only substantial asset, being title to the land on which his cottage was erected, to Mrs Johnson.

[43] See discussion in ch 4, at 111–12.

[44] *Johnson v Buttress* (1936) 56 CLR 113 (High Court of Australia).

[45] The circumstances did not support a finding of active exercise of influence by Mrs Johnson: *Johnson v Buttress* (1936) 56 CLR 113 (High Court of Australia) 133–34 (Dixon J, Evatt J concurring) 143 (McTiernan J)

There was evidence that the basis of the transfer was that Mrs Johnson and her family would look after Mr Buttress for the rest of his life. A majority of the High Court of Australia found that the circumstances gave rise to an unrebutted presumption of undue influence and that the transfer should be set aside.[46]

Following the transfer of title to Mrs Johnson, and arguably in accordance with its understood basis, Mrs Johnson and her family expended considered time, energy and expense repairing the cottage. They provided Mr Buttress with clothing, some basic necessaries, the net rent from the cottage as a living allowance and allowed him to live on other land owned by them free of charge. Although the point was neither taken nor considered, it is noteworthy that none of these changes of position were taken into account for the purpose of assessing Mrs Johnson's restitutionary liability.

Dixon J explained the doctrine of undue influence thus:

> [T]he parties may antecedently stand in a relation that gives to one an authority or influence over the other from the abuse of which it is proper that he should be protected. When they stand in such a relation, the party in the position of influence cannot maintain his beneficial title to property of substantial value made over to him by the other as a gift, unless he satisfies the court that he took no advantage of the donor, but that the gift was the independent and well-understood act of a man in a position to exercise a free judgment based on information as full as that of the donee.[47]

If the doctrine of undue influence does reflect a strongly protective or prophylactic policy, then arguably, that policy might be undermined by allowing the defendant in the position of influence to retain the benefit, notwithstanding that the influence was not actively exercised.

It is beyond this work to resolve the critical uncertainty surrounding the basis or rationale of the doctrine of undue influence. What must be reiterated, however, is that there does exist an established line of undue influence cases that expressly contemplate what resembles a change of position defence in category (3) type cases. To that extent, therefore, it seems either that there is no absolute policy against recognising the defence in the strong terms considered earlier, or that policy is not consistently applied. In either case, the state of the authorities does not preclude the application of the defence in category (3) cases of undue influence and, in the absence of definite authority to the contrary, it should accordingly be left open.

Further, and for much the same reasons as apply in the case of duress, any policy reasons for barring the defence will be considerably weakened in category (1) cases, where the defendant recipient was not in a position of influence. In such cases, any public interest in encouraging persons in a position of influence to take steps to protect the weaker party do not apply to the defendant. Nor do notions of deterrence have any sensible role to play in respect of this category of the defend-

[46] Latham CJ, Dixon, Evatt and McTiernan JJ. Starke J held that the transaction should be set aside for illegitimate pressure.

[47] *Johnson v Buttress* (1936) 56 CLR 113 (High Court of Australia) 134 (Dixon J, Evatt J concurring).

ant. Policy, principle and precedent therefore all combine to suggest that the change of position defence is, and ought to be, available in this category of case.

D The Innocent Inducer

This leaves the second category of case, where the defendant has actively induced the claimant to transfer the benefit to the defendant, albeit with the best of intentions. We have called this category of defendant the 'innocent inducer'. An example in the undue influence context[48] is found in the Australian case of *Giarrantano v Smith.*[49] In that case, the claimant created a trust of her title to land in the name of herself and her children, at the direction of her father-in-law. She was found to be naïve, unsophisticated, with no business sense or understanding of matters of property and a person easily open to persuasion. The intentions of the father-in-law throughout were selfless. He was solely motivated by a concern that, given her nature, she and her children were vulnerable to exploitation at the hands of others who did not hold their interests at heart. Nonetheless, the claimant succeeded in her claim for rescission of the trust and restitution of the land on the ground of undue influence.[50] Suppose that, in a variation of the facts, the claimant had declared a trust of the land and included the defendant as a beneficiary. Suppose further that, in reliance on this gift, the defendant had persuaded the claimant to enrol her children in a non-government school and had paid for the children's school fees.[51] Had this not occurred, the children would have remained with their former government-funded school for free. Should the defendant be entitled to rely on the change of position defence to the extent of his irreversible change of position?

The category of case of innocent inducer is not limited to claims of undue influence and duress: it also encompasses cases where the defendant innocently induced a claimant's mistaken transfer. For example, suppose a defendant innocently misrepresents to a claimant bank that it owes him money. The misrepresentation is the result of a third party's deception of the defendant. Suppose further that, on receiving the amount from the claimant, the defendant changes his position in reliance on his receipt by paying the money over to the fraudster, who subsequently vanishes. Assuming that in the circumstances of the fraud, it

[48] An example in the context of illegitimate pressure is *Williams v Bayley* (1866) LR 1 HL 200, discussed above, at 174; see also *Mutual Finance Ltd v John Wetton & Sons Ltd* [1937] 2 KB 389 (HL).

[49] *Giarrantano v Smith* (1985) NSW ConvR 55-267 (New South Wales Supreme Court). For a more recent example, see: *Winefield v Clarke* [2008] NSWSC 882 (New South Wales Supreme Court), where the defendant's change of position conferred a benefit on the claimant and thus is perhaps better analysed as involving a counterclaim by way of set-off for restitution: see ch 4, at 94–95, 103–07 and n 113.

[50] The claim was subject to a small interest in favour of the children due to a contribution by the father-in-law.

[51] Whether it is ever reasonable for a defendant in a position of influence to rely on his receipt will strongly depend on the view taken of the policy behind the doctrine, as to which see below, at 181–82.

was reasonable for the defendant to rely on his receipt, should the defendant nonetheless be barred from relying on the defence because of his role in innocently inducing the transfer?

We have seen in part one that there is some (albeit not entirely consistent) support in the estoppel, payment over and rescission case law for excluding the defence in cases of this kind.[52] Further support is discernible from *Saronic Shipping*,[53] considered in the previous section. On the other hand, the bar was rejected in the Australian case of *Mercedes-Benz (NSW) Pty Ltd v National Mutual Royal Savings Bank Limited*[54] on the ground that mere inducement did not constitute the defendant a 'wrongdoer' or *mala fides*. The same reasoning underpinned Henderson J's recent rejection in *Test Claimants in the FII Group Litigation v Revenue and Customs Commissioner*[55] of the suggestion that the Revenue should be denied the defence where it was responsible for the unlawful tax that had caused the claimants' mistaken payments. While it is no doubt correct that an 'inducer' may be neither a 'wrongdoer' nor *mala fides*, this conclusion should not end the enquiry. There may be further and independent reasons supporting the recognition of an innocent inducer bar, in addition to any wrongdoer bar and notwithstanding the *bona fides* of the defendant. This possibility was not considered by the courts in the *Mercedes* and *FII* cases. Its investigation is the task of the balance of this section.

One argument in favour of recognising a bar to innocent inducers is that having been himself 'a factor' in the claimant's vitiated decision to transfer the benefit, the defendant has interfered with the claimant's autonomy in decision-making. This interference counteracts or defeats the defendant's own complaint that he has changed his position in reliance on his receipt. Having been the author, at least in part, of his unjust enrichment, the defendant must bear the risks arising from the claimant's vitiated decision—including the risk that the received benefit might independently devalue or be destroyed, or that the defendant might change his position in reliance on his receipt.[56] We saw a similar, autonomy-based argument at play in estoppel.[57] Further, the innocent inducer can be said to have been at fault in the weak sense of having induced the claimant's impaired decision. Some commentators have argued that a liability rule that takes into account the fault of the parties in transferring or receiving benefits encourages them to take

[52] For estoppel, see: ch 2, at 54–59; 'payment over' defence, ch 3, at 82. The rescission case law is more sympathetic to the innocent inducer: ch 4, at 109–14.

[53] *Saronic Shopping Co Ltd v Huron Liberian Co* [1979] 1 Lloyd's Rep 341 (QB (Comm Ct)). The bar is also noted in *R v Secretary of State for the Environment ex p Camden London Borough Council* (1996) 28 HLR 321 (QB) 326 (Schiemann J).

[54] *Mercedes-Benz (NSW) Pty Ltd v National Mutual Royal Savings Bank Limited* (New South Wales Court of Appeal 27 February 1996) [23] (Sheller JA, with whom Priestly and Clarke JJA concurred).

[55] *Test Claimants in the FII Litigation v Revenue and Customs Commissioner* [2008] EWHC 2893 (Ch) [342].

[56] The same sort of bar, founded on this same rationale, is found in German law in the context of public law claims: M Jewell, 'The Boundaries of Change of Position—A Comparative Study' [1999] *Restitution L R* 1, 47.

[57] Ch 2, at 58–59.

reasonable precautions against mistakes.[58] This seems a justifiable concern and is largely consistent with the 'reasonable reliance' requirement that constitutes a core element of the change of position defence.

However, Professor Birks[59] and others[60] have argued that the fault of the defendant in inducing the claimant's impaired decision should not be taken into account, because to do so would be inconsistent with the strict liability approach otherwise applicable in the law of unjust enrichment. Given that fault on the part of the claimant is irrelevant to establishing her prima facie claim, why should the fault of the defendant be taken into account for the defence?

The answer is that the contexts in which the questions arise, and the focus of the enquiry in each instance, are quite distinct.[61] Where the defendant has not changed his position, the claimant will always have a better claim to the return of the benefit, whether or not she has been at fault. The fact that she has transferred the benefit to the defendant as a result of an impaired decision will always supply her with a strong normative claim. And, given the nature of the relief sought (restitution, rather than compensation, for example), the defendant suffers no harm from being required to make restitution of the benefit.

The position changes where the defendant has irreversibly changed his position. In those circumstances, to require the defendant to make restitution in full will harm the defendant. Yet, unless he is required to make full restitution the claimant will suffer harm. At this point, someone must lose out. In those circumstances, it is arguable that 'considerations of fault inevitably intrude'.[62]

A further argument against allowing consideration of the role of the innocent inducer to inform the court's decision is that it leads to uncertain and unpredictable exercises in comparison of incommensurable fault.[63] However, the same can be said of other areas of the law where comparisons of fault are routinely undertaken: the significant familiarity of tort law with the concept of contributory negligence is an obvious example. If the exercise is not too unpredictable or

[58] J Beatson and W Bishop, 'Mistaken Payments in the Law of Restitution' (1986) 30 *U Toronto L J* 149 (describing it as a 'comparative fault' approach) and H Dagan, 'Mistakes' (2001) 79 *Texas L Rev* 1795. These commentators argue that both claimant and defendant should be encouraged to take reasonable precautions, not only the defendant, as to which see further below, at 180–81.

[59] P Birks, *Unjust Enrichment* (2nd edn, OUP, Oxford 2005) 214.

[60] Most notably, R Grantham and C Rickett, 'Change of Position in New Zealand' [1999] *New Zealand Business LQ* 77, 77–78; R Grantham and C Rickett, 'Change of Position and Balancing the Equities' [1999] 7 *Restitution L Rev* 162, 162–63, adopted in *Dextra Bank and Trust Co Ltd v Bank of Jamaica* [2002] 1 All ER (Comm) 193 (PC) [45].

[61] E Bant and P Creighton, 'The Australian Change of Position Defence' (2002) 30 (2) *U Western Australia L Rev* 208, 225; E Bant and P Creighton, 'Mistake of Fact and Change of Position: Sound Advice from the Privy Council?' (2002) 2 *Oxford U Common L J* 271, 277–80. *Cf* H Dagan, *The Law and Ethics of Restitution* (Cambridge University Press, Cambridge 2004) 33 who collapses the defence into the primary claim.

[62] *National Bank of New Zealand Ltd v Waitaki International Processing (NI) Ltd* [1999] 2 NZLR 211 (New Zealand Court of Appeal) 229 (Thomas J).

[63] J Dawson, 'Restitution without Enrichment' [1981] 61 *Boston U L Rev* 563 and P Birks, 'Change of Position and Surviving Enrichment' in W Swadling (ed) *The Limits of Restitutionary Claims: A Comparative Analysis* (The United Kingdom Committee of Comparative Law, Glasgow 1997) 41 adopted in *Dextra Bank and Trust Co Ltd v Bank of Jamaica* [2002] 1 All ER (Comm) 193 (PC) [45].

discretionary in that context, why is it assumed to be so in the context of the change of position defence?

Chapter two suggests at least one good reason why a contributory negligence approach should be avoided. A contributory negligence approach would require the court both to identify and-crucially-measure the role of the defendant in inducing the impaired decision to transfer. This is then weighed against any part played in coming to the vitiated decision by the carelessness of the claimant. Chapter two explained that it is arguably impossible and inappropriate to place values or relative weights on the various factors that together produce a claimant's decision to transfer a benefit on any particular occasion.[64] This is why estoppel and (it is argued)[65] the change of position defence adopt an 'a factor' approach to causation rather than the alternative 'but-for' or 'NESS' tests familiar to torts law. If correct, it may be that the contributory negligence approach, borne from an area in which the causal inquiry generally involves involuntary objects, does not fit the kinds of causal issues involved in cases of change of position.

An alternative comparative fault methodology would be to reject a comparison of the parties' fault in *contributing* to the vitiated transfer (a 'contributory negligence' approach), in which as we have seen problems of measuring causation loom large, in favour of measuring the comparative failure of the parties to reach the standard of conduct of a reasonable person in their respective circumstances (a 'comparative fault' approach). Provided that the fault of each party was 'a factor' in inducing the impugned transaction, the subsequent assessment of the comparative culpability of the parties could proceed divorced from the threshold causal considerations. For example, suppose as in the earlier hypothetical a defendant made a misrepresentation to the claimant bank due to the deceit of a third party. His misrepresentation was a factor in the claimant's decision to make a payment to the defendant. Suppose the defendant could have done little to avoid making that mistake, given his state of knowledge, education, experience and the fraud of the third party, but the bank could easily have checked its accounts and so uncovered the fraud. The bank's failure to check was thus also a factor in its decision to make the impugned payment. Both parties therefore caused the impugned transfer in an 'a factor' sense. In those circumstances, a court could put aside the threshold considerations of causation and instead assess the degree by which each party fell below the standard of care of a reasonable person in their circumstances. The consequence would be to adjust the defendant's restitutionary liability according to the comparative culpability of claimant and defendant. The exercise would not involve comparison of the parties' *causal* responsibility for the impugned transfer (in the language used earlier, it would not assess their *contributory* negligence). Rather, it would assess their comparative fault.

A comparative fault approach seems a more sensitive means of helping to determine where loss should lie for the purposes of the change of position defence than

[64] Ch 2, at 33–34.
[65] *Ibid*, at 41–42 and ch 5, at 145, 147–148.

simply deciding that fault should be irrelevant. It would also have the incidental benefit of encouraging the parties, and others in a like position, to take reasonable steps to avoid the costs of mistakes. It would allow courts to consider the respective natures of the parties, for example that the claimant is a sophisticated banking institution or insurance company as compared to a private individual.[66] An incidental outcome of adopting the approach is that it would provide a strong incentive to institutional payers to take reasonable precautions to prevent mistakes in transfer transactions.

Notwithstanding these benefits, outside the New Zealand context[67] (which is heavily influenced by the applicable statutory regimes), there is evidence of strong judicial reluctance to engage in this kind of comparative approach in cases of mistake.[68] And the examples of the bar found in the broader context of estoppel, payment over and rescission appears to focus on the fault of a defendant in inducing the claimant's impaired decision to transfer. It is only fault in this specialised (and one-sided) sense that matters.

Is there any implicit support for a comparative fault approach discernable from other areas of the law? Consider the earlier undue influence hypothetical. Many would argue that it is not unreasonable for a father-in-law to attempt to safeguard the future of his daughter-in-law and her children. But, echoing the earlier discussion of the possible policy bases of undue influence, it might be considered unreasonable for him to fail to ensure that she receives independent legal or other emancipating advice in relation to the impugned transaction.[69] This failure to provide emancipating advice is a key trigger for restitutionary liability for undue influence. From that perspective, it could be argued that the doctrine of undue influence already incorporates a reasonableness standard in imposing liability. It also suggests that unless such advice is provided, any reliance by a defendant in a position of influence cannot be reasonable. If correct, this enquiry into fault in the context of undue influence is notably one-sided. The law does not pause to question whether the claimant should have been more independent and strong-willed and thus more like a 'reasonable woman'.[70] In these cases, therefore, it seems that the defendant influencer will always be more at fault than the claimant and so (on

[66] A consideration that has troubled many commentators with respect to cases like *Scottish Equitable Plc v Derby* [2001] EWCA Civ 369, [2001] 3 All ER 818, considered in ch 5, at 153 and *National Bank of New Zealand Ltd v Waitaki International Processing (NI) Ltd* [1992] 2 NZLR 211 (New Zealand Court of Appeal), considered below, at 188–89.

[67] eg *National Bank of New Zealand Ltd v Waitaki International Processing (NI) Ltd* [1992] 2 NZLR 211 (New Zealand Court of Appeal), considered below, at 188–89 and ch 10, at 251–54 and *Thomas v Houston Corbett* [1969] NZLR 151 (New Zealand Court of Appeal), considered in ch 10, at 252–54.

[68] eg *Mercedes-Benz (NSW) Pty Ltd v National Mutual Royal Savings Bank Limited* (New South Wales Court of Appeal 27 February 1996) [10]–[11] (Sheller JA, with whom Priestly and Clarke JJA concurred); *Scottish Equitable Plc v Derby* [2001] EWCA Civ 369, [2001] 3 All ER 818; *Dextra Bank and Trust Co Ltd v Bank of Jamaica* [2002] 1 All ER (Comm) 193 (PC).

[69] Above, at 175–76.

[70] It is for this same reason that some commentators reject any requirement in duress that a claimant must have had 'no reasonable alternative' open to her before she can recover: see Burrows, *The Law of Restitution* 2nd edn, above n 2, at 229; Jones, above n 19, at [10-032].

a comparative fault analysis) the defence should always be excluded in cases where the defendant recipient is in the position of influence.

But this conclusion runs directly contrary to those undue influence authorities discussed earlier that support recognition of a change of position defence in cases of 'spontaneous' decisions to transfer a benefit to the defendant, where the defendant is in the position of influence and thus 'ought' (perhaps) to know of the need for emancipating advice. This inconsistency undermines the existence of any implicit reasonableness requirement or comparative fault approach in the undue influence case law. It also seems to preclude the conclusion that it can never be reasonable for a party in a position of influence to rely on his receipt. The only way to reconcile these authorities is to focus not on the comparative fault of the parties, but on the role of the defendant in inducing the impaired transaction. In cases of spontaneous decisions to transfer, the defendant is not causally implicated in the claimant's impaired decision to transfer and the defence may still apply. In cases where the defence has actively induced the transfer, on the other hand, the defendant is at fault in having interfered with the claimant's autonomy. It is only the defendant's fault in this limited, one-sided and clearly causal sense that operates as a bar to the defence. On balance, it thus seems that the evidence supporting either express or implicit judicial recognition of a comparative fault bar is weak.

There are two further alternative approaches to fault that could be adopted were it accepted that the role of the defendant in inducing the impugned transaction may be relevant to the defence. The first is to deny the defence only where it can be shown that the defendant was more at fault in inducing the impugned transfer than the claimant, the so-called 'relative fault' approach.[71] This would involve the same kinds of difficulties inherent in any attempt to quantify causation in decision-making that were explored in the context of the contributory negligence approach. It follows that a relative fault approach could only apply where the defendant clearly played a decisive role in inducing the impugned transfer. The onus would lie in practice on the claimant to establish the bar, with the consequence that any borderline or uncertain cases would be resolved in favour of the defendant.

Consider again the earlier hypothetical of a bank which carelessly made a payment to a private individual (the defendant) in reliance on the defendant's innocent misrepresentation that the amount was due to him. On the relative fault approach, the onus would lie on the bank to demonstrate that the defendant's fault in being duped by the fraudster and therefore misleading the bank, was greater than that of the bank's. Given that most financial institutions might reasonably be expected to check their accounts before paying out moneys, the likely result in

[71] Nolan, above n 19, at 157. An example of the relative fault approach is contained in American Law Institute, *Restatement of the Law of Restitution* (American Law Institute Publishers, St Paul 1937) ch. 9, §142(2), which states that: 'Change of circumstances may be a defense or partial defense if the conduct of the recipient was not tortious and he was no more at fault for his receipt, retention or dealing with the subject matter than was the claimant.'

most cases of that type would be that the defendant's fault would not operate as a bar and he would be entitled to the full benefit of the defence.

A relative fault approach would bring the claimant's fault in making the impugned transfer into account against the fault of the defendant in inducing the claimant's transfer, without engaging in the sorts of fine causal assessments that bedevil the contributory negligence approach. On the other hand, as with the comparative fault approach, a relative fault approach would allow courts to consider the respective natures of the parties, for example that the claimant is a sophisticated banking institution or insurance company as compared to the defendant individual. It may also have the incidental benefit of providing an incentive to institutional payers to take reasonable precautions to prevent mistakes in transfer transactions.

However, and again as with the comparative fault approach, there is little support in the mistake case law for this approach outside the New Zealand context.[72] And in cases of undue influence, its adoption would again tend to dictate a blanket bar of the defence in cases where the defendant occupied the position of influence, rather than permit the defence to operate in cases of 'spontaneous' decisions to transfer a benefit, as some cases appear to contemplate. Further, part one in particular demonstrated that the focus has tended to be on whether the defendant induced the transaction, not on the relative (or comparative) fault of the parties. Nor does it seem possible that a relative fault approach could be adopted in addition to a defendant-oriented innocent inducer bar. This is because there is a real possibility that innocent inducers in mistaken payment cases will often be less at fault than careless claimants, particularly in the context of cases involving institutional payers such as banks. If that is correct, adoption of a relative fault bar would have a propensity to produce contradictory results to those suggested by a defendant-orientated bar. In the bank hypothetical, for example, the application of the relative fault approach would indicate that no bar applies. On a solely defendant-oriented innocent inducer bar, the defendant induced the bank's mistaken payment and therefore must be precluded from relying on the defence. This means that unless some method is developed for regulating their interaction, adoption of one form of bar will tend to exclude the adoption of the other.

This brings us to the final alternative. It is that the defence should be denied where the defendant played any part (however innocent) in inducing the claimant's vitiated decision to transfer the benefit.[73] On this approach, it is not necessary for the court to weigh the role of the defendant in inducing the claimant's vitiated decision, nor the degree of fault demonstrated by each party during the impugned transaction. It is sufficient for the claimant to demonstrate that the defendant's actions played a role (were 'a factor') in inducing the mistake, for example, on which the claimant subsequently acted. In other words, provided that the defendant caused the claimant's vitiated decision, the defence should be

[72] eg *Scottish Equitable Plc v Derby* [2001] EWCA Civ 369, [2001] 3 All ER 818.

[73] *Cf* the 'contributory fault' approach in Beatson and Bishop, above n 58, at 149.

denied. Notably, on this approach, the defendant would need to be shown to have been causally responsible in some part for the pleaded unjust factor. It would not be enough, for example, for a claimant to demonstrate that the defendant asked the claimant to pay what was due and the claimant, in response to that request, incorrectly assessed what she owed to the defendant. If the claimant did in fact owe the defendant money but assessed it incorrectly, then it cannot be said that the defendant's mistake was made in reliance on the defendant's request.

Of the three approaches to fault considered in this section, it is submitted that the third, in which the defence is barred if the defendant has been a factor in inducing the claimant's vitiated decision to transfer, is the best 'fit' with the preponderance of undue influence, duress and mistake cases that have contemplated an innocent inducer bar. Furthermore, it is supported by the arguments from autonomy discussed earlier and avoids the problems inherent in attempting to weigh the relative causal contributions to the claimant's decision-making processes. Finally, there is some express support for this approach from the estoppel case law, where courts have held that a defendant will be precluded from raising the defence where his own actions were a factor in the claimant making the particular representation.[74]

E Illegality and Legal Stultification

The fifth context in which the role of fault arises for consideration is where defendants have been involved in illegal conduct. There are now three English decisions in which the change of position defence was addressed in cases of illegality.[75] The first is *Barros Mattos Junior v MacDaniels.*[76] In that case, a Brazilian bank had millions of dollars stolen from it by fraudulent SWIFT transfers. The defendants received $8 million which they thought was for genuine foreign exchange transactions (a matter not challenged on the summary judgment application). In response to the bank's claim for restitution, the defendants argued that they had changed their position by converting the claimant's money into Nigerian currency and distributing it. It was assumed for the purposes of the case that the defendants were entirely innocent throughout and changed their position in good faith. Nonetheless, the defence failed because the exchange occurred pursuant to a foreign exchange contract that was illegal under Nigerian law. Laddie J held that the illegality prevented reliance by the defendants on a change of position defence.

[74] Ch 2, at 54–59.

[75] The issue has arisen in a number of other jurisdictions: eg *Garland v Enbridge Gas Distribution Inc* [2004] 1 SCR 629 (Supreme Court of Canada); *Equiticorp Industries Group Ltd v R (No 47)* [1998] 2 NZLR 481 (New Zealand High Court).

[76] *Barros Mattos Junior v MacDaniels* [2004] EWHC 1188 (Ch), [2005] 1 WLR 247.

Professor Tettenborn has argued that the result in *Barros Matteos* is difficult to justify.[77] If the defendants were the innocent recipients of the proceeds of fraud and had irreversibly changed their position in reliance on their receipt, it seems harsh that their 'technical infraction'[78] of the Nigerian exchange laws should operate to deny them the defence. In that context, it is enlightening to contrast the Australian approach to illegality, where illegality will bar the change of position defence only if there is an overriding public or statutory policy that would be stultified by recognising the defence.[79] In *Nelson v Nelson*,[80] McHugh J expressed the Australian approach to illegality thus:

> [Courts] should not refuse to enforce legal or equitable rights simply because they arose out of or were associated with an unlawful purpose unless: (a) the statute discloses an intention that those rights should be unenforceable in all circumstances; or (b)(i) the sanction of refusing to enforce those rights is not disproportionate to the seriousness of the unlawful conduct; (ii) the imposition of the sanction is necessary, having regard to the terms of the statute, to protect its objects and policies; and (iii) the statute does not disclose an intention that the sanctions and remedies contained in the statute are to be the only consequences of a breach of the statute or the frustration of its policies.

On this approach, it is necessary to determine whether the policy of the statute or the legal prohibition *requires* the exclusion of the defence. The nature and extent of any statutory penalty provisions will be of key importance in determining this question. In general, where a penalty is already provided, courts should be slow to add to those consequences a further sanction, in the form of the denial to the defendant of rights (in this case, a defence) he would otherwise hold.[81] This echoes another of Tettenborn's criticisms of *Barros Mattos*, that there is a distinction between taking away a cause of action in order to promote public policy and 'artificially disabling a defence', particularly where the latter can lead to 'wildly arbitrary results'.[82]

The Australian approach is, in essence, the same approach to illegality that we saw employed in cases of estoppel and payment over in part one.[83] In that context, and given the problems with the illegality bar as applied in *Barros Mattos*, it is submitted that the same approach should apply to the change of position defence. On this approach, the bar would apply both to illegality in receiving the impugned benefit and illegality in how the defendant changed his position.[84] For example,

[77] AM Tettenborn, 'Bank Fraud, Change of Position and Illegality: The Case of the Innocent Money-Launderer' [2005] *Lloyd's Maritime and Commercial L Q* 6–8.

[78] *Ibid*, at 6, 9.

[79] The Australian approach to illegality is discussed in detail in J Edelman and E Bant, *Unjust Enrichment in Australia* (OUP, Melbourne 2006) 294–300 and 337–38.

[80] *Nelson v Nelson* (1995) 184 CLR 538 (High Court of Australia) 613.

[81] *Yango Pastoral Co Pty Ltd v First Chicago Australia Ltd* (1978) 139 CLR 410 (High Court of Australia) 429 (Mason J). A recent Australian example of the change of position defence operating in the context of illegality is *Tonkin v Cooma-Monaro Shire Council* [2006] NSWCA 50, (2006) 145 LGERA 48 (New South Wales Court of Appeal).

[82] Tettenborn, above n 77, at 6, 8.

[83] Ch 2, at 62 and ch 3, at 85–86.

[84] *Cf* Tettenborn, above n 77, at 6–8.

suppose a woman receives an overpayment, in reliance on which she kills her husband on whom she had formerly relied for her income. The crime could never constitute a relevant change of position, notwithstanding satisfying the elements of the defence.[85] A less extreme example is a case where the unjust factor permitting restitution is a reason of policy which would be stultified by the application of the defence, such as a policy to promote adherence to the law which requires restitution following the reversal of a judgment,[86] or a policy to prevent agreements that compromise criminal proceedings.[87] As these further examples show, the bar is better understood as a 'legal stultification' bar, rather than one of illegality per se. It would also apply, for example, where the effect of applying the change of position defence would be to undermine the protection given by statute to a protected class.[88]

The second English case that considered the change of position defence in the context of an illegal transaction is the Court of Appeal decision in *Abou-Rahmah v Abacha*.[89] It will be recalled from chapter five that the majority in that case found that the defendant bank had changed its position in good faith in paying moneys to its clients who were involved in a fraudulent scheme.[90] This was so notwithstanding the fact that at the time of opening the account, the bank suspected that its clients might be involved in money-laundering.

The majority considered the relevance of the bank's suspicions, and the illegality of the transaction in which the bank had taken part, only in the context of determining whether the requirement of good faith was satisfied. However, as chapter five and this chapter demonstrate, good faith and illegality are distinct concepts, albeit ones that tend to overlap factually in case scenarios. The majority thus ought to have separately addressed the significance of the illegality of the transaction at the heart of the pleaded defence. Further, on the legal stultification approach to the bar, there were strong policy reasons for denying the defence. As Rix LJ, dissenting, pointed out, the effect of allowing the defence was to undermine Nigeria's attempts to stop the 'vice of money laundering'.[91] Therefore, even were the primary elements of the defence satisfied,[92] it is arguable that public policy considerations should have operated to deny the bank the defence.

[85] It might be objected that the defendant's reliance in this case is not reasonable. However, even though the change of position *itself* was not reasonable, that is not the focus of the requirement: ch 5, at 151. The reliance may well have been based on a reasonable understanding of the basis of her receipt and that basis may have been a reasonable one on which to decide to act, thereby satisfying the reasonableness requirement. See also: Birks, *Unjust Enrichment* 2nd edn, above n 59 at 261 (money spent on procuring child for sexual abuse would not sustain the defence).

[86] *White v Tomasel* [2004] QCA 89, (2004) 2 Qd R 438 (Queensland Court of Appeal), discussed further in ch 7, at 203.

[87] *Williams v Bayley* (1866) LR 1 HL 200 221 (Lord Westbury), discussed above, at 174–75.

[88] *Jeffrey v Fitzroy Collingwood Rental Housing Association Ltd* [1999] VSC 335 (Victorian Supreme Court) may be an example of this category of case.

[89] *Abou-Rahmah v Abacha* [2006] EWCA Civ 1492, [2007] 1 All ER (Comm) 827.

[90] Ch 5, at 158–60.

[91] *Abou-Rahmah v Abacha* [2006] EWCA Civ 1492, [2007] 1 All ER (Comm) 827 [50], [55].

[92] As to which, see: ch 5, at 158–60.

The final case in the trilogy is the recent decision of Henderson J in *Test Claimants in the FII Group Litigation v Revenue and Customs Commissioner*.[93] As with *Abou-Rahmah v Abacha*, the case highlights the dangers of failing to appreciate the significance of an independent stultification bar. It will be recalled that the claimants had paid tax to the Revenue pursuant to a mistaken belief that the applicable taxation regime was lawful. In truth, the system of taxation was in breach of what are now Article 43 (freedom of establishment) and Article 56 (free movement of capital) of the EC Treaty, with the consequence that the claimants were *prima facie* entitled to restitution of their mistaken payments.

Alongside their mistake claims, the claimants also had, in theory,[94] independent '*Woolwich*'[95]-style claims against the Revenue arising out of its unlawful taxation demands. Henderson J correctly considered that the change of position defence was automatically precluded in such claims. Although Henderson J reached this conclusion on the basis of the 'wrongdoer' exception, the better reason for it lies in the independent stultification bar. The *Woolwich* principle reflects a longstanding and vital public interest in prohibiting unlawful exaction of taxes by public authorities. This policy would be wholly undermined or stultified if the defence was permitted to apply to such claims. Henderson J effectively endorsed this view when he stated:[96]

> Subject to the need to bring his claim within a reasonable limitation period, the right of a private citizen to recover tax which has been unlawfully levied by an executive arm of the government should, as a matter of principle, be unfettered.

However, because Henderson J regarded the applicable bar as the 'wrongdoer' bar, he concluded that the public policy considerations that excluded the defence in *Woolwich*-style claims, did not apply to non-wrongful claims such as mistake.[97] The consequence was that the Revenue was entitled to rely on the change of position defence to defeat the mistake claims. This mis-characterisation of the relevant bar in terms of wrongdoing rather than stultification obscured the relevant policy considerations. The claimants' mistaken payments were entirely caused by the unlawful taxation regime. In those circumstances, to allow the change of position defence so as to permit the Revenue to retain the benefit of its unlawful imposts undermined the strong policy reasons supporting restitution.

F Fault in the Defendant's Change of Position

The final type of fault to be considered as a potential bar to the defence is the fault of the defendant in dealing with the received benefit. Some commentators have

93 *Test Claimants in the FII Litigation v Revenue and Customs Commissioner* [2008] EWHC 2893 (Ch).
94 Subject to an important limitation period point, as to which see discussion at [243]–[244].
95 *Woolwich Equitable Building Society v IRC* [1992] 3 All ER 737 (HL).
96 *Ibid*, [340].
97 Above at 168–69.

argued that fault in this sense is irrelevant, provided that the defendant has acted in reasonable reliance on his receipt.[98] This is because the defendant is entitled to act in a manner consistent with the reasonably understood basis of his receipt. If, for example, the defendant reasonably believes himself entitled to a payment, he is also entitled in reliance on that belief to tear up the received notes, gamble them away or invest them unwisely. A defendant comes under no duty of care with respect to a receipt he reasonably believes to be unimpeachable.

While this can be accepted, the position is less clear when it comes to defendants who know or suspect that they are not entitled to their receipt. It will be recalled that the reasonableness requirement applies not only to the basis of the belief on which the defendant acts: the belief must also be one on which a reasonable person would act. Arguably, where a defendant knows or suspects that he is not entitled to his receipt, he only acts in reasonable reliance on his receipt where he acts consistently with the known (or suspected) basis of the receipt. Where he deals with the benefit other than by transferring the benefit to that entitled party, or (perhaps) placing it in a reasonably secure location pending return to the entitled party,[99] he does so at his peril.[100]

Taking a slightly different approach to the problem, Birks argued that if a defendant is aware that he is not entitled to the benefit, but must hold it for the benefit of a third party or the claimant, the defendant comes under a duty of care similar to that of a trustee, to take reasonable care to protect the benefit pending its safe transfer to the third party or the claimant.[101] If the defendant then fails to exercise that care and the benefit is lost, destroyed or devalued as a result, then the defendant may lose any entitlement to rely on the defence.

There is some support in the change of position case law for this kind of bar to the defence. In *National Bank of New Zealand Ltd v Waitaki International Processing (NI) Limited*[102] a bank insisted on paying money to the defendant, despite the latter's repeated protests that it was not entitled to the payment. The defendant invested the money with a small finance company to be held so that it could be repaid when the bank realised its error. But by the time the bank did so, the finance company had gone into liquidation and, for reasons which were not entirely clear, the security was worthless. The New Zealand Court of Appeal accepted that the defence applied because the defendant had invested the money

[98] Notably Bant and Creighton, 'The Australian Change of Position Defence' above n 61, at 227–28 and Edelman and Bant, above n 79, at 335.

[99] This choice of investment location was a key problem in *National Bank of New Zealand Ltd v Waitaki International Processing (NI) Ltd* [1992] 2 NZLR 211 (New Zealand Court of Appeal), as to which see immediately below and ch 10, at 253–54.

[100] Nolan, above n 19, at 155. *Cf* Cleasby B's aphorism in *Fowler v Hollins* (1872) LR 7 QB 616 (Exch) 639: 'persons deal with the property in chattels or exercise acts of ownership over them at their peril'.

[101] P Birks, 'A Bank's Mistaken Payments: Two Recent Cases and Their Implications' (2000) 6 *New Zealand Business L Q* 155, 90.

[102] *National Bank of New Zealand Ltd v Waitaki International Processing (NI) Ltd* [1999] 2 NZLR 211 (New Zealand Court of Appeal). A similar duty is identified in *Citibank Ltd v Department of Public Works and Services* [2001] NSWSC 1066 (New South Wales Supreme Court) [31] (Newman AJ).

so that it would be available to repay the plaintiff at a later time and was acting consistently with its knowledge of the nature of the receipt. That is, the defendant had relied on its receipt. Nonetheless the court discounted the value of the defence because of the defendant's failure to ensure that there was sufficient security for its invested funds.[103]

Further support for this bar can be found in the rescission case law. The Australian case of *Alati v Kruger*[104] was considered in chapter four.[105] It will be recalled that the defendant had fraudulently induced the claimant to purchase a business. The defendant also took an assignment of the lease for the premises from which the business operated. After the claimant took control of the business, it deteriorated for reasons unrelated to the misrepresentations. The High Court of Australia held that this did not preclude *restitutio in integrum*. However, of particular pertinence to this discussion are the further facts that after the claimant had elected to rescind the transaction and after the trial judge had made preliminary findings of fact in his favour, the claimant discontinued the business and left the premises. The landlord accordingly repossessed the premises. All this occurred before the trial judge's final judgment was handed down. The claimant therefore could not make counter-restitution to the defendant of the business or lease.

In a joint judgment, Dixon CJ, Webb, Kitto and Taylor JJ considered that had the claimant acted 'unconscientiously', as by discontinuing the business and abandoning the premises without giving the defendant a reasonable opportunity to get them back, the court might refuse relief consequent on rescission.[106] However, following the preliminary findings of fact made against him by the judge, the defendant knew that the case was going against him. In those circumstances, the onus fell on him to take steps to protect the value of the business and lease. In other words, following the preliminary findings of fact against the defendant, the risk of the property devaluing fell back on the defendant:

> [The defendant] took his chance, contenting himself with such maintenance of the business as the [claimant's] continuing conduct of it might afford . . . [T]he [claimant] was not under a duty to go on indefinitely, working for nothing and incurring losses . . ..[107]

Fullagar J, in a separate judgment, stated that a party remaining in possession of a benefit after giving a notice to rescind 'is under a duty to take reasonable care to preserve the property, so that what he has received from the other party may . . . be restored to the other party'.[108] In the circumstances of the case, however, Fullagar J agreed with the majority that the defendant had failed to establish that

[103] The defence was initially reduced by one-third to reflect this fault, then increased to 90% to reflect the claimant's fault in insisting on payment in the first place: on this 'comparative fault' approach to fault, see above, at 180–81.

[104] *Alati v Kruger* (1955) 94 CLR 216 (High Court of Australia). *Cf Munchies Management Pty Ltd v Belperio* (1989) 58 FCR 274 (Federal Court of Australia) 288–89 (Fisher, Gummow and Lee JJ).

[105] At 104–5, 116.

[106] *Alati v Kruger* (1955) 94 CLR 216 (High Court of Australia) 225.

[107] *Alati v Kruger* (1955) 94 CLR 216 (High Court of Australia), at 226.

[108] *Ibid*, at 228.

any loss had been caused through any breach of duty or unreasonable conduct on the part of the claimant.[109]

It is doubtful whether this bar should be framed in terms of a duty of care, which might suggest, for example, that the duty is actionable and could give rise to compensation. However, the case law does support the more limited proposition that in circumstances where the defendant knows that he is not entitled to his receipt, he should be precluded from relying on the change of position defence if he fails to take the care a reasonable man would in the circumstances, in particular, knowing that the benefit must be accounted for to another.

In principle, this bar should apply as much to cases of independent changes of position as defendant-instigated changes. However, this general position is subject to the caveat we saw in chapter five, namely that the change of position defence only becomes relevant in cases where the defendant has initially accepted the benefit, so that he can sensibly be said to have been enriched by his receipt.[110] In cases where there is an independent change of position, there will often have been no acceptance of the benefit and so considerations of fault do not apply. For example, in the case where a defendant leaves a valuable painting exposed on his front porch, when he might easily have moved it indoors out of harm's way, it will still be open for the defendant to say that he never accepted the benefit and therefore cannot be expected to take any positive steps to protect it. To find otherwise would be to impose a positive obligation to preserve a benefit that the defendant never accepted.

The final question to be addressed in respect of this category of fault is, once again, whether it should operate as a complete bar to the defence, or whether the defendant's fault should be quantified and the defence diminished proportionately. In *Waitaki*, the second approach was taken. This has the attraction of leaving the defendant some measure of protection where his degree of fault was not great. Further, this area does not suffer from the same sorts of causal difficulties that bedevil the contributory negligence and relative fault approaches considered earlier in the context of 'innocent inducers'. We saw that one objection to those approaches was that courts were being asked to assess the impact of the defendant's actions on the claimant's decision-making processes. In contrast, in cases where the defendant has been at fault in the manner in which he has changed his position, the court is not being asked to make this kind of comparative and quantitative assessment.

That said, it is not easy to see what criteria should be taken into account in assessing the degree of fault in this context. One approach would be to determine the extent to which the defendant's conduct fell below that of the reasonable man in his position and to discount the defence by that percentage. Alternatively, the bar could operate completely, thereby obviating any need to engage in assessments of this kind. While this would fit with the 'reasonable reliance' approach to the

[109] *Ibid*, at 229.
[110] At 147.

problem considered earlier,[111] its consequences may be too harsh for courts to accept.

G Conclusion

This chapter has demonstrated that even where a defendant can establish the primary elements of the change of position defence, his fault taken together with the broader policy not to stultify the law's existing prohibitions and protections will often operate to deny him the change of position defence. The ramifications of this finding flow into the issue of the ambit of operation of the defence, to which we now turn.

[111] Above, at 188.

7

Ambit of Operation

A Introduction

THIS CHAPTER CONSIDERS the categories of claims to which the change of position defence applies. This question can be divided into two sub-issues. The first is whether the defence applies to all claims in unjust enrichment. The second is whether the defence operates beyond unjust enrichment to other categories of claim.

Much of the necessary groundwork for this chapter has already been covered. In many cases, the requirement of an irreversible change of position, reasonable reliance or the operation of bars to the defence will determine this issue. The main work of this chapter, therefore, will be to draw out and summarise the conclusions either explicit or implicit in the earlier portions of this book.

The chapter begins by considering examples of claims in unjust enrichment, before turning to consider the application of the defence beyond that category of claim. In that regard, it must be recognised that the classification of many unjust factors is disputed. We have noted previously the debate over whether undue influence operates as a wrong or an unjust factor, or indeed some other category of legal event.[1] Settling those sorts of controversies is beyond the scope of this book. Rather, this chapter will consider some of the main categories of claims said to come within and outside the law of unjust enrichment and the kinds of considerations that will impact on the availability of the change of position defence. In this way, even if the categorisation itself is disputed, the underlying reasons for the application or denial of the change of position defence will be revealed.

B Application to Claims in Unjust Enrichment

(1) Mistake

This book commenced by noting that spontaneous mistake claims are the paradigm example of claims to which the change of position defence will apply.[2] In

[1] Ch 4, at 111–112.
[2] Ch 1, at 2–3.

contrast, the following chapters revealed that induced mistake claims will be far less likely to attract the defence. Often, this will be because a defendant incidentally[3] revealed to be guilty of deceit or negligent misrepresentation, for example, will not be able to demonstrate the reasonable reliance[4] necessary for the defence in cases of defendant-instigated changes of position. For example, a defendant who deliberately tricks a claimant into transferring a benefit to him will know of, or suspect, the claimant's mistake. It follows that any subsequent decision to change his position cannot have been made in reliance, or reasonable reliance, on his receipt.[5] Further, a defendant who induces a claimant into the same transaction in breach of his duty of care by definition has not acted as would a reasonable man. In those circumstances, it will be highly unlikely that any decision to change his position will have been made in reasonable reliance on his receipt.

In cases of independent changes of position, the defence is unlikely to be available to the incidental wrongdoer for two reasons. The first and main reason is that in the context of wrongfully-induced mistakes, to allow the defence may undermine the policies that make deliberate or negligent misrepresentation tortious.[6] There are two factors that must be brought into account, however, before coming to that conclusion. The first is that the claimant herself chose to bring a claim in unjust enrichment, to which the defence prima facie applies. The second is that where the law already supplies a regime in one context for addressing wrongful behaviour, courts should only deny a defence applicable outside that context where it is clearly necessary to protect the policy underlying the law's existing prohibition. Whether it is necessary in this sense to exclude the change of position defence in cases of incidentally-revealed deceit and negligent misrepresentation has yet to be expressly addressed by the courts.

The second reason why the defence is unlikely to be available in cases of wrongfully-induced mistakes is that, wrongdoing aside, the defendant induced the claimant's vitiated decision to enter into the impugned transaction. This 'innocent inducer' bar provides an additional reason for excluding the defence in cases of incidentally-revealed cases of wrongful inducement.[7] It also provides an independent reason why even innocent (non-wrongful) inducers of a claimant's mistake, for example an innocent misrepresentor, may be precluded from relying on the defence.[8] Taken together, these considerations indicate that the ambit of operation of the change of position defence within mistake claims will be quite limited.

[3] An 'incidental wrongdoer': see ch 6, at 166.
[4] Ch 5, at 147–55.
[5] Ch 2, at 28–30 and ch 5, at 148, 154–55.
[6] Ch 6, at 166–67.
[7] *Ibid*, at 168.
[8] Ch 6, at 177–84.

(2) Duress and Undue Influence

In cases of duress and undue influence, we saw in chapter six[9] that there are only two limited circumstances where a defendant may be able to rely on the defence: first, where the duress or undue influence came from a third party[10] and secondly (in cases of undue influence only), where the claimant's decision was 'spontaneous', in the sense that the defendant did not actively exercise his influence over the claimant.[11]

The potential operation of the defence can be illustrated by considering examples of the two classes of case.[12] The position of defendants who receive benefits as a result of the influence of third parties arose for consideration in the case of *Bridgeman v Green*.[13] There, a gentleman subject to the influence of his butler made a number of gifts of money to the butler's wife and brother. The wife and brother were not parties to the influence, nor was there any indication that they were aware, or suspected, that the gifts were the result of excessive influence. Nonetheless, they were required to make full restitution of the received benefits. Suppose that the brother, in reasonable reliance on his gift, had spent its value on an around-the-world trip. In those circumstances, and on the approach taken to the defence in this work, he should be permitted to raise the change of position defence. The only remaining basis for precluding the defence would be that it undermines the reasons for the law's prohibition of undue influence. This bar would need to be considered independently and by reference to the facts of each particular case.[14]

A modification of the facts of *Reid v Reid*[15] illustrates the second class of case. There, a formerly independent young adult was severely injured in a car accident and nursed back to health by his mother. The young man never quite regained his former faculties, remaining dependent on his mother's assistance and guidance in many aspects of his life. On receiving compensation, he spontaneously determined to buy a house in which he and his parent could live. However, he purchased the property in the joint names of himself and his mother, expressing to her that it was a measure of his gratitude for her ongoing love and support. In those

[9] At 172–77.

[10] As in *Bridgeman v Green* (1757) Wilm 58, 97 ER 22; *Huguenin v Baseley* (1804) 14 Ves Jun 273, 33 ER 526; *Giarrantano v Smith* (1985) NSW ConvR 55-267 (New South Wales Supreme Court).

[11] As in *Quek v Beggs* (1990) 5 BPR 11,766 (New South Wales Supreme Court); *Smith v Smith* (New South Wales Supreme Court 12 July 1996); *Reid v Reid* (New South Wales Supreme Court 30 November 1998); *Hartigan v International Society for Krishna Consciousness Incorporated* [2002] NSWSC 810 (New South Wales Supreme Court), discussed in ch 3 at 112–14 and ch 6, at 173.

[12] See also examples considered in ch 6, at 173–75.

[13] *Bridgeman v Green* (1757) Wilm 58, 97 ER 22. A duress case with the same fact pattern, considered in the context of the payment over defence, is *D Owen & Co v Cronk* [1985] 1 QB 265 (CA), considered in ch 3, at 80 and ch 6, at 174–75.

[14] An example of the kind of public policy reasoning in play is discussed in ch 6, at 175–76.

[15] *Reid v Reid* (New South Wales Supreme Court 30 November 1998). As noted in ch 4, a number of cases of rescission for undue influence appear to contemplate a change of position defence in circumstances where the claimant's decision to enter into the transaction was spontaneous: ch 4, at 112–114.

circumstances, an unrebutted presumption of undue influence arose, given the nature of the relationship and the size and imprudence of the gift.

Suppose, however, in reasonable[16] reliance on the gift and the financial freedom from rent it entailed, that the mother had decided to have the hip surgery that she had always wanted but could not previously afford. Could she rely on the change of position defence in diminution of her restitutionary liability? In the case itself, Bryson J held that the mother held her interest in the property on trust for her son. We will see in section (6) below that the fact that a trust was held to arise might provide an independent reason for denying the application of the defence. Suppose, however, that the transfer was analysed as giving rise to a proprietary power to rescind the transaction, of the same nature as we saw operate in the context of rescission.[17] On the approach to the defence adopted in this book (and subject to any further bars), the change of position defence should be available.

Apart from these two classes of case, a combination of the 'reasonable reliance' requirement,[18] public policy considerations[19] and the role of the defendant as 'innocent inducer'[20] all suggest that the defence may be denied in cases of undue influence and duress. In particular, in cases of an innocent inducement of the claimant's impaired decision to act, the fact that the recipient's intentions were selfless will not be sufficient to permit the defence. Suppose, for example, the mother in *Reid v Reid* had actively suggested that she became a joint proprietor of the property, not because she wished to benefit personally but because she feared that her son was incapable of managing the property in his best interests by himself.[21] Notwithstanding her chaste motives, her role as innocent inducer would be sufficient (if that bar is adopted) to preclude her from relying on the defence. In any event, it may be determined that to allow her to rely on the defence, given her active role in procuring the benefit, would overly undermine the deterrent and protective aims of the doctrine and should be denied on that policy ground.

[16] See discussion in ch 6, at 181–82 on the interplay between applicable policy and the reasonableness requirement where the defendant is in the position of influence.

[17] As was held by a majority in *Allcard v Skinner* (1887) 36 Ch D 145 (CA), Cotton LJ in the minority preferring the vested trust model and in *Quek v Beggs* (1990) 5 BPR 11,766 (New South Wales Supreme Court), both cases discussed in ch 4, at 112–13 and both consistent with an application of a change of position defence.

[18] Ch 6, at 181–82.

[19] *Ibid*, at 174–77.

[20] *Ibid*, at 177–84.

[21] *Cf Winefield v Clarke* [2008] NSWSC 882 (New South Wales Supreme Court), where the defendant arranged for the claimant's property to be transferred into their joint names for the claimant's protection. The defendant changed her position by discharging the mortgage over the property, thereby conferring a benefit on the claimant that was the proper subject of a counter-claim for restitution for total failure of consideration: see ch 4, at 94–95, 103–07 and n 113.

(3) Failure of Consideration

Turning to cases of failure of consideration, or failure of basis, the key feature of this category of claim is that the transfer of the benefit is conditional. Applying the elements of the defence identified in this book, a defendant who understands that a benefit is conferred on a conditional basis but, before the condition is fulfilled, acts as if his interest were absolute, will not be entitled to the defence. His change of position is not a consequence of his knowledge of the circumstances of the receipt and, accordingly, the required element of reliance is not satisfied. A prime example of this category of case is *Goss v Chilcott*,[22] discussed in chapter one.[23] In that case, Lord Goff explained that the defendants could not rely on the defence because, knowing that in due course the loan received by them would need to be repaid, they had allowed the money to be paid to a third party. As the loan was conditional on repayment, the defendants dealt with it (other than by repaying it) at their own risk.

Although this is the starting point, it is not impossible that the defence can, and should, apply in some cases of failure of consideration. In particular, a defendant who has not knowingly taken the risk of the failure of condition at the time he changes his position may have relied on his receipt. The most obvious class of case of this type is frustration, now largely covered in England by subsections 1(2) and 1(3) Law Reform (Frustrated Contracts) Act 1943.[24] The structure and operation of that legislation and its relationship with the change of position defence are considered in chapter ten.[25] In cases where the Act applies, the common law defence will be excluded. However, as chapter ten explains, the statute's coverage is piecemeal and its equivalent has not been adopted throughout the Australian states. It follows that courts both in England and Australia will still be required to consider from time to time whether the change of position defence applies in cases of frustration. In such cases, it is possible that a defendant may have changed his position in reasonable reliance on his receipt of contractual rights.[26] Certainly, it is difficult in the light of the definition of what constitutes a frustrating event to conceive of the defendant as a risk-taker. In those circumstances, as a matter of principle (and subject to the usual bars), the defence ought to be available.

The same conclusion may be reached in cases of initial failure of consideration. Where the basis of a transfer failed from the outset, for example, because it was

[22] *Goss v Chilcott* [1996] AC 788 (PC) 799. To same effect is *State Bank of New South Wales Ltd v Swiss Bank Corporation* (1995) 39 NSWLR 350 (New South Wales Court of Appeal) discussed in ch 5, at 152–53; *Sanwa Australia Finance Ltd v Finchill Pty Ltd* [2001] NSWCA 466 (New South Wales Court of Appeal) [29]–[30] (Davies AJA, Beazley and Heydon JJA concurring); *Gilsan (International) Ltd v Optus Networks Pty Ltd* [2004] NSWSC 1077 (New South Wales Supreme Court) [358]–[81] (McDougall J) and *Saba Yachts Limited v Fish Pacific Ltd* [2006] NZHC 1452 (New Zealand High Court) [59]–[62] (Winkelmann J) citing *Goss v Chilcott.*

[23] At 12.

[24] An equivalent statutory regime is found in Australia in Frustrated Contracts Act 1958 (Vic).

[25] At 244–50.

[26] As in *Fibrosa Spolka Akcyjna v Fairbairn Lawson Combe Barbour Ltd* [1943] AC 32 (HL).

transferred pursuant to a void contract, and the defendant was not aware of the failure at the time of irreversibly changing his position, he may be able to bring himself within the defence provided that his reliance was reasonable and no bars to the defence apply. The reason for the failure of the basis will be of great significance in determining these issues. If, for example, the transaction is void because the defendant was *non est factum*, there is no policy reason for excluding the defence. Indeed, the defence may serve to further the protective policy of the law in cases involving parties who lack transactional capacity.[27] This scenario can be contrasted with a case in which, for example, a contractual clause was void because of the application of a statutory provision designed to protect a class of payer to which the *claimant* belongs. Here, there will be strong reasons to refuse the application of the defence in order not to defeat or stultify the policy of the statute.[28] Courts may also be less likely to regard reliance as reasonable where it was made in the face of express statutory prohibition of the transaction in question.

The other class of case arising from a failure of consideration to which the defence may apply are cases where there was a independent change in the received benefit. In this category of case, there is no 'reasonable reliance' requirement and so the fact that a defendant realised his receipt was insecure will not of itself preclude the operation of the defence. In those circumstances, and provided that no bars to the defence pertain, the defence may still apply.

(4) No Intention to Benefit

The controversial unjust factor of 'no intention to benefit' is said to operate as an '*a fortiori*' extension of the unjust factors of mistake, duress and failure of basis.[29] On this approach, the umbrella unjust factor of 'no intention to benefit' harbours three sub-categories of claim: first 'ignorance', a stronger version of mistake; secondly 'powerlessness', a stronger version of duress; and, thirdly, 'anti-beneficial basis' a stronger version of failure of basis. Whether this analysis is correct is beyond the scope of this book. However, assuming for the moment that it is, in theory, the change of position defence ought to apply to these categories of claim, subject to the same considerations that apply with respect to their 'weaker' counterparts.[30]

[27] *Cf Perpetual Trustees Victoria Limited v Ford* [2008] NSWSC 29 (New South Wales Supreme Court).

[28] *David Securities Pty Ltd v Commonwealth Bank of Australia* (1992) 127 CLR 353 (High Court of Australia) 384. This form of bar is discussed in ch 6, at 184–87.

[29] The following analysis of the unjust factor of ignorance is adopted from J Edelman and E Bant, *Unjust Enrichment in Australia* (OUP, Melbourne 2006) ch 12. For an important contrary view, see W Swadling, 'Ignorance and Unjust Enrichment: The Problem of Title' (2008) 28 *OJLS* 627

[30] *Lipkin Gorman (a firm) v Karpnale Ltd* [1991] 2 AC 548 (HL) itself is regarded by some commentators as an ignorance-based claim, to which the change of position defence applied: see further below, at 208–09. Other cases that could be analysed as involving 'ignorance' claims that considered but rejected the defence on grounds unrelated to the unjust factor include: *Cressman v Coys of Kensington (Sales) Ltd* [2004] EWCA Civ 47, [2004] 1 WLR 2775 and *Barros Mattos Junior v MacDaniels* [2004] EWHC 1188 (Ch), [2005] 1 WLR 247. *Re Diplock's Estate* [1948] 1 Ch 465 (CA) 546 may also be an

On this analysis, a thief who has instigated a change of position will not be able to rely on the defence in response to a claim brought by the victim on the ground of 'ignorance' because, as with cases of fraudulent misrepresentation, he will not be able to prove reasonable reliance. Nor will he be able to rely on the defence should there have been a independent change of position in relation to the stolen benefit. This is not because of the 'reasonable reliance' requirement (which does not apply with respect to independent changes of position) but because of the application of the 'wrongdoer' and 'stultification' bars.[31] In particular, to allow a thief to rely on the defence would entirely undermine the law's prohibition of his act of theft.

Similarly, a defendant who robs a claimant of her watch, having tied her to a chair so as to prevent any struggle, will fail to defend a claim for restitution based on 'powerlessness' for much the same reasons as apply in the case of duress. Most obviously, he will be unable to prove reasonable reliance in cases of defendant-instigated changes of position. He will also fall foul of the 'wrongdoer' and 'stultification bars to the defence in cases of independent change of position, given that the benefit was transferred as a result of his assault and to allow him to rely on the defence would directly undermine the law's prohibition of that wrong.

Finally, a defendant who knows that a benefit is transferred on the basis that is not to be enjoyed by him personally ('anti-beneficial basis'), but then deals with it for his own benefit, will face the same hurdles in proving reasonable reliance as were discussed earlier in the context of failure of consideration. For example, suppose a woman transfers property to her children on the understanding that it will be held for her benefit.[32] The children then mortgage the property to finance their personal business venture. The business fails and the property is sold to repay their debts. In those circumstances, it will not be possible for them to raise the change of position defence because they acted contrary to the known basis of their receipt. On the other hand, and again consistent with the weaker form of claim, it will remain possible for a defendant to rely on the defence where the change was independent of, rather than instigated by the defendant. For example, suppose in a variation of the earlier hypothetical, that the house was destroyed by an earthquake. In those circumstances, the defence may remain open.

In contrast with these scenarios, and again as with cases of mistake, duress and failure of basis, a defendant who receives the claimant's asset from a third party in circumstances where he is entirely unaware of the vitiating factor of 'no intention to benefit' may, in theory and subject to the usual bars, be entitled to rely on the

early example of a successful, albeit intuitive, application of the defence. In Australia, a number of cases fit the ignorance analysis and either applied the defence, or considered that it was, in theory, available: *State Bank of New South Wales Ltd v Swiss Bank Corporation* (1995) 39 NSWLR 350 (New South Wales Court of Appeal); *Gertsch v Atsas* [1999] NSWSC 898, (1999) 10 BPR 18 431 (New South Wales Supreme Court); *Port of Brisbane Corp v ANZ Securities* [2002] QCA 158, [2003] 2 Qd R 661 (Queensland Court of Appeal); *Spangaro v Corporate Investment Australia Funds Management Ltd* [2002] QCA 158, [2003] 2 Qd R 661 (Queensland Court of Appeal).

31 Discussed in ch 6, at 167–69.

32 As in *Nelson v Nelson* (1995) 184 CLR 538 (High Court of Australia).

defence to a claim in unjust enrichment.[33] For example, suppose a defendant receives the claimant's watch from a third party. Unbeknown to him, the benefit was forcibly removed from the claimant by the third party while the claimant was tied up and helpless to prevent the robbery. In those circumstances, the recipient is entirely innocent of the circumstances of powerlessness that led to his enrichment. Provided that he satisfies the elements of the defence, he may be entitled to rely on it to reduce his restitutionary liability. This analysis, however, is subject to any further considerations that may arise from the claimant retaining proprietary rights to the watch, considerations to which we will return below.[34]

Although the preceding analysis is fairly straightforward as a matter of principle, the position as a matter of precedent is less clear. This is largely because, contrary to the position assumed above, the juristic bases of the claims that potentially come within the 'no intention' category are not settled as a matter of authority. For example, it is in this category of case that one would expect to find cases where there has been a misapplication or misdistribution of trust or estate assets.[35] The juristic basis of these kinds of claim is highly contentious. In particular, debate continues over whether what are traditionally known as claims in 'knowing receipt'[36] can be brought within an unjust enrichment rubric, or whether a separate unjust enrichment analysis can apply as an alternative avenue of claim arising from the same facts. The most recent English[37] and Australian[38] authorities have not been receptive to applying a 'strict liability in unjust enrichment plus change of position defence' analysis in preference to, or in addition to the traditional knowing receipt claim. Whether this stance is justified cannot be addressed here. However, a number of points can be made about the position taken in the authorities to the application of the defence to knowing receipt claims in particular, and 'no intention to benefit' type claims in general.

[33] Above n 30.

[34] At 202 and 204–09. Examples in the UK case law arguably fitting this fact pattern include *Re Diplock's Estate* [1948] 1 Ch 465 (CA) 546; *Lipkin Gorman (a firm) v Karpnale Ltd* [1991] 2 AC 548 (HL), discussed below, at 208–09; *Cressman v Coys of Kensington (Sales) Ltd* [2004] EWCA Civ 47, [2004] 1 WLR 2775 and *Barros Mattos Junior v MacDaniels* [2004] EWHC 1188 (Ch), [2005] 1 WLR 247. In Australia, see: *State Bank of New South Wales Ltd v Swiss Bank Corporation* (1995) 39 NSWLR 350 (New South Wales Court of Appeal); *Gertsch v Atsas* [1999] NSWSC 898, (1999) 10 BPR 18 431 (New South Wales Supreme Court); *Port of Brisbane Corp v ANZ Securities* [2002] QCA 158, [2003] 2 Qd R 661 (Queensland Court of Appeal); *Spangaro v Corporate Investment Australia Funds Management Ltd* [2002] QCA 158, [2003] 2 Qd R 661 (Queensland Court of Appeal).

[35] *Gertsch v Atsas* [1999] NSWSC 898, (1999) 10 BPR 18 431 (New South Wales Supreme Court); *Spangaro v Corporate Investment Australia Funds Management Ltd* [2002] QCA 158, [2003] 2 Qd R 661 (Queensland Court of Appeal).

[36] Pursuant to the first limb in *Barnes v Addy* (1874) 9 Ch App 244.

[37] *Bank of Credit and Commerce International (Overseas) Ltd v Akindele* [2001] Ch 437 (CA(Civ Div)), followed in *Criterion Properties Plc v Stratford UK Properties LLC* [2002] EWCA Civ 1783, [2003] 1 WLR 2108, *Charter plc v City Index Ltd* [2007] EWCA Civ 1382, [2008] 2 WLR 950; *Uzinterimpex JSC v Standard Bank Plc* [2008] EWCA Civ 819. But cf *Charter plc v City Index (Gawler & ors)* [2007] EWCA Civ 1382, [2008] Ch 313 [29] (Carnwath LJ, Mummery LJ concurring) [74] (Arden LJ).

[38] *Farah Constructions Pty Ltd v Say-Dee Pty Ltd* [2007] HCA 22, (2007) 230 CLR 89 (High Court of Australia).

First, we saw in chapter six that it is arguable that it is the limited nature of the relief sought (restitution), rather than the nature of the claim (unjust enrichment) that attracts the application of the defence.[39] It follows that in theory, the defence could apply to claims for restitution of value received by a defendant in breach of trust, where the trigger for liability is both receipt of the benefit plus some level of knowledge of the reason for restitution. That is, the fact that a claim is regarded as one in 'knowing receipt' rather than 'unjust enrichment' does not automatically preclude the operation of the defence. However, what will generally prevent its operation, at least in cases of defendant-instigated changes of position, is the requirement that the defendant must have reasonably relied on his receipt.[40] This means that the defence will not readily apply to claims in knowing receipt nor, indeed, any form of claim for restitution[41] where prima facie relief is dependent on proof of knowledge of the reason for restitution on the part of the defendant.

Secondly, and notwithstanding the recent hostility to any unjust enrichment analysis in cases of misapplied trust assets, there do exist isolated pockets in the law where the change of position defence has been applied or considered applicable, in circumstances that closely approach those that would attract a knowing receipt analysis. In the Australian case of *Gertsch v Atsas*,[42] for example, the defence was applied with respect to distributions from a deceased estate made pursuant to a forged will. An earlier possible example is the case of *Re Diplock*, in which the recipients of mis-distributed funds from a deceased estate successfully defended claims for proprietary relief on the basis that the funds had been spent on alterations to the recipient's property, which alterations had not necessarily raised the value of the property and could not be severed and reversed. And in *Spangaro v Corporate Investment Australia Funds Management Ltd*,[43] the court considered that the change of position defence could in theory be available to a third party who received unauthorised trust distributions. Further, as Professor Bryan has

[39] At 171.

[40] Noted in *K & S Corp Ltd v Sportingbet Australia Pty Ltd* [2003] SASC 96, (2003) 86 SASR 313 (South Australian Supreme Court) [156]–[59] (Besanko J).

[41] eg it would automatically preclude the operation of the defence in cases of 'knowledge-based' constructive trusts of the type found in *Wambo Coal Pty Ltd v Ariff* [2007] NSWSC 589 (New South Wales Supreme Court), even before consideration of matters peculiar to proprietary restitutionary rights, as to which see below, at 204–09.

[42] *Gertsch v Atsas* [1999] NSWSC 898, (1999) 10 BPR 18 431 (New South Wales Supreme Court).

[43] *Spangaro v Corporate Investment Australia Funds Management Ltd* [2002] QCA 158, [2003] 2 Qd R 661 (Queensland Court of Appeal).

[44] M Bryan, 'The Liability of the Recipient' in S Degeling and J Edelman (eds) *Equity in Commercial Law* (Lawbook Co, Sydney 2005) ch 13.

[45] Cases include *State Bank of New South Wales Ltd v Swiss Bank Corporation* (1995) 39 NSWLR 350 (New South Wales Court of Appeal); *Port of Brisbane Corp v ANZ Securities* [2002] QCA 158, [2003] 2 Qd R 661 (Queensland Court of Appeal); *Finlay v Silcon Industries Pty Ltd* [2003] SASC 236 (South Australian Supreme Court) [121]–[24] (Doyle CJ, Nyland and Lander JJ concurring); *Spangaro v Corporate Investment Australia Funds Management Ltd* [2002] QCA 158, [2003] 2 Qd R 661 (Queensland Court of Appeal). *Primlake Limited (In Liquidation) v Matthews Associates* [2006] EWHC 1227 (Ch) is an English case of potentially the same sort, although in the unjust factor was rather doubtfully identified as 'absence of basis': at [335], as to which see ch 1, at 10–12. The facts of the case would accommodate a 'no intention to benefit' analysis (probably based on powerlessness, rather than

demonstrated,[44] there is a respectable body of Australian case law[45] that has applied a strict liability approach to receipt of benefits transferred in breach of fiduciary duty. In cases sharing this fact pattern, liability has been imposed at common law rather than in equity and by reference to *Lipkin Gorman v Karpnale*,[46] rather than the concept of knowing receipt. Given the nature of the relief sought and that, contrary to the position taken in claims of knowing receipt, restitutionary liability is not dependent on proof of knowledge (in some degree), the change of position defence in theory ought to be available in this category of case.

The strength of such cases as authorities in support of the application of the change of position defence to knowing receipt-style claims or, more broadly, to 'no intention to benefit' cases, is weakened by two factors. The first is that the reason for restitution (variously argued as unjust enrichment,[47] a 'proprietary' claim[48] or some form of wrongdoing[49]) is usually not identified and thus, it is said,[50] cannot be regarded as constituting support for the existence of a 'no intention to benefit' category of unjust factor. However, the important point is surely not whether the courts have adopted a particular label but the fact that there exists a body of case law bearing the same fact pattern and outcome, which reflects or is consistent with the proposed rationalisation.[51] A second and more significant deficiency is the lack of discussion in the cases as to whether the nature of cases bearing a 'no intention to benefit' fact pattern might raise considerations for the application of the change of position defence *additional* to those discussed earlier that apply with respect to the 'weaker' (mistake, duress and failure of basis) forms of claim.

Indeed, in these cases there is arguably an additional factor to consider. That is that the claimant may have retained, or obtained,[52] a proprietary interest in the benefit received by the defendant, for example because the claimant's consent to the transaction was entirely absent or fundamentally impaired. Where this is the case, it might be argued that the change of position defence should not apply, as to do so would allow the defence to undermine the protection otherwise afforded by the law to the claimant's proprietary interest in the benefit received by the defendant. Given this is a concern about the 'fit' between the change of position defence and proprietary rights to restitution, it will be considered in that context below.

ignorance). Notably, Lawrence Collins J appeared to leave open whether an innocent recipient in this category of case could rely on a change of position defence: [336].

[46] *Lipkin Gorman (a firm) v Karpnale Ltd* [1991] 2 AC 548 (HL).

[47] eg P Birks, 'The English Recognition of Unjust Enrichment' [1991] *Lloyd's Maritime and Commercial L Q* 473; AS Burrows, *The Law of Restitution* (2nd edn, Butterworths, London 2002) 191–93; Edelman and Bant, above n 29, at 274–75.

[48] eg G Virgo, *The Principles of the Law of Restitution* (2 edn, OUP, Oxford 2006) 570–71.

[49] eg W Swadling, 'Some Lessons from the Law of Torts' in P Birks (ed) *The Frontiers of Liability* (OUP, Oxford 1994).

[50] *Farah Constructions Pty Ltd v Say-Dee Pty Ltd* [2007] HCA 22, (2007) 230 CLR 89 (High Court of Australia) [156] (the Court).

[51] Bryan, above n 44, at 337.

[52] Pursuant to a trust, for example.

(5) Policy-motivated Unjust Factors

The final category of unjust factor to be considered contains those claims squarely based on policy considerations, the so-called 'policy-motivated unjust factors'.[53] These include (in England at least) 'Woolwich' style claims,[54] claims for reversal of judgment restitution, claims based on incapacity and claims based on illegality. The chief question in this context is whether allowing the defence of change of position would undermine or stultify the policy behind allowing restitution. The Australian case of *White v Tomasel*[55] provides a good example of these concerns. In that case, court orders were set aside on appeal as irregular but, in the interim, White had transferred the property the subject of the dispute to Tomasel pursuant to the orders. McMurdo J of the Queensland Court of Appeal stated:

> [A] successful appellant's right is a personal one in the sense that restitution can be ordered only against a person to the judgment. The risk that money paid or property transferred pursuant to a judgment will have been paid or transferred away by the respondent by the conclusion of the appeal often provides a basis for staying a judgment under appeal. But whether a stay is sought, of if sought is granted, does not affect an unsuccessful respondent's obligation to restore to the appellant what was the appellant's property prior to the judgment.[56]

It appears, therefore, that a key concern in this area is whether a litigant's right to restitution following a successful appeal should be subject to the change of position defence.[57] On the approach taken in this book, the change of position defence should be denied where its recognition would stultify the policy reason for ordering restitution.

It is this question of stultification that will prove the most significant hurdle to public authorities seeking to rely on the defence in circumstances where they have received a benefit pursuant to an unlawful demand.[58] Both the *Woolwich* principle and the principle of duress *colore officii* rest on judicial recognition of a long-standing and vitally important public interest in prohibiting unlawful demands by public authorities. The policy of prohibiting such demands would be entirely undermined if a public authority were effectively permitted to keep the benefit of the unlawful demand by relying on the defence of change of position.[59] This

[53] Edelman and Bant, above n 29, ch 13.

[54] *Woolwich Equitable Building Society v IRC* [1992] 3 All ER 737 (HL).

[55] *White v Tomasel* [2004] QCA 89, (2004) 2 Qd R 438 (Queensland Court of Appeal).

[56] *White v Tomasel* [2004] QCA 89, (2004) 2 Qd R 438 (Queensland Court of Appeal).

[57] *Cf Woodgate v Keddie* [2006] FCA 1728 (Federal Court of Australia); appeal dismissed on other grounds in *Woodgate v Keddie* [2007] FCAFC 129 (Full Federal Court of Australia).

[58] The actual ground for relief in such cases will vary according to the facts, but could include mistake, duress *colore officii* and a 'Woolwich' style claim: see generally: Edelman and Bant, above n 29, at 297–98.

[59] A point not considered in *Sempra Metals Limited v Commissioners of Inland Revenue* [2007] UKHL 34, [2008] 1 AC 561. It was correctly identified in *Test Claimants in the FII Litigation v Revenue and Customs Commissioner* [2008] EWHC 2893 (Ch) with respect to the Woolwich claim, but wrongly concluded to be inapplicable to the alternate mistake claim, discussed in ch 6, at 168–69, 187.

conclusion may, of course, be pre-empted, for example because the authority can readily reverse its changes of position by raising additional money from the public and therefore cannot satisfy the primary elements of the defence.[60] It may also be fortified if an 'innocent inducer' bar to the defence is recognised.[61]

(6) Cases of Proprietary Restitution

Finally, before leaving the application of the defence to claims in unjust enrichment, it is necessary to consider whether the defence should apply where the claimant demonstrates a proprietary restitutionary right to the benefit received by the defendant, rather than a personal right to restitution. There are instances of a change of position defence applying in the context of cases involving proprietary restitutionary rights.[62] However, the theoretical basis for applying the defence in respect of cases of proprietary restitutionary rights has never expressly been addressed and, as we will see below, there are countervailing arguments to be found in the law against extending the defence to such cases. This uncertainty is exacerbated by the deep controversy that rages over the very availability of and justification for proprietary restitutionary rights.[63] It is not feasible to resolve that controversy here.[64] If it is never possible to obtain proprietary restitutionary rights then, of course, the question how the change of position defence relates to proprietary rights becomes irrelevant. Accordingly, this section proceeds on the basis that it is possible to obtain proprietary restitutionary rights in response to an event of unjust enrichment. On that assumption, the question remains whether there is some reason or reasons why the defence should be precluded where the rights generated are proprietary, rather than personal.

[60] Burrows, above n 47, at 358. This point was misunderstood and rejected as an irrelevant by Henderson J in *Test Claimants in the FII Litigation v Revenue and Customs Commissioner* [2008] EWHC 2893 (Ch) [347], seemingly on the basis that it raised general hardship issues.

[61] Discussed in ch 6, at 177–84.

[62] eg *Allcard v Skinner* (1887) 36 Ch D 145 (CA), discussed in ch 4, at 178–79; *Gertsch v Atsas* [1999] NSWSC 898, (1999) 10 BPR 18 431 (New South Wales Supreme Court). *Re Diplock's Estate* [1948] 1 Ch 465 (CA) 546 may also be an early example.

[63] Cp, eg, W Swadling, 'A New Role for Resulting Trusts?' (1996) 16 *Legal Studies* 110, cited with approval by Lord Browne-Wilkinson (Lords Slynn and Lloyd agreeing) in *Westdeutsche Landesbank Girozentrale v Islington LBC* [1996] AC 669 (HL) 703 with the approach taken by R Chambers, *Resulting Trusts* (OUP, Oxford 1997), supported by Lord Millett, delivering the advice of the Privy Council in *Air Jamaica Ltd v Charlton* [1999] 1 WLR 1399 (PC) 1412. Controversy also exists over the form of proprietary right that should arise in response to unjust enrichment, in particular, whether it should conform to the 'vested' or 'proprietary power' models: cp Edelman and Bant, above n 29, ch 3 and P Millett, 'Proprietary Restitution' in S Degeling and J Edelman (eds) *Equity in Commercial Law* (Thompson, Sydney 2005) 319–22. This debate is considered further below, at 205–09. An important new contribution to that topic is contained in B Häcker, 'Consequences of Impaired Consent Transfers: A Strucural Comparison of English and German Law' (Mohr Siebeck, Tübingen 2009) ch 4. Dr Häcker's arguments have also been developed in 'Proprietary Restitution After Impaired Consent Transfers: A Generalised Power Model' (Conference paper presented on 24 July 2008 at the Obligations IV Conference, Singapore), to be published in (2009) *CLJ* (forthcoming).

[64] In so far as the discussion touches on rescission, it adopts the analysis of rescission in ch 3.

Some commentators have argued that it is unacceptable for a claimant to be able to avoid the consequences of the change of position defence by switching to rely on her proprietary rights.[65] This is particularly so given that the availability of a proprietary claim will often turn on the purely fortuitous, continued existence of the original benefit transferred or its identified substitute. For example, returning to our core case, suppose a claimant pays money to the defendant by mistake. The defendant changes his position in reliance on his receipt by withdrawing money from a separate account and using it to pay for a luxurious meal. Assuming the original notes received from the claimant are still identified in his wallet and the facts give rise to a proprietary right to restitution,[66] it would be odd if the defendant could rely on the defence in response to the personal claim for restitution of the value of the payment, but not in response to a proprietary claim in respect of the notes themselves.

On the other hand, as we saw in chapter six, the law generally accepts that claimants may choose between different causes of action and may rely on different rights to their advantage.[67] If the change of position defence does not apply to proprietary restitutionary rights, it would be extraordinary to remove the option of relying on those rights from the claimant for that reason. Therefore, the only relevant question must be the anterior one, namely does the change of position defence apply to proprietary restitutionary rights? To answer this question, it is necessary to identify relevant factors that may influence the outcome.

One factor might lie in the very difference between proprietary and personal rights. Professor Chambers argues that the basic difference between proprietary and personal restitutionary rights is that the former involves a right to restitution of the enrichment itself, whereas the latter involves a right against the defendant to restitution of its value.[68] To have a proprietary right to restitution thus requires both identification of the location of the specific thing the subject of the claim and that the thing be of a nature that can be subject to property rights. The value of the thing, however, is irrelevant. In contrast, a personal right to restitution is not a right to any specific thing, but rather a right to payment from a particular person. In this context, what matters is not the identification and form of the enrichment, but its value to the particular defendant.

This analysis has some interesting ramifications for the present discussion.[69] We saw in chapter five that some commentators have argued that the change of

[65] P Birks, 'Change of Position: The Nature of the Defence and its Relationship to other Restitutionary Defences' in M McInnes (ed) *Restitution: Developments in Unjust Enrichment* (LBC Information Services, North Ryde 1996) 55–56; P Birks, 'Change of Position and Surviving Enrichment' in W Swadling (ed) *The Limits of Restitutionary Claims: A Comparative Analysis* (The United Kingdom Committee of Comparative Law, Glasgow 1997) 43; Burrows, above n 47, at 527.

[66] *Chase Manhattan NA v Israel-British Bank (London) Ltd* [1981] 1 Ch 105 (Ch D).

[67] At 166–69.

[68] R Chambers, 'Resulting Trusts' in AS Burrows and Lord Rodger of Earlsferry (eds) *Mapping the Law: Essays in Memory of Peter Birks* (OUP, Oxford 2006) 256.

[69] Indeed, taken to its full logical extent, it could suggest that claims to assert proprietary restitutionary rights are fundamentally different in structure to claims in unjust enrichment, but see now R Chambers, 'Two Kinds of Enrichment' in R Chambers, C Mitchell and J Penner, *Philosophical Foundations of the Law of Unjust Enrichment* (Oxford, OUP 2009).

position defence applies only in cases of 'disenrichment' and operates to counter the 'enrichment' element of the primary claim in unjust enrichment. In substance, it requires that a balance sheet approach be taken to any pleaded change of position: the value of any change being offset against the original benefit received. Chambers' analysis suggests that, if the disenrichment approach is adopted, the change of position defence should never apply to cases of proprietary restitutionary rights. This is because in these cases the value of the received enrichment is irrelevant.[70]

This blanket ban can, however, be avoided by taking the view of the defence adopted in this book, namely that the defence is concerned with the broader protection from harm of defendants who (in most cases)[71] have irreversibly changed their position in reliance on their receipt. On this approach, the question becomes whether there is something inherent in the nature of the claimant's proprietary right to restitution that should preclude the application of the defence (which would otherwise be available).

For the purpose of answering this question it is important to distinguish between the different forms of proprietary restitutionary rights. The two main[72] forms of proprietary restitutionary rights that are said to arise in response to unjust enrichment are a vested proprietary interest arising under a trust and the proprietary restitutionary power, the latter most commonly encountered in the context of the power to rescind.[73] These two models of proprietary rights have different characteristics. In that context, it is worth considering whether those differences may have ramifications for the change of position defence.

Turning first to the case of a proprietary power to rescind, its main characteristic is that the claimant has a proprietary power in respect of the received benefit, which arises as soon as the benefit is received. Once exercised, that power has the effect of revesting or facilitating the revesting of title to the received benefit in the claimant.[74] We saw in chapter four that in the area of rescission courts have come to recognise that the defendant's changes of position made or suffered prior to the exercise of a claimant's power to rescind can be taken into account when making orders consequent on rescission. This can be done in a variety of ways, such as by making any orders for specific restitution subject to an obligation on the claimant

[70] R Chambers, *ibid*, at 275–76. *Cf* P Millett, 'Proprietary Restitution' in S Degeling and J Edelman (eds) *Equity in Commercial Law* (Thompson, Sydney 2005) 324–25. For a contrary view, see: Burrows, above n 47, at 527.

[71] Other than in cases of independent changes of position, where tracing rules often approximate the effect of a change of position defence.

[72] A lien may also be granted to secure restitutionary rights: *cf* R Chambers, 'Resulting Trusts' in AS Burrows and Lord Rodger of Earlsferry (eds) *Mapping the Law: Essays in Memory of Peter Birks* (OUP, Oxford 2006) 247, 256–57.

[73] Ch 4. For a compelling thesis in favour of a more generalised adoption of a power model, see B Häcker, 'Proprietary Restitution After Impaired Consent Transfers: A Generalised Power Model' above n 63.

[74] Ch 4, at 90–91.

to pay a specified amount to the defendant,[75] or by granting personal relief only in the form of a monetary award.[76]

This analysis suggests that proprietary restitutionary powers should be subject to the change of position defence.[77] Should the same be said, though, of proprietary restitutionary rights that arise under a trust? Assuming that these types of rights are truly proprietary in nature,[78] a claimant beneficiary has a vested equitable proprietary interest in the benefit received by the defendant which arises as soon as the benefit is received. This is unlike the proprietary power which, as we have seen, only vests legal or equitable title to the transferred benefit once it is exercised. This distinguishing feature arguably brings the vested right arising under the trust into the same category of case as that where the claimant's title never passed to the defendant, or where the claimant exercised her proprietary power to revest title to an asset prior to the defendant's change of position. Whatever the nature of the event that generates the right (which may differ from case to case),[79] in all these cases, the claimant has a vested proprietary right in respect of the received benefit prior to the defendant's change of position. This common feature is important because it raises the question whether the change of position defence should be refused on the ground that it undermines the law's protection of the claimant's vested proprietary interest in the asset. As Dr Fox has noted[80]:

> It is alien to the security of property interests that the conduct of a person who receives the plaintiff's asset should affect the plaintiff's right to enforce his property in it. It is in the nature of a proprietary interest that it should remain enforceable against persons generally, provided that the conditions for its continued survival are fulfilled.

[75] As contemplated in *Winefield v Clarke* [2008] NSWSC 882 (New South Wales Supreme Court), where Barrett J considered that the proceeds of any sale of the property the subject of the claim should be subject to a lien in favour of the defendant: see ch 4, at n 84 and n 113. See also *Nelson v Nelson* (1995) 184 CLR 538 (High Court of Australia) and *Gertsch v Atsas* [1999] NSWSC 898(1999) 10 BPR 18 431 (New South Wales Supreme Court).

[76] Ch 4, at 107.

[77] The main difficulty then becomes determining when a proprietary power arises, as opposed to a vested proprietary right, eg Birks argued that a claimant's proprietary restitutionary right in respect to substituted assets is better analysed as being in the nature of a proprietary power, rather than a vested right: P Birks, 'Overview: Tracing, Claiming and Defences' in P Birks (ed) *Laundering and Tracing* (Clarendon Press, Oxford 1995) 307–11; P Birks, *Unjust Enrichment* (2nd edn, OUP, Oxford 2005) 183–84, 198–99. If correct, this would vastly expand the category of proprietary claims subject to the change of position defence. See also discussion of *Lipkin Gorman (a firm) v Karpnale Ltd* [1991] 2 AC 548 (HL) below, at 208–09.

[78] McFarlane has recently argued that beneficiaries' rights that arise under a trust are never proprietary, properly so-called. Rather, they are a *sui generis* form of 'right against a right' that mimic some characteristics of property rights (in particular, the quality of persistence), without sharing their other core features: B McFarlane, *The Structure of Property* (Hart Publishing, Oxford, 2008) ch 2. On his approach, a claim against a defendant based on a pre-existing persistent right is not subject to the change of position defence, whereas a claim based on a power to create a persisting right is: see at 333–35. Although the distinction is based on a different analysis of the structure of property rights, in terms of its significance for the application of the change of position defence, it roughly correlates with the vested interest/proprietary power distinction drawn in this section.

[79] See text to n 81 and following.

[80] D Fox, 'Legal Title as a Ground of Restitutionary Liability' [2000] *Restitution L Rev* 465, 488.

Fox is prepared, however, to draw a distinction between 'restitutionary actions which aim directly at the vindication of title' and those 'where the plaintiff's title is itself created in response to unjust enrichment'.[81] This reflects a distinction between existing proprietary rights that persist through the transfer to the defendant and new proprietary restitutionary rights that arise in response to unjust enrichment. Fox would allow the change of position defence to operate in the latter case, but not in the former. However, it is difficult to see why the event generating the vested proprietary right should make any difference to the application of the defence, or why the distinction between persisting and new proprietary rights should matter. In both cases, the claimant has a vested proprietary right to the thing held by the defendant at the moment of receipt and, in both cases, to allow the defence would arguably undermine the protection generally afforded to such rights. The change of position defence has never been available in respect of cases of conversion. It has recently been rejected as a defence to actions that seek to enforce proprietary rights arising for reasons other than unjust enrichment.[82] There must be some reason why it should apply, extraordinarily, with respect to vested proprietary rights that arise as a result of unjust enrichment.[83]

On the approach taken in this book, this reason cannot be (as is suggested by Fox and others)[84] because the change of position defence is inextricably linked to the cause of action in unjust enrichment. This book has demonstrated that it is far more likely that the defence is linked to the limited nature and purpose of the relief sought (restitution) than the cause of action to which that relief responds.[85] It follows that, unless some further explanation is found, and unless there is a change of judicial policy with respect to the protection to be afforded to vested proprietary rights, it remains doubtful that the change of position defence does or should apply with respect to those rights.

This conclusion would still leave it open for the change of position defence to apply with respect to proprietary restitutionary powers. In that respect, it is worth reconsidering the facts of *Lipkin Gorman v Karnale*.[86] In that case, a rogue partner (Cass) had withdrawn amounts from his law firm's client account. He then gambled the amounts with the defendant casino. The claimant firm was entirely ignorant of his actions throughout. The House of Lords held that the claimant firm was entitled to restitution from the defendant of the value of the received bets, subject to the change of position defence. The precise basis on which the claimant was

[81] *Ibid*; also: Burrows, above n 47, at 527.

[82] P Millett, 'Proprietary Restitution' in S Degeling and J Edelman (eds) *Equity in Commercial Law* (Thompson, Sydney 2005) 325, explaining *Foskett v McKeown* [2001] 1 AC 102 (HL) 129 (Lord Millett, with whom Lord Hoffman agreed).

[83] For an article that, inter alia, explores the economic arguments against the application of the defence to proprietary rights, see C Rotherham, 'Tracing Misconceptions in *Foskett v McKeown*' [2003] *Restitution L R* 57, 73–76.

[84] P Birks, 'Change of Position: The Nature of the Defence and its Relationship to other Restitutionary Defences' in M McInnes (ed) *Restitution: Developments in Unjust Enrichment* (LBC Information Services, North Ryde 1996) 55; Burrows, above n 47, at 527.

[85] Ch 6, at 171.

[86] *Lipkin Gorman (a firm) v Karpnale Ltd* [1991] 2 AC 548 (HL).

entitled to claim restitution of the amount received, and whether the case was one of unjust enrichment, has been a matter of significant controversy.[87] However, assuming for the moment that the claim did rest in unjust enrichment, there is academic support for the view that the relevant unjust factor was 'ignorance'.[88]

For the purposes of the current discussion it is notable that although Cass had obtained good title to the withdrawn amounts,[89] Lord Goff took the view that the claimant firm had a continuing proprietary right to the money.[90] Commentators adopting an unjust enrichment analysis of the case have suggested that the claimant's proprietary right was in the nature of a restitutionary power *in rem*.[91] If this is correct, then even had the claimant sought to exercise its proprietary power (for example, because the amounts paid to the casino by Cass were still identified in the casino's safe), rather than rely (as was arguably the case) on the personal right to restitution generated by the receipt of the assets the subject of that power,[92] the property right should still have been subject to the change of position defence.

C Application to Claims Outside Unjust Enrichment

The second ambit of operation issue surrounding the change of position defence is whether the defence operates beyond claims in unjust enrichment. Again, the work required to answer this question has been completed in the context of the earlier portions of this book. Accordingly, this section will simply seek to summarise the earlier findings relevant to this question.

The previous section suggested that, in theory, the change of position defence could apply beyond claims in unjust enrichment, for example, to claims for restitution for wrongs, or to claims to vindicate the claimant's continuing proprietary interest in a benefit received by the defendant. This is because it is the nature and purpose of the relief sought which is the key to the availability of the change of position defence.[93] Where restitution is sought, the aim of which is to reverse

[87] eg Swadling, 'Some Lessons from the Law of Torts in P Birks (ed), *The Frontiers of Liability*, above n 49; LD Smith, 'Unjust Enrichment, Property and the Structure of Trusts' (2000) 116 *LQR* 412; LD Smith, 'Restitution: the Heart of Corrective Justice' (2001) 79 *Texas L Rev* 2115–175; Virgo, above n 48, at 570–71.

[88] Birks, 'The English Recognition of Unjust Enrichment', above n 47; Burrows, above n 47, at 191–93; Edelman and Bant, above n 29, at 274–75.

[89] *Lipkin Gorman (a firm) v Karpnale Ltd* [1991] 2 AC 548 (HL) 573 (Lord Goff).

[90] *Ibid*, at 573–74.

[91] Indeed, the point seems to have been conceded by counsel for the Club: [1991] 2 AC 548, 555.

[92] On the personal claim, identification of the claimant's proprietary right in the received asset arguably is only necessary to demonstrate that the defendant's enrichment was at the claimant's expense: P Birks, '"At the Expense of the Claimant": Direct and Indirect Enrichment in English Law' in D Johnston and R Zimmermann (eds) *Unjustified Enrichment: Key Issues in Comparative Perspective* (CUP, Cambridge 2002) 514–16; Burrows, above n 47, at 191; Edelman and Bant, above n 29, at 135–36.

[93] P Hellwege, 'The Scope of Application of Change of Position: A Comparative Study' [1999] *Restitution L R* 92, 96–100.

transfers of value so as to restore the parties to the *status quo ante*, it is generally no hardship to the defendant to return the received benefit to the claimant provided that he has not changed his position in such a way that he cannot be returned to the *status quo ante*. Where he has so changed his position, however, there must be some additional reason for requiring full restitution.

We also saw that usually, the additional reasons for requiring full restitution notwithstanding the defendant's change of position will be ones of policy: in particular, the policy of not stultifying the law's existing (and overriding) prohibitions or protections by allowing the change of position defence. For example, as we saw earlier, allowing the change of position defence in cases where the claimant's action is based on their vested proprietary right to the benefit (such as claims of conversion, or claims to vindicate a pre-existing property right) may be regarded as undermining the law's traditional protection of proprietary rights.[94] Likewise, the overriding need to deter breaches of fiduciary duty may preclude the application of the defence, even where the breaching fiduciary acted with the best of intentions and ignorant of their breach.[95] In the absence of clear evidence of a shift in judicial attitude to the balance of policy interests in these cases, it would be premature to say that the change of position defence should apply to these kinds of claims. This conclusion does not mean that the defence can never apply in respect of claims for restitution for wrongs, merely that each category of wrong must be individually examined to determine whether permitting the defence would undermine or stultify the reason for the law's prohibition. That task is beyond the scope of this book, which can only suggest the relevant considerations that should inform such an undertaking.

D Conclusion

Taken together with chapters five and six, this chapter provides ample support for Lord Goff's prediction that the change of position defence will be available only rarely.[96] The combination of the reasonable reliance requirement, the role of fault as a bar to the defence and the policy against stultifying overriding legal protections and prohibitions operate to restrict the application of the defence significantly. This is so notwithstanding that in theory the defence operates beyond the confined concept of 'disenrichment' and thus is not necessarily restricted to rebutting an element of the primary claim in unjust enrichment. This role of the defence beyond disenrichment in turn raises the question of its rationale, to which we now turn.

[94] *Cf* ch 6, at 170–72.

[95] *Ibid.*

[96] *Lipkin Gorman (a firm) v Karpnale Ltd* [1991] 2 AC 548 (HL) 580.

8

Rationale

A Introduction

THE PREVIOUS THREE chapters have identified the elements, bars to and ambit of operation of the change of position defence. It remains to this chapter to identify its underlying rationale or rationales, as revealed through the identified characteristics of the change of position defence.[1] At least four possibilities have been identified during the course of this book: 'disenrichment', 'autonomy,' 'security of receipt' and a 'harm-based' rationale. This chapter will consider each of these possibilities in turn, before concluding the most likely rationale(s) of the defence.

B Disenrichment

The concept and role of disenrichment has already been examined in detail in chapter five and so needs only be briefly addressed here. Disenrichment is a common feature of change of position cases and its presence is a strong indicator of when the defence may apply. However, chapter five demonstrated that it is a too restrictive concept to explain the sorts of cases which may, and arguably should, attract the operation of the change of position defence.[2] For example, the defence should be capable of applying in cases where the defendant's change of position is irreversible but defies a balance-sheet analysis, as where a defendant decides to conceive a child in reliance on his receipt, or remains enriched on a balance-sheet approach but has re-ordered his life radically and irreversibly in reliance on his receipt. The fact that the disenrichment approach struggles to accommodate these cases suggests that unless they are to be excluded, the rationale(s) for the defence must lie elsewhere.

[1] Perhaps the most obvious example of 'bottom up' reasoning employed in this book: see ch 1, at 18–19.

[2] At 126–38.

C Autonomy

A strong candidate for at least partially underpinning the change of position defence is the need to protect the defendant's autonomy in decision-making. We saw that this concern resounded throughout the estoppel case law and gave normative force to the otherwise causal requirement of reliance.[3] Further, the rescission case-law suggests that restitutionary relief should be denied where, because of the defendant's change of position, an order to make restitution in part or in full would leave him in a worse position than he occupied prior to his receipt. Importantly, we saw that the concept of 'worse' includes positions that are 'entirely different' from that occupied prior to his receipt.[4] The reason for this is that to force a defendant, through the award of restitution, into a state entirely different from that originally occupied by him and thus one he never chose, does not afford adequate protection to his right to autonomy.

In the context of the change of position defence, this concern with autonomy is manifested in the reliance requirement in cases of defendant-instigated changes of position, and in the reversibility requirement which (as in rescission) protects the defendant from being forced to assume a position entirely different from any originally chosen by him.[5] Further, a concern to protect the parties' autonomy arguably characterises the law of unjust enrichment, the main context in which the defence applies.[6] For example, if a claimant seeks restitution of a benefit transferred to the defendant on the basis that her intention to transfer the benefit was imperfect in some way (because of mistake, undue influence, the failure of the basis on which it was transferred etc), it is at least arguable that her claim is based on her right to deal with her assets with unimpaired autonomy. However, corrective justice[7] demands that she accord equal respect to the defendant's right to autonomy following his receipt of the benefit. Where a defendant changes his position under the mistaken belief that he is entitled to the received benefit, he is as much entitled to the law's protection as the claimant.

On balance, it seems clear that the need to protect the defendant's autonomy in decision-making informs the change of position defence. However, as the following discussion demonstrates, it does not account for and is not consistent with the whole of the defence. Indeed, in some cases, the policy to protect the defendant's autonomy is subordinated to or, indeed, trumped entirely by other concerns.

[3] Ch 2, at 40–41, 58–59.

[4] Ch 4, at 113–4, 118–19.

[5] The reversibility requirement is not wholly supportive of an autonomy-based rationale: see below, at 213.

[6] LD Smith, 'Restitution: the Heart of Corrective Justice' (2001) 79 *Texas L Rev* 2115; H Dagan, 'Mistakes' (2001) 79 *Texas L Rev* 1795.

[7] Recalling 'reciprocity', discussed briefly in ch 4, at 118–19. On the corrective justice analysis, see: Smith, *ibid* and, in the context of change of position, R Grantham and C Rickett, 'A Normative Account of Defences to Restitutionary Liability' (2008) 67 *CLJ* 92, 121–22.

First, if the change of position defence were solely concerned with the autonomy of the defendant, it is arguable that it should look different from the way it does. Professor Dagan has argued convincingly that the receipt of a benefit can impact on a defendant's autonomy in all sorts of subtle ways.[8] Quite apart from changes of position, it can engender expectations and hopes and interfere with a defendant's life-plans in a significant manner that might, of themselves, merit relief. Indeed, as Dagan notes, it is not completely contrary to recognising the claimant's autonomy in decision-making to make her abide by the consequences of her actions, particularly where the defendant's own autonomy is affected significantly as soon as a benefit is received. If these points were taken to their logical conclusion, it is arguable that the change of position defence should operate as a complete defence, rather than *pro tanto*, as it does currently. The law's obvious choice to intervene only in more limited circumstances and to a more limited degree reflects a deviation from, or at least a dilution of, the autonomy model. We return below to explore possible reasons for that choice.

A second area which possibly demonstrates a lack of fit between the defence as developed and an exclusive autonomy rationale has already been alluded to. We saw in chapter five[9] that the fact that a defendant's intention was impaired may well operate to defeat his pleaded change of position defence: for example, if he can easily reverse his change of position vis-à-vis a third party (for example, by recovering overpaid tax on the ground that he paid it pursuant to a mistake). Where that is the case, it seems the impairment of the defendant's autonomy (resulting in the change being reversible) has undermined his right to protection as regards the claimant. Against this, it could be argued that the law does give protection to his autonomy by recognising a claim against the third party, so that this restriction is not necessarily determinative of the issue. But the problem remains that, vis-à-vis *the claimant*, the defendant's right to protection of his autonomy is being limited.

The final and arguably most important area which demonstrates a deviation from an exclusively autonomy-based rationale is the role of fault within the defence. We have seen that fault in a variety of manifestations is incorporated throughout the defence: in the integration of good faith in reliance, in the requirement that reliance be reasonable, the 'wrongdoer' and 'incidental wrongdoer' bars and the concerns to respond to situations of illegality and stultification. This incorporation of concepts of fault within the defence as a condition or limitation on its protection cannot reflect a concern to *protect* the defendant's autonomy. This does not mean that considerations of autonomy are entirely irrelevant: they still inform many (albeit not all) of the fault-based features of the defence. Where, for example, a defendant knows that the claimant's decision to transfer was vitiated, there is no need to protect his autonomy, because his change of position reflected an unimpaired exercise of his decision-making capacity. We have also

[8] H Dagan, *The Law and Ethics of Restitution* (Cambridge University Press, Cambridge, 2004) ch 3. An earlier version of his arguments is found in Dagan, 'Mistakes', above n 6. There is an interesting contrast with estoppel on this point: see ch 10, at 229–30.

[9] At 131, 139–43.

seen that where the defendant induced the claimant's impaired decision to transfer a benefit, his interference with her autonomy undermines his own right to protection. In these cases, the relevance of fault can be seen as reflecting an autonomy-based rationale. But the requirement that the defendant's reliance must be reasonable cannot be explained in terms of a concern to protect a defendant's autonomy in decision-making. It is an independent normative requirement that is concerned to limit the scope of protection of the defence.[10] It follows that the rationale(s) of the defence must be sufficiently broad or contextured to incorporate the reasonableness requirement.

D Security of Receipt

Professor Birks was an early champion of a 'security of receipt' rationale for the change of position defence[11] and, for many commentators,[12] it remains the most likely option. However, the term is slippery: reflecting this, it has been adopted by both champions[13] (Birks included) and opponents[14] of the disenrichment rationale of the defence and has been inextricably linked with the arguments from autonomy. As such, close attention must be paid to what comes within the attractive label: like 'unconscionability', the concept of security of receipt requires a definite content if it is to have explanatory force.

At its base, the security of receipt rationale reflects the idea that a defendant ought generally to be able to make decisions in reliance on the apparent basis of his asset holdings. He is entitled to deal freely with those receipts he reasonably regards as unimpeachable, and he should be able to deal with assets apparently held for other people in accordance with that belief. If it then appears that his receipt was insecure because subject to a claim by another, or was to be held for the benefit of someone else, the defendant is entitled to protection. This description encompasses the disenrichment rationale. However, the security of receipt rationale extends beyond simple dealings with receipts to much broader life choices consistent with the defendant's understanding of the basis of his asset holdings.[15] There is no reason to suppose that it is limited to disenriching changes of position.

[10] Ch 2, at 45–47; ch 5, at 151.

[11] eg P Birks, 'Change of Position and Surviving Enrichment' in W Swadling (ed), *The Limits of Restitutionary Claims: A Comparative Analysis* (The United Kingdom Committee of Comparative Law, Glasgow, 1997).

[12] Goff and Jones argued in their sixth edition that this rationale was accepted by the Privy Council in *Dextra Bank and Trust Co Ltd v Bank of Jamaica* [2002] 1 All ER (Comm) 193 (PC) [38]: G Jones (ed), *Goff and Jones The Law of Restitution* 6th edn (Sweet & Maxwell, London, 2002) [40-003] fn 38, but with respect, the passage is ambiguous and the point does not appear in the seventh edition.

[13] AS Burrows, *The Law of Restitution* 2nd edn (Butterworths, London, 2002) 509.

[14] J Edelman and E Bant, *Unjust Enrichment in Australia* (OUP, Melbourne, 2006) 322.

[15] Dagan, *The Law and Ethics of Restitution*, above n 8, at 47.

The security of receipt rationale arguably tracks more closely with the argument from autonomy. A defendant who changes his position in reliance on a mistaken belief as to his entitlement ought to be protected because, if recipients were required to hold themselves always ready to give back any benefits they received, their autonomy would be severely affected.[16]

However, like the argument from autonomy, the security of receipt rationale struggles to explain some of the concrete and core elements of the change of position defence unless, that is, the defendant's right to the security of his receipt is narrowly circumscribed. If, for example, the defence is concerned to protect the defendant's security of receipt, it is not immediately obvious why there is a reversibility requirement to the defence. If the defendant is entitled to the security of his receipt, why should it matter that changes made in reliance on his receipt are reversible? The obvious answer is that the defendant's right to the security of his receipt is not absolute: weighing against it is the claimant's right to restitution.[17] Where the defendant can be substantially restored to the position he occupied prior to his receipt, he will suffer relatively little harm and, to that extent, the defendant's right to the security of his receipt is subordinated to the claimant's right to restitution.

But this answer seems less about protecting the defendant's security of receipt and more about the need to protect the defendant from the harm that would flow from a requirement to make restitution or restitution in full. Security of receipt is here playing a subsidiary role. It says that the defendant should get some protection, but not how much nor when that protection should be withdrawn. It does not suggest, in other words, how the defendant's right to security of his receipt should be reconciled with the claimant's right to restitution, and it is with this balancing act that the change of position defence is primarily concerned.

E A Harm-based Rationale

Dagan notes that reconciling parties' conflicting rights to autonomy is a core task of tort law.[18] He argues that, analogously to tort cases, there are two core concerns of the change of position defence. These are: (1) to prevent the harm that may be caused by a legal reversal of the claimant's mistake; and (2) to encourage both parties to take reasonable steps to avoid their mistakes (either on the part of the claimant, in making the original transfer, or on the part of the defendant in changing his position).

[16] Birks, above n 11, at 36, 50–51; Dagan, *ibid*, at 45–46.

[17] *Alpha Wealth Financial Services Pty Ltd v Frankland River Olive Company Ltd* [2008] WASCA 119 (Western Australia Supreme Court of Appeal) [201] (Buss J, Steytler P concurring) set out below, at n 22.

[18] *The Law and Ethics of Restitution*, above n 8, at 46–47.

Arguably, of all the analyses of the defence's rationale, Dagan's most closely tracks the elements of and bars to the defence identified in this book. It highlights the fact that the defence arises where the order to make restitution would, because of the defendant's change of position, leave him in a worse position than he was in prior to his receipt. It accommodates the requirements of reasonable reliance and irreversibility that characterise the primary elements of the defence and allows for the defendant's fault to have a legitimate role in barring the defence.

There remains, however, one significant concern with adopting Dagan's analysis. This is that the previous chapters have demonstrated that the defence operates only in the context of claims for restitution, the purpose of which is to reverse transfers of value so as to restore the parties to the *status quo ante*. We have seen that this contextual feature is crucial to explaining the requirement of irreversibility and the concern of that requirement with non-disenriching changes of position. The change of position defence is not concerned, for example, with compensating the defendant for consequential losses. It is restricted in its concept of harm to the discrete context of an award of restitution the purpose of which is to restore the parties to the *status quo ante*. It is only harm in the restricted sense of irreversibility that counts. Unless Dagan's concept of 'harm' is understood to equate to irreversibility, it runs the risk of misrepresenting this defining feature of the change of position defence.

The core purpose of restitution being to reverse transfers of value so as to restore the parties to the *status quo ante* also explains why the fault of the defendant, irrelevant in the context of the primary claim,[19] becomes relevant in the context of the defence.[20] Where the parties cannot be restored to the *status quo ante* because of the defendant's change of position, and the defence is prima facie established, the question is then whether there are any factors that should determine on whom the loss (in Dagan's terms, the harm) should fall. It is in this context that fault has a role to play.

Dagan argues that the fault of both parties should be taken into account to determine this question. Indeed, Dagan's approach tends to feed considerations of fault back into the primary claim in unjust enrichment. However, this approach to incorporating fault is both contrary to established authority[21] and tends to assume an inextricable link between unjust enrichment and the defence of change of position. We have seen that it is far more likely that the defence responds to the nature of the remedy being sought (restitution). Moreover, chapter six demonstrated that Anglo-Australian courts seem to have set their face against any approach that attempts to bring the claimant's fault into the account. Rather, the question for Anglo-Australian courts has been whether the fault of the defendant (in the various manifestations discussed in chapter six) should operate to exclude or bar him from the protection to which he would otherwise be entitled. It is a fairly one-sided enquiry, the claimant's fault only coming in at a contextual level (for example, the claimant's involvement with the defendant in an illegal scheme).

[19] *Kelly v Solari* (1841) 9 M & W`54, 152 ER 24.
[20] Discussed in ch 6, at 179.
[21] *Kelly v Solari* (1841) 9 M & W`54, 152 ER 24.

F A Mixed Rationale of Protection and Prophylaxis

Given these concerns, it would be potentially misleading to adopt Dagan's harm-based analysis as the rationale of the defence. However, what his analysis does highlight is that the change of position defence is not solely concerned with the defendant's autonomy. The defence has two distinct aims, two pincers that are required before the defence will grip. The first (and very specific) aim is to protect the defendant from the harm he would suffer where an order to make restitution in part or in full would leave him in a worse (including entirely different) position than he was in prior to his receipt. This harm-orientated limb serves to protect the defendant's autonomy, for example by preventing him from being placed in an entirely different position from that which he occupied prior to the receipt. It also, however, implicitly requires the claimant's competing right to restitution to be taken into account. The defendant's right to protection of his autonomy is not absolute. Even where he has acted in reliance on his receipt, so that his autonomy in decision-making has been affected, he must demonstrate that his change is irreversible. If not, then the claimant's right to restitution (whether that right is based solely on a competing right to protection of her autonomy or other concerns) trumps the defendant's right to protection. To avoid confusion as to the nature of harm in issue, this rationale can be called 'irreversibility protection'.[22]

This brings us to the second aim or pincer of the defence, namely to restrict the level of protection given to the defendant by reference to the defendant's fault. We saw earlier that the requirement that the defendant's reliance must be reasonable cannot be explained in terms of a concern to protect a defendant's autonomy in decision-making. Rather, it reflects a policy choice (incidentally supported by the innocent inducer bar) that protection of the defendant's autonomy is limited and the defendant is expected to take reasonable steps to protect himself against the possibility that a receipt might be impeachable. It has the secondary effect of encouraging defendants in like circumstances to take reasonable steps to avoid the costs (both to them and to the claimants) of reversing vitiated-consent transfers. This second feature of the defence thus incorporates more overtly instrumentalist concerns than the harm-orientated pincer. It could be said that rather than having an aim of irreversibility-protection, its aim is prophylactic in nature.

Any label for this mixed rationale must reflect both pincers of the defence. Although somewhat unwieldy, it is submitted that 'irreversibility protection and prophylaxis' accurately encapsulates the mixed rationale of the defence.

[22] *Alpha Wealth Financial Services Pty Ltd v Frankland River Olive Company Ltd* [2008] WASCA 119 (Western Australia Supreme Court of Appeal) [201] (Buss J, Steytler P concurring):

> The rationale for change of position as a defence to a restitutionary claim based on mistake lies in the inherent unfairness of requiring a recipient to make restitution where the recipient has received the payment in good faith and has irreversibly and materially altered his or her position, on the faith of the receipt, to his or her detriment. In those circumstances, the recipient has a proper interest in the security of the receipt.

G Conclusion

The discussion in this chapter reflects the links between the change of position defence and the estoppel and rescission case law and highlights the value of the analyses completed in part one. It reinforces the view taken throughout this book that is only once relevant insights from the surrounding case law have been identified that a sensible assessment of the disputed features of the change of position defence can be made. Now that assessment is complete, it is possible to articulate a comprehensive definition of the defence. That is the task of the next and concluding chapter of part two.

9

Conclusion

THE PRIMARY AIM of this book is to provide a comprehensive definition of the change of position defence. One of its core themes is that it is necessary to place the change of position defence within its broader historical and legal context in order to see how its disputed features might be resolved. To that end, part one of the book examined three defences that together shed considerable light on the potential shape and operation of the change of position defence. Chapter five then proceeded both to consider the modern case law and use the lessons derived from the defences considered in part one to determine the contested primary elements of the change of position defence.

As a result of that process, the core elements of the change of position defence are clear:

- The defendant must have suffered an irreversible change of position.
- Subject to the exceptional cases of anticipatory changes of position, the irreversible change of position must have been caused by the defendant's receipt of the enrichment the subject of the primary claim (the 'causation' requirement).
- The causal test that must be satisfied to establish causation will depend on the nature of the pleaded change of position. Where there has been an independent change to the received benefit, but-for causation will generally be satisfied. Where, however, the pleaded change of position is defendant-instigated, the change must have been made by the defendant in reliance on his receipt.
- Broken into its constituent elements, reliance requires, first, that the receipt of the benefit must be 'a factor' in the defendant adopting an assumption and, secondly, that this assumption formed 'a factor' in the defendant's decision to change his position.
- Where reliance is required, it must be reasonable.

The same process of examining the change of position case law in the light of the insights obtained in part one revealed three main bars to the defence, addressed in chapter six. Of primary importance is that the change of position defence must not be permitted to undermine or stultify overriding legal rules or prohibitions. The application of this 'legal stultification' bar will often determine whether wrongdoers (those in breach of a legal or equitable duty) sued in that capacity, or 'incidental' wrongdoers, will be entitled to the defence. The conclusion reached was that, barring major changes in policy, wrongdoers will find it difficult to rely on the defence. Secondly, it was argued that there is some support both in the case law and in principle for barring the defence in cases of 'innocent inducers'. Finally, both precedent and principle suggest that a defendant who knows that he is not entitled to his receipt should be precluded from relying on the change of position defence if he fails to take the care a reasonable man would in the circumstances, in particular, knowing that the benefit must be accounted for to another.

Chapter seven addressed the ambit of operation of the defence. In essence, it demonstrated that because of the combination of the irreversibility and 'reasonable reliance' requirements and the bars to the defence, the change of position defence is more limited in its operation than perhaps previously perceived. The consequence is that, in general, it will be limited to claims in unjust enrichment and even there its ambit of operation will be closely circumscribed.

Finally, chapter eight drew together all the threads from the previous sections to conclude that the rationale of the defence has two aspects, or pincers, both of which must be engaged before the defence can grip. The first is to protect the defendant from the harm he would suffer where an order to make restitution in part or in full would leave him in a worse (including entirely different) position than he occupied prior to his receipt ('irreversibility protection'). The second is to restrict the protection afforded to the defendant by reference to the defendant's fault. In particular, the defendant is expected to take reasonable steps to protect himself against the possibility that his receipt might be impeachable. This 'prophylactic' aspect of the defence's rationale has the secondary effect of encouraging defendants in like circumstances to take reasonable steps to avoid the costs (both to them and to claimants) of reversing vitiated-consent transfers.

This concludes part two of the book. The final part considers some of the ramifications of adopting the definition of the defence advocated in part two. In particular, it addresses the light that definition sheds on the relationship between the change of position defence and other, related defences.

Part Three

Ramifications

10

Ramifications

A Introduction

THE FINDINGS OF this book have significant ramifications beyond the change of position defence. Most obviously, they raise the issue of the ongoing relationship between that defence and other, related defences, including those raised in part one.

Ideally, to ensure that any comparison between the defences proceeded on a sure footing, one would replicate this book's enquiry into the change of position defence for each of the other defences, so that the elements of, bars to and rationales of each of the other defences were clearly identified. That is neither feasible nor appropriate within the confines of this work. However, it remains possible to make some suggestions as to the possible relationship and interaction between the change of position defence and other, related defences, accepting that the analysis is subject to any uncertainty pertaining to those other defences. That is the task of this final chapter of the book.

The first three sections of this chapter consider defences that overlap in whole or in part with those defences the subject of part one of the book. In particular, they explore the nature of the ongoing relationship between those defences and the change of position defence in the light of its definition in this work. In contrast, the last three sections consider other defences that are 'related' to change of position only in the limited sense that, at first sight, they display apparent similarities with that defence that might suggest a degree of overlap between them. The sections demonstrate, however, that any similarities are superficial and should not be allowed to obscure the clear demarcation between the defences. As explained in chapter one, this conclusion also accounts for the absence of these defences from the analysis in part one.[1] Responding to different questions from those posed by change of position cases, the defences form an unsuitable foundation for resolution of its disputed features.

[1] At 20–21.

B Estoppel by Representation

We saw in chapter two that both change of position and estoppel require a detrimental change of position on the part of the defendant.[2] However, unlike the change of position defence, the focus of estoppel by representation is not on any changes of position that may preclude the defendant from being returned to his position prior to the impugned transaction. Rather, it operates to protect the defendant from the harm that would otherwise arise from his change of position if the claimant were permitted to resile from her representation. A detrimental change of position is required but it has a distinct point of reference. No doubt for this reason, the defence traditionally operates to prevent any detriment by preventing the claimant from asserting a position contrary to that represented, thereby compelling adherence to the defendant's assumption. The consequence is that, once established, the estoppel operates as a complete defence. In contrast, the change of position defence operates to protect the defendant against the harm that he would suffer were he now required to make restitution, given his irreversible change of position. The relief offered by the defence is accordingly *pro tanto*—to the extent of the value of the defendant's irreversible change of position, measured against his primary obligation to make restitution in full.

Although its complete operation makes sense in the light of the detriment the defence seeks to avoid, in some cases, the all-or-nothing approach of estoppel appears to work inequitably. A case in point is *Avon City Council v Howlett.*[3] It will be recalled from chapter two that an employer sought restitution of moneys mistakenly overpaid to its employee. For the purposes of the case, the employee was treated as having spent only part of the overpayment in reliance on his employer's representations. The question squarely in issue was whether the defence operated to bar the claimant's action completely, or *pro tanto*, to the extent of the employee's change of position. By a majority, the Court of Appeal held that, as estoppel by representation operated as a rule of evidence, it operated as a complete bar to the claim.

In this case, the protection offered by the estoppel defence is liable to criticism as being disproportionate. If estoppel by representation operates to protect the defendant from the harm that would flow from his change of position if the claimant were now permitted to resile from her representation, why does it not operate *pro tanto*? The members of the court were alive to this objection. Each member of the majority expressly qualified their finding, stating that there may be cases where it would be 'unconscionable'[4] or be an 'injustice'[5] to permit the

[2] Consistent with the approach taken in ch 2, this chapter will continue to refer to the representee as the defendant and the representor as the claimant, unless otherwise stated.

[3] *Avon City Council v Howlett* [1983] 1 WLR 605 (CA), considered in ch 2, at 25.

[4] *Ibid*, at 612 (Everleigh LJ).

[5] *Ibid*, at 624 (Slade LJ).

defence to operate absolutely.[6] In the minority, Cumming-Bruce LJ refused to consider the hypothetical facts and held in favour of the defendant on the basis that, on the facts as proven, the defendant had spent all the money. His Lordship went on to state that he did not consider that 'where on the facts it would be clearly inequitable to allow a party to make a profit by pleading the estoppel, this court will necessarily be powerless to prevent it'.[7] The court, however, left for future cases the further development and elucidation of the circumstances that might attract this 'unconscionability' exception.

Since this case, a number of English courts have refused to apply an all-or-nothing approach to estoppel by representation, where to do so would leave the defendant seemingly enjoying a windfall. A variety of methods have been employed to that end. The first is to declare that, where estoppel and the change of position defence are both available, the latter should be preferred.[8] This is because, being a *pro tanto* defence, it provides a degree of protection that better reflects (is better tailored to) the particular defendant's interest in the security of his receipt.

However, this approach is objectionable as a matter of principle. There is no obvious reason why estoppel by representation, a defence applicable across the law, should uniquely be excluded from the law of unjust enrichment. Further, it assumes that the only purpose of estoppel is to protect a defendant's security of receipt. As we saw in chapter two, there are other possibilities, such as that it operates to protect a defendant's autonomy in decision-making.[9] Another, raised by Professor Birks in his later work adopting a juristic reasons approach to unjust enrichment, is that estoppel operates to hold parties to their word (in this case, their representation) in a manner similar to contract.[10] On this analysis, estoppel provides a juristic reason for the transfer, thereby negating the claim in unjust enrichment. Indeed, notwithstanding the change of heart on the topic of unjust factors, Birks consistently argued that estoppel was an 'unjust-related' defence, rather than an 'enrichment-related' defence as (he also argued) in the case of change of position. Prior to his recantation of the unjust factor approach to unjust enrichment, his analysis was that once a claimant made a representation on which the defendant had relied, the claimant was precluded from resiling from the representation and pleading an unjust factor. On this analysis estoppel thus pre-empts and disables the unjust factor.[11] Whether this analysis, or the others considered above, is correct is beyond the scope of this book. The simple point is that, if the purpose of estoppel goes beyond protecting a defendant's interest in the

[6] Considered further below, at 226.

[7] At 608.

[8] *Lipkin Gorman (a firm) v Karpnale Ltd* [1991] 2 AC 548 (HL) 579 (Lord Goff); *Philip Collins Ltd v Davis* [2000] 3 All ER 808 (Ch); *Scottish Equitable Plc v Derby* [2001] EWCA Civ 369, [2001] 3 All ER 818.

[9] At 40–41, 58–59.

[10] P Birks, *Unjust Enrichment* (2nd edn, OUP, Oxford 2005) 234–35.

[11] P Birks, 'Change of Position: The Nature of the Defence and its Relationship to other Restitutionary Defences' in M McInnes (ed) *Restitution: Developments in Unjust Enrichment* (LBC Information Services, North Ryde 1996) 67–68. *Cf* the 'ingenious' argument relating to enrichment considered below, at 226–27.

security of his receipt, then there must be some additional reason to preclude the defendant from raising the defence to protect that further interest.

The second method that has been adopted to avoid the all-or-nothing application of estoppel has been to appeal to the 'unconscionability' exception alluded to in *Avon City Council v Howlett.*[12] On this approach, it is said to be 'unconscionable' for the defendant to rely on estoppel as a complete defence where the value of the defendant's change of position bears no relation to the amount sought to be recovered. However, as Professor Burrows notes,[13] provided the extent of the defendant's change of position can be proven to be less than the amount sought to be recovered, it presumably will always be unconscionable to retain any clear windfall benefit. The consequence is that the so-called exception becomes the rule, subject perhaps to some *de minimus* cases. This both flies in the face of the actual decision in *Avon City Council v Howlett* and highlights the difficulty of applying an exception that is grounded in the ambiguous concept of 'unconscionability'.

Thirdly, there is the argument raised by junior counsel on appeal in *Scottish Equitable plc v Derby.*[14] Described as by Walker LJ as 'ingenious and convincing', the argument was that detriment for the purposes of estoppel must be assessed at the time of trial. At that time, any 'detriment' that might otherwise flow from the claimant resiling from her representation would be pre-empted and negated by the application of the change of position defence. However, there are clear difficulties with this argument.

The first and most obvious is that, as we saw in chaptert two, detriment for the purposes of estoppel is assessed at the time the representee seeks to resile from her representation, not at the time of trial.[15] This fatally undermines any 'pre-emption' argument.

Secondly, as noted at the start of this discussion, the detriment that applies for the purposes of estoppel is that which will be suffered if the claimant is permitted to resile from her representation. In contrast, detriment for the purpose of the change of position defence is measured by the extent of the irreversible change of position, seen in the light of the primary purpose of any order for restitution made against the defendant to reverse transfers of value so as to restore the parties as closely as possible to the *status quo ante.* While the measures of detriment may coincide in some cases, the differing focus of their detriment requirements suggests they will not always do, even in those classes of estoppel that contemplate the possibility of *pro tanto* operation, as in proprietary estoppel. For example, suppose a claimant pays £50,000 to a defendant. She makes a clear and unambiguous representation that the payment is made to secure the defendant's participation in a property development venture with the claimant, in which the defendant will earn a certain interest in the properties the subject of the venture. The value of that

[12] *Avon City Council v Howlett* [1983] 1 WLR 605 (CA).
[13] AS Burrows, *The Law of Restitution* (2nd edn, Butterworths, London 2002) 537.
[14] *Scottish Equitable Plc v Derby* [2001] EWCA Civ 369, [2001] 3 All ER 818 [45] (Robert Walker LJ).
[15] At 48–49.

interest is estimated at £10 million. In reliance both on his receipt and on the representation, the defendant performs all the tasks required of him pursuant to the arrangement with the claimant. The claimant subsequently seeks to resile from her representation because it was induced by her mistaken belief that she had planning approval for the proposed development. There is no contract between the parties.

Assuming that both the elements of proprietary estoppel and the change of position defence are made out, what will be the measure of relief? The detriment for the purposes of the change of position defence will be the value of the defendant's time, effort and any irreversible financial outlay spent in completing his part in the arrangement. It is unlikely that the detriment for the purposes of proprietary estoppel will be the same. A recent case suggests that the detriment is more likely to be the loss of the interest that the representation indicated would be earned through the defendant's efforts.[16] Although the court's reasoning was not entirely clear, the result reflects the view that detriment for the purpose of estoppel is measured by reference to the detriment that will be suffered if the claimant is permitted to resile from her representation, not by reference to any need to restore the parties to the *status quo ante.* In the hypothetical case, by the time the defendant completes his side of the arrangement, he stands to lose the interest in the project that he has notionally earned (if the claimant resiles from her representation) not his simple reliance costs.

The example demonstrates that the potential difference in value of the detriments in estoppel and change of position is considerable, even in a class of estoppel that contemplates proportionality in detriment. The example suggests that where the representation relates to a matter or benefit that is independent of the received benefit, the amount of the detriment in estoppel and change of position may differ. If this is correct, it is only where the claimant's representation concerns the entitlement of the defendant to the received benefit that the measures of the detriment in estoppel and change of position will coincide.

The final reason for doubting the 'pre-emption' argument raised in *Scottish Equitable v Derby* is that there is no obvious reason why the application of estoppel by representation should be dependent on prior proof of some other, substantive defence. The availability of any defence must depend on the proven facts of the case. A finding that the change of position defence applies is not a 'fact' that can determine the application of estoppel by representation. This point is highlighted by the fact that the change of position defence may not even be pleaded. Indeed, given its traditional characterisation as a rule of evidence, there is every reason to think that estoppel should apply first, to establish the facts on which the legal issues (including the availability of a change of position defence) should apply.

[16] *Cobbe v Yeoman's Row Management Ltd* [2006] EWCA Civ 1139, [2006] 1 WLR 2964. On appeal, the House of Lords held that the alleged proprietary interest that was to be obtained pursuant to the agreement in principle was insufficiently certain to support the recognition of a proprietary interest pursuant to proprietary estoppel. However, Lord Scott (with whom Lords Hoffmann, Walker, Brown and Mance relevantly agreed) noted the distinction between the measure of awards in cases of proprietary estoppel and restitution in terms consistent with the above analysis: *Yeoman's Row Management Limited v Cobbe* [2008] UKHL 55 [4], [14]–[16], [42]–[44].

The fourth way in which commentators have suggested that the all-or-nothing approach of estoppel by representation may be avoided is where either the claimant's representation, or the defendant's detrimental reliance on the representation, is severable.[17] For example, Burrows argues that in *Avon City Council v Howlett*, the claimant ought to have been free to deny that the amount that had not been spent by the defendant belonged to him. The severance was possible, and not overly artificial, because there was more than one payment and therefore more than one possible representation.

However, as Justice Handley (writing extra-judicially) has noted, the defendant in that case was unable to bring proof of each change of position made in reliance on his receipt.[18] Moreover, given the employer's representations and arguably their duty to pay the correct amount to the defendant, it was unreasonable for him to be required to do so. It was the employer's representations that made the defendant believe that he was free to spend the money as he wished, without keeping strict records of his expenditure.[19]

There is no doubt that normally the onus of proving the change of position in estoppel lies on the defendant. If the claimant is permitted to divide up her overall representation by reference to each separate payment, and require proof of each change of position by reference to each representation, the onus of proof may become crushing on defendants. The burden seems particularly harsh given it was the claimant's representation that lulled the defendant into believing that his receipt was secure. Given these difficulties, it seems that the claimant should only be permitted to sever her representations, or the defendant's detrimental reliance, where the separate characters of each representation or act of reliance are clearly evidenced on the facts and severance does not place too great an evidential burden on the defendant.

The fifth and final way of avoiding the all-or-nothing operation of the estoppel defence is again directed to the nature of the representation. Birks argued that a reasonable person would understand most representations of entitlement as 'prospectively revocable in the event of the representor's discovering a mistake'.[20] That construction would bind the claimant pending any notification. Once notified of a mistake, however, the estoppel would end, presumably because any subsequent changes of position would not be made in reasonable reliance on any assumption induced by the claimant. Birks argued that if this approach were adopted, recognition of an estoppel would rarely produce results disproportionate in comparison with the change of position defence. However, there are two related problems with this analysis. First, it is debatable that reasonable people

[17] Burrows, *The Law of Restitution* 2nd edn, above n 13, at 534; K Handley, *Estoppel by Conduct and Election* (Sweet & Maxwell, London 2006) [5-026]–[5-027], [5-033].

[18] Handley, *ibid*, at [5-027], [5-033].

[19] Echoing the Canadian Court of Appeal's concerns in *RBC Dominion Securities Inc v Dawson* (1994) 111 DLR (4th) 230 (Newfoundland Court of Appeal) in the context of the change of position defence, discussed in ch 5, at 138.

[20] Birks, *Unjust Enrichment* 2nd edn, above n 10, at 235–36.

faced by an unconditional statement 'We have checked this out and you may rely on us that all is in order'[21] would think it is obviously subject to the implied condition 'unless and until we notify you to the contrary'.[22] Secondly, as *Avon City Council* itself demonstrates, the practice of the courts has not been to find, or find readily, this sort of implied term.

Given the difficulties identified above with any argument that would seek to render the defence of estoppel by representation otiose in cases of unjust enrichment, or would render its operation *pro tanto*, the preferable view remains that the two defences continue to have a separate, albeit overlapping existence, as has been the case in Australian courts to date.[23] Any further or different conclusions must await judicial clarification of the purpose of the estoppel (is it also concerned, for example, with protecting expectations, or the defendant's autonomy in decision-making?), its operation (is it truly a rule of evidence or is it substantive?) and any 'exceptions' to its all-or-nothing operation. Although these enquiries are critically important, they cannot be the subject of this work. Any further examination into them involves a switch in focus entirely away from change of position to the rationale and operation of estoppel.

That being said, it is notable that, aside from the need for a representation and the difference in focus between the detriment requirement for estoppel and change of position, chapters two and five identified another significant difference between the two defences.[24] This is the requirement in estoppel that the claimant must be responsible for the defendant's mistaken assumption on which the defendant subsequently acts. A related point arises from chapter two, namely that a concern for the defendant's autonomy in decision-making may be at the core of estoppel by representation.[25] These features support the view taken above that estoppel and the change of position defence are independent defences that should

[21] *Ibid*, at 236.

[22] *Ibid.*

[23] *David Securities Pty Ltd v Commonwealth Bank of Australia* (1992) 127 CLR 353 (High Court of Australia) 385 (Mason CJ, Deane, Toohey, Gaudron, and McHugh JJ). Both change of position and an estoppel were pleaded by way of defence in *City of Sydney v Burns Philp Trustee Co (In liquidation)* (New South Wales Supreme Court 13 November 1992) (estoppel by representation); *Civil Aviation Authority v Jorm* (Australian Capital Territory Supreme Court, 18 October 1994) (estoppel by representation); *Commonwealth Bank of Australia v Webster* (Victorian Supreme Court, 27 July 1995) (estoppel by representation); *National Australia Bank Ltd v Budget Stationery Supplies Pty Ltd* (1997) 217 ALR 365 (New South Wales Supreme Court of Appeal) (estoppel by representation); *Australian Breeders Co-operative Society Ltd v Jones* (1997) 26 ACSR 26 (Federal Court of Australia) (estoppel by representation); *Gilsan (International) Ltd v Optus Networks Pty Ltd* [2004] NSWSC 1077 (New South Wales Supreme Court) (estoppels by representation and convention); *Woodgate v Keddie* [2006] FCA 1728 (Federal Court of Australia) (estoppel by representation); *Ethnic Earth Pty Ltd v Quoin Technology Pty Ltd (in liq) (No 3)* [2006] SASC 7, (2006) 94 SASR 103 (South Australian Supreme Court) (estoppel by representation); *Alpha Wealth Financial Services Pty Ltd v Frankland River Olive Company Ltd* [2008] WASCA 119 (Western Australia Supreme Court of Appeal) (estoppel by convention). Estoppel and change of position were mentioned as independent defences in *Ovidio Carrideo Nominees Pty Ltd v Dog Depot Pty Ltd* [2004] VSC 400 (Victorian Supreme Court) [38] (Kaye J) and *Perpetual Trustees Victoria Limited v Ford* [2008] NSWSC 29 (New South Wales Supreme Court) [116] (Harrison J).

[24] Ch 2, at 27–31; ch 5, at 150–51.

[25] Ch 2, at 40–41, 58–59.

be pleaded separately. They may also present substantive reasons (over and above any characterisation of that estoppel as a rule of evidence) why estoppel by representation should operate as a complete defence, rather than *pro tanto* as does the change of position defence. If the defence is concerned with protecting the defendant's autonomy, and it can be shown that the claimant was responsible for vitiating the defendant's decision to change his position, it might be thought that protection of the defendant's autonomy in decision-making calls for a complete defence.[26] Echoing the earlier discussion of causation in decision-making,[27] the role played by the representation on the defendant's decision to change his position cannot be measured or weighed. If the law is concerned to protect the defendant's autonomy, it would at least make sense to intervene by providing a complete defence. This assessment is not inconsistent with an 'unjust-related' analysis of the defence.[28] On the latter approach, the claimant's right to the protection of her autonomy in decision-making and thus to restitution of benefits transferred pursuant to, for example, a mistake, is undermined by having made a representation on which the defendant has relied. The claimant is responsible for the defendant's vitiated decision to change his position. From the perspective of autonomy, for the claimant to resile from her representation would be to deny the defendant the same respect for and protection of his autonomy in decision-making on which the claimant now seeks to base her claim. If that is correct, then again it at least makes sense for the defence to operate completely to preclude the claimant from resiling from her representation.[29]

In summary, it is premature to conclude that estoppel by conduct is subsumed or rendered redundant by the change of position defence. Until there is clearer guidance from the courts as to its rationale, operation and the application of any 'exceptions' to its application, estoppel can and should continue to be pleaded separately as an independent defence.

C Payment Over and Ministerial Receipt

In contrast to estoppel by representation, the analysis of the payment over defence contained in chapter three suggests that, subject to one caveat, it is capable of being subsumed within the change of position defence. Both defences are characterised by the requirement that the defendant has irreversibly changed his position in reasonable reliance on his receipt and their bars largely correlate. The caveat is that

[26] A similar analysis is developed in R Grantham and C Rickett, 'A Normative Account of Defences to Restitutionary Liability' (2008) 67 *CLJ* 92, 106–09.

[27] Ch 2, at 32–35, 41–42.

[28] Above, at 225.

[29] This analysis could co-exist with Birks' argument that the representation may be 'prospectively revocable': the complete operation of the defence would only affect the irrevocable representation: see above, at 228–29.

the payment over defence appears to be available only in cases of disclosed agents.[30] There is no such restriction in the change of position defence. However, the requirement of reasonable reliance in the change of position defence may have the consequence that an undisclosed agent will not be able to rely on the defence in any event. Knowing that the claimant assumes she is dealing with a principal, the defendant also knows that the claimant is transferring any benefit to him under a mistake. In that context, the undisclosed agent arguably makes any irreversible payment over to his principal at his own risk.

If the reasonable reliance requirement does not cover the field of cases where undisclosed agents are denied the payment over defence, it is submitted that the restriction of the defence to disclosed agent should be abandoned, so as to bring it in line with the change of position defence. Arguably, the restriction makes far more sense in the context of the stronger agency defence—ministerial receipt—considered briefly in chapter three, and should be restricted to that context.[31] It will be recalled from chapter three that in contrast with the payment over defence, this broad agency defence applies at common law[32] and in equity[33] and whether or not the agent has paid the benefit over to his principal. Effectively, it denies that an agent who receives ministerially (that is, solely in his capacity as agent) is the proper defendant to proceedings to recover the transferred benefit, even if the benefit is retained in the agent's hands.[34]

The position of ministerial receipt as a separate defence has not been free from controversy. Professor Stevens has argued that the common law cases involving recovery of deposits,[35] which a number of commentators identify as supporting a

[30] *Holland v Russell* (1861) 1 B & S 424, 121 ER 773; *Agip (Africa) Ltd v Jackson* [1990] Ch 265 (Ch); *Portman Building Society v Hamlyn Taylor Neck (a firm)* [1998] 4 All ER 202 (CA) 207 (Millett LJ). Contra is *Transvaal and Delgoa Bay Investment Co Ltd v Atkinson* [1944] 1 All ER 579.

[31] At 66–67.

[32] A classic case is *Sadler v Evans* (1766) 4 Burr 1984, 98 ER 34, approved on appeal: 4 Burr 1984, 1986; 98 ER 34, 35 (Lord Mansfield) and followed in *Greenway v Hurd* (1792) 4 TR 553, 555; 100 ER 1171, 1173 (Lord Kenyon); *Miller v Aris* (1800) 3 Esp 231, 233; 170 ER 598, 599 (Lord Kenyon).

[33] eg *Agip (Africa) Ltd v Jackson* [1990] Ch 265 (Ch) 291–92 (Millett J); approved on appeal [1991] Ch 457; *El Ajou v Dollar Land Holdings plc* [1994] 2 All ER 685 (CA) 700 (Lord Hoffmann); *Eagle Trust plc v SBC Securities Ltd* [1993] 1 WLR 484 (Ch) 490, 501 (Vinelott J); *Evans v European Bank Limited* [2004] NSWCA 82, (2004) 61 NSWLR 75 (New South Wales Court of Appeal); *Nimmo v Westpac Banking Corp* [1993] 3 NZLR 218 (New Zealand High Court) 224–25 (Blanchard J); *Air Canada v M & L Travel Ltd* [1993] 3 SCR 787 (Supreme Court of Canada) 810–11; *Citadel General Assurance Co Ltd v Lloyd's Bank Canada* [1997] 3 SCR 805 (Supreme Court of Canada); *Gold v Rosenberg* [1997] 3 SCR 767 (Supreme Court of Canada).

[34] The common law and equitable authorities are explored in Burrows, *The Law of Restitution* 2nd edn, above n 13, at 600–01; J Moore, *Restitution from Banks* (D Phil thesis, University of Oxford 2000) 250–53; J Edelman and E Bant, *Unjust Enrichment in Australia* (OUP, Melbourne 2006) 362–63. *Cf* R Stevens, 'Why do agents "drop out"?' [2005] *LMCLQ* 101.

[35] *Duke of Norfolk v Worthy* (1808) 1 Camp 337, 170 ER 977; *Bamford v Shuttleworth* (1840) 11 Ad & E 926, 113 ER 1083; *Hurley v Baker* (1846) 16 M & W 26, 153 ER 1083; *Edgell v Day* (1865) Law Rep 1 CP 80 (CCP); *Ellis v Goulton* [1893] 1 QB 350 (CA); *Christie v Robinson* (1907) 4 CLR 1338 (High Court of Australia); *North Eastern Timber Importers v Ch Arendt & Sons* [1952] 2 Lloyd's Rep 369 (QB); *Burt v Claude Cousins & Co Ltd* [1971] 2 QB 426 (CA) 435 (Lord Denning); *Goodey and Southwold Trawlers Ltd v Garrick, Mason and Millgate* [1972] 2 Lloyd's Rep 369 (QB); *Tudor v Hamid* [1988] 1 EGLR 251 (CA); *Arnhem Technology Ltd v Dudley Joiner* (Ch 31 January 2001). *Cf Wilder v Pilkington* [1956] JPL 739 (QB).

defence of ministerial receipt,[36] do no such thing.[37] He argues that in those cases, the claim for restitution was based on failure of consideration and it was because this primary claim failed on the facts that the agent escaped liability, not because of the operation of any so-called agency defence. He gives the example of A agreeing to paint B's house for £100 payable in advance. B deposits the cheque for this amount into A's account with bank C. A now refuses to carry out the work. B clearly has a claim against A for restitution on the ground of failure of consideration. However, Stevens argues, B would not be able to make out a claim of failure of consideration against C. In the example, C has 'no notion'[38] of the basis of the payment: so far as it is concerned, no condition has been attached and so the claim against it must fail.

There are a number of difficulties with this analysis. First, a claim for failure of consideration may succeed even though the basis is not subjectively shared by the defendant: it is arguable that the basis of a transaction is determined objectively.[39] Further, the reason for the requirement that the basis of a transaction must be (objectively) shared is to exclude claims where the claimant was a risk-taker.[40] The claimants in the deposit cases generally pay the deposit pursuant to a contractual obligation the basis for which subsequently wholly fails and thus cannot properly be said to be risk-takers. In that context, it should be enough for their prima facie claim to succeed that the objective basis on which the claimants paid the deposit (that is, that the underlying transaction would proceed) fails.

It could be argued in support of Stevens' thesis that one basis on which the agents in the deposit cases received the deposit was that it should be paid to the principal. That basis did not fail and so the primary claims against the agents were unsuccessful for that reason (rather than because of the existence of any defence). But there are also a number of problems with this argument. The first is that it assumes that there can only be one basis for a transaction. That clearly is not the case. Further, the agents in the deposit cases received the deposit on more than one basis—the most obvious other one being that the underlying transaction in respect of which the deposit is paid should proceed. In that event, even if one basis for the payment did not fail, there remained another viable failure of basis claim against the agent and the agent's escape from liability must have another explanation. Further, at least one of the cases on which Stevens relies supports alternative analysis of the basis of the claim as lying in mistake, not failure of consideration.[41]

[36] Burrows, *The Law of Restitution* 2nd edn, above n 13, at 600–01; Moore, above n 34, at 250–53; Edelman and Bant, above n 34, at 362–63.

[37] Stevens, above n 34, at 116–17.

[38] *Ibid*, at 117.

[39] *Fostif Pty Ltd v Campbells Cash & Carry Pty Ltd* [2005] NSWCA 83, (2005) 218 ALR 166 (New South Wales Court of Appeal) 210–12 (Mason P, Sheller and Hodgson JJA agreeing), discussed in Edelman and Bant, above n 34, at 362–63.

[40] *Gilbert & Partners v Knight* [1968] 2 All ER 248 (CA); *Burgess v Rawnsley* [1975] Ch 429 (CA); F Maher, 'A New Conception of Failure of Basis' [2004] *Restitution L Rev* 96, 101, discussed in Edelman and Bant, *ibid.*

[41] *Duke of Norfolk v Worthy* (1808) 1 Camp 337, 340; 170 ER 977, 978 (Lord Ellenborough).

So collapse of a claim grounded in failure of basis should not have proved fatal to the claim. Finally, as a more general observation, the deposit cases repeatedly emphasise that payment to the agent is *eo instanti*, payment to the principal.[42] Therefore, the emphasis of the cases lies in the status of the agent in the transaction, rather than the basis of the transaction itself.

It seems, therefore, that there remain strong grounds for saying that there exists a separate defence of ministerial receipt. Given that it regards any payment over by the agent as irrelevant, that defence must have a distinct rationale or rationales (and thus elements) from that underpinning the change of position defence. In that regard, there are two possible rationales for the defence of ministerial receipt. The first is that, coming under an immediate obligation to pay over the received benefit to his principal, the agent is not net enriched by his receipt so as to become primarily liable in unjust enrichment for restitution of the received benefit.[43] This rationale clearly cannot apply with respect to the change of position defence, which proceeds on the basis that the elements of the primary claim—including that of enrichment—are satisfied.

The second reason underlying the defence of ministerial receipt is the policy need to protect agents in cases of claims for restitution for unjust enrichment[44] from what has been called 'the agent's dilemma'.[45] This dilemma arises because on receipt of a benefit, the agent generally will come under an immediate obligation to account to his principal for his receipt. Faced with a claim for restitution of the benefit by the claimant, what is the agent to do? If he pays over the benefit to his principal after notice of the claim, he will not be entitled to the defence of payment over (or, by analogy, the change of position defence) if it subsequently turns out that the claim succeeds. Yet a failure to pay over, even after notice of the claim, will put him in breach of his obligations to his principal. Lord Millett has expressed the view that, in those circumstances, the agent should interplead.[46] However, in practice, this is not a satisfactory answer. Even if that process can protect the agent from liability with respect to the claimant, it does not protect the principal who has changed his position in reliance on the receipt by his agent of moneys which the principal believed to be unimpeachable.[47] The defence of ministerial receipt resolves this dilemma as a matter of policy, by identifying the principal as the proper party to any claim in unjust enrichment. Notably, this

[42] eg *Duke of Norfolk v Worthy* (1808) 1 Camp 337, 339; 170 ER 977, 978 (Lord Ellenborough); *Hurley v Baker* (1846) 16 M & W 26, 30; 153 ER 1083 1085 (Rolfe, B); *Edgell v Day* (1865) Law Rep 1 CP 80 (CCP), 84 (Erle CJ); *Christie v Robinson* (1907) 4 CLR 1338 (High Court of Australia) 1350 (O'Connor J); *Burt v Claude Cousins & Co Ltd* [1971] 2 QB 426 (CA) 435 (Lord Denning).

[43] Stevens, above n 34, at 111.

[44] Different considerations apply where the agent is a tortfeasor, or is the defendant to a claim for breach of a contract to which the agent was a signatory: see Stevens, above n 34.

[45] M Bryan, 'Recovering Misdirected Money from Banks: Ministerial Receipt at Law and in Equity' in FD Rose (ed) *Restitution and Banking Law* (Mansfield Press, Oxford 1998) 168; Moore, above n 34, at 269. Cf *BMP Global Distribution Inc v Bank of Nova Scotia* [2009] SCC 15 (Supreme Court of Canada) [63] Deschamps J (McLachlin CJ and Binnie, Le Bel and Rothstein JJ concurring).

[46] *Portman Building Society v Hamlyn Taylor Neck (a firm)* [1998] 4 All ER 202 (CA) 207 (Millet LJ).

[47] Moore, above n 34, at 268.

rationale is specific to claims in unjust enrichment made against agents and must be limited to that context. It cannot inform or affect a more general defence of change of position.

It follows from this analysis that the change of position defence and the defence of ministerial receipt are entirely separate defences with different rationales, elements and operation. Where a defendant has received a benefit in his capacity as agent, the defence of ministerial receipt will tend to outflank the change of position defence because it does not require proof of any change of position caused by the defendant's receipt. However, it must be emphasised that its application is dependent on the receipt being by an agent acting in that capacity. Recipients may act as agents in some transactions but not in others, even when dealing with the same payer. For example, banks may act as agents in the receipt of some payments from a claimant, but not always: all too often it is forgotten that banks regularly act as principals in transactions in which they receive payments for their own benefit and profit. More must be done in that context to ascertain the circumstances in which banks truly operate in a ministerial capacity.

D *Restitutio in Integrum*

Turning to the final defence considered in part one of this book, chapter four demonstrated that there exists a very close relationship between the concepts of *restitutio in integrum* and the change of position defence. Both aim to reverse transfers of value so as to protect defendants from being placed in a worse or entirely different position from that which they occupied prior to their receipt. In that context, it is important that the similarities between the concepts are articulated and rationalised to their fullest possible extent.

It is, however, premature to say that the concepts are identical: much more needs to be done to explore the similarities and differences between the concepts of *restitutio in integrum* and the change of position defence and between rescission and restitution. For example, one conclusion of chapter six was that there was support in the authorities for recognition of a bar to the change of position defence in the case of innocent inducers.[48] However, we also saw in chapter four that the rescission case law was more sympathetic to the plight of innocent inducers than were the estoppel, payment over and change of position authorities.[49] Although the position was not consistently maintained, there was clear support in the rescission authorities for permitting innocent inducers to rely on changes of position made in reliance on their receipts in diminution of their restitutionary liabilities.

It is unsatisfactory that the position of innocent inducers should be treated inconsistently depending on whether the claim is for unilateral restitution or for mutual rescission. It is to be hoped that future cases will soon provide the oppor-

[48] Ch 6, at 177–84.
[49] Ch 4, at 110–14.

tunity for courts to resolve this ambiguity—whether it is in favour of the innocent inducer, or against. At the very least, if a difference in treatment of this category of defendant is to continue, clear justification must be found for it, justification that is not presently obvious.

We also saw that while rescission is a predominantly restitutionary process, the precise nature of the relationship between it and restitution remains unclear. Recently, commentators have argued that common law and equitable rescission operate by quite separate mechanisms: rescission at common law is an act of the parties whereas rescission in equity arises by order of the court.[50] While both forms of rescission are subject to the influences of equity in adjusting the rights of the parties on rescission, their independence should be maintained for reasons of principle and practice. If that is correct and the distinction is strictly maintained, it could impact on the rationalisation of *restitutio in integrum* and the change of position defence in a number of ways.

First, it would mean that the time at which detriment is to be assessed differs at common law and in equity, being at the time of the act of the rescinding party at common law and (presumably) at the time of the court order in equity. This in turn will dictate whether a claimant may rely on a careless change of position affecting the benefit she received from the defendant. If rescission occurs at common law, we have seen[51] that the claimant might be precluded from relying on her change of position where she acted unreasonably in the light of her obligation to account for the benefit to the defendant. For example, in *Alati v Kruger*,[52] the court considered whether rescission was precluded because the business the subject of the proceedings had deteriorated under the claimant's direction. If rescission occurs in equity, the timing of rescission (being the act of the court) will render this bar redundant.

Secondly, the analysis suggests that where a rescinding party insists on her common law rights, the defence of counter-restitution impossible must be applied. This is because at the time the claimant purports to rescind the transaction, the courts have nothing to say in the matter. The act of rescission is the act of the party and it is complete—or not, as the case may be—at the time the act takes place. It is only subsequently, if the matter comes to court, that a court will be able to review the purported act of rescission and determine if counter-restitution was possible and adequately made, or make orders to enforce the defendant's right to counter-restitution. If full counter-restitution was not made and is impossible at the time of the court hearing, then it is too late retrospectively to impose conditions on the act of rescission, so as to satisfy the requirement of *restitutio in integrum*. In those circumstances, the purported act of rescission will have failed.

Although this seems to present a significant difficulty for any rationalisation of *restitutio in integrum* and the change of position defence, in practice it may be more apparent than real. A party faced with the prospect of her act of rescission

50 D O'Sullivan, S Elliot and R Zakrzewski, *The Law of Rescission* (OUP, Oxford 2008).

51 Ch 4, at 115–16 and ch 5, at 189–90.

52 *Alati v Kruger* (1955) 94 CLR 216 (High Court of Australia), considered in ch 6, at 189–91.

being defeated by the principle of *restitutio in integrum* is far more likely either to make full counter-restitution at the time of rescission or to submit to the concurrent jurisdiction exercised by equity in cases of fraud and duress, rather than risk the continuation of the impugned transaction by insisting on her common law rights.

The final area which requires further consideration, if common law and equity indeed have distinct rescission mechanisms, is the consequences of rescission for any right to counter-restitution. The learned authors argue that when rescission occurs at common law, it gives rise to an automatic right to counter-restitution on the part of the defendant.[53] This is consistent with the analysis in chapter four. However, they also contend that no equivalent right automatically arises in equity: there, counter-restitution is in the discretion of the court and depends on the willingness of the rescinding party to 'do equity' by accepting the terms imposed by the court. The right of the defendant is limited to insisting that all proper allowances are made in the accounting.[54]

As with the previous point, this difficulty may be more apparent than real. Given that the right to rescind in equity is conditional on the claimant accepting the court's conditions of rescission that encompass counter-restitution, or submitting to an account in which the defendant must be given his proper allowances, claimants are unlikely to deny the defendant the full benefits of his (limited) right to counter-restitution.

However, this is not an entirely satisfactory way of dealing with the problem. As we saw in chapter four, the characterisation of the defendant's right to counter-restitution as one that arises automatically on the rescission of the impugned transaction underpins the entire analysis linking the change of position defence and the doctrine of *restitutio in integrum*. If there is no right to counter-restitution, that analysis cannot apply. But, with respect, it is difficult to see any reasoned basis for the proposed difference in the nature of the right to counter-restitution at common law and in equity. If a court in equity orders a defendant to make restitution, the basis on which he conferred a benefit on the claimant fails as completely as when the rescission occurs through the act of the rescinding party herself. Given that failure of consideration is an unjust factor that arises equally at common law and in equity,[55] there seems little justification for saying that the defendant who transfers a benefit to a claimant pursuant to a transaction subsequently rescinded in equity obtains no entitlement to counter-restitution, but only a right to all proper allowances in an account. For these reasons, the view taken in this work is that, even if rescission at common law and in equity are distinct processes, the analysis of the countervailing right to counter-restitution in chapter four remains correct.

[53] O'Sullivan, Elliot and Zakrzewski, above n 50, at [14.02], [14.45], [15.60].
[54] *Ibid*, at [15.51], [15.57].
[55] *Muschinski v Dodds* (1985) 160 CLR 583 (HCA) 618–620 (Deane J, Mason J concurring).

E Good Consideration

In *Barclays Bank Ltd v WJ Simms, Son and Cooke (Southern) Ltd*,[56] Lord Goff cited 'good consideration' as one of a number of defences that can arise in response to a claim for restitution of a benefit transferred pursuant to a mistake. Another of the defences cited was a change of position defence. Although Lord Goff clearly regarded the defences as distinct,[57] subsequent courts have from time to time suggested that the defence of good consideration is merely an example of the change of position defence in play.[58] It is thus important to be clear about what the defence entails and its relationship to the change of position defence.

Analysis of the cases reveals that two distinct defences have come to harbour under the umbrella term of 'good consideration'. The first has already been examined in the context of rescission.[59] It arises where the defendant provided a benefit to the claimant in return for his own receipt. If required to make restitution of the receipt, the basis of his transfer of benefit will fail. This defence is also known by the label 'failure of consideration' or, from the perspective of the claimant, the defence of counter-restitution required. It operates as a counterclaim by way of set-off for failure of consideration and its rationale is to prevent the unjust enrichment of the claimant. As we saw in chapter four, one of the consequences of characterising the defence in this way is that the defence of change of position in theory applies with respect to the counterclaim.

The second is that the benefit was received in satisfaction of an existing right. This seems most likely to be the form of the defence Lord Goff had in mind in *Barclays Bank v Simms*, when his Lordship gave as an example of the defence, cases where,

> money is paid to discharge, and does discharge, a debt owed to the payee (or a principal on whose behalf he is authorised to receive the payment) by the payor or by a third party by whom he is authorised to discharge the debt.[60]

An example of this category of case is *Lloyds Bank plc v Independent Insurance Co Ltd*.[61] A customer instructed its bank (the claimant) to make a payment to its

[56] *Barclays Bank Ltd v WJ Simms, Son and Cooke (Southern) Ltd* [1980] QB 677 (QB (Comm Ct)) 695.

[57] See also: *Australia and New Zealand Banking Group Ltd v Westpac Banking Corporation* (1988) 164 CLR 662 (High Court of Australia) 673 (the Court) and *David Securities Pty Ltd v Commonwealth Bank of Australia* (1992) 127 CLR 353 (High Court of Australia) 381 (Mason CJ, Deane, Toohey, Gaudron and McHugh JJ).

[58] eg *Lloyds Bank plc v Independent Insurance Co Ltd* [2000] 1 QB 110 (CA) 126 (Waller LJ) and *K & S Corp Ltd v Sportingbet Australia Pty Ltd* [2003] SASC 96, (2003) 86 SASR 313 (South Australian Supreme Court) [161] (Besanko J).

[59] Ch 4, at 93–95, 103–107. Cases applying this defence and adopting the good consideration terminology include *Aiken v Short* (1856) 1 H & N 210, 126 ER 1180 and *Lloyds Bank plc v Independent Insurance Co Ltd* [2000] 1 QB 110 (CA), both discussed immediately below; *Ovidio Carrideo Nominees Pty Ltd v The Dog Depot Pty Ltd* [2006] VSCA 6, [2006] V Conv R 54-713 (Victorian Supreme Court of Appeal), considered in ch 4, at 101; *R & Z Mazzei Nominees Pty Ltd v Aegean Food Import Export Pty Ltd* [2006] VSC 210 (Victorian Supreme Court) and *Ragi Pty Ltd v Kiwi Munchies Pty Ltd* [2007] NSWADT (New South Wales Administrative Decisions Tribunal).

[60] *Barclays Bank Ltd v WJ Simms, Son and Cooke (Southern) Ltd* [1980] QB 677 (QB (Comm Ct)) 695.

[61] *Lloyds Bank plc v Independent Insurance Co Ltd* [2000] 1 QB 110 (CA).

creditor (the defendant) in order to discharge a debt due and owing from the customer to the defendant. The bank did so under the mistaken belief that there were sufficient funds credited to the customer's account to satisfy the payment. The Court of Appeal refused the bank's claim for restitution of the value of the payment on the ground that the defendant creditor had given 'good consideration' for it, by discharging the debt owed to it by the customer. In Australia, the High Court of Australia has likewise recognised that a claim for restitution based on mistake (of law) would not succeed where,

> the moneys were paid under a mistaken belief that they were legally due and owing under a particular clause of a particular contract when in fact they were legally due and owing under another contract.[62]

The key features of this defence are: (1) that the liability must be due and owing at the time of the payment; and (2) that the payment must be effective to discharge that liability. It follows that the defence may be defeated if the claimant can undermine the basis of the defendant's right, for example by demonstrating that the contract on which the right depends is void, or voidable and has subsequently been rescinded, or that the payment was not effective to discharge the liability. For example, in *Barclays Bank v Simms* itself, the defence of good consideration (receipt in satisfaction of a right) failed because the claimant bank paid the defendant on its client's cheque, overlooking the client's stop order. As the payment was unauthorised, it was not effective to discharge the client's debt to the defendant. Finally, the defence may fail where it can be demonstrated that the right was not presently exercisable, as where a defendant holds a debt which is not presently due and owing at the time the payment is received.[63]

Given the chief characteristics of the defence of receipt in satisfaction of a right, its likely rationale is that it negates any allegation that the defendant was enriched by his receipt. Prior to his receipt, the defendant held a valuable asset, for example a debt. This asset was extinguished by the receipt and discharge of the debt, such that there was no net change to his assets.[64] Importantly, although the usual case involves payment of a debt, there is no reason why the defence should not extend to other transfers in discharge of a duty owed to the defendant.

The preceding analysis demonstrates that although the two defences of 'good consideration' harbour under the same label, they are distinct. The distinction becomes obvious on considering two of the leading cases in the area. We saw previously that in *Lloyds Bank plc v Independent Insurance*,[65] the claimant bank's payment

[62] *David Securities Pty Ltd v Commonwealth Bank of Australia* (1992) 127 CLR 353 (High Court of Australia) 376 (Mason CJ, Deane, Toohey, Gaudron and McHugh JJ).

[63] *Equiticorp Finance Ltd (in liq) v Bank of New Zealand* (1993) 32 NSWLR 50 (New South Wales Court of Appeal) 151 (Clarke JA and Cripps JA).

[64] W Swadling, 'Restitution and *Bona Fide* Purchase' in W Swadling (ed) *The Limits of Restitutionary Claims: A Comparative Analysis* (United Kingdom National Committee of Comparative Law, London 1997) 102; K Mason, JW Carter and G Tolhurst, *Mason and Carter's Restitution Law in Australia* (2 edn, LexisNexis Butterworths, Sydney 2008) [440], [520].

[65] *Lloyds Bank plc v Independent Insurance Co Ltd* [2000] 1 QB 110 (CA).

discharged a debt owed to the defendant, a creditor of the bank's client. Clearly, the creditor did not have any claim by way of set-off against the bank for failure of consideration. Rather, its defence was that it had discharged a debt owed to it by the bank's client. Likewise, in *Aiken v Short*,[66] the claimant bank paid a debt owed by a third party to the defendant in order to remove the defendant's charge over property held by the third party. The property was then transferred from the third party to the bank. It subsequently transpired that the third party did not have good title to the property and thus neither did the bank. When the bank sought to recover the money paid to the defendant, a majority held that the defendant had given good consideration by discharging the debt owed by the third party. As in *Lloyds Bank*, there was no defence, or set-off, of failure of consideration in this case because the debt was owed by the third party, not the bank. Rather, the defence succeeded because the defendant had received the payment in satisfaction of an existing right.

The final question to consider is the relationship between these defences and the change of position defence. We saw in chapter four that the defence of failure of consideration operates as a counterclaim by way of set-off to the claimant's action and thus is quite distinct from the change of position defence.[67] Indeed, the change of position defence may operate with respect to the counterclaim.

Likewise, the defence of receipt in satisfaction of a right is autonomous. Its core features differ significantly from the change of position defence. Its bars may also differ. Given that the focus of the defence is the satisfaction of a valid and existing right held by the defendant, so that there is no net enrichment of the defendant, there is little reason to think that any bad faith or fault on the part of the defendant in receiving the payment should matter. Even if, for example, the payment is received as a result of the defendant's duress, the defence should still apply provided the payment was received pursuant to a pre-existing right (untainted by the duress), which was due and excisable at the time of receipt.[68]

F *Bona Fide* Purchase

The final common law defence to consider is the defence of bona fide purchase of legal title in good faith and without notice (the 'bona fide purchase defence'). This defence arises where a defendant has purchased a legal title to an asset in good faith, for value and without notice of any right or interest affecting that title, from a person whose title to the asset is defective or absent. Once raised, the defence operates to confer on the defendant a fresh legal title to the asset, free from any defects that may have affected the transferor's title. It therefore operates as an exception to the general rule of property law, *nemo dat quod non habet* (no one can

[66] *Aiken v Short* (1856) 1 H & N 210, 126 ER 1180.
[67] At 93–95, 103–107.
[68] *Equiticorp Finance Ltd (in liq) v Bank of New Zealand* (1993) 32 NSWLR 50 (New South Wales Court of Appeal) 151 (Clarke and Cripps JJA).

give what he does not have). Finally, the defence extinguishes once and for all any prior titles to the asset that would otherwise compete with the defendant's new right. It follows from these features of the defence that it operates completely, by conferring on the defendant a new title, rather than simply responding to the value of the defendant's change of position (usually, the value paid for his purchase).

The defence of bona fide purchase exists at common law and in equity. However, at common law, its operation is ad hoc, targeting certain limited classes of transactions. Its main area of operation involves situations where money passes into currency. For example, the defence applies generally where defendants provide goods and services in exchange for money, extinguishing any prior, competing title to the money even in cases where the precise coins or notes can still be identified. This application of the defence reflects the importance of currency in maintaining an efficient market economy.[69] Other instances of the defence at common law (for example, the now largely historical rule of sale in market *ouvert*)[70] display the same, efficiency-based rationale.

In equity, the defence operates more generally to protect good faith purchase of legal title without notice. It also operates to protect good faith purchase of an equitable interest, where the prior conflicting right is a 'mere equity',[71] such as a restitutionary right to rescind a transaction for fraud or innocent misrepresentation.[72] The defence does not, however, operate to protect good faith purchase of a subsequent equitable estate against a prior, conflicting equitable estate.[73] In such cases, equity also follows the *nemo dat* rule, albeit known in equity by a different name, *qui prior est tempore potior est jure* (he who is first in time is better in law).

Although it is sometimes said that the reason for the bona fide purchaser defence in equity is lack of jurisdiction to interfere with the legal title,[74] this rationale does not explain its application in cases where legal title has not been purchased. Although the matter is not without difficulty,[75] the manner of operation

[69] Swadling, 'Restitution and *Bona Fide* Purchase' in Swadling (ed), above n 64, at 82–85; D Fox, '*Bona Fide* Purchase and the Currency of Money' (1996) 55 *CLJ* 547, 565.

[70] Still applicable in Australia through the state Sales of Goods legislation but only of historical interest in England. This and other exceptions to *nemo dat* at common law are discussed in Swadling, 'Restitution and *Bona Fide* Purchase' in Swadling (ed), above n 64, at 82–89.

[71] Perhaps better described as proprietary powers: see ch 7, at 206–07.

[72] *Phillips v Phillips* (1861) 4 De GF & J 208, 215; 45 ER 1164, 1166 (Lord Westbury); *Latec Investments Ltd v Hotel Terrigal (in liq)* (1965) 113 CLR 265 (High Court of Australia) 277 (Kitto J).

[73] *Cave v Cave* (1880) 15 Ch D 639; *Rice v Rice* 2 Drew 73, 61 ER 646; *Latec Investments Ltd v Hotel Terrigal (in liq)* (1965) 113 CLR 265 (High Court of Australia).

[74] *Pilcher v Rawlins* (1872) 7 Ch App 265.

[75] The problem lies in determining which purchases merit protection and why: Swadling, 'Restitution and *Bona Fide* Purchase' in Swadling (ed), above n 64, 90. Although outside the scope of this work, it is suggested that the distinction between proprietary powers and vested proprietary rights may also have some explanatory force in this context: see ch 7, at 206–07. Consistent with that distinction is the discussion of Kitto J in *Latec Investments Ltd v Hotel Terrigal (in liq)* (1965) 113 CLR 265 (High Court of Australia) 277–78 of those classes of case

> in which an equity is asserted which *must be made good* before an equitable interest can be held to exist. In [such] cases the equity is distinct from, because logically antecedent to, the equitable interest, and it is against the equity and not the consequential equitable interest that the defence [of bona fide purchase] must be set up. (Emphasis added).

of the defence in equity is consistent with the common law's policy of protecting security of purchase and can be understood on that basis.

What is the relationship between this defence and the defence of change of position? Although at first sight superficially similar, in that both require a change of position in good faith, and in both the concept of notice has a role to play, there remain significant differences in their elements, ambits of operation and rationales. First, we have seen from chapter five that the defence of change of position is not limited to changes of position by way of purchase. Even taking the narrowest 'enrichment' approach to what counts as a change of position, the defence clearly may apply where the change of position involves a gift to a third party.

Secondly, the change of position defence operates *pro tanto*, by reference to the extent of the change of position. In contrast, the bona fide purchaser defence is concerned to identify a valuable consideration paid for the purchase but, once that is identified, the defence operates completely, without further reference to the quantity of the purchase price. The point can be illustrated by reference to *Lipkin Gorman v Karpnale.*[76] It will be recalled that a rogue solicitor (Cass) withdrew money from his firm's client account and spent it at the defendant's casino. The defendant changed its position by permitting Cass to lay bets and by paying out on his winning bets. The casino's defence of bona fide purchase failed because the chips Cass purchased did not count as good consideration (having been given pursuant to void wagering contracts)[77] and because the right to use the chips to purchase food and drink was not sufficiently valuable consideration for the money exchanged. However, had the chips counted as good consideration,[78] the defence would have operated to defeat the firm's claim completely. In contrast, the change of position defence only operated to the extent of the value of the winnings paid to Cass, a considerably lesser amount. As Lord Goff stated:

> The defence of change of position is akin to the defence of bona fide purchase: but we cannot simply say that bona fide purchase is a species of change of position. This is because change of position will only avail a defendant to the extent that his position has been changed; whereas, where bona fide purchase is invoked, no inquiry is made (in most cases) into the adequacy of the consideration.[79]

Thirdly, it will be apparent from the earlier discussion that the bona fide purchase defence does not apply in the generality of two-party unjust enrichment cases, in which claimants usually confer good title to the enrichment on defendants. Rather, a typical example of a case in which it will apply involves three parties, for example, where a thief has stolen the defendant's money and exchanged it for the defendant's goods or services. It follow that its most likely areas of contact with unjust enrichment cases are where the claimant's benefit was transferred to the

[76] [1991] 2 AC 548 (HL).
[77] Pursuant to the Gaming Act 1845 s 18, subsequently repealed by the Gambling Act 2005.
[78] As they presumably now would: *ibid.*
[79] *Lipkin Gorman (a firm) v Karpnale Ltd* [1991] 2 AC (HL) 580–81.

defendant without her consent, for example in 'ignorance' cases.[80] This stands in stark contrast with the change of position defence, which clearly operates where the defendant has received good title to the asset and changes his position in reliance on that receipt.

Fourthly, the defence of bona fide purchase applies to claims for proprietary restitution. It must also operate with respect to claims for personal restitution[81]: any other conclusion would entirely undermine or stultify the operation of the defence in conferring a good title to the enrichment on the defendant in order to protect the security of the transaction and promote transactional efficiency. For example, suppose a claimant brings a claim for proprietary restitution of her money exchanged by a thief for goods or services provided by the defendant. Assuming proprietary restitution is possible, it would not make sense for the defence of bona fide purchase to apply to cure the defendant's title to the money, yet permit the claim for personal restitution for the amount of the money receipt. This aspect of the ambit of operation of the defence again stands in contrast with the change of position defence, where its application to claims for proprietary restitution is highly contentious precisely because of its capacity to undermine the law's protection of proprietary rights.

Fifthly, the respective ambits of operation of the defences discussed above demonstrate that their focuses are different: one defence is concerned with irreversibility protection, the other with conferring good title to protect security of purchase transactions in certain limited cases, for reasons of market efficiency. It could be said that change of position is focused on the claims of the particular defendant to protection from the consequences of his irreversible change of position. Bona fide purchase, by contrast, is less concerned with the position of the particular defendant and more concerned to protect the class of transactions of which his is but one example.

Although the defences are distinct, a further question arising from the last point is whether the work done by bona fide purchase might nonetheless be effectively subsumed or rendered redundant by the change of position defence. It is submitted that it cannot: the defence of bona fide purchase extinguishes prior, competing titles and confers a fresh, non-derivative title on the defendant. The consequence is that the defendant is then able to convey that fresh title on parties

[80] This discussion assumes the existence of this category of claim and the possible of proprietary restitution. If neither exists, then the role of the defence within unjust enrichment law must be extremely limited: Swadling, 'Restitution and *Bona Fide* Purchase' in Swadling (ed), above n 64; Grantham and Rickett, above n 26, at 113. *Cf* G Virgo, *The Principles of the Law of Restitution* (2 edn, OUP, Oxford 2006) 656, who argues that the defence applies only to proprietary restitutionary claims and that this category of claims fall outside the law of unjust enrichment.

[81] Implicit in the House of Lords' treatment of the defence in *Lipkin Gorman (a firm) v Karpnale Ltd* [1991] 2 AC 548 (HL) and that of the Privy Council in *Dextra Bank and Trust Co Ltd v Bank of Jamaica* [2002] 1 All ER (Comm) 193 (PC). See also: K Barker, 'After Change of Position: Good Faith Exchange in the Modern Law of Restitution' in P Birks (ed) *Laundering and Tracing* (OUP, Oxford 1995) 213; P Birks, 'Change of Position and Surviving Enrichment' in W Swadling (ed) *The Limits of Restitutionary Claims: A Comparative Analysis* (The United Kingdom Committee of Comparative Law, Glasgow 1997); Birks, *Unjust Enrichment* 2nd edn, above n 10, at 240.

in future transactions. This is simply not the concern of change of position, which never operates to confer any benefit on the defendant additional to that which he received pursuant to the original transfer. Rather, it operates to protect him from the harm that may arise from an order for restitution, given his irreversible change of position, by restricting his liability to make restitution or restitution in full.

Barker has argued for a broader role for the bona fide purchaser defence, namely that it operates to protect the sanctity of exchange transactions.[82] Where a benefit is received by a defendant pursuant to a valid contract with the claimant, then the contract governs the parties' rights. Claims in unjust enrichment that might undermine the contractual allocation of risks are excluded.[83] The defendant's good faith is relevant in that context because it permits the defendant to rely on the objective principle of contract law to exclude evidence of any subjective vitiation of the claimant's intention. Where, on the other hand, a defendant has received a benefit by way of exchange with a party other than the claimant, the defendant is unprotected against claims by the claimant, who is immune from risk-allocations in contracts to which she is not a party. In these circumstances, the defence of bona fide purchase applies to prevent the contract between the defendant and the third party from being undermined, unless the defendant was dishonest or had notice of the facts entitling the claimant to restitution of the benefit conferred pursuant to the contract. On Barker's approach, therefore, both the bona fide purchase defence and the objective principle of contract law are concerned with the same need to protect parties engaged in exchange transactions.

Even if this is so, the defence of bona fide purchase must remain separate from the change of position defence in which, as we have seen, relevant changes of position extend well beyond changes in exchange. However, given the focus of the bona fide purchase defence on curing title and its sporadic application to limited forms of exchange transactions, it is submitted that its rationale is better understood, at least at present, as concerned with security of purchase in cases where that protection is essential to the efficient operation of a market economy. Although this overlaps somewhat with a concern to protect security of exchange transactions, it is not co-extensive with that concern and has a distinctly different focus.

G Statutory Change of Position Defences

The final class of defences that fall for consideration are those statutory defences that are analogous to the change of position defence. This section will first consider those analogous defences that arise both in England and Australia pursuant to

[82] Barker, above n 81.

[83] Claims in unjust enrichment are not always inconsistent with the continuing existence of a contract: see, eg *Roxborough v Rothmans of Pall Mall Ltd* (2001) 208 CLR 516 (High Court of Australia), discussed in Edelman and Bant, above n 34, at 266–67.

frustrated contracts legislation, before turning to consider the variety of other statutory defences found in Australia that respond to defendants' changes of position in a restitutionary context. The aim is not to examine each exhaustively, but rather to provide some insight into the form and features of those defences and their interaction with and differences from the common law change of position defence.

The Law Reform (Frustrated Contracts) Act 1943 (UK) and the Frustrated Contracts Act 1958 (Vic) govern restitution of benefits transferred pursuant to certain classes of frustrated contracts in their respective jurisdictions of operation.[84] In so doing, they also provide means for taking into account certain changes of position of recipients of those benefits in a manner broadly analogous to the change of position defence. The following analysis will primarily focus on the terms of the English legislation, on which the Victorian legislation is modelled. The legislation treats restitution of money payments (the subject of section 1(2)) separately from restitution of other benefits (section 1(3)). Section 1(2) reads:

> All sums paid or payable to any party in pursuance to the contract before the time when the parties were so discharged (in this Act referred to as 'the time of discharge') shall, in the case of sums so paid, be recoverable from him as money received by him for the use of the party by whom the sums were paid, and, in the case of sums so payable, cease to be so payable: *provided that, if the party to whom the sums were so paid or payable incurred expenses before the time of discharge in, or for the performance of the contract, the court may, if it considers just to do so, having regard to all the circumstances of the case, allow him to retain it or, as the case may be, recover the whole or any part of the sums so paid or payable, not being an amount in excess of the expenses so incurred.* (emphasis added)

The italicised proviso has been rationalised as a statutory change of position defence.[85] It has also been identified as manifesting a concern with loss apportionment,[86] a matter entirely alien to the common law change of position defence.[87] If

[84] The Acts do not apply if there is a provision to the contrary in the contract. It would seem, therefore, that they are intended to operate as a code (compare the other statutory defences, considered below, at n 135). The UK provision excludes charterparties, contracts for the carriage of goods by sea other than by charterparty, contracts of insurance and contracts for the sale of goods where the goods have perished. The Victorian legislation extends to contracts for the sale of goods that have been 'avoided' under s 12 Goods Act 1958 (Vic).

[85] *BP Exploration Co (Libya) v Hunt (No 2)* [1979] 1 WLR 783 (QB) 800 (Robert Goff J) affirmed on other grounds in *BP Exploration Co (Libya) Ltd v Hunt* [1981] 1 WLR 232 (CA) and *BP Exploration Co (Libya) Ltd v Hunt (No 2)* [1983] 2 AC 352 (HL). Contrast *Gamerco SA v ICM/Fair Warning (Agency) Ltd* [1995] 1 WLR 1226 (QB) 1237 (Garland J) (deriving no specific assistance from the suggestion and stating that there was 'no question of any change of position as a result of the plaintiff's advance payment'), as to which see further below, at 247–48. E McKendrick, 'Frustration, Restitution and Loss Apportionment' in AS Burrows (ed) *Essays on the Law of Restitution* (Clarendon Press, Oxford 1991) 154–65 also argues that the provision enacts a restitutionary response to the frustration of the contract in which the proviso works much like a change of position defence.

[86] A Haycroft and D Waksman, 'Frustration and Restitution' [1984] *JBL* 207, 255; Burrows, *The Law of Restitution* 2nd edn, above n 13, at 363–66. McKendrick, above n 85, considers that any loss apportionment is restricted to exercise of the court's discretion to award a 'just' sum.

[87] It is for this reason that this work does not examine the New South Wales and South Australian frustrated contracts legislation which are expressly concerned with loss apportionment: see Frustrated Contracts Act 1978 (NSW) and Frustrated Contracts Act 1988 (SA).

the proviso does enable loss apportionment, its relationship to the change of position defence must be tenuous at best. As Burrows has commented, however, the case for loss apportionment must be made out and cannot be assumed.[88] Indeed, it is submitted that on closer consideration, the proviso is generally consistent with, although more limited in its scope of operation to, its common law counterpart. It does not demand an excursus into loss apportionment.

The proviso clearly operates more narrowly than the common law defence in a number of respects. First, it only applies to 'expenses' incurred and thus does not extend to the broader, non-pecuniary changes of position encompassed by the common law defence.[89] It also excludes those pecuniary changes of position that were not made 'in or for the purposes of the performance of the contract'. Therefore, a party who receives a payment and changes his position in reliance on his receipt by purchasing a lavish dinner for his personal enjoyment falls outside the proviso.

In other respects, however, the proviso can be interpreted in a manner largely consistent with the common law defence. First, although framed as a proviso, the section has been interpreted as an independent enactment, the onus lying on the party seeking to rely on the proviso to satisfy its requirements.[90]

Secondly, a party is only entitled to rely on the proviso where sums have been paid, or were payable to him pursuant to a contract. That is, there is a requirement that the party has received a benefit in the form of a sum paid or payable. Burrows argues that the reference to 'payable' means that a party can rely on the proviso even though he has received no benefit. He reluctantly concludes that the proviso must be partly concerned with loss apportionment.[91] However, if one accepts that actionable benefits for the purposes of the law of unjust enrichment extend to contractual rights,[92] receipt of an accrued right to a sum must be as much a benefit as receipt of the sum itself. Once that step is taken, and subject to the question of anticipatory changes of position which is dealt with further below, any apparent inconsistency between this aspect of the common law defence and statutory proviso is resolved.

Thirdly, the requirement that a party to whom sums were paid or payable has incurred expenditure 'pursuant to' the contract establishes the required causal link between receipt of the sum, or right to the sum, and his change of position. It requires the court to consider the party's reasons for his expenditure and thus is consistent with a reliance requirement.

Fourthly, the proviso is clearly broad enough to encompass anticipatory, precontractual expenditure, provided it was incurred 'for the purpose of the performance of the contract'. Given the expenditure must be incurred in anticipation of a

88 Burrows, *The Law of Restitution* 2nd edn, above n 13, at 361.

89 Ch 5, at 132–34.

90 *Lobb v Vasey Housing Auxiliary (War Widows Guild)* [1963] VR 239 (Victorian Supreme Court) 247 (Hudson J); *Gamerco SA v ICM/Fair Warning (Agency) Ltd* [1995] 1 WLR 1226 (QB) 1236 (Garland J), 'assisted' in his reasoning by the decision of Hudson J.

91 Burrows, *The Law of Restitution* 2nd edn, above n 13, at 363.

92 Discussed in ch 4, at 91.

contract, it must be incurred in anticipation of the receipt of contractual rights. This is the same link between the anticipatory change of position and subsequent receipt of a benefit that is required for the common law defence.[93]

Finally, any amount that is retained or recovered pursuant to the proviso must not exceed the expenses incurred. Further, even if the incurred expenses exceed the amount of the sum paid or payable, then the defendant is limited to retain (or recover) the sum paid or payable. This limits the value of the defendant's change of position to the value of the benefit received, therefore ensuring that the proviso operates by way of defence, rather than being an independent source of rights to compensation or a means of apportioning loss, for example.[94]

Therefore, the proviso contains significant points of similarity to the change of position defence. On the other hand, the proviso does contain a discretionary element that has the potential to render it significantly distinct from the change of position defence. This is the apparently broad discretion[95] given to a court to allow relief to a qualified recipient 'if it considers it just to do so, having regard to all the circumstances of the case'.

However, in the absence of express indications in the statute to that effect,[96] it should not be too readily assumed that the discretion operates as an invitation to engage in loss apportionment.[97] The discretion can be exercised in accordance with established principles of the common law, in particular by reference to those considerations applicable to the common law change of position defence. This approach would permit consideration of issues such as the reversibility of any change of position, the reasonableness of the recipient's reliance and the matters underlying the bars to the common law defence, such as the defendant's fault and any illegality affecting the transaction. It would not extend to more general considerations unconnected with the circumstances of the case,[98] those being the receipt of the benefit and the change of position. It would thus exclude broad considerations of hardship to the respective parties.[99] This approach to the exercise of the discretion would both give a definite content to the provision and allow the statutory defence to operate as consistently as possible with the common law defence—an important consideration given the piecemeal application of the statute.[100]

The case law to date on the proviso is arguably consistent with this approach to the exercise of the discretion. In *Lobb v Vasey Housing Auxiliary (War Widows Guild)*, a woman paid £1250 to the defendant in accordance with a contract pursuant to which she was to obtain the exclusive right to possess a flat (to be built by the defendant) for the balance of her lifetime. She died before the flat was

93 Ch 5, at 156–57.
94 Haycroft and Waksman, above n 86, at 217.
95 *Gamerco SA v ICM/Fair Warning (Agency) Ltd* [1995] 1 WLR 1226 (QB) 1237 (Garland J).
96 As contained in Frustrated Contracts Act 1978 (NSW) and Frustrated Contracts Act 1988 (SA).
97 *Cf* McKendrick, above n 85, at 158–59.
98 *Gamerco SA v ICM/Fair Warning (Agency) Ltd* [1995] 1 WLR 1226 (QB) 1238 (Garland J).
99 *Scottish Equitable Plc v Derby* [2001] EWCA Civ 369, [2001] 3 All ER 818.
100 Above, n 84.

completed. Her executrix sought recovery of the value of the payment on the ground that the basis of, or consideration for, the payment had entirely failed. The primary claim for restitution of the value of the payment was accepted by Hudson J of the Supreme Court of Victoria. His Honour then proceeded to consider section 3 of the Frustrated Contracts Act 1959 (Vic), the equivalent of section 1(2) of the UK Act. His Honour noted that if, as could be assumed, the defendant had gone on to complete the flat and dispose of it for a value at least equivalent to the amount paid by the deceased, 'justice would not demand that the defendant should be allowed to retain any part of the sum'.[101] Although framed in terms of a broad discretion, the court's reasoning supports a familiar and principled requirement that, in order for the proviso to apply, the recipient party's change of position must be irreversible.

A principled approach to the exercise of the discretion is also discernible in the sole English case on point, *Gamerco SC v ICM/Fair Warning (Agency) Ltd.*[102] In that case, a rock concert to be held in Spain had to be cancelled a few days before it was due to take place because the proposed venue was declared unsafe. The claimants had paid $412,500 to the defendants and owed them a further sum by the date frustration occurred. Both the claimants and defendants had incurred expenses in preparation for the concert: $450,000 (which amount included the earlier payment to the defendants) by the claimants and $50,000 by the defendants. Garland J held that the claimants were entitled to restitution of the $412,500 payment and that there should be no deduction for the defendant's expenses under the proviso.

Although Garland J purported to be exercising a broad discretion,[103] the matters taken into consideration in coming to that conclusion[104] indicate that Garland J was intuitively offsetting the amount of the defendants' expenses against those incurred by the claimants. In other words, Garland J considered that the discretion permitted consideration of any expenses incurred *by the party seeking restitution* in, or pursuant to, the performance of the contract. Far from being an unprincipled exercise of a broad discretion, however, this reasoning is reminiscent of the analysis contained in chapter four, in which it was argued that a rescinding claimant is also entitled to have taken into account her changes of position made in reliance on the receipt of benefits from the defendant pursuant to a contract.

On the facts of *Gamerco*, the defendant's change of position was counterbalanced to the tune of $37,500 by the claimants' changes made in reliance on their receipt of contractual rights. A precise calculation would perhaps have permitted a further offset against the claimant's payment of the defendants' expenses of $12,500. However, given that the defendants bore the onus of establishing their

[101] As this issue had not been investigated at trial, the trial was adjourned to allow the defendant to bring further evidence and argument on the point. Judgment was subsequently entered by consent for an amount slightly less than the amount of the original payment.

[102] *Gamerco SA v ICM/Fair Warning (Agency) Ltd* [1995] 1 WLR 1226 (QB).

[103] *Ibid*, at 1238.

[104] *Ibid*, at 1236.

expenses and given the judge's expressed dissatisfaction with the evidence adduced by the defendants to support their claim,[105] the result does not appear entirely unreasonable and certainly is not solely explicable on the basis of an completely unbridled discretion to do what is fair and just. Indeed, as we will see, it is broadly consistent with one interpretation of the joint effects of section 1(2) and (3). It is to this latter provision that we now turn.

Section 1(3) addresses restitution of non-money benefits. It reads:

> Where any party to the contract has, by reason of anything done by another party thereto in, or for the purposes of, the performance of the contract, obtained a valuable benefit (other than a payment of money to which the last foregoing subsection applies) before the time of discharge, there shall be recoverable from him by the said other party such sum (if any), not exceeding the value of the said benefit to the party obtaining it, as the court considers just, having regard to all the circumstances of the case and, in particular—(a) the amount of any expenses incurred before the time of discharge by the benefited party in, or for the purposes of, the performance of the contract, including any sums paid or payable by him to any other party in pursuance of the contract and retained or recoverable by that party under the last foregoing subsection, and (b) the effect, in relation to the said benefit, of the circumstances giving rise to the frustration of the contract.

There is an obvious symmetry between this subsection and section 1(2). There is the same requirement that a party has received a benefit, albeit in non-monetary form. The value of any just sum is again limited by the value of the benefit received. And the wording of section 1(3)(a) reflects the proviso in section 1(2) relating to the recipient party's change of position. The relationship between the two subsections is highlighted by the direction that the court take into account any award under section 1(2) so as to avoid double counting of expenses incurred. Given the close connection between the subsections, the starting point in interpreting section 1(3) must be that it introduces the same kind of claim, subject to the same sort of statutory change of position defence (notably with the same limitations and subject to the same considerations as its earlier counterpart) as applies under section 1(2).

The only significant difference between the two provisions stems from section 1(3)(b). Burrows argues persuasively that this proviso addresses the case where a benefit is destroyed due to the frustrating event, such as where a partly-built building is destroyed by fire.[106] The proviso permits the court to take this form of change of position into account even though it is not brought about by the recipient party's reliance expenditure. This seems an entirely straightforward and defensible interpretation of the provision. It suggests that the statute draws the same kind of distinction made in this book between independent changes of position and defendant-instigated changes and, in the case of non-money benefits, expressly extends the operation of the proviso to both classes of case.

Unfortunately, this interpretation of section 1(3) is not entirely supported by the only case to have considered the proviso, *BP Exploration Co (Libya) Ltd v*

[105] *Gamerco SA v ICM/Fair Warning (Agency) Ltd* [1995] 1 WLR 1226 (QB), at 1236, 1238.
[106] Burrows, *The Law of Restitution* 2nd edn, above n 13, at 368.

Hunt.[107] It is beyond the scope of this work to consider in detail the enrichment issues raised by that decision in relation to the primary claim to restitution of the benefit transferred.[108] However, so far as section 1(3)(a) and (b) are concerned, there are two important points. The first is that Robert Goff J identified section 1(3)(a) as a statutory change of position defence and applied an interpretation of it consistent with that advocated in this work.[109] The second is that his Lordship collapsed what we have seen could be interpreted as a change of position enquiry contained in subsection (3)(b) into the prior question of whether a benefit was received.[110] On this approach, if a partly-built building is destroyed by fire, there will be no benefit received and thus no award under section 1(3). Although it leads in that case to the same result as would be reached on application of a change of position defence approach, it does so by quite a different route.

With respect, it is difficult to see that section 1(3)(b) merits this distinct treatment. The structure of the provision as a whole strongly suggests that the stated restrictions as to valuation of the received benefit and the calculation of the just sum only apply where a benefit has been received prior to the time of discharge. That is, there must first be an identified and received benefit before subsections (a) and (b) can apply. On this reading, the section seems to fall naturally into two main parts: the first dealing with the non-discretionary identification of benefit and the second with the valuation of the 'just sum' (which amount is not permitted to exceed the value of the received benefit), in which discretion plays an important role. In that context, it seems odd that the provision should switch from identification of a recoverable benefit in the main section, to issues going to valuation of the just sum in section 1(3)(a), only to switch back to identification of benefit issues in section 1(3)(b).

It is submitted that the analysis that accords more closely with the wording and structure of the section is that section 1(3) is the counterpart to section 1(2) and its subsections reflect the same sort of change of position concerns that we have seen developed independently in a common law context. Indeed, taken together, section 1(2) and (3) suggest a process for unwinding mutual contracts much like that espoused in chapter four of this book. Both payments and non-monetary benefits that have been transferred pursuant to a frustrated contract must be restored, subject to change of position defences in favour of each receiving party. In this way, the primary claims and defences mirror each other and result in a complete and mutual unwinding of the contract, so as to restore the parties as closely as possible to the *status quo ante*.

The preceding discussion has examined statutory defences analogous to the common law change of position defence that arise in the context of some classes of frustrated contract. There is a plethora of further statutory defences in

107 *BP Exploration Co (Libya) v Hunt (No 2)* [1979] 1 WLR 783 (QB).

108 For discussion of the benefit issues, see: McKendrick, above n 85, at 160–63; Burrows, *The Law of Restitution* 2nd edn, above n 13, at 368–71.

109 *BP Exploration Co (Libya) v Hunt (No 2)* [1979] 1 WLR 783 (QB) 804.

110 *Ibid*, at 801–02.

Australia[111] that apply to other forms of transactions—typically mistaken payments and distributions—and in varied contexts, such as trust and estate distributions,[112] mistaken payments generally[113] and cy-près distributions.[114] An example of the statutory defences is contained in section 125(1) Property Law Act 1969 (WA):

> Relief, whether under section 124 or in equity or otherwise, in respect of any payment made under mistake, whether of law or fact, shall be denied wholly or in part if the person from whom relief is sought received the payment in good faith and has so altered his position in reliance on the validity of the payment that in the opinion of the Court, having regard to all possible implications in respect of the parties (other than the plaintiff or claimant) to the payment and of other persons acquiring rights or interests through them, it is inequitable to grant relief, or to grant relief in full.

The statutory defences share features that render them analogous to the common law defence. In particular, each requires that the defendant has received a benefit in good faith and so altered his position that it is 'inequitable' to grant relief wholly or in part. From this perspective, the provisions are not very far from the seminal description of the common law defence in *Lipkin Gorman v Karpnale.*[115] However, as we will see, the statutory provisions contain a number of differences from the common law defence, both in terms of their core requirements and in determining in what circumstances it will be 'inequitable' to grant relief.

There are three core requirements for the statutory defences to arise: a change of position, reliance and good faith. Turning first to the requirement that a defendant has 'altered his position', it is clear that as at common law, both acts and omissions may give rise to a relevant change of position. For example, in *Wendt v Orr,*[116] Commissioner Johnson QC considered that a recipient's decision made in reliance on receipt of moneys pursuant to an estate distribution, not to make a claim against the estate pursuant to the Inheritance (Family and Dependants Provisions) Act 1972 (WA) as well as a decision not to make an application for payment of capital pursuant to the will would both count as relevant 'alterations in position' for the purposes of Trustees Act 1962 (WA) section 65(8).

On the other hand, any alterations in position must result from reliance: that is, only defendant-instigated changes of position count. It follows that independent

[111] Trustee Act (NT) 50AA(2)(c); Trusts Act 1973 (Qld) 109(3); Succession Act 1981 (Qld) 53(5); Perpetuities and Accumulations Act 1992 (Tas) 24(2)(c); Property Law Act 1969 (WA) 125; Trustees Act 1962 (WA) 65(8).There is also a plethora of New Zealand provisions, many in very similar terms to their Australian counterparts. New Zealand authorities considering those provisions will therefore be referred to where relevant.

[112] Trusts Act 1973 (Qld) 109(3); Succession Act 1981 (Qld) 53(5); Trustees Act 1962 (WA) 65(8).

[113] Property Law Act 1969 (WA) 125.

[114] Trustee Act (NT) 50AA(2)(c); Perpetuities and Accumulations Act 1992 (Tas) 24(2)(c).

[115] [1991] 2 AC 548 (HL) considered in ch 5, at 125.

[116] *Wendt v Orr* [2004] WASC 28 (Western Australian Supreme Court) [219]. See also *TRC Consultants Ltd v Higgs* [2007] NZHC 1551 (New Zealand High Court) considering s 296(3) Companies Act 1993 (NZ) (the recipient's decision made in reasonable reliance on the validity of its receipt to continue providing services and consequential loss of opportunity to refuse to complete its contract constituted relevant alteration of position).

changes of position, such as where a benefit is destroyed by a third party or natural event, or where a benefit spontaneously devalues, will not count for the purposes of the defence. This is a clear point of distinction between the statutory and common law defences.

It is uncertain whether the statutory provisions extend to anticipatory changes of position. The natural structure and wording of most sections would suggest not: the defendant must have: (1) received the payment in good faith; and (2) have altered his position in reliance on the validity of the payment. However, it remains possible for the statutes to be interpreted consistently with the common law, provided that the elements are read as cumulative rather than consecutive. This approach would be supported by the sorts of policy considerations that support extension of the common law defence to this category of claim[117] and also by some New Zealand authorities.[118]

Turning to the reliance requirement, all statutory defences require that the defendant has relied on the validity of his receipt.[119] This suggests that the defendant must have acted on an assumption that there was no ground for reversing the transaction: that the receipt of the benefit was 'free from challenge or attack'.[120] A defendant who is aware that a claimant has transferred the benefit pursuant to a mistake, for example, cannot rely on the defence, no matter how blameless he was for the original transfer or for any subsequent loss of the benefit and notwithstanding that he dealt with the benefit in accordance with his understanding that it must eventually be returned to the claimant. Hence in *National Bank of New Zealand v Waitaki*,[121] the defendant was unable to rely on the statutory defence contained in section 94B Judicature Act 1908 (NZ) (the terms of which are substantially mirrored in section 125 property Law Act (WA)) because he was aware of the paying bank's mistake. This was notwithstanding that he initially refused to receive the payment, did his best to bring the bank's mistake to its attention and, once he had received the payment, invested the sum in a manner consistent with recognition of the bank's right to the mistaken payment. By contrast, we saw in chapter five[122] that it is possible for a defendant to rely on his receipt for the purposes of the common law defence even

[117] Discussed in ch 5, at 156–57.

[118] *Thomas v Houston Corbett* [1969] NZLR 151 (New Zealand Court of Appeal); *Re Island Bay Masonry Ltd* (1998) 8 NZCLC 261 discussed by P Watts, 'Company Law' [1999] NZLR 23

[119] The precise wording differs: eg in Trustees Act 1962 (WA) 65(8), the recipient must have 'altered his position in reliance on his having an indefeasible interest in the asset or assets'. Under the Property Law Act 1969 (WA) 125, the recipient must have 'altered his position in reliance on the validity of the payment'. Trusts Act 1973 (Qld) 109(3) and Succession Act 1981 (Qld) 53(5) require the recipient to have acted in reliance on 'the propriety of the distribution'. A New Zealand statute, the Administration Act 1969 (NZ) s 51 perhaps spells out this common requirement most clearly, requiring that the recipient must have altered his position in the reasonable belief that the 'distribution was properly made and would not be set aside'; Companies Act 1993 (NZ) s 296(3) and Insolvency Act 1967 (NZ) s 58(6)(a) share the same requirement.

[120] *National Bank of New Zealand Ltd v Waitaki International Processing (NI) Ltd* [1992] 2 NZLR 211 (New Zealand Court of Appeal) 217 (Henry J).

[121] *National Bank of New Zealand Ltd v Waitaki International Processing (NI) Ltd* [1992] 2 NZLR 211 (New Zealand Court of Appeal).

[122] At 148–49.

if aware that it was the result of a mistaken transfer, provided that he acts consistently with the known basis of his receipt and takes an appropriate level of care in dealing with the benefit.

On the other hand, and consistent with the common law defence, the statutory defences do not require that the defendant must have considered himself entitled to the receipt in order to prove reliance: provided he honestly assumes that the payment is valid and acts in accordance with that assumption, it does not matter if he believes the benefit is to be held for the benefit of a third party. For example, in *Thomas v Houston Corbett & Co*,[123] the claimant was induced by a fraudulent employee, Cook, to pay £1381 to the defendant. Cook then told the defendant that he was entitled to retain part of the sum but that the balance was payable to other parties. The defendant then paid the balance to Cook in reliance on what he understood to be the basis of his receipt. The New Zealand Court of Appeal found that the defendant had changed his position in reliance on the validity of the payment for the purposes of section 94B Judicature Act 1908 (NZ), even though he had not believed himself entitled to all of it.

Finally, so far as the good faith requirement is concerned, as with the common law defence, it is difficult to see what additional work is done by this element that is not covered through the concept of reliance. What is clear is that good faith, whether subsumed within reliance or not, is a matter to be proven by the defendant.[124] The statutory defences will therefore not countenance the kind of reversal of onus that has marred some cases contemplating the common law defence.[125]

Once the criteria of good faith, a change of position and reliance are established, the statutory question that arises is whether it is 'inequitable' to grant relief against the defendant wholly or in part. As with the 'just sum' discretion under the frustrated contracts legislation, the issue is whether there is anything in these terms to require a different approach from that adopted in the common law defence.

There is certainly nothing on the face of the provisions to exclude the core requirement of the common law defence that any change of position must be irreversible. Echoing *Lobb v Vasey*, where a change is readily reversible, it will presumably not be inequitable to grant relief.

Further, the inclusion of a reliance requirement suggests that the focus is on inequity that will occur *as a result of* the defendant's change of position: general hardship that is causally unconnected with the change will not count.[126] Therefore,

[123] *Thomas v Houston Corbett* [1969] NZLR 151 (New Zealand Court of Appeal).

[124] *Alpha Wealth Financial Services Pty Ltd v Frankland River Olive Company Ltd* [2008] WASCA 119 (Western Australia Supreme Court of Appeal), [39] (Pullin JA) [210]–[12] (Buss JA, with whom Steytler P concurred) discussed in ch 5, at 160; *GE Finance and Insurance Trading As GE Commercial Finance v Heath and Meltzer as Liquidators of Phoenix Freight Ltd* [2007] NZHC 1029 (New Zealand High Court), considering s 296(3) Companies Act 1993 (NZ).

[125] As in *Abou-Rahmah v Abacha* [2006] EWCA Civ 1492, [2007] 1 All ER (Comm) 827, discussed in ch 5, at 158–60.

[126] Contrast s 86(9)(a) Social Security Act 1964 (NZ) which expressly requires courts to take into account the 'financial circumstances' of the defendant in exercising its discretion: considered in *Owens v Social Development* [2007] NZSC 8 (New Zealand Supreme Court).

in *Wendt v Orr*,[127] Commissioner Johnson QC refused to take into account the recipient's 'advanced age and increasingly poor state of health . . . as well as the fact that it will be far more difficult emotionally for her to make any necessary application under [the terms of the will] or to otherwise assert her rights or meet her needs'. Rather, these matters should be taken into account only in determining the method of repayment.[128]

Unlike the common law defence, many of the statutory provisions require the court to have regard to the implications for third parties in assessing whether it would be inequitable to grant relief. For example, in *Alpha Wealth Financial Services Pty Ltd v Franklin River Olive Company Ltd*,[129] Commissioner Sanderson of the Western Australian Supreme Court considered the application of the statutory change of position defence contained in section 125 Property Law Act 1969 (Western Australia).[130] Commissioner Sanderson noted that if the defendant was ordered to make restitution there was a real prospect that the investment scheme in which the claimant, defendant and third parties were involved would be forced to come to an end. He concluded that the interests of those third parties strongly supported the application of the statutory change of position defence.

The other possible criterion that may be taken into account in determining whether it would be inequitable to grant relief is fault. The New Zealand Court of Appeal has been robust in its recognition of fault as a relevant consideration under section 94B Judicature Act. In both *National Bank of New Zealand Ltd v Waitaki International Processing (NI) Ltd*[131] and *Thomas v Houston Corbett*,[132] the New Zealand Court of Appeal took into account the recipient's carelessness in losing the benefit in determining the extent of protection offered under section 94B Judicature Act (NZ), as well as the claimant's fault in making the payment in the first place.

While it is clear that that the statutory defences are sufficiently broad to encompass considerations of fault, it is submitted that the discretion to do so should be guided by the sorts of considerations discussed in detail in chapter six. In particular, it is important to be very clear about whose fault counts, the kind of fault in issue and the extent to which any fault can be 'weighed' to make fine adjustments

127 *Wendt v Orr* [2004] WASC 28 (Western Australian Supreme Court) [220]. *Cf Menzies v Bennett* (New Zealand Supreme Court 14 August 1969) in which Beattie J did take into account the defendant's financial hardship in applying Judicature Amendment Act 1958 (NZ) 94B, considered in R Sutton, 'Case and Comment: More on Money Paid Under Mistake' [1997] *NZLJ* 5 .

128 Under Trustees Act 1968 (WA) s 65(9).

129 *Alpha Wealth Financial Services Pty Ltd v Frankland River Olive Company Ltd* [2006] WASC 70, 199 FLR 91 (Western Australian Supreme Court); reversed on another ground in *Alpha Wealth Financial Services Pty Ltd v Franklin River Olive Company Ltd* [2008] WASCA 119 (Western Australia Supreme Court of Appeal).

130 The provision is considered in detail in E Bant and P Creighton, 'The Statutory Change of Position Defences in Western Australia' (2003) 31 *U Western Australia L Rev* 47.

131 *National Bank of New Zealand Ltd v Waitaki International Processing (NI) Ltd* [1992] 2 NZLR 211 (New Zealand Court of Appeal) considered in ch 6, at 188–89.

132 *Thomas v Houston Corbett* [1969] NZLR 151 (New Zealand Court of Appeal) considered above, at 252.

to the measure of relief. In that regard, it is submitted that courts considering the exercise of a statutory discretion should consider whether the defendant's reliance was reasonable,[133] as well as those matters that go to preclude a defendant from relying on the common law defence such as his fault or illegality affecting the transaction. However, courts should be wary of adopting a different or broader attitude to 'balancing the equities' than applies in the context of the common law change of position defence. If, for example, it not acceptable as a matter of principle for courts to engage in exercises that purport to measure a defendant's role in inducing a mistaken payment for the context of the common law defence,[134] then those same considerations of principle must weigh against their adoption in a statutory context.

In summary, although the provisions of many of the statutory change of position defences are sufficiently wide to allow broad exercises of discretion, it is equally possible, and very important for the statutory defences to operate in a principled manner. Again echoing the earlier discussion of the frustrated contracts legislation, it is notable that the statutory defences operate in a somewhat piecemeal fashion, covering some areas and excluding others.[135] In those circumstances, there is every reason to hope that they will be interpreted in a way that is as consistent as possible, given their terms, with the common law defence.

H Conclusion

The conclusion of this chapter is that, with the exception of the payment over defence, the other common law defences that potentially arise in response to claims in unjust enrichment continue to operate independently of the change of position defence and to different effect. The change of position defence is thus not some type of super-defence with an apparently endless ability to absorb other well-established defences.[136] Rather, it has its own distinctive mode of operation and limitations that fit it neatly within the existing framework of applicable defences.

Further, the statutory defences are capable of being interpreted in a manner broadly consistent with the common law defence. This is important given the ad hoc application of these defences to common law and statutory claims.

[133] A number of New Zealand provisions require that the defendant has acted in 'reasonable reliance: eg Administration Act 1969 (NZ) s 51; Companies Act 1993 (NZ) s 296(3) and Insolvency Act 1967(NZ) s 58(6)(a).

[134] Examined in ch 6, at 180.

[135] It is likely that the statutory defences do not cover the field, so as to preclude the operation of the common law defence: see Bant and Creighton, above n 130, at 51–53 and *National Bank of New Zealand Ltd v Waitaki International Processing (NI) Ltd* [1992] 2 NZLR 211 (New Zealand Court of Appeal). However, there are areas where the statutory defence clearly apply where it is uncertain that the common law defence operates, as with cases involving proprietary relief: see ch 7, at 204–209.

[136] As would have seemed to be the case if it did absorb or render redundant estoppel by representation (above, at 224–30), good consideration (above, at 237–39) and bona fide purchase (above, at 241–42), for example.

Locating the common law defence within its broader context and ensuring its best 'fit' with other related areas were among the chief aims of this book. This chapter has demonstrated that, when defined properly and within its legal context, the change of position defence operates in an entirely rational and justifiable manner that is largely consistent with the law as a whole. Further, its definition both identifies and invites further clarification of those few remaining areas of the law where anomalies persist.[137] Finally, it is hoped that its definition lays to rest any concern that the defence operates in an unprincipled manner[138] or by reference to 'that vague jurisprudence which is sometimes attractively styled "justice as between man and man"'.[139] Rather, the analysis carried out in this work allows us to see how the defence operates according to defined legal standards and promotes the basic principle of justice that like cases should be decided alike.

137 For example, the uncertain position of 'innocent inducers', discussed above, at 234–35.
138 G Virgo, 'Change of Position: the importance of being principled' [2005] *Restitution L Rev* 34.
139 *Baylis v Bishop of London* [1913] 1 Ch 127 (CA) 140 (Hamilton LJ), noted in ch 1, at 3.

INDEX